Interpreting Company
Reports and Accounts

PEARSON
Education

We work with leading authors to develop the
strongest educational materials in business, finance
and marketing, bringing cutting-edge thinking and
best learning practice to a global market.

Under a range of well-known imprints, including
Financial Times Prentice Hall, we craft high quality
print and electronic publications which help
readers to understand and apply their content,
whether studying or at work.

To find out more about the complete range of our
publishing please visit us on the World Wide Web at:
www.pearsoned.co.uk

Interpreting Company Reports and Accounts

TENTH EDITION

Geoffrey Holmes

Alan Sugden

Paul Gee

 Prentice Hall
FINANCIAL TIMES

An imprint of **Pearson Education**

Harlow, England • London • New York • Boston • San Francisco • Toronto • Sydney • Singapore • Hong Kong
Tokyo • Seoul • Taipei • New Delhi • Cape Town • Madrid • Mexico City • Amsterdam • Munich • Paris • Milan

Pearson Education Limited
Edinburgh Gate
Harlow
Essex CM20 2JE
England

and Associated Companies throughout the world

Visit us on the World Wide Web at:
www.pearsoned.co.uk

First published 1979
Tenth edition published 2008

ISBN: 978-0-273-71141-4

British Library Cataloguing-in-Publication Data
A catalogue record for this book is available from the British Library

Library of Congress Cataloging-in-Publication Data
Holmes, Geoffrey Andrew.
  Interpreting company reports and accounts / Geoffrey Holmes, Alan Sugden, Paul Gee. --
10th ed.
    p. cm.
  ISBN-13: 978-0-273-71141-4
1. Financial statements. 2. Corporation reports. I. Sugden, Alan. II. Gee, Paul. III. Title.
  HF5681.B2H63 2008
  657′.3--dc22
                        2007049783

ARP impression 98

Typeset in 9.75/12 Times by 35
Printed and bound by Ashford Colour Press., Gosport

The publisher's policy is to use paper manufactured from sustainable forests.

Brief contents

Contents

Preface

The aim of this book

In the Preface to the first edition we wrote:

> 'Given a sound knowledge of the basic components of a balance sheet and profit and loss account, *anybody with a reasonably enquiring mind* can learn a great deal about a company by studying its report and accounts and by comparing it with other companies. We have written this book to provide the basic knowledge required . . .'

The aim remains the same, although there have been significant developments since the first edition was published in 1979.

UK GAAP

The Accounting Standards Board (ASB) set up in 1990 has now issued 29 Financial Reporting Standards which, together with earlier standards, are referred to as UK Generally Accepted Accounting Practice (or UK GAAP). ASB's main challenge is now to bring UK GAAP closer in line with International Financial Reporting Standards (IFRS). Much progress has been made but the overall process is likely to take several more years before the project comes to final fruition.

IFRS

In the UK, fully listed companies have had to start complying with IFRS from 2005, whilst AIM-listed companies were given a choice between early adoption (2005) or late adoption (2007). It appears that relatively few unlisted companies have yet adopted IFRS.

Narrative reporting

Corporate governance, business reviews and corporate social responsibility reporting are now a well-established part of corporate life for bigger companies. This current edition addresses the fast-moving developments in this area.

Approach

This edition seeks to provide a bridge between UK GAAP and IFRS. The earlier chapters in the book examine various topics, initially from the perspective of UK GAAP and then conclude with the implications of adopting IFRS. Two chapters pull together the comparisons between UK GAAP and IFRS, and the conversion processes required. The book concludes with an analytical chapter, 'Putting it all together', based on a real company. As with earlier editions, we use the Key Points symbol to help the reader sort out the wheat from the chaff.

Alan Sugden
Paul Gee

Publisher's acknowledgements

We are grateful to the following for permission to reproduce copyright material:

Chapter 1, page 4, a Wiggins Group article from the *Daily Telegraph*, 8 March 2001 (Daily Telegraph, 2001); Chapter 4, pages 26–27, Chapter 9, page 68, Chapter 14, page 113, Chapter 20, pages 161–162 and Chapter 34, pages 285–287, extracts containing information on the Management Consulting Group, from *Management Consulting Group Director's Report 2006, Management Consulting Group Annual Report 2006, Management Consulting Group Interim Report 2005, Management Consulting Group Annual Report and Accounts Year Ending 31 December 2005*, reprinted with permission of Management Consulting Group PLC; Chapter 4, pages 28 and 31 and Chapter 9, pages 65–67, extracts containing information on the Wilmington Group, from *Wilmington Group Director's Report 2006* and *Wilmington Group Annual Report 2006* (Wilmington, 2006); Chapter 14, pages 111, 113–114, Chapter 22, page 183 and Chapter 23, page 194, extracts containing information on First Choice Holidays, from *First Choice Holidays Annual Report 2006* (First Choice, 2006). These examples are taken from the *First Choice Holidays PLC Annual Report* and reflect the trading position at that time. However, First Choice Holidays PLC has since undergone a merger with the tourism division TUI AG to form TUI Travel PLC, and First Choice Holidays PLC is no longer a public listed company; Chapter 19, page 150, from the *Investors Chronicle* extract, 26 March 1993 (*Investors Chronicle*, 1993); Chapter 23, page 185, extracts taken from the *Daily Telegraph*, 6 October 1995 (*Daily Telegraph*, 1995); Chapter 35, pages 293–295, extracts from the *Investors Chronicle*, cuttings since 1998 (*Investors Chronicle*, 1998); Chapter 35, pages 291–292, extracts from Charterhouse Annual Reports/data (Charterhouse Communications, 2002–2007).

In some instances we have been unable to trace the owners of copyright material, and we would appreciate any information that would enable us to do so.

We are grateful to the Financial Times Limited for permission to reprint the following material:

Chapter 6 Tomkins, © *Financial Times*, 1 July 2000; Chapter 8 Revenue recognition, © *Financial Times*, 9 July 2001; Chapter 8 PwC wins costs against Jarvis, © *Financial Times*, 15 July 2000.

We are grateful to the following for permission to use copyright material:

Chapter 8 How accounting executives looked the wrong way from *The Financial Times Limited*, 13 August 2002, © Robert Howell.

CHAPTER 1

Overview of the regulatory scene

Purpose of the book

This book is intended as a practical guide to the interpretation of reports and accounts. In it frequent reference is made to the legal and accounting requirements in the UK, both as regards UK GAAP (UK Generally Accepted Accounting Practice) and IFRS (International Financial Reporting Standards). This is done in the context of interesting information to look out for, rather than how a set of accounts should be prepared.

The regulatory structure in the UK

Introduction

What needs to be included in a set of financial statements is governed by a mixture of company law requirements (presently the Companies Act 1985) and accounting standards. Companies that have a full listing on the London Stock Exchange are required to comply with additional rules set by the Financial Services Authority (FSA), which is the UK Listing Authority.

In the UK, reporting requirements are in a state of flux. Companies listed on the London Stock Exchange and the Alternative Investment Market (AIM) are required to comply with International Financial Reporting Standards (IFRS). Other companies may choose between UK GAAP (shorthand for UK Generally Accepted Accounting Practice – see Chapter 3 for details) and IFRS. These requirements are explained in this and the following chapter.

UK adoption of IFRS

Whether particular categories of company may or must adopt IFRS is referred in Chapter 2. Wherever applicable, the impact of IFRS (International Financial Reporting Standards) is referred to throughout the book at the end each relevant chapter, and in summary in Chapters 33 and 34.

The annual report and accounts

The purpose of the annual report

The report and accounts, normally produced annually, is the principal way in which shareholders and others keep themselves informed of the activities, progress and future plans of a company. *The style and content of the annual report vary somewhat in line with the directors' views on its use as a public relations vehicle.*

What has to be included?

There is a minimum of information that must be disclosed to comply with the law. In addition, the form and content of accounts are subject to Financial Reporting Standards. The detailed requirements of annual reports are dealt with in subsequent chapters.

The financial statements

The financial statements are a key part of a company's annual report. The annual report of the auditors to the company's shareholders begins 'We have audited the financial statements on pages xx to yy, [i.e. the pages containing the financial statements]'. The audit report then goes on to add a lot more detail before concluding (provided the auditors think all is well with the company) with the opinion that 'the financial statements give a true and fair view . . .' (see Chapter 6 for more detail, which includes the audit report on the financial statements of Associated British Foods).

Under UK GAAP, the financial statements include four primary financial statements:

- profit and loss account,
- statement of total recognised gains and losses,
- balance sheet,
- cash flow statement.

Financial statements also include:

- notes to the financial statements,
- statement of accounting policies.

The notes and the primary financial statements form an integrated whole, and should be read as such to obtain a complete picture. *Chapter 4 refers in more detail to the content and structure of the annual report.*

The profit and loss account

The profit and loss account (referred to under IFRS as the income statement) is a record of the company's activities over a stated period of time, usually a year. Chapter 3 explains how the profit and loss account is compiled and prepared. More detailed requirements are dealt with in Chapters 8 to 10.

The balance sheet

The balance sheet is a statement of the company's assets and liabilities at close of business on a given date, referred to as the balance sheet date. Again, Chapter 3 explains how the balance sheet is compiled and prepared. Later chapters deal with specific issues in detail.

The directors' report

The Companies Act 1985 requires a company's annual report to contain a directors' report. This contains a great deal of important information on a wide range of issues, including the principal activities of the business, the names of the company's directors. Listed companies must give details of their shareholdings and share option arrangement. It also contains a business review which should refer to business performance, principal risks and uncertainties, and key performance indicators (KPIs). The directors' report is dealt with in Chapter 4.

Narrative reporting

In recent years 'Narrative reporting' has emerged as a high-profile issue. Annual reports of larger companies contain information over and above that required by law and accounting standards. Sometimes this information has to be provided because the company is fully listed on the London Stock Exchange – see the corporate governance and remuneration report requirements in Chapter 6. Sometimes the information is provided as best practice by companies whose shares are publicly-traded – see Chapter 5. The quality of a company's narrative reporting can impact on its reputation within the financial community.

The various aspects of narrative reporting, including recent developments and trends, are dealt with in Chapters 4, 5 and 6.

The objective of financial statements

Overall objective

The key objective is to provide information about the financial position and performance of an entity that is useful to a wide range of users for assessing the stewardship of management and for making economic decisions (ASB's Statement of Principles (StoP), Chapter 1).

Users and their information needs

Financial information about the activities and resources of an entity is typically of interest to many stakeholders. Although some of them are able to command the preparation of special purpose financial reports in order to obtain the information they need, the rest – usually the vast majority – will need to rely on general purpose financial reports (StoP, para 1.1). As the StoP points out, annual reports and accounts, and interim reports, are of interest not only to investors, but also to:

- lenders (although banks demand and get a lot more timely and detailed information than is generally available);
- suppliers and other trade creditors (to decide how much credit to allow a company);
- customers (e.g., a retailer who needs to assess the financial strength of a potential supplier);
- employees (whether to buy some shares or to start looking for another job);
- governments and their agencies; and
- the general public (e.g. where a company makes a substantial contribution to a local economy by providing employment and using local suppliers).

What users look for

Economic decisions often require *an evaluation of the entity's ability to generate cash* and the timing and certainty of its generation. To do this, users focus on the entity's (i) financial position, (ii) performance, and (iii) cash flows, and use these in predicting expected cash flows.

The *financial position* of an entity encompasses the resources it controls, its financial structure, its liquidity and solvency, and its capacity to adapt to changes in the environment in which it operates. Much, but not all, of the information on financial position needed *is provided by the balance sheet.*

The *performance* of an entity comprises the return obtained by the entity on the resources it controls, including the cost of its financing. Information on performance is *provided by the profit and loss account and the statement of total recognised gains and losses.*

The Financial Reporting Council's role

Introduction

The collapse of ENRON and WORLDCOM in the USA led the government to undertake a wide-ranging review of both accountancy regulation and corporate governance in the UK.

In January 2003, the Secretary of State for Trade and Industry announced that reform would be introduced in three areas:

- raising standards of corporate governance;
- strengthening the accounting and auditing professions;
- providing for an independent system of regulation for those professions.

This reform was to be achieved by means of an enhanced role for the then existing Financial Reporting Council (FRC) which was to become the '*new, single, independent regulator*'.

The Financial Reporting Council (FRC)

The FRC has responsibility for:

- corporate governance;
- setting accounting and auditing standards;
- proactively enforcing and monitoring them;
- overseeing the self-regulatory professional bodies.

Two key bodies which report to the FRS are:

- the Financial Reporting Review Panel (FRRP) and
- the Accounting Standards Board (ASB).

The Financial Reporting Review Panel (FRRP)

The FRRP enquires into financial statements where it appears that the requirements of the Companies Act 1985 (CA 85), principally that the financial statements show a true and fair view, might have been breached. The FRRP is autonomous in carrying out its function. Whilst large private companies are within the Panel's remit, the Panel has announced that it intends to focus its resources on larger listed companies.

The role of the FRRP is to examine departures from the accounting and disclosure requirements of both CA 85 and applicable accounting standards, and if necessary to seek an order from the court to remedy such departures. This may refer either to compliance with UK Financial Reporting Standards (UK GAAP) or with International Financial Reporting Standards (IFRS).

Until comparatively recently, FRRP did not actively scrutinise accounts unless they were brought to its attention. It now has a proactive role and scrutinises accounts of larger companies on a sample basis. In Press Notice 88 (FRRP PN 88, www.frc.org.uk) FRRP noted that it had 'developed a more systematic approach to accounts selection based on business sectors, accounting themes and company-specific factors'. In December 2004, it announced its 2005 Risk-based Proactive Programme, which referred to monitoring activity focusing on five industry sectors: Automobile; Pharmaceutical; Retail; Transport; and Utilities. In December 2005, it announced that it would continue to select accounts from the priority sectors referred to above, but that 'the strategy should be widened to include some companies providing services to these sectors.'

Further details of the Panel's remit and activities are available from the FRRP section of the Financial Reporting Council website (www.frc.org.uk).

Where a company has to revise its accounts, its reputation can be seriously damaged. For example, WIGGINS GROUP had to revise its accounts for the year to 31 March 2000, as the *Daily Telegraph* reported.

Now isn't that an interesting point of view?

The article ended 'Wiggins shares fell $^3/_4$ to $31^1/_4$p', and they went on falling, as Figure 1.1 shows.

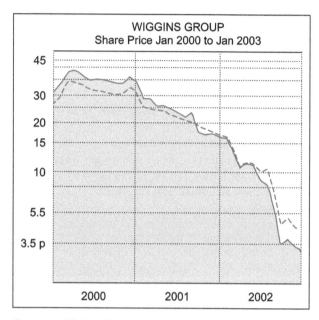

Figure 1.1 Wiggins Group: loss of confidence

WIGGINS GROUP *Extract from Daily Telegraph 8 March 2001*

Wiggins sees profit restated as £10m loss
Wiggins Group, the airport and property manager, yesterday restated its accounts for the second time in six months after regulators intervened.

The new accounts show that the company made a £9.9m pre-tax loss in the year to March 2000 instead of a pre-tax profit of £25.1m.

The restatements mean that Wiggins incurred losses totalling £25.2m in the years 1995 to 2000 rather than making profits of £48.9m as initially recorded.

The Financial Reporting Review Panel said Wiggins had mistakenly booked a £21.5m profit from redeveloping Manston airport, and failed to account for £3m losses from starting an international airport network.

Oliver Iny, Wiggins chief executive, said 'We did wrong, and we've admitted we did so, but it had no impact on the fundamental value of the company . . .'

The FRRP issued a Press Notice in March 2001 dealing with the above company's accounts (FRRP PN 65) available from the FRRP section of the Financial Reporting Council website (www.frc.org.uk), see also page 56.

The Accounting Standards Board (ASB)

The ASB develops and issues UK accounting standards (UK Generally Accepted Accounting Practice or UK GAAP) and keeps them up to date.

An important part of its role now is to help converge UK standards with standards developed by the International Accounting Standards Board (IASB). The IASB's standards are referred to as International Financial Reporting Standards or IFRS (see Chapter 2).

The Urgent Issues Task Force (UITF)

The UITF is a sub-committee of ASB. Its main role is to assist the ASB on emerging issues where there is evidence of unsatisfactory reporting practice. The UITF issues 'Abstracts' to provide interim rules pending the issue of, or amendment to, an accounting standard.

Financial Reporting Standards (FRSs)

CA 85 includes the definition of 'accounting standards' and requires that directors of companies preparing accounts under UK GAAP follow standards issued by the Accounting Standards Board. These include both Financial Reporting Standards (FRSs) issued by ASB, Statements of Standard Accounting Practice (SSAPs) issued by ASB's predecessor body, and Abstracts issued by the Urgent Issues Task Force. Current standards and Abstracts are listed in Appendix 1.

Prior to issue of a standard in final form, ASB issues an exposure draft for comment and discussion (this is referred to as a Financial Reporting Exposure Draft or FRED). FREDs do not have mandatory status until converted into an FRS.

Accounting standards concessions for small companies are dealt with in Chapter 27.

Statements of Recommended Practice (SORPs)

SORPs are developed by bodies recognised by the ASB to provide guidance on the application of accounting standards to specific industries for example, banking, insurance, investment trusts, charities and higher education. Information about current SORPs and where these can be obtained, may be found on www.frc.org.uk.

International Financial Reporting Standards (IFRS)

These are issued by the International Accounting Standards Board (IASB). The activities of IASB, and implications for UK companies, are referred to in Chapter 2 and, where applicable, throughout the remainder of the book.

The current position for UK companies is as follows:

- Fully listed groups are required to adopt IFRS for their group accounts for all accounting periods which started on or after 1 January 2005.

- Companies listed on the Alternative Investment Market (AIM), are required to adopt IFRS for accounting periods which start on or after 1 January 2007. For periods starting before this date, AIM companies may adopt either UK GAAP or IFRS.
- All other categories of companies (including those listed only on PLUS Markets) may presently adopt either UK GAAP or IFRS.

UK company law

The Companies Act 1985 (CA 85) sets out relevant disclosure requirements for companies adopting UK GAAP. These do not apply to UK companies who adopt IFRS which has its own requirements.

Other parts of CA 85 apply to all UK companies, whether they adopt UK GAAP or IFRS. These include audit requirements, rules on distributable profit, filing accounts at Companies House, duties of directors and so on.

The Companies Act 2006 (CA 2006) received Royal Assent in November 2006. CA 2006 will eventually replace most of CA 85. However, different parts of the Act come into force at different times, ranging from early 2007 to late 2008. Commencement procedures will be referred to in the text wherever relevant. Details can be found on www.berr.gov.uk/bbf by clicking on Companies Act 2006 on the left-hand panel.

Categories of companies

Limited companies

The key purpose of forming a company is to limit the liability of its shareholders.

Before the first Companies Act in 1862 introduced the company as a separate legal entity, the *proprietor* of a business (and his or her business partners) had *unlimited* liability. If the business failed, the proprietor(s) were personally liable for settling the debts of the business, even if this required selling the home and personal possessions.

Companies limited by shares

Limited companies are usually formed as limited by shares (see below for companies limited by guarantee). If the shares are fully paid, the members' liability is limited to the money they have put up: the maximum risk a shareholder runs is to lose all the money he has paid for his shares, and no further claim can be made on him for liabilities incurred by the company. In rare cases where shares are issued only partly paid, shareholders can be called upon to subscribe some or all of the unpaid part, but no more than that.

Limited companies may be formed as either private companies or public companies.

Private companies

Most UK limited companies are private – their constitution does not allow their shares to be traded. Many of these companies have only one or two shareholders. The company name ends with the word *limited* (often abbreviated to *Ltd*).

Public companies

A public company is a company which is registered as such. Its share capital must be at least £50,000 and its name must end either with the words 'Public limited company' or with the abbreviation 'PLC' or 'plc'.

A public limited company does *not* automatically have its shares listed on the London Stock Exchange despite popular belief!

In practice, many PLCs are fairly large, and are listed on a market such as the London Stock Exchange, the Alternative Investment Market or PLUS Market. A number of PLCs are companies which have de-listed due to acquisition of shares by private equity groups. Some PLCs are fairly small and are privately-owned businesses.

Fully listed companies

Fully listed companies trade their shares on the London Stock Exchange and are subject to considerable public scrutiny. These companies usually have sophisticated websites that feature important sections on investor relations. These offer quick and easy access to public documents such as annual reports, interim reports, and corporate social responsibility and environmental reports. Many larger companies post presentations to analysts and conference calls.

AIM listed

AIM listed companies shares are traded and share prices published in the financial press. However AIM listed companies vary greatly in size and the extent to which shares are held by major shareholders, directors and financial institutions. Some AIM-listed companies are effectively under the control of one person and family members.

Useful information is available through the following London Stock Exchange links.

- www.londonstockexchange.com/aim
- http://www.londonstockexchange.com/en-gb/pricesnews/statistics/factsheets/aimmarketstats.htm

PLUS Markets

For many regulatory purposes, companies who trade solely on PLUS Markets are regarding as 'unlisted'. The market was previously referred to as OFEX. The PLUS Markets website (www.plusmarketsgroup.com) is extremely comprehensive and gives details of companies whose shares are traded, their share prices and so on.

Small and medium-sized enterprises (SMEs)

Small and medium-sized enterprises (SMEs) are defined by the Companies Act 1985 – please refer to Chapter 27 for the special features of these companies and the financial information which has to be made available.

Unlimited companies

By contrast with a limited company, the members have joint and several liability in the same way as a partnership (each member can individually be held entirely responsible). The principal advantage of forming an unlimited company is that it is not required to file its accounts each year at Companies House. This form of company is relatively uncommon today.

Companies limited by guarantee

This method is used for charitable and similar organisations, where funds are raised by donations and no shares are issued. The liability is limited to the amount each member can personally guarantee, which is the maximum amount each member may be called upon to pay in the event of liquidation. This form of incorporation is not normally used for a commercial business.

Limited liability partnerships (LLPs)

A limited liability partnership (LLP) is a relatively new legal vehicle – the relevant legislation came into force in April 2001. Companies House described it as an 'alternative corporate business vehicle that gives the benefits of limited liability but allows its members the flexibility of organising their internal structure as a traditional partnership. The LLP is a separate legal entity and, while the LLP itself will be liable for the full extent of its assets, the liability of the members will be limited.'

The main difference between an LLP and a limited company is that an LLP has the organisational flexibility of a partnership and is taxed as a partnership. Apart from this, an LLP is very similar to a company. Many large accountancy and legal firms are now constituted as LLPs.

Extracts from published accounts

The book includes practical examples of company accounts presented both in accordance with UK GAAP and with IFRS. These are allocated within the appropriate sections of each chapter.

UK GAAP

Most unlisted companies and a large number of AIM-listed companies continue to use UK GAAP. (However, for AIM listed companies this choice ceases to be available for accounting periods which started on or after 1 January 2007: they will be required to move over to IFRS.)

Many UK GAAP illustrations taken from a few years ago continue to be useful (most of these relate to fully listed companies which have now moved over to IFRS). Where these illustrations give clear presentation and would still be acceptable if published today under UK GAAP, we have retained them. UK GAAP is likely to be around for some time to come.

IFRS

We have provided a large number of IFRS illustrations including reference to useful websites for those readers who want to research further.

CHAPTER 2

International Financial Reporting Standards (IFRS) overview

Introduction

We referred to the International Accounting Standards Board (IASB) in Chapter 1. IASB is an independent body, responsible for developing and setting Standards and Interpretations.

For companies operating within the European Union (EU) and producing accounts under IFRS, the Standards used must have been officially approved ('endorsed') by the EU. Companies in their accounting policies usually start referring to 'basis of preparation' and state words similar to:

'These accounts have been prepared in accordance with International Financial Reporting Standards ("IFRS"), including International Accounting Standards ("IAS") and interpretations issued by the International Accounting Standards Board ("IASB") and its committees, *and as adopted by the EU* [emphasis added] . . .'

Terminology

The terms 'International Financial Reporting Standards' (IFRS) and 'International Accounting Standards' (IAS) *are effectively interchangeable*.

The term IAS originates from the earlier standards issued by the IASB's (International Accounting Standard Board) predecessor body, the International Accounting Standards Committee. These standards are still applicable, although several have been substantially revised in recent years.

The Companies Act 1985 and the relevant tax legislation refer to 'IAS'. However, the more widely-used (and modern) term is IFRS – this is the term we will use throughout the book.

The Standards

The Standards referred to in the extract above are listed in Appendix 1. 'IFRS GAAP' is effectively a combination of International Accounting Standards issued by the former International Accounting Standards Committee (these are referred to as IAS 1, IAS 2, etc.) and International Financial Reporting Standards issued by the current body, the International Accounting Standards Board (these are referred to as IFRS 1, IFRS 2, etc.).

Who must adopt IFRS?

At present in the UK, the only two mandatory categories are companies that are fully listed on the London Stock Exchange and companies whose shares are traded on AIM (the Alternative Investment Market). This position is currently under review.

Fully listed companies

In June 2002, EU Member States adopted the Regulation on the Application of International Accounting Standards (*the 'IAS Regulation'*).

This requires companies governed by the law of a member state to prepare their *consolidated* accounts in conformity with international accounting standards if their securities are admitted to trading on a regulated market of any member state. In the UK, this applies to consolidated accounts of *fully listed* companies.

The IAS Regulation applies to each financial year *commencing on or after 1 January 2005*. For example, a *fully* listed group with a 31 March year-end first had to apply IFRS to its full-year *consolidated* accounts to 31 March 2006.

The above requirement is only applicable to the consolidated accounts (the accounts of the combined group). We refer to the concept of consolidated accounts in Chapter 28. The Companies Act 1985 permits the individual parent company and subsidiary company accounts to be prepared on the basis of either UK GAAP or IFRS.

However, it is the consolidated accounts that are used as the primary basis for analysts.

Alternative Investment Market (AIM) companies

The Rules of the London Stock Exchange require all AIM companies to adopt IFRS for *financial years commencing on or after 1 January 2007*. Several AIM companies adopted IFRS earlier, for example for 31 December 2005 year-ends.

Unlisted companies

For financial years commencing on or after 1 January 2005, all British companies have the *option* of using IFRS as an alternative to UK accounting standards. This option extends to SMEs as well as large unlisted companies.

For unlisted companies, the choice between UK GAAP and IFRS is likely to remain an option for some years to come.

How does this affect different categories of companies?

Examples of the possible impact are summarised in the table below.

The Accounting Standards Board issued a Press Notice on 10 May 2006 (ASB PN 289) setting out proposals for extending the mandatory categories that might be required to adopt IFRS including all public quoted and other publicly accountable entities and UK subsidiaries of group companies that applied IFRS in the group accounts. A further announcement is awaited.

Convergence

What does 'convergence' mean?

The term 'convergence' may be used in two separate but interlinked contexts:

- convergence of UK GAAP with IFRS,
- convergence of IFRS and US GAAP.

Type of company	Application of IFRS
Traded on PLUS Markets (formerly OFEX)	For regulatory purposes, companies whose shares are traded on PLUS Markets are regarded as unlisted and there is therefore no mandatory date for transition to IFRS. However, such companies should consider strategic issues such as how late adoption of IFRS might be viewed in the marketplace, particularly for those companies intending to move over to AIM or the full market.
UK listed parent company	CA 85 offers a choice between adopting UK GAAP and adopting IFRS.
UK subsidiaries of UK fully listed groups	All UK subsidiary companies within a group must adopt either UK GAAP or IFRS (see above). In practice, many adopt IFRS in order to ease the preparation of consolidated accounts under IFRS.
UK subsidiaries of foreign listed groups that are adopting IAS	Although UK company law does not require these subsidiaries to adopt IFRS, the overseas parent may require IFRS accounts from them so that it can itself prepare IFRS consolidated accounts.
Unlisted companies	These companies can for the moment choose whether and when they adopt IFRS. The decision may be affected by a number of considerations, including the desires of the major shareholder(s), whether the company has future plans for 'going public' and its relations with suppliers and customers outside the UK.

Convergence of UK GAAP with IFRS has been taking place for a large number of years, for example the respective standards on accounting for provisions (FRS 12 and IAS 37) are identical. More recent years have seen an acceleration of the convergence process, for example, the areas of accounting for financial instruments and share-based payment transactions such as accounting for share option schemes. We will refer to the extent of convergence in the chapters that follow.

Convergence of IFRS and US GAAP is a relatively recent development. It is hoped that bringing the two accounting frameworks closer together will eventually mean that large UK companies with share listings in the USA will no longer have to publish tables reconciling their respective profits and assets between IFRS and US GAAP.

UK convergence strategy

The ASB's Technical Plan, published on 22 June 2005, set out a 'phased approach'. The original plan was to bring UK standards into line with IFRS by bringing a number of standards on related topics into effect each year over a three to four-year period (e.g. FRSs based on FREDs 25 and 28 were originally planned to be brought into UK GAAP during 2005/06).

At a public meeting held in January 2006, ASB proposed an alternative strategy whereby further changes to UK standards should be introduced with a common effective date.

ASB issued a Press Notice on 10 May 2006 (ASB PN 289), seeking views on the future application of reporting requirements for UK companies. This effectively proposes further extensions to the categories of companies for which IFRS would be mandatory.

Transition from UK GAAP to IFRS

We refer to the 'conversion process' in Chapter 34, including the extent to which invaluable information is available in the investor relations and archive sections of corporate websites.

Approach followed in the book

Whilst fully listed and many AIM companies are now following IFRS, most UK companies are still using UK GAAP. In the current edition of the book, each chapter will initially consider the relevant UK GAAP requirements (including those of the Companies Act 1985) and their implications for the interpretation of company accounts. This will be followed by a concise summary of the key differences for companies that adopt IFRS.

Chapter 33 contains a summary of the key differences over the relevant profit and loss account and balance sheet areas.

CHAPTER 3

Accounting principles

What is UK GAAP?

Terminology

'GAAP' stands for Generally Accepted Accounting Practice (but it can also stand for Generally Accepted Accounting Principles). UK GAAP is effectively a package of principles, rules and guidance statements used by companies to measure profits and assets, and also to determine what disclosures must be given in the company's annual accounts or financial statements.

Main components of UK GAAP

In practice, in the UK, this set of rules and guidance derives from a number of diverse sources, including:

- the Statement of Principles for Financial Reporting (StoP) – issued by the Accounting Standards Board (ASB);
- Statements of Standard Accounting Practice (SSAPs) – issued by the ASB's predecessor body;
- Financial Reporting Standards (FRSs) – issued by the ASB;
- Abstracts – issued by the Urgent Issues Task Force (UITF);
- Companies Act 1985 requirements (as subsequently amended by the Companies Act 2006 and Regulations expected to be issued during 2007);
- Statements of Recommended Practice (SORPs) – issued by ASB-recognised industry committees;
- Reporting Statements, such as the guidance on the Operating and Financial Review (OFR, see Chapter 5) – issued by the ASB;

- best practice – as adopted by leading UK companies (e.g. leading FTSE companies) or sectors; UK GAAP may also reflect best practice in particular industry sectors such as the construction industry;
- guidance from the leading professional bodies, for example, guidance on revenue recognition (see Chapter 8) issued by the Consultative Committee of Accountancy bodies (CCAB);
- feedback from regulators such as the Financial Reporting Review Panel (FFRP) on appropriate company reporting practice.

Accounting principles

Statement of principles for financial reporting

ASB issued its Statement of Principles for Financial Reporting (StoP) in 1999. In the words of ASB:

'This Statement of Principles for Financial Reporting sets out the principles that the Accounting Standards Board believes should underlie the preparation and presentation of general purpose financial statements.

'The primary purpose of articulating such principles is to provide a coherent frame of reference to be used by the Board in the development and review of accounting standards and by others who interact with the Board during the standard-setting process.

'Such a frame of reference should clarify the conceptual underpinnings of proposed accounting standards and should enable standards to be developed on a consistent basis. . . .'

StoP is a lengthy document consisting of eight chapters over some 57 pages (excluding appendices). It was clearly important in the development of the numerous Financial Reporting Standards (FRSs) issued after its publication. It is now rather less important as more recent FRSs such as FRS 25, Financial Instruments – Disclosure and Presentation (see Chapter 24) are based on standards issued by the International Accounting Standards Board following the policy of converging UK GAAP with International Financial Reporting Standards (IFRS) – see Chapter 2. IASB has its own statement of principles referred to as 'The Framework'.

FRS 18 – Accounting policies

The term 'accounting policies' refers to the rules that the company uses for dealing with particular transactions, for example, how they are recognised and presented in the financial statements, and whether assets are stated at historical cost or a current valuation figure. The application to particular transactions and situations will be dealt with in the chapters in the book that deal with individual financial statement topics, for example, fixed assets, revenue recognition and stocks.

FRS 18 sets out principles to be followed in selecting accounting policies and the disclosures required. An example of a typical company accounting policy statement under UK GAAP is included later in this chapter.

FRS 18 does highlight two particular concepts that are crucial in dealing with particular transactions and in preparing and presenting financial statements. These are the going concern assumption and accruals.

Going concern assumption

Financial statements are usually prepared on the assumption that the entity will continue in operational existence for the foreseeable future. The going concern basis is not used if the entity is being liquidated or has ceased trading, or if the directors have no alternative but to liquidate or cease trading.

Accruals

The accruals basis of accounting assumes that revenues and costs are accrued (accounted for) as they are earned or incurred, not as money is received or paid. Revenues are matched with associated costs and expenses to determine profit, by including them in the same accounting period.

Comparability

Users need to be able to able to compare an entity's financial information over time in order to identify trends in its financial performance and financial position. They also need to be able to compare the financial information of different entities in order to evaluate their relative financial performance and financial position.

When companies change their accounting policies, figures for the previous year will be restated in line with the new policy so that current and previous year figures are comparable.

Comparability between companies can be distorted by:

- companies adopting different accounting policies, for example, companies in similar business sectors depreciating similar equipment over different useful lives;
- companies financing assets in different ways, for example, a retailer that owns all its outlets cannot be fairly compared with a similar retailer that rents all its outlets, unless the analyst adjusts the figures to allow for the difference;
- the effects of inflation (see Chapter 31).

Consistency

Consistency is viewed against the objective of comparability, which can be achieved through a combination of consistency and disclosure. The consistency concept assumes that accounting treatment of like items is consistent from one period to the next.

Substance over form

This concept was introduced by FRS 5 but is now incorporated within the Companies Act 1985. It requires transaction to be accounted to reflect their commercial substance rather than their legal form, should these differ.

For example, where a company may not technically be the *legal* owner of an asset but for practical purposes may effectively have the risks and rewards of ownership of the asset. In this situation, the asset should be included in the company's balance sheet. This could occur, for example, in a hire-purchase transaction where a company was already deriving virtually all the commercial benefits from an asset, and had an indefinite option to buy it from its legal owner for a nominal sum.

Materiality

Information is material if its omission or misstatement could influence the economic decisions of users taken on the basis of those financial statements. Materiality must be judged in terms of its significance to the reporting entity.

Estimation techniques

Estimation techniques are the method a company adopts to arrive at estimated monetary amounts – for example:

- depreciation charges;
- provisions for slow-moving or obsolete stock;
- warranty provisions for expected returns.

The profit and loss account – UK GAAP

The profit and loss account (also referred to in IFRS as the income statement) is a record of the activities of a company for a stated period of time. This period, called the accounting reference period, is normally a year.

Example 3.1 shows a typical profit and loss account; the terminology box below explains the terms used.

Example 3.1 A typical profit and loss account

Profit and loss account for the year ended 30 June 2007

	£000	£000
Turnover		7,200
Cost of sales		3,600
Gross profit		3,600
Distribution costs	1,100	
Administrative expenses	1,300	
		2,400
		1,200
Other operating income		95
Trading or operating profit		1,295
Interest receivable		20
		1,315
Interest payable		100
Pre-tax profit on ordinary activities		1,215
Taxation		415
Profit for the year		800

TERMINOLOGY

UK GAAP: Profit and loss account

The **profit and loss account** is a monetary record of the activities of a business during an accounting period, which is normally one year. A balance sheet is drawn up on the last day of the company's accounting period.

Turnover (also called sales) is money received, or to be received, by the business for goods or services sold during the year.

Expenses are costs incurred in producing those goods and services, normally divided into:

(i) **Cost of sales**, i.e. the cost of the goods themselves, e.g. raw materials and wages

Gross profit = Turnover – Cost of sales

(ii) **Distribution costs**, i.e. the cost of getting the goods to the customer

(iii) **Administrative expenses**, i.e. other expenses which cannot be or are not allocated to particular products (i.e. which do not form part of cost of sales) or appear under other headings.

Operating profit or **trading profit** = Turnover – Expenses (i.e. (i) to (iii) above).

Where expenses (i) to (iii) above exceed turnover, the difference is an **operating loss**.

(iv) **Other operating income** is income and expenses which fall outside (i) to (iii) above, e.g. property income of a trading company, or patent income.

(v) **Interest paid** on borrowed money **interest received** represents income from interest on money lent (e.g. deposits at the bank).

Pre-tax profit = Operating profit + (iv) +/– (v)

Depreciation is an expense appearing as part of (i) to (iii) above, as appropriate.

The cost of each fixed asset is written off over its expected life. Using the most common method of depreciation, **the straight line method:**

$$\frac{\text{Depreciation}}{\text{for the year}} = \frac{\text{Cost of asset} - \text{Residual value}}{\text{Expected useful life}}$$

Corresponding figures or 'comparatives' are those for the same item for the preceding accounting period.

Note: Dividends are distributions to the shareholders. **As dividends on equity (or ordinary) shares are not an expense of the business, they are not entered in the profit and loss account** (see Chapter 24).

Accounts are required to include the figures for two periods, normally those for the year being reported on and corresponding (or comparative) figures for the previous year. For simplicity, at this stage we show only figures for the year being reported on.

The balance sheet – UK GAAP

The balance sheet is a statement of the assets and liabilities of a company at the close of business on a given day, i.e. on the balance sheet date. The balance sheet is always drawn up on the last day of the company's accounting period.

Example 3.2 shows a typical balance sheet; the terminology box below explains the main terms used in balance sheets.

Example 3.2 A typical balance sheet

Balance sheet as at 30 June 2007

	£000	£000	£000
Fixed assets			
Freehold land and buildings		950	
Fixtures and fittings		175	
Motor vehicles		535	
			1,660
Current assets			
Stock (of goods)		500	
Debtors		1,040	
Cash		5	
		1,545	
Less: Current liabilities:			
Creditors due within 1 year:			
Trade creditors	860		
Taxation payable	415		
Overdraft	90		
		1,365	
Net current assets			180
Net assets			1,840
Capital and reserves			
Ordinary share capital		1,000	
Profit and loss account		840	
Ordinary shareholders' funds			1,840

Note

Dividends paid are not entered in the profit and loss account, as they are not an expense of the company. Dividends paid are charged direct to reserves (see also Chapter 24). The profit and loss account in last year's balance sheet at 30 June 2006 amounted to £600. The profit for the year amounted to £800 (see Example 3.1). The dividends paid during the year amounted to £560.

The above figures may be reconciled to the closing profit and loss reserves of £840 as follows:

	£
Profit and loss reserves at 1 July 2006	600
Profit for the year	800
Equity dividends paid	(560)
Profit and loss reserves at 30 June 2007	840

TERMINOLOGY

UK GAAP: balance sheet

A **balance sheet** is a statement of the assets and liabilities and ownership interest of an enterprise at the close of business on the balance sheet date.

Assets are things which a business owns and on which a book value can be placed.

Book value is cost less accumulated depreciation or, if the asset has been revalued, it is the valuation figure less any subsequent depreciation.

Liabilities are amounts owed by a business.

Net assets = All assets – All liabilities.

Fixed assets are assets (like land and buildings, plant and machinery) not held for resale but for use by the business.

Fixed assets can be either **tangible**, from the Latin *tango*, I touch (e.g. motor vehicle, land and buildings) or **intangible**, i.e. not susceptible to touch (e.g. patent rights and trademarks).

Current assets are cash and other assets that the company expects to turn into cash (e.g. stock).

Current liabilities, which are usually described as **Creditors due within one year**, are the liabilities that the company expects to have to meet within 12 months.

The **members (shareholders)** of a company provide some or all of the finance in the form of **share capital** (that is, they subscribe for shares) in the expectation that the company will make profits, and pay dividends.

Ordinary shareholders' funds are made up of ordinary share capital and all accumulated reserves.

Financial statements is the term which covers the annual accounts as a whole, i.e. the profit and loss account, balance sheet, cash flow statement and statements forming part of the statutory accounts.

Worked example – putting the accounts together

The initial transactions

A company is formed with a share capital of 300,000 ordinary shares, each with a nominal value of £1. The director/shareholders subscribe for these at par (= nominal value) by payment of cash.

At the same time, the directors of the company negotiate with the bank and agree an overdraft facility of £150,000. As the company is new, the bank requires personal securities from the directors – for example against their personal assets such as their properties. This facility enables the company to overdraw by up to £150,000. However, this figure does not appear in the accounts.

Acquiring assets and getting started – the first year of the business

The company:

1. buys a freehold shop for £200,000
2. acquires fixtures and fittings for £75,000
3. stocks the shop with £200,000 of goods
4. buys a van for £10,000.

The above are all acquired by payment of cash except for the purchase of goods. Half of these are bought for cash and half are bought on credit terms requiring payment within four weeks following delivery (i.e. four weeks

credit). These suppliers become creditors of the company – immediately following receipt of the goods, the amount owing to them is a liability.

No actual trading took place during the year, i.e. no goods were sold and so the entire purchases of £200,000 represent unsold stocks at the end of the year.

The company's cash position at the end of the first year is as follows:

	£
Initial cash introduced by the shareholders	300,000
Freehold shop	(200,000)
Shop fittings	(75,000)
Purchase of goods (50% × £200,000)	(100,000)
Motor van	(10,000)
Overdrawn bank account	(85,000)

The balance sheet of the company at the end of the first year as follows:

	£000	£000
Fixed assets		
Freehold land and buildings		200,000
Fixtures and fittings		75,000
Motor vehicles		10,000
		285,000
Current assets		
Stock (of goods)	200,000	
Current liabilities:		
Creditors	100,000	
Overdraft	85,000	
	185,000	
Net current assets		15,000
		300,000
Capital		
Ordinary share capital		300,000

Comment

Fixed assets are held not for resale but for use by the business. *Current assets* are cash and other assets that the company expects to turn into cash (e.g. stock). *Current liabilities* (usually described as *creditors due within one year*, are all the liabilities that the company expects to have to meet within 12 months. In balance sheets prepared and presented in accordance with UK GAAP, current liabilities are deducted from current assets to arrive at a sub-total referred to as 'net current assets'. Presentation under IFRS may be quite different from this (see Chapter 12).

Trading transactions during the second year of trading

The company:

5. sells goods for £1,200,000
6. buys goods for £850,000
7. incurred expenses for wages and other expenses of £280,000.

Calculating profit for the year

To work out the profit for the year, further information is required:

Closing stock

Some of the goods purchased were not actually sold, so the cost of these goods must be excluded from the profit calculation. They will be included in the year-end balance sheet as a current asset. Assume that the cost of these goods amounts to £250,000.

Depreciation

Allowance must be made for the wear and tear on fixed assets during the year. This is done by means of a provision for depreciation. Depreciation is simply a way of spreading the cost of the fixed asset over the period it is being used. For example, assume a machine costs £5,000 and it will be used for ten years and at the end of this period its value will be negligible. One way of calculating the depreciation charge would be to spread it evenly over the ten years, charging an expense of £500 against the profits of each year.

In practice, fixed assets will usually have some value at the end of their 'useful lives'. This is referred to as residual value (see also Chapter 13).

In our example, using the straight-line method, the depreciation charges for the buildings, fittings and van are set out below. Note that the land element of the land and buildings (assumed to be £75,000) is not depreciated as its life is assumed to be infinite and not subject to wear and tear. The figures below show both the depreciation expense in the profit and loss account (£12,000) as well as the amount for fixed assets in the balance sheet (£273,000).

Calculation of depreciation charge in the profit and loss account using the straight line method (see Chapter 13):

$$\text{Depreciation for the year} = \frac{\text{Cost of asset}}{\text{Expected useful life}}$$

For our company the depreciation charge for the year would be worked out as follows:

Fixed asset	Cost	Life	Annual depreciation £
Buildings	125,000	50 years	2,500
Fittings	75,000	10 years	7,500
Motor van	10,000	5 years	2,000
Depreciation charge for the year			12,000

Net book amount of fixed assets in the balance sheet

	Cost £	Accumulated depreciation £	Net book amount £
Land	75,000	–	75,000
Buildings	125,000	2,500	122,500
	200,000		197,500
Fixtures and fittings	75,000	7,500	67,500
Motor vehicles	10,000	2,000	8,000
	285,000	12,000	273,000

The profit and loss account

The profit and loss account for the second year is as follows:

	£
Sales (or turnover)	1,200,000
Less cost of goods sold	(800,000)

	£
Opening stocks	200,000
Purchases	850,000
	1,050,000
Less: closing stock	250,000
	800,000

	£
Gross profit	400,000
Wages and other expenses	(280,000)
Depreciation	(12,000)
Profit before tax	108,000
Corporation tax	27,000
Profit for the year	81,000

The bank account

The movement on the bank account is summarised as follows:

	£	£
Overdrawn bank account at beginning of year		(85,000)
Receipts from sales		1,120,000

	£
Sales during the year	1,200,000
Less amounts not yet received (represented by debtors)	(80,000)
Cash collected	1,120,000

Payments to suppliers for goods	(830,000)

	£
Owing at beginning of year	100,000
Purchases during the year	850,000
	950,000
Less amounts owing at end of year (represented by creditors)	120,000
Cash paid	830,000

Wages and expenses	(280,000)
Overdrawn bank account at end of year	(75,000)

The balance sheet at the end of year 2

This may now be completed:

	£	£
Fixed assets		
Freehold land and buildings		197,500
Fixtures and fittings		67,500
Motor vehicles		8,000
		273,000
Current assets		
Stock	250,000	
Debtors	80,000	
	330,000	
Current liabilities (or creditors due within 1 year)		
Trade creditors	120,000	
Taxation payable	27,000	
Overdraft	75,000	
	222,000	
Net current assets		108,000
Total assets less current liabilities		381,000

Capital and reserves

	£
Ordinary share capital	300,000
Profit and loss reserves	81,000
	381,000

Format and terminology differences – UK GAAP and IFRS compared

Some of the more common terminology differences are as follows. Other differences will be referred to in specific chapters later in the text.

UK GAAP term	IFRS term
Profit and loss account	Income statement
Turnover	Revenue
Debtors	Trade and other receivables
Stocks	Inventories

Accounting policies – UK GAAP

Financial Reporting Standard 18 (FRS 18) on Accounting policies, states that the standard 'sets out the principles to be followed in selecting accounting policies and the disclosures needed to help users to understand the accounting policies adopted and how they have been applied'.

Example – Statement of accounting policies

This usually appears in the annual report at the start of the section dealing with the notes to the accounts. The statement begins with the accounting convention or basis of accounts, and then deals in turn with each major accounting area. The following is a typical example:

Basis of accounting

The accounts have been prepared under the historical cost convention.

Turnover comprises the fair value of the consideration received or receivable for the provision of printing services, and is net of value added tax.

Turnover is recognised when the service has been provided and all obligations to the customers have been fulfilled.

Amortisation is calculated so as to write off the cost of an asset, less its estimated residual value, over the useful economic life of that asset as follows:

Goodwill – 10% straight line

Depreciation is calculated so as to write off the cost of an asset, less its estimated residual value, over the useful economic life of that asset as follows:

Freehold Property – nil
Plant & Machinery – 20–33% straight line
Computer Equipment – 33% straight line
Motor Vehicles – 33% straight line
Office Equipment – 33% straight line

Stocks are valued at the lower of cost and net realisable value, after making due allowance for obsolete and slow-moving items.

Assets held under **hire-purchase agreements** are capitalised and disclosed under tangible fixed assets at their fair value. The capital element of the future payments is treated as a liability and the interest is charged to the profit and loss account on a straight line basis.

Rentals applicable to **operating leases** where substantially all of the benefits and risks of ownership remain with the lessee are charged against profits on a straight line basis over the period of the lease.

The company operates a defined contribution **pension** scheme for employees. The assets of the scheme are held separately from those of the company. The annual contributions payable are charged to the profit and loss account.

Deferred tax is provided in full in respect of taxation deferred by timing differences between the treatment of certain items for taxation and accounting purposes. The deferred tax balance has not been discounted. Deferred tax assets are recognised only when recovery is likely.

Assets and liabilities in **foreign currencies** are translated into sterling at the rates of exchange ruling at the balance sheet date. Transactions in foreign currencies are translated into sterling at the rate of exchange ruling at the date of the transaction. Exchange differences are taken into account in arriving at the operating profit.

Accounting policies – IFRS

The accounting policies statement under IFRS is more detailed and complex than its UK GAAP counterpart. A typical example for a listed company appears below to give a flavour at this stage in the book. Each topic area under IFRS is referred to at the end of each relevant chapter. Readers may wish to revisit the example below when they have completed the relevant chapters.

ROK PLC *Annual Report 2006*

Notes to the consolidated Financial Statements

1. Accounting Policies

Basis of preparation
Rok plc (the Company) is a company domiciled in
the United Kingdom. Both the Company financial
statements and the Group financial statements have
been prepared and approved by the directors in
accordance with International Financial Reporting
Standards as adopted by the EU (Adopted IFRSs). On
publishing the Company financial statements here
together with the Group financial statements, the
Company is taking advantage of the exemption in
s230 of the Companies Act 1985 not to present its
individual income statement and related notes that
form a part of these approved financial statements.

At the date of issue of these financial statements
the following standards and interpretations, which
have not been applied in these financial statements,
were in issue but not yet effective:

IFRS 7   Financial Instruments Disclosures
IFRIC 7   Applying the Restatement Approach under
            IAS 29 Financial Reporting in
            Hyperinflationary Economies
IFRIC 8   Scope of IFRS 2
IFRIC 9   Reassessment of Embedded Derivatives

The directors anticipate that the adoption of these
standards and interpretations, in future periods will
have no material impact on the financial statements
of the Group.

The financial statements have been prepared on
the historical cost basis, except where otherwise
indicated. The principal accounting policies adopted
are set out below.

Subsidiaries and joint ventures
The consolidated financial statements comprise
the Company and its subsidiaries and the Group's
interest in jointly controlled entities.

The results of subsidiary undertakings acquired or
disposed of are included in the consolidated income
statement from the date of acquisition until the
date of disposal. The Company's investments in
subsidiaries are stated at cost less any impairment.

The consolidated financial statements include
the Group's appropriate share of joint venture
undertakings' post tax profits in the consolidated
income statement after aligning the accounting
policies with those of the Group. Investments in joint
venture undertakings are accounted for under the
equity method, initially stated at cost and adjusted

thereafter for subsequent changes in the Group's
share of net assets.

Revenue and profit recognition

Building
Revenue recognised on building activities reflects
the value of work performed. The amount of profit
attributable to the stage of completion of a contract
is recognised when the outcome of the contract can
be foreseen with reasonable certainty. The results
for the year include adjustments for the outcome of
contracts executed in both the current and preceding
years. These adjustments arise from claims by
customers or third parties in respect of work carried
out and claims and variations on customers or third
parties for variations to the original contract.
Provision for claims against the Group is made
as soon as it is believed that a liability will arise.
Claims and variations made by the Group are
not recognised in the income statement until the
outcome is reasonably certain. Where it is foreseen
that a loss will arise on a contract, provision for the
expected loss is made in the current year.

Maintenance
Revenue and profit is recognised on projects which
have been completed.

Development
Revenue and profit on the Group's development
activities are recognised as follows. Revenue on the
sale of development properties is recognised when
the group has transferred to the buyer the significant
risks and rewards of ownership of the development
property. This is achieved when legal title is
transferred to the buyer if a property is pre-sold
and the Group has construction work to complete
or rental guarantees in respect of un-let space are
outstanding, the Group reviews the nature and extent
of its continuing involvement to assess whether
it is appropriate to recognise revenue. Where the
conditions for the recognition of revenue are met
but the Group still has significant acts to perform,
revenue is recognised as the acts are performed.
Revenue and profit on all other commercial property
development activities is recognised on legal
completion.

Goodwill and other intangible assets
All business combinations are accounted for by
applying the purchase method. In respect of business
combinations that have occurred since 1 January
2004, goodwill represents the difference between the
cost of the acquisition and the fair value of the net

▶

identifiable assets acquired. In respect of acquisitions prior to this date, goodwill is included at the carrying amount recorded under UK GAAP at the date of transition.

Goodwill is stated at cost less any accumulated impairment losses. Goodwill is allocated to cash-generating units and is tested annually for impairment and more frequently if there are indications of impairment. Any excess of the fair value of net identifiable assets acquired over the cost of an acquisition is recognised directly in the consolidated income statement.

Intangible assets other than goodwill acquired by the Group are stated at cost less accumulated amortisation and impairment losses. Amortisation is charged on a straight-line basis over the intangible assets' useful economic life. These have been estimated as follows:

Brands – between 4 and 5 years
Customer relationships – 10 years

Intangible assets are tested for impairment if there are circumstances which indicate that an impairment might have arisen.

Property, plant and equipment
Property, plant and equipment is stated at cost less accumulated depreciation. Depreciation is charged on a straight-line basis so as to write off the cost over their useful economic lives. These have been estimated as follows:

Leasehold improvements – lower of the remaining life of the lease or 10 years
Plant and machinery – between 4 and 7 years
Office and computer equipment – between 3 and 5 years

Work in progress
Development work in progress is carried at the lower of cost and net realisable value, net of progress payments, interest charges incurred in respect of development projects are charged to the income statement as incurred.

Building and Maintenance work in progress is stated at the lower of cost and net realisable value, less interim receipts. Cost comprises direct materials, direct labour and subcontractor costs.

Operating leases
Operating lease rentals paid are charged on a straight-line basis to the consolidated income statement in the period to which the rentals relate.

Finance leases
Assets obtained under finance leases and hire purchase contracts are capitalised at their fair value on acquisition and depreciated over their estimated useful lives, The corresponding liability to the lessor is included in the balance sheet as a finance lease obligation. The finance charges are allocated over the period of the lease in proportion to the capital element outstanding.

Taxation
Income tax on the profit or loss for the year comprises current tax and deferred tax. Income tax is recognised in the consolidated income statement except to the extent that it relates to items recognised directly in shareholders' equity.

Current tax is the tax expected to be payable on the taxable profit for the year, calculated using tax rates enacted or substantively enacted by the balance sheet date, and any adjustment to tax payable in respect of previous years.

Deferred tax is recognised on temporary differences between the carrying amounts of assets and liabilities in the balance sheet and the amounts attributed to such assets and liabilities for tax purposes. Deferred tax liabilities are generally recognised for all taxable temporary differences and deferred tax assets are recognised to the extent that it is probable that future taxable profits will be available against which deductible temporary differences can be utilised.

Deferred tax relating to charges made directly to equity is recognised in equity.

Employee benefits
The Group operates a defined contribution pension scheme 'Rokplan' and contributions to the scheme are charged to the consolidated income statement as incurred.

The Group also has three defined benefit pension schemes which are closed to new members and future service accrual. The assets of the schemes are held separately from those of the Group.

Pension scheme assets are measured using fair values as at the respective balance sheet dates.

Pension scheme liabilities are stated at their present value calculated by discounting at the current rate of return on a high quality corporate bond of equivalent term and currency as the liabilities. The expected return on scheme assets and the increase during the period in the present value of the schemes' liabilities arising from the passage of time are included in other finance charges. Actuarial gains and losses are recognised in equity and presented in the statement of recognised income and expenses.

▶

Share-based payments

Charges for employee services received in exchange for share-based payments have been made for all options granted after 7 November 2002 in accordance with IFRS 2 'Share-Based Payment'.

Options granted under the Group's employee share schemes are equity settled. The fair value of such options has been calculated using a stochastic model, based upon publicly available market data, and is charged to the consolidated income statement over the vesting period.

Cash and cash equivalents

Cash and cash equivalents as stated in the cash flow statement include the Group's cash balances and overdrafts.

Trade receivables

Trade receivables do not carry any interest and are stated at their nominal value as reduced by appropriate allowances for estimated irrecoverable amounts.

Trade payables

Trade payables are not interest bearing and are stated at their normal value.

Dividends

Dividends are recorded in the Group's financial statements in the period in which they are approved or paid.

CHAPTER 4

The annual report

Information other than the financial statements

In this and the following two chapters we look at what can be learned from those parts of the report of a company that are not strictly part of the accounts. The directors' report has long been part of the reporting system and is required by the Companies Act 1985 (to be replaced by the Companies Act 2006). The other documents covered in these chapters include the chairman's statement, the chief executive's review, the operating and financial review, the corporate governance report, and the remuneration report.

What is the annual report?

We referred to the term 'annual report and accounts' in Chapter 1. The annual report is effectively a corporate document that includes a package of information both numerical and narrative. Some of this information is required by law, accounting regulation, the Financial Services Authority (FSA) or the London Stock Exchange. Other information is included as a result of following recommended guidance or industry best practice.

This chapter is concerned with those parts of the annual report that are mandatory. Corporate governance requirements specific to fully listed companies are dealt with in Chapter 6. The operating and financial review and best practice narrative reporting are dealt with in Chapter 5.

 In this and subsequent chapters we refer to a large number of practical examples – either by including extracts from a report or by reference to a website. The relevant hard copy

annual reports are generally available on request from the company's registered office but a quicker way of obtaining the information is to visit the relevant company's website and to look for the section that deals with 'investor relations' (or a similar title).

Most companies archive annual reports and interim accounts so that it is possible to make comparisons over past years.

The mandatory parts of the annual report

This list is a moving target – narrative reporting disclosure requirements for fully listed companies will be extended when the relevant requirements of the Companies Act 2006 come into force for accounting periods commencing on or after 1 October 2007.

The key components and the chapters in which further information is included are as shown below.

Key components	Chapter
Directors' report	4
Business review	4
Annual accounts:	
Profit and loss account (referred to as income statement under IFRS)	7
Balance sheet	12
Equity statement	11
Cash flow statement	26
Notes to the accounts	Various
Remuneration report (directors' remuneration)	6
Corporate governance statement (mandatory for fully listed companies only)	6

Best practice (non-mandatory) parts of the annual report

These include the following – but note the information is structured and packaged in different ways by different companies and groups.

Non-mandatory part	Chapter
Chairman's report	5
Chief executive's report	5
Operating and financial review (OFR)	5
Corporate social responsibility report	5
Environmental report	5
Social and community issues	5

The directors' report

Disclosure requirements

The Companies Act 1985 requires all companies to present a directors' report as part of the annual report presented to shareholders. In practice, information provided in the directors' report may be:

- required by law, in particular the Companies Act 1985;
- required for listed companies by the Financial Services Authority (FSA);
- voluntary information, recommended as best practice disclosure.

Unless indicated otherwise, the following are required by law to be disclosed within the report.

Principal activities

The report must give details of the principal business of the company and its subsidiaries, and any significant changes.

Business review

All companies, except for those that are classified as small in size (see Chapter 27) must include a business review, either as part of the directors' report, or cross-referenced to it. The business review must contain a fair review of the business of the company and other matters – detailed content requirements are referred to later in this chapter.

Results and dividends

These should be disclosed in the directors' report although some companies give fairly brief information and cross-refer to more detailed disclosures elsewhere in the notes to the financial statements. The following example from COMPUTACENTER is typical of the level of disclosure.

COMPUTACENTER *Extract from the Directors' Report 2005*

The Group's activities resulted in a profit before tax of £34.0 million (2004: £9.8 million). Due to the implementation of IFRS, Dividends are now recognised in the accounts in the year in which they are paid, or in the case of a final dividend, when approved by the shareholders. As such, the amount recognised in the accounts, as described in note 10, is made up of last year's final dividend and the interim dividend of this year.

The final dividend, if approved, will be paid on 30 May 2006 to those shareholders on the register as at 5 May 2006. The company paid an interim dividend of £4.6 million on 21 October 2005.

Research and development

The directors' report should include an indication of the activities (if any) in the field of research and development as ENODIS discloses.

ENODIS *Extract from the Directors' Report 2005*

4. Research and development
During the period the Group incurred expenditure on research and development of £11.7m (2005: £10.1m). The Group's major research and development facility, the Enodis Technology Center ('ETC') at New Port Richey near Tampa, Florida, provides a central resource for the Group's research and development activity. Many of the Group's operating companies also have local development facilities.

Directors and directors' interests in shares

The report should disclose names of persons who were directors at any time during the year and their interests in shares or debentures of the company, both at the beginning of the financial year (or date of appointment as director, if later) and at the end of the year.

Unlisted companies are no longer required to present this information for directors' reports that are signed on or after 6 April 2007. Fully listed companies must still give this information because of Listing Rules requirements.

Post-balance sheet events

The report should include particulars of any important events that have occurred since the balance sheet date as WORKSPACE shows (note also the requirements of FRS 21/IAS 10 – see page 215).

WORKSPACE GROUP *Extract from the Directors' Report 2006*

Post-balance sheet events and future developments
Following the year end, the Group's interest in the Stevenage Business Centre was sold for a consideration of £3.2m, Wharf Road for £7.0m and the Group purchased No 1 Morie Street, London SW18 for a consideration of £4.4m. The Group plans to continue the development and expansion of its business and has targeted the acquisition of at least £60m of new property in the current year. Further, the Group plans to extend its activities to exploit the potential for improving, extending and changing the use of selected properties. Following the year end the Group advised that it had reached agreement to sell a portfolio of properties with potential for improvement to a joint venture with a developer, Glebe, in which the Group would take a 50% stake.

Employees with disabilities

Companies with more than 250 employees are required to disclose policies for employment, training, career development and promotion regarding employees with disabilities as MARKS AND SPENCER shows.

MARKS AND SPENCER GROUP *Extract from Directors' Report 2006*

Employees with disabilities
It is our policy that people with disabilities should have full and fair consideration for all vacancies.

During the year we continued to use the Government's 'two tick' disability symbol to demonstrate our commitment to interviewing those people with disabilities who fulfil the minimum criteria, and endeavouring to retain employees in the workforce if they become disabled during employment. We will actively retrain and adjust their environment where possible to allow them to maximise their potential. We continue to work with external organisations to provide workplace opportunities on the 'Workstep Programme'.

Employee consultation and involvement

Companies with more than 250 employees are required to include a statement describing the action that has been taken regarding provision of information, consultation, encouraging involvement in the company's performance through employee share schemes, etc., and achieving awareness of employees in financial and economic factors.

Companies vary in the extent of detail given in this area. Good examples are MARKS AND SPENCER and WORKSPACE GROUP.

MARKS AND SPENCER GROUP *Extract from Directors' Report 2006*

Employee involvement
We have maintained our commitment to employee involvement throughout the business.

Employees are kept well informed of the performance and objectives of the Group through personal briefings, regular meetings and e-mail. These are supplemented by our employee publication, and video presentations. Business involvement Groups in stores, and head office locations represent employees in two-way communication and are involved in the delivery of change and driving business improvement.

The eleventh meeting of the European Council took place last July. This council presents an additional forum for communicating with employee representatives from the countries in the European Community.

Directors and senior management regularly visit stores and discuss, with employees, matters of current interest and concern to the business.

▶

We continue to support employee ownership through long-established employee share schemes, membership of which is service-related, details of which are given on pages. . . .

We maintain contact with retired staff through communications from the Company and the Pension Trust. Elections are currently under way to appoint member-nominated trustees to the Pension Fund Board, including employees and pensioners. Our retired staff have also recently benefited from a significant increase in their M&S discount entitlement.

Equal opportunities
The Group is committed to an active Equal Opportunities Policy from recruitment and selection, through training and development, appraisal and promotion to retirement. It is our policy to promote an environment free from discrimination, harassment and victimisation, where everyone will receive equal treatment regardless of gender, colour, ethnic or national origin, disability, age, marital status, sexual orientation or religion. All decisions relating to employment practices will be objective, free from bias and based solely upon work criteria and individual merit.

The Group is responsive to the needs of its employees, customers and the community at large and we are an organisation that endeavours to use everyone's talents and abilities to the full.

WORKSPACE GROUP *Extract from the Directors' Report 2006*

Employment policies
The Group aims to create a working environment in which every current or prospective employee is given equal opportunity in selection, development and promotion.

During the year a Staff Forum has been established to improve communication and consultation with employees.

[*Additionally, Section 2 of the Workspace Annual Report contains a number of individual reports, one of which is 'Our people' – this sets out the Group's key priorities for its people policies, and refers specifically to: Investment in people; Organisation structure, leadership and succession; Composition of workforce; Training and development; Remuneration, performance and retention; Staff and customer surveys.*]

Health and safety
The Group's policy is to provide and maintain safe and healthy working conditions, equipment and systems of work for all of its employees and to provide such information, training and supervision as they need for this purpose. The Group accepts responsibility for the health and safety of other people who may be affected by its activities.

Whilst all employees of the Group have a responsibility in relation to health and safety matters, certain staff have been designated 'workplace' responsibilities or other co-ordinating responsibilities throughout the Group, and ultimately, at Board level, the Chief Executive has overall responsibility. Reports on health and safety are made to each Board meeting.

Environmental policies

Increasingly, larger companies are providing non-mandatory disclosures on environmental policies either within the directors' report (see AMSTRAD below) or in a separate part of the annual report (see Chapter 5).

AMSTRAD *Extract from the Directors' Report 2005/2006*

Environmental matters
The company seeks to minimise the environmental impact of its business and to operate in accordance with the standards required by law and codes of best practice.

The company is currently preparing for compliance with the Waste Electrical and Electronic Equipment ('WEEE') Directive. The WEEE Directive sets goals for the recycling of electrical goods and is currently planned to come into effect in the UK in 2007. The Restriction of Hazardous Substances in Electrical and Electronic Equipment ('RoHS') Directive came into effect on 1 July 2006 and prohibits the use of lead solder and certain other restricted substances. The Group's products imported after that date comply with the RoHS Directive.

Supplier payment policy

The directors' report should disclose the policy for the payment of creditors and the average period of payment of creditors (often referred to as 'creditor days'). For a group of companies, this should be disclosed for both the group and for the parent company (see MANAGEMENT CONSULTING GROUP below). The number of payment days should be calculated by dividing the aggregate amount of trade creditors at the balance sheet date by the aggregate amount of purchases and expenses for the year.

> **MANAGEMENT CONSULTING GROUP** *Extract from the Directors' Report 2006*
>
> **Creditor payment policy**
> The Group's policy, in relation to all of its suppliers, is to agree the terms of payment when first contracting with the supplier and to abide by those terms provided that it is satisfied that the supplier has provided the goods or services in accordance with the agreed terms and conditions. The Group does not follow any code on payment practice but operates a prompt payment policy on settling invoices. The amount of trade creditors shown in the balance sheet at 31 December 2006 represents 50 days of average purchases during the year (2005: 24 days) for the Company and 20 days (2005: 15 days) for the Group.

Charitable and political donations

If the combined amount of charitable and political donations exceeds £200, the Report should disclose the split between the two totals. Where the amount of an individual political donation exceeds £200, the report should disclose the name of the recipient and the amount given.

MARKS AND SPENCER GROUP give details in their 2006 directors' report of charitable donations. The report also refers to political donations making clear that it is company policy not to make such donations, but also draws attention to the complexities and potential pitfalls of the relevant legislation.

Purchase of own shares

Companies must give detailed disclosures regarding acquisitions of their own shares. MARKS AND SPENCER GROUP is a typical example.

> **MARKS AND SPENCER GROUP** *Extract from Directors' Report 2006*
>
> **Purchase of ordinary shares**
> The company is authorised by the shareholders to purchase, in the market, the Company's own shares, as permitted under the Company's Articles of Association. The Company engages in share buy-backs to create value for the shareholders, when cash flow permits and there is not an immediate alternative investment use for the funds. During the year, no shares were bought back under this authority. This authority is renewable annually and approval will be sought from shareholders at the Annual General Meeting in 2006 to renew the authority for a further year. It is the Company's present intention to cancel any shares it buys back, rather than hold them in Treasury.

Substantial shareholdings

Fully listed companies are required to disclose individual shareholdings which amount to 3% or more of the company's issued share capital (MANAGEMENT CONSULTING GROUP below). There is a separate CA 85 requirement to disclose directors' shareholdings (see above) and there is no *de minimis* for this.

> **MANAGEMENT CONSULTING GROUP** *Extract from the Directors' Report 2006*
>
> **Substantial share interests**
> As at 6 March 2007 (the latest practicable date prior to the issue of this Report), the Company has been notified, in accordance with Chapter 5 of the Disclosure and Transparency Rules issued by the Financial Services Authority, of the following interests in the ordinary share capital of the Company:
>
> | | Number of ordinary shares | Percentage of issued share capital |
> | --- | --- | --- |
> | Schroders PLC | 31,980,090 | 11.8 |
> | Barclays PLC | 23,868,211 | 8.81 |
> | Legal and General Group PLC | 10,861,907 | 4.01 |

Going concern

The directors' report should make reference to the going concern assumption. This is not a legal requirement but is always included in view of its fundamental importance and reference to it elsewhere in the annual report, as WORKSPACE GROUP shows.

WORKSPACE GROUP *Extract from the Directors' Report 2006*

Going concern
After making enquiries, the directors have a reasonable expectation that the Group and the Company have adequate resources to continue in operational existence for the foreseeable future. For this reason, they continue to adopt the going concern basis in preparing the accounts.

Risk management

Companies *other than those which are small* must give an indication in the directors' report of the financial risk management objectives and policies of the company and the exposure of the company to various categories of risk. WORKSPACE GROUP includes this and also cross-refers to detailed extracts elsewhere in its annual report.

WORKSPACE GROUP *Extract from the Directors' Report 2006*

Risk Management
The financial risk management objectives and policies of the Company are set out in note 17(g) to the financial statements and in the Corporate Governance section of the report on page 44.

Corporate Social Responsibility (CSR)

Much of the disclosure under this heading is best practice rather than mandatory, and hence the extent to which

companies disclose varies considerably. Many companies publish separate CSR reports – either as part of the overall annual report or within a specifically designated section of their corporate website. CSR reports are discussed in Chapter 5, but the extract below, relating to MANAGEMENT CONSULTING GROUP, is an example of a company that includes this within its directors' report.

MANAGEMENT CONSULTING GROUP *Extract from the Directors' Report 2006*

Corporate social responsibility
The Group is committed to making a positive social and economic contribution in all the places it operates. This is driven by the Board. Emphasis is placed on ensuring that we continue to create and maintain trust in and loyalty to our Group by all our stakeholders.

The Board annually assess the social, environmental and ethical (SEE) impact of the Group's business and ensures that any risks arising are being managed appropriately as recommended by the Association of British Insurers (ABI). The Board has carried out an assessment of its SEE risks and based on feedback from management has concluded that the Group's exposure to SEE risks is limited, primarily due to the nature of its operations. Further information on the environmental and ethical policies adopted are provided below. . . .

(The Report then continues to provide information covering two pages on the following: Environmental policy; Energy use and climate change; Waste and recycling; Water; Health and Safety; Whistleblowing; Employees. These have not been reproduced below but are available on page 25 of the Annual Report for 2006 – see www.mcgplc.com.)

Statement of directors' responsibilities

This is not a legal requirement but is always included in view of its fundamental importance and reference to it elsewhere in the annual report (e.g. audit report and corporate governance statement), as WILMINGTON GROUP shows. The wording follows that in the Auditing Practices Board Bulletin 2006/6, Appendix 5.

WILMINGTON GROUP *Extract from Directors' Report 2006*

Directors' responsibilities

The Directors are responsible for preparing the annual report and the financial statements in accordance with applicable law and International Financial Reporting Standards as adopted by the European Union. They are also responsible for ensuring that the annual report includes information required by the Listing Rules of the Financial Services Authority.

Company law requires the Directors to prepare financial statements for each financial year which give a true and fair view of the state of affairs of the Company and Group and of the profit or loss of the Group for the period. In preparing these financial statements the Directors are required to:

- select suitable accounting policies and then apply them consistently;
- make judgements and estimates that are reasonable and prudent;
- state whether applicable accounting standards have been followed, subject to any material departures disclosed and explained in the financial statements;
- prepare the financial statements on the going concern basis unless it is inappropriate to presume that the Company will continue in business.

The Directors are responsible for keeping proper accounting records that disclose with reasonable accuracy at any time the financial position of the Company and the Group and enable them to ensure that the financial statements comply with the Companies Act 1985. They are also responsible for safeguarding the assets of the Group and hence for taking reasonable steps for the prevention and detection of fraud and other irregularities.

The Directors are responsible for the maintenance and integrity of the corporate and financial information included on the Company's website. Legislation in the United Kingdom governing the preparation and dissemination of the financial statements and other information included in annual reports may differ from legislation in other jurisdictions.

Disclosure of information to auditors

CA 85 requires that the directors' report must contain a statement to the effect that so far as each director is aware, there is no relevant audit information of which the company's auditors are unaware, and the director has taken all the steps in order to make himself aware of any relevant audit information (see WILMINGTON GROUP below). This requirement applies to all companies, including small companies, *except those that have taken audit exemption.*

WILMINGTON GROUP *Extract from Directors' Report 2006*

Disclosure of information to auditors

Each of the Directors has confirmed that:

(a) so far as he is aware, there is no relevant audit information of which the Company's auditors are unaware, and
(b) he has taken all the steps that he ought to have taken as a Director in order to make himself aware of any relevant audit information and to establish that the Company's auditors are aware of that information.

The business review

Overview of requirements

CA 85 requires the directors of all companies *other than small companies* to include a business review as part of the directors' report. This must contain a fair review of the business of the company, and a description of the principal risks and uncertainties facing the company.

The business review should be a balanced and comprehensive analysis (consistent with the size and complexity of the business) of the development and performance of the business of the company during the financial year, and the position of the company at the end of that year.

The review should include analysis relating to *financial* 'key performance indicators' (KPIs), to the extent necessary to understand the development, performance or position of the business.

Companies other than medium-sized companies are also required to include information relating to *non-financial key performance indicators*.

The above requirement became mandatory for financial years that commenced on or after 1 April 2005.

General disclosure examples

WILMINGTON GROUP Annual Report 2006 – Business
Review, pp. 4–13 (www.wilmington.co.uk)
WOLSELEY Annual Report 2006 – Performance
Review, pp. 20–41 (www.wolseley.com)
DSG INTERNATIONAL Annual Report 2005/6 –
Directors' Report, pp. 30–37 (www.dsgplc.com)

Principal risks and uncertainties

The directors' report must contain a description of the
principal risks and uncertainties facing the company.

A good example from the retail sector is the 2006
annual report of MARKS AND SPENCER GROUP PLC, page 37
(www.marksandspencer.com/the company). The principal
risks and uncertainties are set out in a table covering a page
and are grouped under five main areas:

- clothing and home,
- food,
- people,
- stores,
- business interruption.

For each of these five risk areas, the table sets out
descriptions of the main issues and examples of 'mitigating
activities'.

The relevant extract from the directors' report of
TOROTRAK is as follows.

TOROTRAK *Extract from Directors' Report 2006*

Principal risks
The key risks and uncertainties facing the group
include the following:

Patent protection
The continuing ability to establish, protect and
enforce our proprietary rights is fundamental to
the group. This is principally achieved through the
process of patent application and establishing patent
protection. However, should these applications or
granted patents be challenged, then the defence of
our rights could involve substantial costs and the
outcome cannot be predicted with certainty.

Commercialisation
The Group's commercial progress depends upon
its ability to establish and maintain successful
relationships with appropriate licensees and other
third parties to successfully exploit IVT through
development, manufacturing and distribution
agreements.

Competition
It is possible that competitors may develop
technologies that compete with the group's
technologies. The ability of the group to defend
its competitive advantages rests on maintenance
of appropriate development capacity as well as
securing the commercialisation described above
with appropriate lead times.

Financial
The group's present financial resources, whilst
believed to be sufficient to support the planned
commercialisation of the group's technology, are
limited such that, if sufficient revenue cannot be
generated within anticipated timescales from
royalties, sales of products and services and
dividends from joint ventures, or if new
expenditure is required to exploit additional
business opportunities, it may become necessary
to raise additional funds.

Employees and skills
Retention of key employees remains a critical
factor in the group's successful delivery of its
business plan.
These areas and uncertainties are reviewed,
controlled and mitigated according to risk
procedures described on page 19 [not reproduced].

Other disclosure examples

WS ATKINS Annual Report 2006 – Operating and
Financial Review, p. 41 (www.atkinsglobal.com)
DSG INTERNATIONAL Annual Report 2005/6 –
Directors' Report, pp. 32–35 (www.dsgplc.com)
WILMINGTON GROUP Annual Report 2006 – Business
Review, p. 7 (www.wilmington.co.uk)

Financial key performance indicators (KPIs)

The business review must (to the extent necessary for an understanding of the development, performance or position of the company's business) include analysis using key performance indicators. Examples of financial KPIs include:

- gross profit margins,
- net operating margin,
- return on capital employed,
- gearing/interest cover,
- sales growth,
- sales per employee,
- sales per square foot,
- operating cash flow,
- liquid asset ratio,
- hire income as a percentage of fleet cost.

> **Disclosure examples**
>
> TESCO Annual Report 2006 – Operating and Financial Review (www.tescocorporate.com)
> WOLSELEY Annual Report 2006 – Performance Review, pp. 20–41 (www.wolseley.com)
> DSG INTERNATIONAL Annual Report 2005/6 – Directors' Report, p. 36 (www.dsgplc.com)
> MARKS & SPENCER Annual Report 2006 – Operating and Financial Review (www.marksandspencer.com)

Non-financial key performance indicators (KPIs)

The business review must (to the extent necessary for an understanding of the development, performance or position of the company's business) include *where appropriate* analysis using other key performance indicators including information relating to environmental matters and employee matters. Medium-sized companies are exempt from this disclosure requirement.

Examples of non-financial KPIs include:

- market share,
- number of subscribers,
- customer retention,
- new business from existing customer referrals,
- environmental spillage,
- waste disposal,
- CO_2 emissions,
- employee health and safety,
- accident statistics,
- staff satisfaction levels,
- staff retention levels,
- efficiency (complaints as percentage of total output).

For more details of possible non-financial KPIs appropriate to different business sectors, see the ASB's Reporting Statement on Operating and Financial Review, Implementation Guidance examples.

> **Disclosure examples**
>
> WORKSPACE GROUP Annual Report 2006, pp. 2, 82 (www.workspacegroup.co.uk)
> WORKSPACE GROUP Sustainability Report, p. 32 (www.workspacegroup.co.uk)
> WM MORRISON SUPERMARKETS Corporate Social Responsibility Report 2007, p. 3 (www.morrisons.co.uk)
> GEORGE WIMPEY Annual Report 2006, pp. 20, 21 (www.georgewimpeyplc.co.uk)
> GEORGE WIMPEY Corporate Social Responsibility Report 2006, p. 7 (www.georgewimpeyplc.co.uk/csr)
> TESCO Annual Report 2006, p. 7 (www.tescocorporate.com)
> WS ATKINS Annual Report 2006 – Operating and Financial Review, p. 41 (www.atkinsglobal.com)
> WILMINGTON GROUP Annual Report 2006 – Business Review, p. 7 (www.wilmington.co.uk)

The enhanced business review

New requirements in the Companies Act 2006 will require *fully listed companies* (only) to include additional disclosures in the business review, including main trends and factors likely to affect the future development, performance and position of the company's business. These disclosures referred to in Chapter 5 become mandatory for accounts periods beginning on or after 1 October 2007.

Presenting the business review in practice

The business review is presented by companies in a variety of different ways, including:

- as a separate statement entitled 'Business review';
- as a separate component of the directors' report;
- referred to in the directors' report 'by reference' to other parts of the annual report such as the chairman's statement, the chief executive's statement, the operating and financial review, or the finance director's review.

Different approaches to presenting the business review

Two examples are shown here – WILMINGTON GROUP and ENODIS.

WILMINGTON GROUP *Annual Report 2006*

The Annual Report of Wilmington plc for 2005 is a good example of a self-contained business review which contains the following main headings and sub-headings:

- IFRS (International Financial Reporting Standards);
- Overview of the Group's financial performance;
- Earnings per share;
- Taxation;
- Cashflow;
- Treasury policy;
- Business objectives and strategy;
- Key financial and operational targets (including KPIs);
- Principal risks and uncertainties;
- Wilmington's people;
- Review operations (covering business groupings and operations within each grouping);
- Social and community;
- Environmental policies.

ENODIS *Annual Report 2005*

Enodis plc is a good example of a business Review 'by reference'. The Annual Report for 2005 includes the following paragraph as part of its Directors' report:

2. Enhanced Business Review Requirements

The Group is obliged to comply with the Enhance Business Review disclosures required by the Companies Act 1985 as amended to comply with the EU Modernisation Directive. The Group has chosen to include much of the disclosure within its Operating and Financial Review ('OFR') including the following:

- disclosure of key performance indicators for the Group on page 18;
- disclosure of principal risks and uncertainties affecting the business on page 21;
- disclosure of financial risk management policy including the use of financial instruments on pages 28 and 29 and pages 73 to 77.

In addition the Group has made certain disclosures about its environmental impact in the current year in the Corporate Social Responsibility Statement on pages 30 and 31.

Annual review and summary financial statements

Several large companies take advantage of the CA 85 option to send an annual review and summary financial statements, as an alternative to sending the full annual report and accounts. The relevant qualifying conditions for sending out such statements and what they must include are set out in the Companies Act 1985.

MORRISON SUPERMARKETS *The company issued an Annual Review and Summary Financial Statement 2007, covering the period up to 4 February 2007 (www.morrisons.co.uk), containing the following:*

- Chairman's statement;
- Chief Executive's operating review;
- Board of Directors;
- Summary Directors' Report;
- Summary Corporate governance report;
- Corporate social responsibility report summary;
- Independent auditors' statement to the members;
- Summary financial statement;
- Seven year summary of results;
- Summary Directors' remuneration report;
- Investor relations information.

Other examples

SMITH & NEPHEW Summary Financial Statements 2006
(www.smith-nephew.com)
TESCO Annual Review and Summary Financial
Statements 2006 (www.tesco.com/corporate)

Sequence of study of a report and accounts

It is difficult to lay down a set of rules as to the best order in which to study a report and accounts, and each individual will – indeed should – develop their own method. The important thing is not to miss information regardless of where it is presented.

One stockbroker tells us he always goes straight to the directors' holdings to see if they are reducing their holdings! Indeed, one co-author maintains on file details of all directors' share transactions in their own companies and spends a few minutes each week studying them.

That the directors have sharply reduced their holdings in the company certainly tends to be a warning sign – but it is unwise for a director (or any other investor) to have too many eggs in one basket. Thus reductions are not necessarily a warning signal – an individual director may have special, personal, financial needs at a particular time.

Similarly, an increase in directors' holdings tends to be encouraging particularly where a company's shares seem undervalued or under pressure, but directors can and do get it wrong, personally as well as commercially, pouring good money after bad even when it is their own.

Major own-share activity on the part of one or more directors does, however, focus attention: something seems to be happening. One needs to find out what.

It is certainly helpful to start by glancing at the chairman's statement and the directors' report simply to see whether anything has occurred which would invalidate a straightforward comparison between one year and another. If, for instance, a major acquisition took place early in the year under review, almost all operating and financial ratios are likely to have been affected. This does not mean that the ratios are useless: simply that the analyst must bear in mind that change in composition every time he compares one ratio with another.

Having then studied the accounts (a process we will discuss in detail in Chapters 30 and 35) and having examined any segmental analysis of turnover and pre-tax profits between classes of business and any geographical analysis of turnover and trading results outside the UK, the reader will have a good idea of how the company has fared in the past year, but little idea why (except in the context of happening to know that it was a good, average or bad year for the industry or industries in which the company operates), and little idea of how the company is likely to do in the current year and beyond. It is to the chairman's statement and the operating review, if there is one, that we should look for this information.

A useful website for reviewing directors' dealings in shares is www.digitallook.com. From the home page, click on Investing, then on UK shares, then on directors' dealings.

The need to read the notes

The role of the notes is to amplify and explain the primary financial statements, and it can be very misleading to read the primary statements in isolation.

Memorandum disclosure in the notes to the financial statements is not a substitute for recognition in the financial statements, and does not correct or justify a misrepresentation or omission in the primary financial statements. However, some companies have certainly tried it on in the past, and will probably do so in future. Let us give you two examples from the accounts of now defunct companies:

A year or so before its demise, the Southampton-based golfing and tennis company LEADING LEISURE's P&L account showed a pre-tax profit of £6.7m. Note 1 to the accounts reported that trading profit generated by the disposal of properties to joint ventures amounted to £10m. Note 12 revealed additions to loans to related companies of £35.8m.

A sceptical analyst might suspect that Leading Leisure had loaned its joint venture partner the money to buy a 50% stake in the properties, and that the price of the 50% stake had been pitched to give Leading Leisure a £10m trading profit.

Among other little gems in the notes, note 6 showed an extraordinary item (a now defunct accounting term) of £1.3m 'Reorganisation and aborted fund raising costs'. There was obviously more than one Doubting Thomas about. In the next 12 months or so the share price fell from 96p to 2p, at which point the shares were suspended. A week later the banks called in administrative receivers.

RESORT HOTELS provides our second cautionary tale of the dangers of not reading the notes. As well as running its own hotels, Resort had management contracts to run a number of hotels financed by Business Expansion Schemes (these were schemes that offered a tax break to encourage investment in young and expanding companies).

Resort charged these BES-financed hotels management fees. The hotels were not profitable enough to be able to pay the fees. However, the unpaid fees were counted as income by Resort, thus bolstering Resort's profits and, at the same time, producing an ever-increasing debtor item of management fees due in Resort's balance sheet. Eventually the bubble burst.

In the last report and accounts before its demise, Resort's balance sheet did give a warning clue: an alarming rise in 'Amounts due from managed companies' from £8.646m to £12.987m, an increase of £4.341m.

But you had to read the notes to find out what was actually going on. Note 1 showed a breakdown of turnover between Hotel operations £11.874m and Hotel management fees £4.219m, almost exactly the increase in the amounts due from managed companies.

CHAPTER 5

Chairman's statement and the operating and financial review

Presenting the annual report in practice

The possible contents of an annual report were referred to in the previous chapter. In practice, larger companies use a variety of approaches to the structure of their annual reports. Most (but not all) companies present a chairman's statement, but not all of these present a separate chief executive's report.

Most companies present a finance review (or finance director's review) – sometimes this is presented as a stand-alone feature, sometimes as part of an operating and financial review.

GEORGE WIMPEY *Annual report 2006*

The annual report of George Wimpey plc for 2006 (www.georgewimpeyplc.co.uk) is a good example of a well-structured report. The annual report is divided into five main sections, each with sub-headings, as follows:

Group Overview
Operational highlights
Group overview – our performance
Group overview – Group at a glance

Business Review
Strategy and KPIs
UK Housing
US Housing
Corporate Social Responsibility
Group Financial Review

Governance
Board of Directors
Directors' Report
Corporate Governance Report
Remuneration Report

Financial Statements
Auditors' Report
Group Income Statement
Balance Sheets
Cash Flow Statements
Accounting Policies
Notes to the Accounts
Five Year Review

Shareholder Information
Notice of Meeting
Business Directors
Shareholder Information.

Corporate social responsibility (CSR) report

An increasing number of companies present a corporate social responsibility report, although what is covered in the report may vary significantly between different companies. The report itself is sometimes integrated within the annual report but can also be presented as a separate document. Frequently, the separate document is posted on the company's website.

Chairman's statement

Companies are not required to publish a chairman's statement, but listed companies invariably do. In the case of companies that believe in keeping shareholders well informed, the chairman's statement will usually contain comment on:

- overall trading conditions during the period, current economic climate and general outlook;
- the performance achieved by each activity, current trading and future prospects;
- items of special interest (e.g. closures and new ventures);
- changes in the board;
- company strategy and plans for the future.

Study the chairman's report, not only for what it says, but also for what it does not – where one is left to read between the lines. We find it is useful to read through the whole statement highlighting with a marker pen key phrases and points of interest as we go, before getting down to detailed analysis.

Chief executive's report

Many companies produce, instead of a chairman's statement but more commonly in addition to one, a chief executive's review. This provides a vital part of the information package, often avoiding the stilted form and language of the directors' report and shedding additional light on information in the accounts.

Typically, where a company produces a chairman's statement this is usually devoted largely to overall performance, plans and strategy. The detailed review of operations, usually division by division, is left to the chief executive's review and the operational review (part of the operating and financial review). It is here that one learns in detail what the various parts of the group do, where and how the group's various markets are shaping, and where the focus of management attention lies. Statistics and graphs often present useful information on these aspects and on trends over the years.

Enhanced business review

The statutory business review, required for all companies other than those classified as small, was referred to in Chapter 4. In addition to this, the Companies Act 2006 imposes additional requirements for quoted companies: these are usually referred to as the enhanced or expanded business review requirements.

Note that the Companies Act uses the term 'quoted companies' to refer to fully listed companies. The enhanced business review requirements are not, therefore, mandatory for AIM-listed and Plus Market companies.

These additional narrative reporting requirements for quoted companies will apply for accounting periods starting on or after 1 October 2007 and will require the following information:

- the main trends and factors likely to affect the future development, performance and position of the company's business;
- information relating to environmental matters (including the impact of the company's business on the environment);
- information about the company's employees;
- information about social and community issues;
- persons with whom the company has contractual or other arrangements that are essential to the company's business (the so-called 'supply chain' provision) – this is subject to an exemption where disclosure of information about a person would be seriously prejudicial to that person and contrary to the public interest.

The requirements referred to immediately above are required by law for fully listed companies. By contrast, the operating and financial review (OFR) disclosures referred to below are regarded as best practice. Many fully listed companies have produced OFRs for ten years or longer.

The operating and financial review (OFR)

Introduction

The UK Accounting Standards Board published a reporting statement (RS) in January 2006. In its Summary section the RS states:

'The Reporting Statement is designed as a formulation and development of best practice; it is intended to have persuasive rather than mandatory force.'

References below to the RS should be read in the light of these comments.

What is an OFR?

The OFR should be a balanced and comprehensive analysis of:

- the development and performance of the business during the financial year;
- the position at the end of the year;
- the main trends and factors underlying the development, performance and position of the business *during the financial year*;
- the main trends and factors likely to affect *future* development, performance and position.

The financial review part of OFR

The main purpose of the financial review part of an OFR is to explain the accounts and to shed light on financial performance and strategy:

- Why did interest payable rise (or fall) so much year on year?
- What exactly do the exceptional items represent?
- Why does the effective tax rate differ from the rate of UK corporation tax?
- Where does the group keep its main cash reserves – the UK? If not, why this location?
- What has happened to gearing and why?
- What was the capital expenditure during the year actually used for? How much more is needed to complete the group's plans and where is it coming from? (Is it in place?)
- How was (is) the group affected by exchange rates and interest rates?
- Risk management, with comment on:
  (a) treasury risk management;
  (b) liquidity risk;
  (c) finance and interest rate risk;
  (d) currency risk;
  (e) commodity risk;
  (f) credit risk.
- Which recent accounting standards have been adopted for the first time in the accounts?

A financial review should be regarded by analysts as being, to all intents and purposes, part of the accounts, and studied as such.

OFR structure – general considerations

The OFR should be prepared in a way that assists the owners of the business to assess its strategies and the potential for those strategies to succeed. The disclosure framework for the OFR should address four key aspects:

1. **Nature of business and objectives and strategies.** Nature of the business includes a description of the market and the competitive and regulatory framework in which the business operates.
2. **Development and performance.** This covers the development and performance of the business both in the financial year under review and in the future.
3. **Resources, risks and uncertainties.** This covers factors that may affect the long-term value of the business, namely the resources available, and the principal risks and uncertainties which face it.
4. **Position of the business.** This includes a description of the capital structure of the business, its treasury policies and objectives, and its liquidity, both in the financial year under review and in the future.

Areas covered by the OFR

The RS refers to the following areas:

- description of business and external environment;
- strategy and objectives;
- current developments and performance of the business;
- future developments and performance;
- resources;
- principal risks and uncertainties;
- capital structure and treasury;
- cash flows and liquidity;
- environmental, employee and social issues;
- contractual arrangements/relationships;
- key performance indicators (KPIs) – financial;
- key performance indicators (KPIs) – non-financial.

These criteria are used by the Accounting Standards Board in its 'Review of Narrative Reporting by Listed UK Companies in 2006'.

Description of business and external environment

The OFR should include a description of the business and the external environment in which it operates as a context for the directors' discussion and analysis of performance and financial performance (RS.30).

TATE & LYLE *Operating and Financial Review 2006*

This includes a section entitled 'Operating environment', which discusses: Markets; Solutions; Customers; Competitors; and Government regulation (Operating and Financial Review, p. 21 (www.tateandlyle.com)).

Other examples

WORKSPACE GROUP Annual Report 2006, p. 10 (www.workspacegroup.co.uk)

SMITH & NEPHEW Annual Report 2006, p. 4 (www.smith-nephew.com)

Objectives and strategy

The OFR should discuss the objectives of the business to generate or preserve value over the longer term (RS.33).

The OFR should set out the directors' strategies for achieving the objectives of the business (RS.36).

TATE & LYLE *Extract from the Operating & Financial Review 2006*

Strategy and objectives
Tate & Lyle's purpose is to create the world's leading renewable ingredients business. In order to grow our business and create value for our shareholders, our strategic objectives are to:

- grow the contribution from value added products;
- invest in acquisitions and partnerships;
- unite our business;
- operate efficiently;
- invest in technology and people; and
- serve our customers.

Each of these strategic objectives is explained in more detail below . . .

Other examples

NATIONAL GRID Annual Report 2005/06 – Operating and Financial Review, p. 30 (www.nationalgrid.com)
GEORGE WIMPEY Annual Report 2006, pp. 20, 21 (www.georgewimpeyplc.co.uk)
REGENT INNS Annual Report 2006, p. 7 (www.regentinns.co.uk)

Current developments and performance of the business

The OFR should describe the significant features of the development and performance of the business, focusing on those business segments that are relevant to an understanding of the development and performance as a whole (RS.43).

Example

NATIONAL GRID Annual Report 2005/06 – Operating and Financial Review, p. 30 (www.nationalgrid.com)

Future developments and performance

The OFR should analyse the main trends and factors that the directors consider likely to impact on future prospects (RS.47).

Example

SMITH & NEPHEW Annual Report 2006, p. 48 (www.smith-nephew.com)

Resources

The OFR should include a description of the resources available to the entity and how they are managed (RS.50). It should also set out the key strengths and resources, tangible and intangible, available to the business. This may include:

- corporate reputation and brand strength;
- natural resources;
- employees;
- research and development;
- intellectual capital;
- licences;
- patents;
- copyright and trademarks;
- market position.

Example

NATIONAL GRID Annual Report 2005/06 – Operating and Financial Review, p. 30 (www.nationalgrid.com)

Principal risks and uncertainties

The OFR should include a description of the principal risks and uncertainties facing the entity together with a commentary on the directors' approach to them (RS.52) (see also Chapter 3).

Examples

TATE & LYLE Annual Report 2006 – Operating and Financial Review, p. 24 (www.tateandlyle.com)

WS ATKINS Annual Report 2006 – Operating and Financial Review, p. 41 (www.atkinsglobal.com)

WILMINGTON GROUP Annual Report 2006 – Business review, p. 7 (www.wilmington.co.uk)

Capital structure and treasury

The OFR should contain a discussion of the capital structure of the entity (RS.63). It should also set out the entity's treasury policies and objectives (RS.65).

Example

MANAGEMENT CONSULTING GROUP Annual Report 2006, p. 18 (www.mcgplc.com)

Cash flows and liquidity

The OFR should discuss the cash inflows and outflows during the financial year, along with the entity's ability to generate cash to meet known or probable cash requirements and to fund growth (RS.68).

The OFR should discuss the entity's current and prospective liquidity. Where relevant this should include commentary on the level of borrowings, the seasonality of borrowing requirements (indicated by the peak level of borrowings during that period) and the maturity profile of both borrowings and undrawn committed borrowing facilities (RS.71).

Examples

WILMINGTON GROUP Annual Report 2006 – Business review, p. 7 (www.wilmington.co.uk)

MANAGEMENT CONSULTING GROUP Annual Report 2006, p. 19 (www.mcgplc.com)

ENODIS Annual Report, p. 27 (www.enodis.com)

Environmental, employee and social issues

The OFR should include information about environmental matters, the entity's employees and social and community issues (RS.28). Environmental issues were also referred to in Chapter 4

Other examples

WOLSELEY Annual Report 2006, pp. 20–41 (www.wolseley.com)

GEORGE WIMPEY Annual Report 2006, pp. 20, 21 (www.georgewimpeyplc.co.uk)

WILMINGTON GROUP Annual Report 2006 – Business review, p. 13 (www.wilmington.co.uk)

WS ATKINS Annual Report 2006 – Operating and Financial Review, p. 41 (www.atkinsglobal.com)

TATE & LYLE Annual Report 2006 – Operating and Financial Review, p. 35 (www.tateandlyle.com)

MANGEMENT CONSULTING GROUP Annual Report – Directors' report, p. 26 (www.mcgplc.com)

Employee issues

This was also referred to in Chapter 4.

Further examples

MARKS & SPENCER Annual Report 2006 – Operating and Financial Review (www.marksandspencer.com)

GEORGE WIMPEY Annual Report 2006, pp. 20, 21 (www.georgewimpeyplc.co.uk)

WORKSPACE GROUP Annual Report 2006, pp. 2, 82 (www.workspacegroup.co.uk)

WS ATKINS Annual Report 2006 – Operating and Financial Review, p. 41 (www.atkinsglobal.com)

Social and community issues

TATE & LYLE *Extract from the Operating & Financial Review 2006*

Communities
Tate & Lyle aims to play a positive role in all the communities in which we operate. Over the years we have developed a Group-wide community involvement policy that forms one of the core components underpinning our ethical behaviour. Our programme involves building long-term relationships with local partners to deliver a shared objective: establishing strong safe and healthy communities by investing time and resources into projects that directly address local needs.

Our community partnerships are very well supported by employees, many of whom take part in local community programmes. These benefit our employees by enhancing their own local communities, offering significant personal development opportunities and making Tate & Lyle a company for which they are proud to work. . . .

[The report then sets out calendar year highlights including: charitable donations; key achievements in the UK, mainland Europe, Americas and Vietnam; and employee volunteering].

Other examples

GEORGE WIMPEY Annual Report 2006, pp. 20, 21 (www.georgewimpeyplc.co.uk)

WS ATKINS Annual Report 2006 – Operating and Financial Review, p. 41 (www.atkinsglobal.com)

WOLSELEY Annual Report 2006 – Performance Review, pp. 20–41 (www.wolseley.com)

WILMINGTON GROUP Annual Report 2006 – Business Review, p. 7 (www.wilmington.co.uk)

Contractual arrangements/relationships

The OFR should include information about persons with whom the entity has contractual or other arrangements that are essential to the business of the entity (RS28.d).

The OFR should include information about significant relationships with stakeholders, other than members, which are likely, directly or indirectly, to influence the performance of the business and its value (RS.57).

TATE & LYLE *Extract from the Operating & Financial Review 2006*

Commercial partners/suppliers
Long-term, good relationships with our partners and suppliers are very important at Tate & Lyle. We have a consistent Group-wide approach, based on our Code of Conduct, which covers purchasing strategies at global, regional and local levels. We pride ourselves on our supply chain ethics, and are committed to sharing best practice and improving standards among suppliers.

[The report then covers in detail Calendar year 2005 highlights including: Audit of supplier relationships; standards applied to raw material suppliers; initiatives aimed at improving supply chain practices; safety; environment; sustainable procurement; Tate & Lyle's Business Code of Conduct.]

Further example

WOLSELEY Annual Report 2006 – Performance Review, pp. 20–41 (www.wolseley.com)

Key performance indicators (KPIs)

The OFR should include the key performance indicators, both financial and, where appropriate, non-financial, used by the directors to assess progress against their stated objectives (RS.38).

Financial and non-financial KPIs, including examples, were dealt with in Chapter 4.

Further example

TATE & LYLE Annual Report 2006 – Operating and Financial Review, p. 23 (www.tateandlyle.com)

Estimating current year profits

A rough estimate of profits for the current year can be constructed (for each activity which is separately reported on) by quantifying the chairman's comments (and those by the chief executive and finance director in related reports – for simplicity we will refer to the chairman), bearing in mind prevailing conditions and prospects for the industry concerned; e.g. POLYGON HOLDINGS PLC (see Example 5.1 below).

The chairman may also give an overall indication, e.g. POLYGON HOLDINGS' turnover in the first three months of the current year has been 22% higher than the same period last year, the paper division's order-book is now four months, compared with one month last year, and,

despite constant pressure on margins and the increasing ineptitude of government, the outlook for the group is encouraging. 'Outlook encouraging' sounds to us like a 20–25% increase in pre-tax profits, i.e. to £4.3–£4.5m, pointing to the middle of the range we constructed division by division.

Other points to bear in mind in making a profits estimate are these:

1. Loss-makers discontinued will not only eliminate the loss but should, in addition, improve liquidity (and thus reduce interest charges, assuming there is an overdraft). But have all terminal losses been provided for?
2. What is the chairman's previous record? Has he been accurate, cautious, unduly optimistic, erratic? Have past assurances of better times ahead remained unfulfilled?
3. Remember, too, that one of the chairman's most important jobs is to maintain general confidence in the company, so he is likely to concentrate on the good points and only touch briefly or remain silent on the weaker aspects of the company. Here it is a good idea to jot down questions one would like the answer to, even if the analyst or shareholder is unlikely to have the opportunity of putting them to the company, because it focuses the mind and helps to establish what the chairman has not revealed and whether any unexplained area is likely to be significant. Good questions to ask oneself are (i) 'What are the company's main problems?' and (ii) 'What is being done about them?'
4. Beware of vague statements, such as:
   (a) 'Turnover in the first ten weeks of the current year has exceeded the corresponding figure for last year.' It could be 1% ahead in value because

---

Example 5.1 Estimating current year profits: POLYGON HOLDINGS PLC

Activity	Industrial climate	Chairman's remarks	Previous year £m	Reported year £m	Estimate of current year £m
Building	Continued recession	'Further decline inevitable'	1.0	0.8	0.5–0.6
Paper	Cyclical upturn	'Marked improvement'	2.2	1.8	2.4–2.8
Bookmaking	One of the UK's few growth industries	'Continued progress'	1.0	1.2	1.4–1.5
Plastic extrusions	Demand flat	'Market share increasing but lower margins'	0.6	0.75	0.6–0.8
Interest charges	Rates down 2%	'Improvement in liquidity likely'	−0.8	−1.0	−0.8
		Pre-tax total	4.0	3.55	4.1–4.9

inflation more than covered the 4% drop which occurred in volume.

(b) 'Unforeseen difficulties have occurred in . . . and a provision of £1.3m has been made.' Unless there is some indication of the likely overall cost of overcoming these difficulties, or of abandoning the activity altogether, the company should be assumed to have an open-ended loss-maker on its hands.

Longer-term prospects

The chairman of a company should be continually looking to the future and, unless he and his board have good sound ideas on where the future growth in profits is likely to come from, and are steering the company in that direction, then above-average profits growth is unlikely. Although there must, of course, be some restrictions on what a chairman discloses about plans for the future, because of competition, he will usually include some indication of where he thinks the company is going in his annual statement.

A good past growth record is clearly encouraging (a no-growth company is likely to stay a no-growth company unless the management or the management's attitude changes), but what indications are there of future growth? Possibilities to look for are the following:

1. **Better margins on existing business.** This is an unreliable source of growth unless the company *either*
    (a) has some very strong competitive advantage, such as patents or lucrative long-term contracts, or
    (b) has spent large sums of money building up brand images and carving out market share, and is now beginning to reap the benefits;
   even then the profits growth will only last until the patents expire, the long-term contracts run out or the brand images tarnish.
2. **Further expansion of existing activities within the UK.** Is there any scope for this, or is the company in a position like BOOTS or W.H. SMITH, with a store in every town of any size, or like PILKINGTON, with 90% of the UK glass market?
3. **Diversification within the UK.** This was BOOTS' answer to its saturation problem with chemist shops: it widened the range of goods sold to include records and tapes, hi-fi, cameras, binoculars, even sandwiches. BOOTS was using its retailing expertise in wider product ranges, rather than going into some totally unrelated

activity, and there does need to be some logic in diversifications or they can come very badly unstuck.

4. **Acquisition within the UK.** Has the company got a successful record of acquisitions, or would this method of growth be new to it (and therefore more risky)? This was part of W.H. SMITH's solution for further growth: in 1986 it took over the recorded music chain OUR PRICE, with 130 outlets, added 40 music outlets it already had and by 1990, with further acquisitions, built the chain up to around 300 outlets.
5. **Exports.** Is the product suitable for export, or would transport costs make competitiveness overseas unlikely or impossible (e.g. bricks)? Does the company export already, is it a significant amount, and is it growing? The chairman may report that 'exports are 80% up on last year', but if this is an increase from 0.1% to 0.18% of turnover, it is hardly thrilling, and one should be wary of the chairman whose efforts to paint a rosy picture involve misleading statements like that, which should in honesty be qualified by some phrase like 'albeit from a very low base'.
6. **Are there opportunities for overseas growth** like W.H. SMITH's acquisition of the US news and gifts chain ELSON, specialising in shops in hotels and airports, or PILKINGTON putting down float-glass plants overseas, either on its own or in joint ventures, or by licensing the process to foreign glass manufacturers? There are, however, a good many hazards in opening up operations abroad, apart from the initial expense: different business ethics and practices, language, law, accounting and tax systems, and so on. For manufacturing abroad, cost levels and exchange rates may change over time, so that what today looks a good investment may prove otherwise in years to come if the cost of living rises faster in that country than elsewhere.
7. **Is the company spending money on, and attaching importance to, developing new products?** This is particularly important for pharmaceutical companies; GLAXOSMITHKLINE, for instance, in 2003 reported £2,791m spent on research and development, representing 13.0% of the group's turnover.

   Although any manufacturing company that isn't developing new products is almost certainly going downhill, it is also bad news if the chairman is always eulogising about new products that never come to anything: the company's track record on product development should be checked.
8. **Is the company ploughing profits back?** Profits in most industries cannot expand beyond a given point

unless the asset base (needed to support the trading needed to generate the profits) is also expanded. There is a limit to gearing up, while acquisitions and rights issues do not necessarily enhance e.p.s.: only steady ploughback gives scope for steady growth in e.p.s.

In the context of future growth, it is also worth checking press cuttings for stories on the company, which often contain glimpses of the company's thoughts on the future (many people use the FT McCarthy press cutting service).

Information on the quality of management

Returning to the business of assessing the strength of the management, perhaps the most encouraging facet is when the chairman admits to a mistake or to being caught wrongfooted, and reports what is being or has been done about it. A classic example comes from the 'rag trade': the chairman's statement for WEARWELL in 1976, a year in which trading results had fallen from £1m profit to £28,000 loss on turnover down from £7.1m to £6.2m and with over £½m in terminal losses, contained the following comments:

WEARWELL *Extracts from chairman's report 1976*

. . . in 1973 we operated what was basically a cash and carry operation. [In 1974 and 1975 the company made two acquisitions for cash and we] found ourselves in the business of building up stock and financing customers for considerable periods . . . sales not as buoyant as expected . . . liquidity difficulties in the opening weeks of 1976 instituted immediate measures, namely:

1. Closure of the mail order supply business which has required the financing of substantial stocks.
2. Cutting out much of the credit business with chain stores.
3. The waiver by directors of a substantial part of their salary entitlement together with a waiver of between 94.0% and 99.9% of their total entitlement to the interim dividend.
4. Strenuous efforts were made to liquidate stocks.

. . . your company operates now only in the cash and carry type business which is where your management has proved its expertise.

Wearwell's drastic action paid off. The company just managed to get out of the red in 1977, and from then on

pre-tax profits grew steadily; five years later the chairman, Asil Nadir (of POLLY PECK fame, the group which Wearwell subsequently joined) was able to report pre-tax profits in excess of £4m.

Wearwell's shareholders had a bumpy ride: from an offer for sale price of 30p (adjusted for subsequent scrip and rights issues) in July 1973 they saw the ordinary share price fall to a low of 8p in November 1976, and received no dividends at all in 1977 and 1978. But if they got out in time (i.e. before Polly Peck bit the dust) they were amply rewarded: in 1984 Wearwell merged with Polly Peck, whose chairman was also Mr Asil Nadir. The deal gave Wearwell shareholders 53 Polly Peck shares for every 100 Wearwell shares, valuing Wearwell's ordinary shares at 164p each: 20 times the 1976 level.

In contrast, the chairman of a housebuilding company reported proudly in 1974 that 'notwithstanding all these problems [the three-day week, the shortage of mortgage funds, rising interest rates and increases in building costs] your company increased its turnover to a new record level'. The turnover had risen from £25.4m to almost £44m on an equity base of less than £2m net of goodwill and after writing £8.7m off the value of the land bank, by then in the books at a mere £24.4m plus £23.4m work in progress. Apart from the feeling that the chairman was steering his company straight into the eye of a financial typhoon, and his failure to even mention the year's pretax loss of £6.3m in his statement, there were a number of fairly conspicuous danger signals scattered around the report:

- the notice of the AGM included a resolution to appoint a top London firm of accountants to be joint auditors with the existing provincial firm of auditors;
- the directors' report contained a little paragraph on 'financial arrangements', which revealed that the group's bankers had agreed to 'roll up' interest on group borrowings.

But perhaps the most telling fact was an omission: the group's habit of including a historical summary (which in the previous year's accounts had shown a seven-year progression in pre-tax profits from £142,000 to over £7m) had been discontinued! The fall into loss was too painful to face. Liquidation followed quite shortly afterwards.

Corporate Governance developments – including the respective roles of Chairman and Chief Executive and non-executive directors – are referred to in Chapter 6.

CHAPTER 6

Corporate governance and the auditors' report

Corporate governance

Background

Corporate governance, the system by which companies are managed and controlled, has existed since the creation of the first company.

However, it was the publication of the Cadbury Committee's Code of Best Practice in 1992 that focused particular attention on it. Interest was reinforced by a series of incompetencies and scandals, which had made clear that assumptions on the part of investors of the competence and honesty of boards was misplaced.

The Cadbury Committee Report was followed in 1994 by the Greenbury Committee Report on directors' remuneration. Shortly after this, the Hampel Committee published a report recommending that directors should review the effectiveness of all internal controls, financial and otherwise. Subsequent guidance on internal controls was published in September 1999 in the Turnbull Report.

In July 2003, the Financial Reporting Council (www. frc.org.uk) issued a revised version of the Combined Code on Corporate Governance. The 2003 version reflects the publication of yet more reports:

- review of the role and effectiveness of non-executive directors (the Higgs report);
- Combined Code guidance on audit committees (the Smith report).

The Code was amended in June 2006, with companies being 'encouraged' to apply the revised version for reporting periods beginning on or after 1 November 2006.

The Financial Reporting Council referred to 'the limited nature of the changes', so the 2003 version of the Combined Code is largely the version used today. The extract below relating to GEORGE WIMPEY refers to the 2006 changes.

The Combined Code

Introduction

The UK Listing Authority's Combined Code contains main and supporting principles and provisions that are applicable to listed companies. The Code consists of 17 principles of good governance and 48 code provisions, and is in four parts:

- A – Directors
- B – Directors' remuneration
- C – Accountability and audit
- D – Relations with shareholders.

These are discussed below.

Practical guidance on applying the Code includes:

- Internal Control: Revised Guidance for Directors on the Combined Code, Financial Reporting Council (www.frc.org.uk), October 2005;
- Corporate Governance Guidelines for AIM Companies, Quoted Companies Alliance (www.qcanet. co.uk), 2005.

Although much of the information disclosed as a result of the Combined Code does not directly help in interpreting the accounts proper, it does provide useful background information relating to the company, for example as regards internal controls, risk management systems and the operation of the audit committee. The significance of this information can be seen from some of the examples referred to below.

Disclosure statements

The FSA's Listing Rules, paragraph 9.8.6 require companies that are listed (i.e. fully listed on the London Stock Exchange) to make a disclosure statement in two parts in relation to the Code:

- In the **first part of the statement**, a company is required to report on how it applies the principles in the Code. Form and content are not prescribed, as the FSA intends that companies should have a free hand in explaining their governance policies, including reference to any special circumstances applying to them (resulting in a particular approach).
- In the **second part of the statement**, the company has either to confirm that it complies with the Code's provisions or, where it does not comply, provide an explanation. This 'comply or explain approach' offers flexibility (particularly for some smaller listed companies), and enables shareholders to evaluate the corporate governance statement.

The example below shows a compliance statement that reflects the June 2006 changes:

GEORGE WIMPEY *Extract from Annual Report 2006*

The Board is fully committed to high standards of corporate governance and corporate responsibility throughout the Group. The Board supports the Combined Code on Corporate Governance ('Combined Code') as published in July 2003 and updated in June 2006. The Listing Rules of the Financial Services Authority require the Company to include a statement to allow shareholders to evaluate how it has applied the principles and provisions of good governance as set out in Section 1 of the Combined Code.

This Report, together with the information set out in the *Remuneration Report* on pages 44 to 50 [not reproduced here], is published pursuant to the Combined Code which deals with directors, directors' remuneration, relations with and accountability to shareholders and the audit of the company. Together, the two reports are intended to explain how the Company has applied the principles in Section 1 of the Combined Code and provide an insight into how the Board and management run the business for the benefit of shareholders.

. . .

Statement of Compliance
As a result of the Company adopting early one of the principal changes of the 2006 Combined Code, which lifted the restriction on a company chairman serving on the remuneration committee, John Robinson, who was considered independent on his appointment as Chairman, was appointed to the Remuneration Committee on 18 October 2006. This was ahead of the date on which the Financial Reporting Council recommended that companies should voluntarily adopt the Combined Code, namely 1 November 2006. Otherwise, the Board considers that it has complied with the provisions of Section 1 of the Combined Code throughout the year.

George Wimpey also describes the 2006 changes:

GEORGE WIMPEY *Extract from Annual Report 2006*

Statement of compliance
The principal changes of the 2006 Combined Code are set out below:

- to amend the existing restriction on the company chairman serving on the remuneration committee to enable him or her to do so where considered independent on appointment as chairman;
- to provide a 'vote withheld' option on proxy appointment forms to enable shareholders to indicate if they have reservations on a resolution but do not wish to vote against; and
- to recommend that companies publish on their website the details of proxies lodged at a general meeting where votes are taken on a show of hands.

As a matter of best practice, for a number of years, the Company had already complied with the second and third changes set out above.

Directors

Introduction

Part A of Section 1 refers to the role of the board, the chairman and chief executive, and composition of committees, as well as issues regarding appointments, professional development, evaluation of performance and re-election.

The roles of chairman and chief executive

Attitudes have changed sharply in the past five years. In the ninth edition of this book we included the following comment from the Lex column of the Financial Times:

FINANCIAL TIMES *Extract from LEX column,*
1 July 2000

Tomkins
Tomkins is, belatedly, doing some sensible things: improving corporate governance, buying back its unloved shares and – when it actually happens – selling Rank Hovis McDougall. What a shame the conglomerate did not do all this three or four years ago. Greg Hutchings is finally giving up his dual role as chairman and chief executive. Bringing in a non-executive chairman and putting some heavyweight outsiders on the board is good news. The company will start listening to its shareholders now. Though, with the stubborn Mr Hutchings continuing as chief executive, more than a few investors will continue to give Tomkins a wide berth.

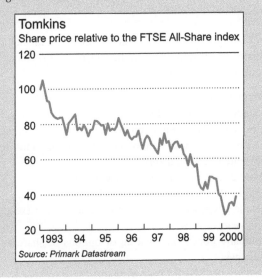

Tomkins
Share price relative to the FTSE All-Share index
Source: Primark Datastream

Selling RHM is long overdue. It was a disastrous acquisition. Tomkins shares have underperformed the market by 60 per cent since it acquired the food group in 1992. . . .

It is very hard to see this phoenix rising from the flames.

The June 2006 version of the Combined Code on Corporate Governance sent out a crystal clear instruction on this issue:

'There should be a clear division of responsibilities at the head of the company between the running of the board and the executive responsibility for the running of the company's business. No one individual should have unfettered powers of decision' (Main Principle A.2).

Non-executive directors

Non-executive directors are valuable provided, and only provided, they:

- are of a healthily independent disposition;
- devote sufficient time to the company to have a good grasp of its affairs (i.e. to know what is going on);
- are prepared to make a stand/resign if they disagree on important issues; and
- bring relevant experience to the boardroom.

The Combined Code states:

'The Board should include a balance of executive and non-executive directors (and in particular independent non-executive directors) such that no individual or small group of individuals can dominate the board's decision taking.' (Main Principle A.3)

Board Committees

The Combined Code refers to the following committees:

- an audit committee
- a remuneration committee
- a nomination committee.

The nomination committee is referred to below. The audit committee and the remuneration committee are referred to later in this chapter.

Nomination committee

The Code states that a separate section of the annual report should describe the work of the nomination committee, including the process it has used in relation to board appointments, for example National Grid Annual Report 2006/7, Corporate Governance Report, lists the items for which the Nominations Committee has responsibility, as follows:

NATIONAL GRID *Extract from Annual Report 2006/7, Extract from Corporate Governance Report*

The key items for which the Nominations Committee has responsibility and that it has discussed during the year include:

- recommending individuals for appointment to the Board following the procedures laid down by the Board in conjunction with the Nominations Committee, including the appointments during the year of Linda Adamany (Non-executive Director) and Mark Fairbairn (Executive Director);
- reviewing the size of the Board, its structure and composition, including considering Board members' independence (where appropriate), skills and experience to ensure these remain relevant to National Grid;
- considering the external commitments of all Directors, to ensure it is satisfied that these do not conflict or interfere with their duties as Directors of the Company;
- reviewing and refreshing the membership of Board Committees, particularly following the appointment of new Directors to the Board;
- considering succession planning for Board members, noting that during the year this focused on the smooth transition of responsibilities to the new Chief Executive;
- development and succession plans for senior management, as developed by the Chief Executive and the Group Human Resources Director; and
- Board and Committee performance evaluation.

Directors' remuneration

Introduction

The Code sets out requirements regarding level of remuneration, remuneration policy (including detailed provisions in a separate appendix of the Code, Schedule A), service contracts and compensation.

Remuneration committee

The Code also sets out procedures including the establishment of a remuneration committee consisting of at least three (and, in the case of smaller companies, two) independent non-executive directors.

J SAINSBURY PLC *Extract from Annual Report 2007, Extract from Remuneration Report*

The responsibilities of the Committee include:

- determining and agreeing with the Board the broad remuneration policy for the Chairman, Chief Executive, Chief Financial Officer and the Operating Board Directors;
- setting individual remuneration arrangements for the Chairman, Chief Executive and the Chief Financial Officer;
- recommending and monitoring the level and structure of remuneration for those members of senior management within the scope of the Committee, namely the Operating Board Directors; the Company Secretary and any other executive whose salary exceeds that of any Operating Board Director; and
- approving the service agreements of each Executive Director, including termination arrangements.

The Committee's terms of reference are available on the Company's website (www.j-sainsbury.co.uk/governance).

Remuneration report

The Listing Rules require listed companies to include a report to the shareholders by the board of directors. This report must deal with:

- company policy;
- remuneration of each director analysed between salary, fees, benefits in kind, bonuses and compensation for loss of office (with total amount for the previous year), presented in tabular form;
- share option information for each director;
- details of long-term incentive schemes;
- details of service contracts with a notice period exceeding one year;
- company policy on granting of options or share award schemes;
- pension benefits for each director;
- arrangements for non-executive directors.

The resultant report tends to be long and detailed – for example, the Remuneration Report of J Sainsbury (see website reference above) runs to seven pages.

Accountability and audit

Internal control

The Code requires the board of directors to 'maintain a sound system of control to safeguard shareholders' investment and the company's assets'.

The board are required to conduct a review, at least annually, of the effectiveness of the group's system of internal controls. They should report to shareholders that they have done this. The review should cover all material controls, including:

- financial controls;
- operational controls;
- compliance controls;
- risk management systems.

The importance of this area is particularly felt when we recall cases in earlier years cited by banks, merchant banks, local authorities and major listed companies that firmly believed they had appropriate controls in place only to find to their cost, that these had not worked.

One gains some reassurance from descriptions of internal controls, such as the comprehensive controls listed in the example below relating to Enterprise Inns.

ENTERPRISE INNS PLC *Extract from Annual Report 2006, Extract from Corporate Governance Statement*

Internal control
The Board is responsible for the overall system of internal control for the Group and for reviewing its effectiveness. It carries out such a review at least annually covering all material controls including financial, operational and compliance controls and risk management systems.

An ongoing process on internal control has been established for identifying, evaluating and managing risks faced by the Group. This process is reviewed regularly by the Board and, with advice from its Audit Committee, is satisfied that this meets the requirements of the guidance 'Internal Control: Guidance for Directors on the Combined Code' issued by the Institute of Chartered Accountants in England and Wales in 1999 and the Turnbull guidance. The risk management process and systems of internal control are designed to manage rather than eliminate the risk of failure to achieve the Group's strategic objectives. It should be recognised that such systems can only provide reasonable and not absolute assurance against material misstatement or loss. This process has been in place since the start of the financial year and up to the date of approval of the accounts.

The key procedures which the directors have established with a view to providing effective internal control are as follows:

- regular Board meetings to consider a schedule of matters reserved for directors' consideration;
- the Board carries out an annual review of corporate strategy which includes a review of risks facing the business, and how these risks are monitored and managed on an ongoing basis within the organisation. This process is regularly reviewed by the Board;
- an established organisational structure with clearly defined lines of responsibility and delegation of authority;
- an established internal audit function which implements the annual internal audit plan as agreed by the Committee;
- documented and enforced policies and procedures;
- appointment of staff of the necessary calibre to fulfil their allotted responsibilities;
- comprehensive budgets and forecasts, approved by the Board, reviewed and revised on a regular basis, with performance monitored against them and explanations obtained for material variances;
- a detailed investment approval process, requiring Board approval for major projects. Post-investment appraisals are conducted and are reviewed by the Board; and
- the Audit Committee of the Board, comprising non-executive directors, considers significant financial control matters as appropriate.

The audit committee

The main board is required to establish an audit committee which consists of at least three independent non-executive directors (two members in the case of smaller companies).

The committee's main roles and responsibilities should include:

- to monitor the integrity of the company's financial statements and any formal announcements;
- to review the company's internal *financial* controls;
- to review the company's internal control and risk management systems (except where examined by a separate risk company or the main board itself);
- to monitor and review the effectiveness of the company's internal audit function;
- to make external audit appointment recommendations to the board;
- to review and monitor the external auditors' independence;
- to develop and implement policy on the engagement of the external auditor to supply non-audit services.

The extract below is taken from the Corporate Governance section of the 2007 Annual Report of Vodafone.

> **VODAFONE GROUP PLC** *Extract from the Annual Report 2007, Extract from Corporate Governance Report*
>
> **Audit Committee**
> The Audit Committee is comprised of financially literate members having the necessary ability and experience to understand financial statements. Solely for the purpose of fulfilling the requirements of the Sarbanes-Oxley Act and the Combined Code, the Board has designated John Buchanan, who is an independent non-executive director satisfying the independence requirements of Rule 10A-3 of the US Securities Exchange Act 1934, as its financial expert on the Audit Committee. Further details of John Buchanan can be found in 'Governance – Board of Directors and Group Management'.
>
> Under its terms of reference, the Audit Committee is required, amongst other things, to oversee the relationship with the external auditors, to review the Company's preliminary results announcement, interim results and annual financial statements, to monitor compliance with statutory and listing requirements for any exchange on which the Company's shares and debt instruments are quoted, to review the scope, extent and effectiveness of the activity of the Group Internal Audit Department, to engage independent advisers as it determines is necessary and to perform investigations.
>
> The Audit Committee reports to the Board on the quality and acceptability of the Company's accounting policies and practices, including without limitation, critical accounting policies and practices. The Audit Committee also plays an active role in monitoring the Company's compliance efforts for

> Section 404 of the Sarbanes-Oxley Act and receives progress updates at each of its meetings.
>
> At least twice a year, the Audit Committee meets separately with the external auditors and the Group Audit Director without management being present. Further details on the work of the Audit Committee and its oversight of the relationships with the external auditors can be found under 'Auditors' and the 'Report from the Audit Committee' which are set out on pages 72 and 74.

Further examples describing the functions and workings of the audit committee are contained in the UNIQ Annual Report 2006, pages 30 to 31 (www.uniq.com) and NATIONAL GRID Annual Report 2005/06, page 70 (www.nationalgrid.com).

Whistleblowing

The Code requires the audit committee to review arrangements by which staff of the company may, in confidence, raise concerns about possible improprieties in matters of financial reporting or anything else. The committee must ensure that appropriate arrangements are in place, as described in the example below:

> **GEORGE WIMPEY** *Extract from Annual Report 2006*
>
> **Statement of Compliance**
> During the year, a formal whistleblowing procedure was put in place across the Morrison Homes business. Whistleblowing is a standing item on the agenda of each meeting of the Audit Committee, at which time the Committee reviews the whistleblowing procedures in place across the Group in line with the Combined Code.

Non-audit services

If the auditor provides non-audit services, the annual report should explain to shareholders how auditor objectivity and independence is safeguarded.

Relations with shareholders

The Code refers to dialogue with large and institutional shareholders, and constructive use of annual general meetings. Companies are required to disclose in their annual report the steps they have taken to ensure that the members of the board, and in particular the non-executive directors, develop an understanding of the views of major shareholders about their company. The Code refers to: direct face-to-face contact; analysts' or brokers' briefings; and surveys of shareholder opinion. These are described in the example below relating to Tesco.

TESCO *Extract from Corporate Governance Statement 2007*

Relations with stakeholders
We are committed to having a constructive dialogue with all stakeholders to ensure we understand what is important to them and allow ourselves the opportunity to present our position. Engagement helps us identify new risks and opportunities to ensure that our long-term strategy is sustainable. In some instances we find that working with stakeholders in partnership can help deliver shared goals. We might not be able to satisfy all stakeholder concerns all the time but through engagement we can do our best to balance competing demands. We know that customers need to be able to trust our business and they will only trust us if we do the right thing by all our stakeholders. Our programme of engaging with stakeholders including customers, staff, suppliers, investors, non-governmental organisations and others, is set out in more detail in the Corporate Responsibility Review and on our website. The launch of the Community Plan has helped to demonstrate our commitment to tackling a wide range of social and environmental issues and we carry out external research to help us understand how well we are addressing stakeholder concerns.

We are committed to maintaining a good dialogue with shareholders through proactively organising meetings and presentations as well as responding to a wide range of enquiries. We seek shareholder views on a range of issues from strategy to corporate governance and SEE [social, environmental and ethical] issues. We recognise the importance of communicating appropriately any significant Company developments. This shareholder communication is mainly co-ordinated by the Investor Relations department. During the year, the Group met with 97 of our leading shareholders representing over 53% of the issued shares of the Company. To complement this programme, the Chairman meets with major shareholders independently from the Executive team. Shareholders also have the opportunity to meet with the Senior Independent Non-executive Director. The Board is kept updated on the views of stake-holders.

It is normal that institutional shareholders may be in more regular contact with the Group than others, but care is exercised to ensure that any price-sensitive information is released to all shareholders, institutions and private, at the same time in accordance with applicable legal and regulatory requirements.

The AGM is an excellent opportunity to communicate directly with all shareholders. The whole Board attends the meeting and are available to answer questions from the shareholders present. To encourage shareholder participation, we offer electronic proxy voting and voting through the CREST electronic proxy appointment service. At our last AGM in July 2006, all resolutions were voted by way of electronic poll. This follows best practice guidelines and allows the Company to count all votes, not just those of shareholders attending the meeting.

Every shareholder may choose to receive a full Annual Report and Financial Statements or the Annual Review and Summary Financial Statement. At the half-year, all shareholders receive an Interim Report. These reports, together with publicly-made trading statements, are available on the Group's website, www.tesco.com/corporate.

Going concern

Under the listing rules, the annual report must include a statement by the directors that the business is a going concern, for example:

GEORGE WIMPEY *Extract from Annual Report 2006*

The Directors are required under the Financial Services Authority's Listing Rules and the Combined Code to have satisfied themselves as to the Group's ability to continue in existence for the foreseeable future. A review has been carried out and the Directors have concluded that the Group has adequate resources and is justified in using the going concern basis in preparing the financial statements.

The auditors' report

The auditors' report has to encompass the reporting requirements of International Auditing Standards issued by the Auditing Practices Board as well as those of Financial Services Authority listing rules in relation to corporate governance. A clear example of a report giving an unqualified opinion appears below. We have added comments on the significance of various component parts.

ASSOCIATED BRITISH FOODS PLC *Annual Report 2007*

Independent auditors' report to the members of Associated British Foods plc
We have audited the group and parent company financial statements (the 'financial statements') of Associated British Foods plc for the year ended 15 September 2007 which comprise the consolidated income statement, the consolidated and parent company balance sheets, the consolidated cash flow statement, the consolidated statement of changes in equity, the parent company reconciliation of movements in equity shareholders' funds, and the related notes. [1] These financial statements have been prepared under the accounting policies set out therein. [2] We have also audited the information in the Remuneration report that is described as having been audited. [3]

This report is made solely to the Company's members, as a body, in accordance with section 235 of the Companies Act 1985. Our audit work has been undertaken so that we might state to the Company's members those matters we are required to state to them in an auditors' report and for no other purpose. To the fullest extent permitted by law, we do not accept or assume responsibility to anyone other than the Company and the Company's members as a body, for our audit work, for this report, or for the opinions we have formed.

Respective responsibilities of directors and auditors
The directors' responsibilities for preparing the annual report and the group financial statements in accordance with applicable law and International Financial Reporting Standards (IFRSs) as adopted by the EU, [4] and for preparing the parent company financial statements and the directors' remuneration report in accordance with applicable law and UK Accounting Standards (UK Generally Accepted Accounting Practice) are set out in the statement of directors' responsibilities on page 46. [5]

Our responsibility is to audit the financial statements and the part of the directors' remuneration report to be audited in accordance with relevant legal and regulatory requirements and International Standards on Auditing (UK and Ireland). [6]

We report to you our opinion as to whether the financial statements give a true and fair view and whether the financial statements and the part of the directors' remuneration report to be audited have been properly prepared in accordance with the Companies Act 1985 and, as regards the group financial statements. Article 4 of the IAS Regulation. We also report to you whether in our opinion the information given in the Directors' report is consistent with the financial statements. The information given in the Directors' report includes that specific information that is cross referred from the Business review section of the Directors' report. [7]

In addition we report to you if, in our opinion, the Company has not kept proper accounting records, if we have not received all the information and explanations we require for our audit, or if information specified by law regarding directors' remuneration and other transactions is not disclosed.

We review whether the corporate governance statement reflects the Company's compliance with the nine provisions of the 2003 Combined Code specified for our review by the Listing Rules of the Financial Services Authority, and we report if it does not. We are not required to consider whether the board's statements on internal control [8] cover all risks and controls, or form an opinion on the effectiveness of the group's corporate governance procedures or its risk and control procedures.

We read the other information contained in the annual report and consider whether it is consistent with the audited financial statements. We consider the implications for our report if we become aware of any apparent misstatements or material inconsistencies with the financial statements. Our responsibilities do not extend to any other information.

Basis of audit opinion
We conducted our audit in accordance with International Standards on Auditing (UK and Ireland) issued by the Auditing Practices Board. An audit includes examination, on a test basis, of evidence relevant to the amounts and disclosures in the financial statements and the part of the Remuneration report to be audited. It also includes an assessment of the significant estimates and judgements made by the directors in the preparation of the financial statements, and of whether the accounting policies are appropriate to the group's

and Company's circumstances, consistently applied and adequately disclosed.

We planned and performed our audit so as to obtain all the information and explanations which we considered necessary in order to provide us with sufficient evidence to give reasonable assurance that the financial statements and the part of the Remuneration report to be audited are free from material misstatement, whether caused by fraud or other irregularity or error. In forming our opinion we also evaluated the overall adequacy of the presentation of information in the financial statements and the part of the Remuneration report to be audited.

Opinion
In our opinion:

- the consolidated financial statements give a true and fair view, in accordance with IFRSs as adopted by the EU, of the state of the group's affairs as at 15 September 2007 and of its profit for the year then ended;
- the consolidated financial statements have been properly prepared in accordance with the Companies Act 1985 and Article 4 of the IAS Regulation;
- the parent company financial statements give a true and fair view, in accordance with UK Generally Accepted Accounting Practice, of the state of the parent company's affairs as at 15 September 2007; [9]
- the parent company financial statements and the part of the Remuneration report to be audited have been properly prepared in accordance with Companies Act 1985; and
- the information given in the Directors' report is consistent with the financial statements.

KPMG Audit Plc
Chartered Accountants
Registered Auditor
8 Salisbury Square
London
EC4Y 8BB
6 November 2007

Authors' comments:

[1] The financial statements referred to by the audit report comprise those of the group (which effectively combines those of the parent company and all the subsidiaries – see Chapter 28) and those of the individual parent company.

[2] The group financial statements have been prepared on the basis of International Financial Reporting Standards (IFRS) – see page 52 of the annual report. Those of the parent company and subsidiaries have been prepared on the basis of UK GAAP – see page 96 of the annual report.

[3] The UK listing rules issued by the Financial Services Authority (FSA) require the company to present a remuneration report and specify which parts fall within the scope of the audit report.

[4] International Financial Reporting Standards and interpretations used in the UK require endorsement by the European Union.

[5] See Chapter 4, page 27.

[6] International Standards on Auditing are issued by the UK Auditing Practices Board. APB activities are referred to on the FRC website (www.frc.org.uk).

[7] The directors' report must include a business review which complies with the requirements of the Companies Act 1985 (to be replaced in due course by equivalent requirements in the Companies Act 2006). The relevant information may be provided elsewhere, for example in the operating and financial review, provided it is adequately cross-referenced from the directors' report.

[8] The statement on internal control required by the Combined Code was referred to above.

[9] The group audit report includes separate opinions on the consolidated financial statements prepared under IFRS and on the parent company balance sheet (state of the parent company's affairs) prepared under UK GAAP.

Audit reports other than those which are unqualified

The Auditing Practices Board has published a Bulletin (2006/6) entitled 'Auditors' Reports on Financial Statements in the United Kingdom'. This includes a large number of specimen reports, covering a diverse range of situations. This area is extremely technical, but the above Bulletin is helpful for those who require a detailed insight into this area.

CHAPTER 7

The profit and loss account:
overall structure

Introduction

The aim of this chapter is to set out the structure of the profit and loss under UK GAAP, and its international equivalent, the income statement, under IFRS.

Chapter 8 deals with the first line in the profit and loss account, turnover (or 'revenue' under IFRS). Chapter 9 deals with additional elements and disclosures concerning the profit and loss account, whilst Chapter 10 deals specifically with interpretative and analytical issues.

The format of the profit and loss account under UK GAAP

Chapter 3 contains simple illustrations of the profit and loss account under UK GAAP, and the main items of terminology. As described in that chapter, the profit and loss account is a score-card of how the company did in the period reported on, normally the last year. The Companies Act 1985 offers companies a choice of several profit and loss account formats. The two most popular formats in the UK, Formats 1 and 2, are 'modern' single-page vertical formats.

The upper parts of Formats 1 and 2 are shown in Examples 7.1 and 7.2 respectively. The difference between them is the way they show operating costs:

- Format 1 breaks down operating costs by function:
  - *cost of sales* (which will include all costs of production, such as factory wages, materials and manufacturing overheads, including depreciation of machinery);
  - *distribution costs* (costs incurred in getting the goods to the customer);

  - *administrative expenses* (e.g. office expenses, directors' and auditors' fees).
- Format 2 breaks down operating costs into:
  - raw materials and consumables;
  - *staff costs*: wages and salaries; social security costs; other pension costs;
  - *depreciation* and other amounts written off fixed assets;
  - other external charges;
  - *change in stock* of finished goods and work in progress.

Example 7.1 Profit and loss account: Format 1

	£000	£000
Turnover		7,200
Cost of sales		3,600
Gross profit		3,600
Distribution costs	1,100	
Administrative expenses	900	
		2,000
		1,600
Other operating income		50
[Operating or trading profit]		1,650
Income from interests in associated undertakings (see Chapter 29)		40
Income from other fixed asset investments		5
Other interest receivable		120
		1,815
Amounts written off investments	15	
Interest payable	600	
		615
[Profit on ordinary activities before tax]		1,200

The formats reflect the disclosure requirements of the European Union Fourth Directive as incorporated in Schedule 4 of the Companies Act 1985. Items in square brackets have been included because they are important to the analyst, although they do not actually appear in the formats in Schedule 4. Most companies now adopt Format 1, though some use a combination of Formats 1 and 2.

Example 7.2 Profit and loss account: Format 2

	£000	£000
Turnover		7,200
Changes in stocks of finished goods and work in progress	160	
Other operating income	50	210
		7,410
Raw materials and consumables	1,700	
Other external charges	1,120	
Staff costs		
Wages and salaries	2,050	
Social security costs	300	
Other pension costs	120	
Depreciation and other amounts written off tangible and intangible fixed assets	400	
Other operating charges	70	
		5,760
[Operating or trading profit]		1,650
Income from interests in associated undertakings (see Chapter 29)		40
Income from other fixed asset investments		5
Other interest receivable		120
		1,815
Amounts written off investments	15	
Interest payable	600	
		615
[Profit on ordinary activities before tax]		1,200

Comparatively few companies adopt Format 2. One which does, but puts most of the detail in the notes to its accounts, is SYGEN INTERNATIONAL, the profit and loss account of which is shown below. We look at SYGEN INTERNATIONAL again later in this chapter in connection with audit fees and interest paid.

Profit before taxation

As shown in Examples 7.1 and 7.2:

- trading profit, *plus*
- income from interests in associated undertakings and from other participating interests (see Chapter 29), *plus*
- income from other investments and other interest receivable, *less*
- interest payable and any amounts written off investments,
- leaves the profit before tax, or 'pre-tax profit'.

The format of the income statement under International Financial Reporting Standards (IFRS)

Under UK GAAP, the format of the profit and loss account is specified by a combination of Companies Act 1985 requirements and FRS 3 (Reporting financial performance) requirements.

Under IFRS, format and content rules are set out in the less prescriptive IAS 1, Presentation of financial statements.

Example 7.3 uses Format 1 (Analysis of expenses by purpose or function). As with UK GAAP, companies are free to analyse and present expenses according to the nature of the expense (see above).

Under IFRS, certain items go through the income statement, even though under UK GAAP they would be required to be passed through reserves. An example is the treatment of the increase in value of investment properties (see below and Chapter 13).

Example 7.3 Income statement under IFRS 1: Format 1

	£000
Revenue[1]	4,163
Cost of sales	3,157
Gross profit	1,006
Other operating income[2]	101
Distribution costs	(239)
Administrative expenses	(325)
Operating profit[3]	543
Finance revenue[4]	23
Finance costs[5]	10
Profit before tax	576
Income tax expense[6]	(172)
Profit for the period	404

1. Revenue is the IFRS term for 'turnover'.
2. This could relate to a variety of items, for example income from royalties or rents received from letting out buildings. Under IFRS it could also include, for example, gains on the increase in the value of investment properties (see Chapter 13).
3. Operating profit continues to be a widely used term under IFRS (some companies refer to this as 'profit from operations').
4. This might consist of interest received from cash deposits, and dividends received on shares held.
5. Under IFRS, this might consist of a variety of items including for example: bank interest, foreign currency gains and losses (see Chapter 29), and gains and losses on derivatives (see Chapter 23).
   The note to the financial statements relating to finance costs will provide a list of the main items making up this total (see Chapter 9).
6. This is the total tax charge, consisting of current tax and deferred tax.

CHAPTER 8

The profit and loss account: turnover and revenue recognition

Turnover and revenue

Under UK GAAP, a company's annual sales are described in the profit and loss account as 'turnover'.

Turnover is defined in the Companies Act 1985 as the amount derived from the provision of goods and services falling within the company's ordinary activities (after deduction of trade discounts and before adding VAT and other sales-based taxes). Companies are required by the standard formats of the Companies Act 1985 to disclose turnover (i.e. total sales) in their profit and loss account. The following must also be given:

(a) Under Sch. 4, para. 55(1), if a company carried on two or more classes of business during the year which in the directors' opinion differ substantially from each other, it should describe the classes and show each one's turnover and pre-tax profit.

(b) If in the year a company supplied geographical markets which in the directors' opinion differ substantially, the turnover attributable to each should be stated (Sch. 4, para. 55(2)).

However, this information need not be disclosed if, in the opinion of the directors, it would be seriously prejudicial to the interests of the company to do so; but the fact that it has not been disclosed must be stated (Sch. 4, para. 55(5)).

Segmental reporting (SSAP 25) is considered in Chapter 10.

Under IFRS, the company's sales are referred to as 'revenue'.

The term 'revenue recognition' is used in both UK GAAP and IFRS to refer to recognition of the sales number (whether referred to in the financial statements as turnover or revenue) as opposed to recognition of profit.

Revenue recognition under UK GAAP

A good place to start fiddling

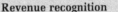

This was how revenue recognition was viewed not that many years ago. As the *Financial Times* put it in July 2001:

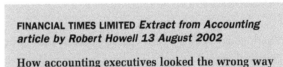

FINANCIAL TIMES *Extract from the LEX column 9 July 2001*

Revenue recognition
If you want to defraud investors by fiddling your company accounts, there are few better places to start than the field of revenue recognition.

A subsequent *FT* article, published on 13 August 2002, warmed to the theme:

FINANCIAL TIMES LIMITED *Extract from Accounting article by Robert Howell 13 August 2002*

How accounting executives looked the wrong way
One of the most basic issues is revenue recognition ... many of the recent failures stem from this issue.

ENRON, acting as a broker between sellers and buyers of energy, took sales credit for the total size of the transaction, rather than only the fee involved, which made the company's size and growth rate look much stronger than it really was.

GLOBAL CROSSING and QWEST COMMUNICATIONS, among other companies, bought and sold capacity from each other and took sales credit at both ends, overstating both companies' revenue.

No UK Accounting Standard

The former International Accounting Standards Committee issued IAS 18 Revenue as long ago as 1993 (and this replaced an earlier version originally issued in 1982).

In the UK, it was not until July 2001 that the Accounting Standards Board issued a Discussion Paper on Revenue with the intention of using this as the basis for the development of a full standard on revenue recognition. This Paper was followed in November 2003 by a 'mini-standard': FRS 5, Application Note G (AN G) on revenue recognition. Mary Keegan, ASB Chairman at the time commented that 'Recent reports of questionable practice have highlighted the need for us to set out best practice. AN G was not the final word however. Differences of opinion remained as to how the statement should be interpreted in relation to accounting for contracts for the provision of services. This resulted in the issue by the Urgent Issues Task Force of Abstract 40, Revenue recognition and service contracts.

Concerns expressed by the ASB related to quite diverse situations: in some cases, policies used by businesses resulted in overstatement of revenue by recognising it in earlier accounting periods than might have been appropriate. In other cases, policies used resulted in delaying the recognition of revenue. For businesses whose shares were publicly traded the main concern was overstatement of revenue. However, for many smaller businesses the main concern of the authorities was exactly the opposite, i.e. the understatement of revenue and profit.

Aspects of revenue recognition that have caused particular concern

The various areas of concern can be grouped into three main categories:

1. those where accounting policies had the effect of accelerating the recognition of turnover as well as profits;
2. those where accounting policies had the effect of exaggerating the total turnover number (but without affecting profit);
3. those where accounting policies had the effect of delaying the recognition of revenue (and also profits).

Examples of policies that accelerated the recognition of revenue and profit

1. Taking the profit on a large deal before contracts have been exchanged

In the absence of an accounting standard dealing with revenue recognition, the Financial Reporting Review Panel (FRRP) has had to consider this issue on a number of occasions. The most notable of these concerned the accounts of the WIGGINS GROUP for each of the five years to 31 March 2000 (see also page 4):

WIGGINS GROUP *Extract from FRRP Press Notice 65*

Revenue recognition
It is the company's accounting policy to recognise revenue in respect of commercial property sales on exchange of contract . . . One of the contracts was conditional upon the company obtaining planning permission on terms satisfactory to the purchaser without which he had certain rights not to proceed.

A second contract had the appearance of a financing transaction rather than an outright sale which, under FRS 5, should not be recognised until the risks and rewards of ownership pass at a future date.

In the particular circumstances, the panel was of the view that neither contract could be recognised in the 2000 accounts.

The directors subsequently agreed to revise the previously published accounts in line with the Panel's views.

2. Booking sales as soon as an order has been placed

This is an old chestnut. Under the practice sometimes referred to as *pre-despatching*, goods were recorded as sold as soon as the order was placed. This caused problems, particularly in the retail sector.

A 'cause celebre' was ALLIED CARPETS, which referred in its 1998 accounts to 'a breakdown of financial controls in respect of sales recognition procedures'. The cumulative effect of the error was an overstatement of sales of £6.4m.

Another example was the furniture group MFI which, in its 1999 accounts, changed its accounting policy on turnover:

MFI *Extract from 1999 accounts*

Accounting policies
During the period the sales recognition policy of MFI Furniture Centres Limited was changed from recognising sales on an order basis to a despatch basis. Prior to the adoption of this accounting policy MFI Furniture Centres Limited recognised sales in full, together with the retail element of the profit, at the time the customer placed the order and paid the deposit . . .

The effect of the change was to reduce the company's net assets at year end 24 April 1999 by £19.2m.

Application Note G, subsequently issued by the ASB in November 2003, limits the circumstances where sales can be booked before the goods have been physically delivered. These rules, dealing with 'Bill and hold sales', would not have been satisfied by MFI's old sales recognition policy.

3. Including annual support and maintenance revenue in full in the year of receipt

Until recently several companies would include revenue in full in the year of receipt, even though some of the revenue related to the provision of services after the balance sheet date.

Adverse press comment (followed in some cases by a falling share price) caused some companies to reconsider their accounting policy, e.g. NETCALL:

NETCALL *Extract from 2003 accounts*

Note 3 Prior year adjustment
During the year the group changed its accounting policy for maintenance and support income for the first year of a supply agreement. Previously this income had been recognised in full upon installation of the system.

The current policy is to spread the first year support and maintenance income over the year rather than in full upon installation . . . a prior year adjustment has been made.

---

4. Sales returns

The terms of contractual arrangements may allow customers to return goods that they have purchased.

Application Note G requires the sales value of estimated returns to be excluded from turnover, and estimates of returns should be reviewed at each balance sheet date. See, for example, PROTHERICS:

PROTHERICS *Extract from accounting policies 2003*

Turnover
Turnover represents amounts receivable in respect of the sales of goods and services, license agreements and intellectual property to customers during the year, net of trade discounts and value added tax.

Turnover is partly recognised upon the shipment of products to the distributor with further amounts being recognised in accordance with the contractual terms upon the shipment to the end user.

Certain medical products sold by the Group can be returned should they remain unused by the expiry date and provision is made for these items. Turnover is stated net of these provisions.

---

5. Extended warranties

Some retailers took full credit for revenue from extended warranties in the period in which the sale of the product took place rather than spreading it over the period of cover.

6. Long-term contracts

Long-term contracts are covered in Chapter 16 (pages 127–128). Because contractors' margins are often thin, and the sums involved may be very large, this can be an area for disagreement between company and auditor, but their differences are normally settled behind closed doors. Not so JARVIS:

FINANCIAL TIMES *Article of 15 July 2000 by Charles Batchelor*   FT

PwC wins costs against Jarvis
Jarvis, the rail maintenance company, took 'an aggressive approach to the recognition of the income and profits on long-term contracts', against the advice of its auditors, a High Court judge said yesterday.

▶

Mr Justice Lightman ordered Jarvis to pay the full legal costs of PwC, its former auditors . . . From the date of its appointment as auditor in 1996, PwC had differences with Jarvis over how income should be recognised in its accounts, Mr Justice Lightman said.

These differences became acute in relation to the March 1999 accounts. 'Jarvis wished to include two claims totalling £15.2m which PwC could not satisfy themselves were sufficiently certain of recovery . . . without actual payment or acknowledgement by Railtrack that the sum was due.

'Ultimately, when PwC threatened to qualify their audit report unless Jarvis excluded £12m, Jarvis reluctantly agreed to exclude this sum. PwC were plainly correct in the line they took for, when Jarvis finally settled accounts with Railtrack, Jarvis had to write off this £12m and a further £6.8m besides.'

Examples of policies which exaggerated the annual turnover number (but without affecting profit)

1. Using sales promotions to boost the top line

Accountancy Age commented on the likely effect of AN G on this practice:

ACCOUNTANCY AGE *December 2003*

Supermarkets and big stores than run 'two-for-one' offers will only be able to record the revenue actually taken, rather than use the notional value of the goods sold.

BIG FOOD GROUP (formerly ICELAND) is an example of a company which changed its accounting policy:

BIG FOOD GROUP *Extract from 2002 accounts*

Accounting policies
Following the implementation of FRS 18, the Group has reviewed its accounting policies.

The only significant effect is to restate the comparative amounts for turnover and cost of sales by £329.2m for the 65 weeks ended 31 March 2001, reflecting the Group's revised policy of excluding sales incentives from turnover.

Turnover and cost of sales for the 52 weeks ended 29 March 2002 would have been £293.3m higher without the change in policy.

---

2. Adding concessionaires' sales to the turnover of the main store

Application Note G included an example of a department store which provided space for concessionaires to sell products and which received a fixed amount of rental income in consideration. AN G stated that the department store should *not* include within its turnover the value of the concessionaires' sales.

In December 2003, *Accountancy Age* noted that the MERCHANT RETAIL GROUP's interim turnover was £51.4m compared with £60.7m on the previous 'industry basis'.

3. Showing turnover at full transaction value when acting in an agency capacity

Where the seller is acting as principal, turnover should be based on gross amount received or receivable.

However where the seller is acting as agent, turnover reported should be based on commission receivable in return for the seller's services.

Application Note G stops, for example, the previous practice of some Internet retailers of booking, say, £1,000 of revenues and costs of £900, for earning £100 commission on the sale of a £1,000 flight provided by a travel company for which the Internet retailer was acting as agent.

EBOOKERS is an example of a company which changed its accounting policy *prior to* the issue of Application Note G:

EBOOKERS *Extract from 2002 accounts*

Accounting policies
During the year the presentation of negotiated fare turnover has been changed from a gross to a net basis.

Negotiated fare tickets are tickets that are bought by the Group or other independent third parties to fulfil existing commitments to the Group's customers.

. . . all turnover is now recorded at the margin earned rather than the amount invoiced to customers.

LASTMINUTE.COM made a clear distinction in its 2003 accounts between full transaction value (which it referred to as 'total transaction value' or 'TTV') and statutory turnover.

LASTMINUTE.COM *Extract from 2003 accounts*

Total Transaction Value ('TTV')

TTV . . . does not represent the Group's statutory turnover.

Where the Group acts as agent or cash collector, TTV represents the price at which goods or services have been sold across the Group's various platforms. In other cases (for example the reservation of restaurant tables), a flat fee is earned. . . . In such cases TTV represents the flat fee commission earned. Where the Group acts as principal, TTV represents the price at which goods or services have been sold across the Group's various platforms.

Turnover

Turnover represents the aggregate amount of revenue from products sold. . . .

Where the Group acts as agent and does not take ownership of the products or services being sold, turnover represents commission earned less amounts due or paid on any commission shared. Where the Group acts as principal and purchases the products or services for resale, turnover represents the price at which the products or services have been sold across the Group's various platforms.

Examples of policies which delayed the recognition of revenue (and also profits)

Many organisations supplying professional services did not record any revenue until the work was completed or an invoice raised for partly completed work (a method of accounting commonly use prior to the issue of UITF Abstract 40, and referred to as the 'completed contract method').

In some cases revenue in respect of completed work was only recognised when a sales invoice had been raised.

This is further referred to below under 'Abstract 40'.

Application Note G – general considerations

Application Note G requires a seller to recognise revenue under an exchange transaction with a customer when and to the extent that the seller obtains the right to consideration in exchange for its performance.

Performance is defined in AN G as the 'fulfilment of the seller's contractual obligations to a customer through the supply of goods and services'.

At the point of revenue recognition, the seller will also recognise a new asset (usually a debtor).

Example accounting policy – sale of goods

Revenue from the sale of goods is recognised when the significant risks and rewards of ownership of the goods have passed to the buyer and the amount of revenue can be reliably measured.

Profit is recognised at the time of sale.

When a seller receives payment from a customer in advance of performance, it recognises a liability. This liability equals the consideration received and represents the seller's obligation under the contract.

Partial performance

In many cases, a seller may obtain a right to consideration when some but not all of its contractual obligations have been fulfilled. Revenue should be recognised to the extent that the seller has obtained the right to consideration through its performance.

Example accounting policy – extended warranty

In addition to the sale of goods, the retailer receives a payment in respect of extended warranty cover.

The revenue should be recognised over the term of the contract. The excess of the money received over the revenue recognised in the profit and loss account should be included within creditors as a payment in advance.

As performance takes place and the seller obtains right to consideration, the liability is reduced and the amount of the reduction is reported as revenue.

Example – advertising consultancy

An advertising consultancy company enters into a contract with a client regarding an advertising campaign. The contract specifies a fixed fee of £20,000 which will be paid on completion of the campaign. At the balance sheet date the company has delivered approximately 30% of the work required under the contract. The company calculates that attributable costs to date amount to £3,600.

Prior to AN G the company may have adopted an alternative accounting policy and included £3,600 as work in progress carried forward to the following period with no revenue or profit included in the current period.

Under AN G, the consultancy company is regarded as having obtained a right to consideration in relation to work done up to the balance sheet date. The proportion of the fee earned by the balance sheet date is assessed by reference to the stage of completion of the project (the percentage of completion method).

Assuming a percentage of 30%, revenue recognised in the profit and loss account will be £6,000 and costs incurred amounting to £3,600 will be offset against this amount to determine a potential operating profit for the period of £2,400. However, the consultancy will also need to consider the requirements of SSAP 9 to assess the outcome of the total contract before determining whether it is appropriate to recognise any profit. The balance sheet will include a debtor (usually described as 'accrued income' of £6,000).

Example – seller of software

A company sells software to a customer and in addition receives additional consideration of £12,000 in relation to a maintenance and support contract covering a period of 12 months. Five months of the period covered falls in the supplier's current year and seven months in the following year. £12,000 is received upfront at the beginning of the contract period.

Prior to AN G, the suppliers might have taken credit in the current period for revenue of £12,000 and included a creditor in the balance sheet for any costs expected to be incurred in the seven months falling in the following period.

Under AN G, the income of £12,000 would be spread over the period of the contract, so that only $^5/_{12}$ (= £5,000) would be recognised in the current period. In the balance sheet, the £7,000 deemed to be received 'in advance' would be included as a creditor.

Abstract 40, Revenue recognition and service contracts

Abstract 40 was issued by the Urgent Issues Task Force to help clarify how AN G should be applied in specific situations relating to contracts for the provision of services.

The general rules is that a contract for services should be accounted for as a long-term contract where contract activity falls into different accounting periods. This is subject to the proviso that contracts for services should not be accounted for as long-term contracts unless they involve the provision of a single service, or a number of services that constitute a single project.

Where the substance of a contract is that the seller's contractual obligations are performed gradually over time, revenue should be recognised as contract activity progresses to reflect the seller's partial performance of its contractual obligations. The amount of revenue should reflect the accrual of the right to consideration as contract activity progresses by reference to value of the work performed.

Where the substance of a contract is that a right to consideration does not arise until the occurrence of a critical event, revenue is not recognised until that event occurs. This only applies where the right to consideration is conditional or contingent on a specified future event, the occurrence of which is 'outside the control of the seller'. For example, suppose a lawyer acts for a client in a court case on a 'no win no fee' basis. The lawyer would not be entitled to recognise revenue in the current period unless the law case had been decided in the client's favour before the balance sheet date.

Example accounting policy – provision of services

Turnover represents revenue earned under a wide variety of contracts to provide professional services and advice to third parties.

Revenue is recognised as earned when, and to the extent that, the firm obtains the right to consideration in exchange for its performance under those contracts.

It is measured at the fair value of the right to consideration, which represents amounts chargeable to clients, including recoverable expenses and disbursements, but excluding VAT.

For incomplete contracts, an assessment is made of the extent to which revenue has been earned. This assessment takes into account the nature of the assignment, its stage of completion and the relevant contract terms.

Revenue in respect of contingent fee arrangements (over and above any minimum agreed fee) is recognised when the contingent event occurs and the recoverability of the fee is assured.

Unbilled revenue is included in debtors under accrued income.

Revenue recognition under IFRS

IAS 18, Revenue, applies to accounting for revenue from the following transactions:

- sale of goods,
- rendering of services,
- income from interest, royalties and dividends.

Recognition of revenue

IAS 18 requires income to be recognised when it is probable that future economic benefits will flow to the entity *and* these benefits can be measured reliably.

Revenue is measured at the fair value of the consideration received or receivable. For a transaction involving sale of goods, revenue is recognised when the entity has transferred to the buyer the significant risks and rewards of ownership of the goods and the amount of revenue can be measured reliably.

Revenue for a transaction involving the rendering of services is recognised as work is performed. For services that will be provided beyond the balance sheet date, revenue should be recognised by reference to the stage of completion at the balance sheet date, provided particular conditions can be satisfied.

Disclosures

Companies should disclose their accounting policies for revenue recognition, including methods used to determine the stage of completion of transactions involving the rendering of services (see, for example, ROK PLC in Chapter 3).

Companies should also disclose the amount of each significant category of revenue recognised during the period.

CHAPTER 9

The profit and loss account: further disclosure areas

Introduction

The aim of this chapter is to explain the accounting and disclosures for various income and expenditure items. Some of these items will be presented separately on the face of the profit and loss account. Others, such as cost of sales or administrative expenses (see Chapter 7), will form part of a larger total and are therefore not shown separately on the face of the profit and loss account. Instead they will form part of the notes to the accounts.

Basic disclosure areas

As explained in Chapters 1 and 4, disclosure requirements may come from a variety of sources, depending on company size and whether its shares are unlisted or listed on the London Stock Exchange.

Below, we consider some of the more important areas regarding disclosure of income and expenses.

Directors' and staff costs

Directors' emoluments

CA 1985 requires the following to be disclosed:

(a) aggregate, for all directors, of each of: emoluments (salaries, fees and bonuses); gains on exercise of share options; amounts in respect of long-term incentive schemes; employers' pension contributions under money purchase (defined contribution) schemes;
(b) number of directors accruing benefits under each of money purchase schemes and defined benefit (final salary) schemes;
(c) details of emoluments of highest paid director where aggregate of items in (a) above, excluding employers' pension contributions, exceeds £200,000;
(d) aggregate of excess retirement benefits;
(e) aggregate amount of compensation for loss of office;
(f) sums paid to third parties in respect of directors' services.

The UKLA Listing Rules require fully listed companies to provide detailed information on each director (see Chapter 6). Details must be given for each director, as shown in the extract from ST IVES, below.

ST IVES *Extract from Directors' Remuneration Report 2003*

	Basic salary	Bonus	Benefits in kind	Pension contributions (Note 1)	Total remuneration 2003	Total remuneration 2002
	£000	£000	£000	£000	£000	£000
Executive						
Wayne Angstrom	197.0	–	14.3	6.1	**217.4**	239.8
Brian Edwards	239.4	–	21.1	–	**260.5**	248.5
Miles Emley	261.9	–	16.0	76.9	**354.8**	344.6
Raymond Morley	176.0	–	0.6	–	**176.6**	176.0
Non-executive						
Lorraine Baldrey	20.0	–	–	–	**20.0**	20.0
Graham Menzies	20.0	–	–	–	**20.0**	20.0
David Wilbraham	25.0	–	–	–	**25.0**	20.0
	939.3	–	52.0	83.0	**1,074.3**	1,068.9

Miles Emley is the highest paid director.

Notes

1. Pension contributions shown under individual directors' remuneration are in respect of money-purchase schemes only. In the case of Miles Emley the sum includes a salary payment of £19,473 (2002, £17,117) in addition to basic pay . . .

Particulars of staff

Under this heading are disclosed the average number employed during the year, and the aggregate amounts of their (a) wages and salaries, (b) social security costs and (c) other pension costs.

Other expenses

Auditors' remuneration

Under this heading is disclosed the auditors' remuneration in their capacity as such, including expenses. Remuneration for services other than those of auditors should be shown separately.

A sharp increase in the auditors' remuneration (i.e. more than merely keeping pace with inflation) may be an indication of difficulties; for example SOCK SHOP paid their auditors £60,000 for the 17 months ended 28 February 1989 compared with £10,000 for the previous year, and went into receivership in 1990. Or to take a recent example:

SYGEN INTERNATIONAL *Extract from note 4 to the accounts for the year ended 30 June 2003*

	2003 £m	2002 £m
Statutory audit	0.4	0.5
Tax compliance and advisory	0.4	0.7
Other non-audit	0.1	0.1
	0.9	1.3

Tax compliance and advisory fees relate to work in respect of statutory tax compliance, general tax advice and other tax advice for the Group's fundamental restructuring which took place in 1998.

Depreciation

Depreciation and impairment in relation to fixed assets must be disclosed in the notes to the financial statements. For companies adopting profit and loss account Format 2, depreciation and impairment will be shown separately on the face of the profit and loss account (see Chapter 7). For companies using Format 1, the total depreciation charge will be allocated between cost of sales, administrative expenses and distribution costs but only the total charge is disclosed in a note.

Methods of calculating depreciation are referred to in Chapter 13.

Operating lease rentals

Rentals on operating leases must be charged to the profit and loss account on a straight line basis over the lease term. The total of operating lease rentals charged as an expense for the year must be disclosed in a note, distinguishing between amounts relating to hire of plant and machinery, and other operating leases (SSAP 21, Accounting for leases and hire purchase contracts).

Disclosure of operating lease commitments is dealt with in Chapter 25.

Foreign exchange

Foreign exchange gains and losses are dealt with in Chapter 29.

Pension costs (retirement benefits)

Accounting for company pension costs has proved to be a controversial subject in the UK. For accounting periods beginning on or after 1 December 2005, Financial Reporting Standard 17, Retirement benefits, replaced the former standard SSAP 24. As a result of this changeover, UK GAAP is far closer to International Financial Reporting Standards.

Types of pension schemes

Pension schemes can be either funded or unfunded:

- In a *funded* scheme, the company's contributions (and the employees' contributions if it is a 'contributory' rather than a 'non-contributory' scheme) are paid away to be invested externally to meet future pension liabilities, and the assets of the scheme are held in trust outside the company.

- In an *unfunded* scheme, which is the norm in some foreign countries, the company makes a provision for future liabilities in its accounts.

The two main types of pension scheme in the UK are:

1. Defined contribution schemes.
2. Defined benefit schemes.

Defined contribution schemes and defined benefit schemes are invariably funded.

Defined contribution schemes

In a defined contribution or 'money purchase' scheme, the employer has no obligation beyond payment of the contributions he has agreed to make. The benefits may vary with the performance of the investments purchased by the contributions, but this risk is borne by the employees.

The cost of providing pensions is thus straightforward: it is the amount of contribution due for the period, and will be charged against profits, see, for example, TESCO:

TESCO *Note on pension commitments 2003*

26. Pensions

. . .

The Group operates a number of schemes worldwide, the majority of which are defined contribution schemes. The contributions payable for non-UK schemes of £8m (2002, £7m) have been fully expensed against profits in the current year.

Smaller companies tend to run this type of scheme, or to contribute to SERPS – the State Earnings Related Pension Scheme – or to employees' own personal pension plans, in order to avoid taking on any open-ended future commitment. Indeed, a number of larger companies have in recent years closed defined benefit schemes and moved to defined contribution schemes to avoid this liability.

Defined benefit schemes

In a defined benefit or 'final salary' scheme, the pensions to be paid depend on the employees' pay, normally the pay in the final year of employment, so the employer's liability is open-ended.

Because of the complexities of estimating the contributions needed to provide for pensions based on wages or salaries often many years hence, consulting actuaries are used to carry out periodic valuations, usually every three years, and to determine the contribution rate required.

FRS 17, Retirement benefits

The key points of FRS 17 are as follows:

- Full actuarial valuations of pension scheme liabilities will be required at least three-yearly, with updates in other years.
- The balance sheet will include one-line items for pension fund asset (assuming a surplus) and pension fund reserve. The pension fund asset is the amount by which the total value of the scheme assets exceeds the present value of the scheme liabilities.
- The profit and loss account will include two charges or credits: (1) operating profit will be charged with current service cost and past service cost; (2) finance income will be credited (debited) with the amount by which the expected return on scheme assets exceeds (falls short of) the interest on pension scheme liabilities.
- The statement of total recognised gains and losses will pick up actuarial gains and losses.
- Movement in surplus or deficit in schemes over the period will be analysed with reconciliation of surplus/deficit to the balance sheet asset/liability.
- A company will have to build up to a five-year statistical summary.

Main points of interest for users of accounts will be:

- The balance sheet will show the pension scheme's surplus or deficit to the extent that the employer company expects to benefit or suffer from it.
- The profit and loss account will show the ongoing service cost, interest cost and expected return on assets.
- The statement of total recognised gains and losses will record and reflect market fluctuations in interest rates and share prices.
- A trend picture will be highlighted by the disclosure of a five-year history of actuarial gains and losses – making users aware of when actuarial assumptions are consistently not being met.

Disclosure requirements

The existing disclosure requirements in FRS 17 will be replaced by requirements based on IFRS (IAS 19, Employee benefits). This change will take place with effect from accounting periods that started on or after 6 April 2007. This affects disclosure requirements only; the accounting treatment outlined above is unchanged.

WILMINGTON GROUP below is an example of what the disclosure requirements will soon look like under UK GAAP. The example clearly uses IFRS terminology, namely:

- Income statement = Profit and loss account;
- Statement of recognised income and expense = Statement of total recognised gains and losses.

WILMINGTON GROUP *Annual Report 2006*

Note 28 – Staff and their pay and benefits

c) Retirement benefits
The valuation used for IAS 19 calculations has been based on the most recent actuarial valuation at 31 March 2004 and updated by the same qualified independent actuaries to take account of the requirements of IAS 19 in order to assess the liabilities of the Scheme at 30 June 2006. Scheme assets are stated at their market value at 30 June 2006.
    Main assumptions:

	30 June 2006 per cent per annum	30 June 2005 per cent per annum	30 June 2004 per cent per annum
Rate of increase in salaries	4.2	3.8	4.2
Rate of increase to pensions in payment	3.0	2.6	3.0
Discount rate	5.3	5.2	5.7
Inflation assumption	3.0	2.6	3.0

▶

The assets and liabilities of the scheme and the expected rates of return were:

| | 30 June 2006 | | 30 June 2005 | | 30 June 2004 | |
	Long-term rate of return expected per cent	*Value £000*	*Long-term rate of return expected per cent*	*Value £000*	*Long-term rate of return expected per cent*	*Value £000*
Equities	7.5	2,268	7.5	1,762	7.5	1,459
Bonds	5.0	136	5.0	118	5.3	120
Cash and other assets	4.5	69	4.5	153	4.0	94
Total market value of assets		2,473		2,033		1,673
Present value of Scheme liabilities		(2,727)		(2,411)		(2,151)
Pension liability before deferred tax		(254)		(378)		(478)
Related deferred tax asset		76		113		143
Net pension liability		(178)		(265)		(335)

Amounts recognised in income statement:

	Year ended 30 June 2006 £000	Year ended 30 June 2005 £000
Recognised within operating expenses		
Current service cost	86	98
	86	98
Recognised within finance costs		
Expected return on assets	147	120
Interest on liabilities	(128)	(124)
	19	(4)

Actuarial gain recognised in statement of recognised income and expenditure ('SORIE').

	Year ended 30 June 2006 £000	Year ended 30 June 2005 £000
Actuarial return less the expected return on assets	231	166
Experience gains and losses on liabilities	2	–
Loss due to changes in assumptions	(137)	(46)
Actuarial gain recognised in SORIE	96	120

Changes in the present value of the defined benefit obligation are as follows:

	Year ended 30 June 2006 £000	Year ended 30 June 2005 £000
Opening defined benefit obligations	2,411	2,151
Current service cost	86	98
Interest cost	128	124
Actuarial losses	135	46
Benefits paid	(33)	(8)
	2,727	2,411

▶

Changes in the fair value of Scheme assets are as follows:

	Year ended 30 June 2006 £000	Year ended 30 June 2005 £000
Opening fair value of scheme assets	2,033	1,673
Expected return	147	120
Actuarial gains	231	166
Contributions by employer	95	82
Benefits paid	(33)	(8)
	2,473	2,033

History of experience gains and losses:

	Year ended 30 June 2006 £000	Year ended 30 June 2005 £000	Year ended 30 June 2004 £000	Year ended 30 June 2003 £000	Sixteen months ended 30 June 2002 £000
Scheme assets	2,473	2,033	1,673	1,421	1,412
Defined benefit obligation	(2,727)	(2,411)	(2,151)	(2,194)	(1,843)
Scheme deficit	(254)	(378)	(478)	(773)	(431)
Experience gains/(losses) on scheme assets					
Amount (£000)	231	166	62	(181)	(419)
Per cent of scheme assets	9.3%	8.2%	3.7%	(12.7)%	(29.7)%
Experience gains/(losses) on scheme liabilities					
Amount (£000)	2	–	402	125	(15)
Per cent of the present value of scheme liabilities	0.0%	0.0%	18.7%	5.7%	(0.8)%

Defined contribution scheme
The Group contributes to a defined contribution pension scheme. Total contributions to the scheme during the year were £295,000 (2005: £274,000).

International Financial Reporting Standards

The nearest equivalent standard to FRS 17, IAS 19 on employee benefits, covers a far broader range of territory, including:

- short-term employee benefits, profit-sharing and bonus plans;
- defined contribution and defined benefit pension schemes;
- termination and redundancy benefits.

Accounting and disclosure for defined contribution schemes in IAS 19 is identical to FRS 17.

For defined benefit schemes, IAS 19 offers a range of options for dealing with actuarial gains and losses. FRS 17 offers no choice – actuarial gains and losses must not go through the profit and loss account, they must be taken through the statement of total recognised gains and losses (see under FRS 17 above).

In practice, relatively few UK companies have to date taken advantage of the options offered by IAS 19. The great majority, like WILMINGTON above, have chosen to deal with actuarial gains and losses outside the income statement (the equivalent of the profit and loss account), and have taken them through the statement of recognised income and expense (the equivalent of the STRGL).

Share option charges

Share-based payment arrangements

The various share-based payment arrangements, including share options offered to staff and directors, are described in Chapter 24. These arrangements involve offering share options and share wards to employees and others, subject to certain conditions being satisfied. These may, for example, be simple conditions such as remaining in the company's employment for a specified number of years, the company achieving specified profit growth, or the company's total shareholder return (TSR including share price growth and dividends) exceeding a specified target derived from comparator companies.

Determining the profit and loss account charge

The rules in FRS 20 are complex. In many cases the charge can only be determined after a special valuation has been carried out by an expert (usually an accountant or actuary). The fair value of the overall share-based payment package will be charged to the profit and loss account over a determined number of years.

For example, suppose a company grants 100 share options to each of its 500 employees. The condition attaching to each is that the options will vest only if an employee continues to work for the company for three years. Subject to this condition, if the options vest then the employee will be entitled to subscribe for shares for cash. The price to be paid will be specified at the outset – it is referred to as the *exercise price*.

To work out the appropriate charge, the first step is to value the options at the date they are granted (i.e. on the first day of the three-year period). The valuer will advise on which valuation model is appropriate (Black–Scholes, binomial, etc.) and the information required from the company in order to determine the appropriate inputs to the option pricing model.

Suppose the valuer determines the value of each share option at £15 per option. Potentially the fair value of all the options in play at the outset is 50,000 × £15 = £750,000. The company would have to estimate the number of options likely to vest, i.e. determine how many of the original 500 employees will be there at the end of the three years. Suppose the directors make an estimate at the end of the first year that they expect 400 employees to be with the company, i.e. 80% of the employees originally granted the options.

The fair value of the options estimated to vest is 80% of £750,000, i.e. £600,000. This would be spread over three years so assuming that the 80% estimate is not subsequently revised this would mean an annual charge to the profit and loss account of £200,000. The other side of the accounting entry is to reserves within shareholders' equity.

This is a very simple example. However FRS 20 contains Implementation Guidance with 13 numerical examples covering calculations for a range of situations (see also page 203).

International Financial Reporting Standards

FRS 20, Share-based payment, is identical to IFRS 2 with the same title. There is an implementation difference – under IFRS the rules came into effect for 2005 but for UK GAAP the rules came in a year later.

Disclosure requirements

The disclosure requirements of FRS 20/IFRS 2 are detailed and extensive. MANAGEMENT CONSULTING GROUP explains its accounting policy and discloses its share option charges as shown below.

MANAGEMENT CONSULTING GROUP Annual Report 2006

Accounting policy – Share-based payments (extract)
Share options are awarded to selected employees on a discretionary basis. Awards are measured at their fair value (which is measured using the stochastic pricing model at the date of grant) and is recognised as an employee benefits expense on a straight line basis over the vesting period based on the Group's estimate of shares that will eventually vest and adjusted for the effect of non-market based vesting conditions, with a corresponding increase in the share compensation reserve. The expected life used in the valuation model has been adjusted, based on management's best estimate, for the effects of non-transferability, exercise restrictions and behavioural considerations.

Note 5 – Staff numbers and costs (extract)
Wages and salaries includes £804,000 (2005: £640,000) relating to charges in respect of share options.

(See www.mcgplc.com for detailed disclosures in Directors' Remuneration Report on page 37 and Note 19 Share Capital on page 78.)

Research and development expenditure

SSAP 13, Research and development, requires all expenditure on pure and applied research to be charged to the profit and loss account of the year in which the expenditure is incurred. Development costs that satisfy a number of conditions (see Chapter 14) may be accounted for under UK GAAP in one of two ways:

1. charged (expensed) to profit and loss account in the period in which the expenditure is incurred; or
2. capitalised and included in the balance sheet as an intangible fixed asset (referred to in the standard as deferred development expenditure) and charged to the profit and loss account of a number of years (see Chapter 14).

SSAP 13 requires companies to disclose their R&D charge in the notes to the accounts. The note should break this total down between expenditure incurred in the current period and amounts amortised from deferred expenditure.

Historically, most UK companies have adopted the first policy. However, this will change in the future as UK GAAP converges with IFRS. IAS 38, Intangible assets, requires development costs that satisfy specified conditions to be capitalised as intangible assets with the expenditure charged against profits over a number of years (see also page 112).

Exceptional items

Definition

FRS 3, Reporting financial performance, defines exceptional items as 'material items which derive from events or transactions that fall within the ordinary activities of the reporting entity and which individually, or, if of a similar size, in aggregate, need to be disclosed by virtue of their size or incidence if the financial statements are to give a true and fair view'.

FRS 3 divides exceptional items into two categories that affect how they are positioned in the profit and loss account in relation to operating profit.

The first category, often referred to as 'operating exceptional items', is charged in arriving at operating profit.

The second category, often referred to as 'non-operating exceptional items', is positioned in the profit and loss account *immediately after operating profit but before finance costs*.

Operating exceptional items

These comprise all exceptional items apart from those that are separately required by FRS 3 paragraph 20 to be shown below operating profit, i.e. so-called non-operating exceptional items.

Abnormal stock and contract bad debt write-offs are examples of operating exceptional items.

Non-operating exceptional items

These include any items that fall into one of the three following categories:

1. profits or losses on the sale or termination of an operation;
2. costs of a fundamental reorganisation or restructuring having a material effect on the nature and focus of the reporting entity's operations;
3. profits or losses on the disposal of fixed assets.

Presentation and disclosure

'Operating exceptional items' should be separately disclosed, either on the face of the profit and loss account, or by way of note. Separate disclosure on the face of the profit and loss account is required if 'that degree of prominence is necessary in order to give a true and fair view'. 'Non-operating exceptional items' must always be shown on the face of the profit and loss account, immediately below operating profit.

SYGEN present exceptional items in a separate column of the profit and loss account:

SYGEN INTERNATIONAL *Extract from group profit and loss account for the year ended 30 June 2003*

	Operations before exceptional items £m	Exceptional items £m	2003 £m	2002 £m
Turnover				
Continuing operations				
Group and share of joint ventures	143.2	–		175.3
less: share of joint ventures	(10.5)	–	—	(10.6)
Group turnover	132.7	–	—	164.7
Group operating profit	4.7	4.6	9.3	11.1
Share of operating profit of joint ventures	0.3	–	0.3	1.1
Total operating profit	5.0	4.6	9.6	12.2
Fundamental restructuring				
– Sale and closure of businesses	–	(2.2)	(2.2)	(2.9)
– Other consequential income	–	(0.8)	(0.8)	1.9
Net interest receivable	0.4	0.1	0.5	1.5
Profit/(loss) on ordinary activities before tax	5.4	1.7	7.1	12.7

The accounts must analyse all exceptional items (whether operating or non-operating) between those that relate to continuing operations and those that relate to discontinued operations. These terms are defined below.

Headline or normalised earnings

Headline earnings exclude the following items:

- profits or losses on the sale or termination of an operation;
- profits or losses on the disposal of fixed assets;
- expropriation of assets;
- amortisation of goodwill;
- bid defence costs;
- diminution in the value of fixed assets;
- profit or loss on the capital reorganisation of long-term debt;
- profits or losses on the disposal of trade investments.

The former Institute of Investment Management and Research (IIMR) approach, focusing on the trading activities of a company, has been followed by most leading stock brokers, to produce what are termed *normalised earnings*, but with some variations.

The main variation between brokers is that some follow the IIMR recommendation to include 'costs of a fundamental reorganisation or restructuring having a material effect on the nature and focus of the reporting entity's operations' (one of the items shown separately below operating profit), while others exclude it on the grounds of abnormality and of being unlikely to recur.

The trouble with excluding it is that doing so encourages companies to classify relatively minor reorganisations as 'fundamental' in order to avoid the costs reducing 'normalised' profits and earnings per share.

The other problems with adjusting or 'normalising' earnings are taxation and minority interests. With the three items that have to be disclosed separately after operating profit (sale or termination of an operation, fundamental reorganisation and restructuring, and disposal of fixed assets), FRS 3 requires relevant information on the effect of these items on the tax charge and on any minority interests (see Chapter 28) to be shown.

With the other items listed by the IIMR for stripping out (e.g. expropriation of assets), the effect on the tax charge may have to be estimated by the analysts. And the effect on minorities will not be known unless disclosed by the company (note that IIMR is now UKSIP – see page 80).

International Financial Reporting Standards

IFRS does not use the term exceptional item. IAS 1 paragraph 86 simply requires that 'when items of income and expense are material, their nature and amount shall be disclosed separately'. Paragraph 87 includes the followings examples:

- inventory and plant write-downs (and reversals of such write-downs);
- restructuring costs;
- disposals of items of property, plant and equipment;
- disposals of investments;
- discontinued operations;
- litigation settlements;
- other reversals of provisions.

Discontinued and continuing operations

Discontinued operations

These are defined by FRS 3 as operations of the reporting entity that are sold or terminated during the year and which satisfy all of the following conditions:

- the sale or termination is completed either before the balance sheet date *or* the earlier of three months after the commencement of the subsequent period and the date on which the directors approve the financial statements;
- if the operations are terminated, the former activities have ceased permanently;
- the sale or termination has a material effect on the nature and focus of the entity's operations;
- the assets, liabilities, results of operations and activities are clearly distinguishable.

Continuing operations

These are operations that do not satisfy all of the above conditions relating to 'discontinuing'.

International Financial Reporting Standards

IFRS 5, Non-current assets held for sale and discontinued operations, defines a discontinued operation as a component of an entity that either has been disposed of or is classified as held for sale and which:

- represents a separate major line of business or geographical area of operations, *or*

- is part of a single coordinated plan to dispose of a separate major line of business or geographical area of operations, *or*
- is a subsidiary acquired exclusively with a view to resale.

Under IFRS 5, the net effect on profit of a discontinued operation is shown as a *single line item on the face of the income statement.* A detailed breakdown of how this amount is arrived at should be disclosed in the notes to the accounts. This contrasts with FRS 3, which includes the effect of discontinued operations on each line item in the profit and loss account (see, for example, SYNERGEN above).

Comparative figures

The analysis of comparative figures between continuing and discontinued operations is not required on the face of the profit and loss account. Nevertheless, experience suggests that most companies do show it there.

Whichever method is employed, the composition of the comparative figures needs to be understood. As paragraph 64 of the Explanations to FRS 3 states:

> To aid comparison, the comparative figures in respect of the profit and loss account should be based on the status of an operation in the financial statements of the period under review and should, therefore, include in the continuing category only the results of those operations included in the current period's continuing operations. . . . the comparative figures for discontinued operations will include both amounts relating to operations discontinued in the previous period and amounts relating to operations discontinued in the period under review, which in the previous period would have been included as part of continuing operations.

Finance costs

Interest paid

The Companies Act 1985 requires the disclosure of the interest paid on bank loans and overdrafts, on loans repayable within five years and on other loans. Most companies show a single figure in their profit and loss account, giving details in a note which may include: (i) some netting out of interest received; (ii) discount amortisation of deep discount bonds; (iii) interest capitalised and other adjustments; as, for example, the note explaining 'net interest' in SYGEN INTERNATIONAL's 2003 accounts:

SYGEN INTERNATIONAL Extracts from the accounts for the year to 30 June 2003

Note 5 Interest	2003	2002
	£m	£m
Interest payable and similar charges:		
On bank loans and overdrafts	(0.1)	(0.4)
Other interest payable	–	(0.3)
Unwind of discount on surplus property provision	(0.3)	(0.3)
Interest receivable	0.9	2.5
Net interest receivable	0.5	1.5

Net interest receivable for the year ended 30 June 2002 includes exceptional interest receivable of £1.0m, relating to tax refunds from prior year tax returns in connection with the disposal of certain businesses in 1998.

Although all this information may be shown on the face of the profit and loss account, it rarely is. In general one finds it early in the notes to the accounts, in a note entitled something like 'Profit on ordinary activities before tax', though there is then usually a separate note on employment costs and/or directors' emoluments.

Preference dividends

Some preference shares entitle the holder to a fixed rate of dividend, provided there are sufficient distributable profits. Such dividends are obligatory from the company's perspective and are not at the discretion of the directors (see Chapter 24).

Preference dividends, which are discretionary, should be accounted for in the same way as equity dividends (see Chapter 11).

Capitalisation of borrowing costs

In certain circumstances, finance costs incurred in relation to a construction project may be capitalised and included as part of the fixed asset. The rules are set out in FRS 15, Tangible fixed assets.

Capitalisation is not mandatory, but if a company adopts a policy of capitalisation:

1. It must be consistently applied to all finance costs directly attributable to the construction of tangible assets.
2. The amount capitalised in any period may not exceed finance costs incurred in that period, so notional interest may not be capitalised.
3. Capitalised finance costs must be 'directly attributable', i.e. they must be incremental, avoidable if there had been no expenditure on the asset.
4. Finance costs are to be capitalised gross, i.e. before the deduction of any tax relief attributed.
5. All finance costs, as defined by FRS 4 Capital instruments, have to be capitalised, not just the interest on the debt. This means that issue costs that are deducted in arriving at the net proceeds of the debt instrument will be capitalised to the extent that they form part of the finance charge.
6. If a company borrows funds specifically to construct an asset, the costs to be capitalised are the actual finance costs during the period.
7. If the project has been financed from the company's general borrowings, a detailed calculation method is laid down.
8. Capitalisation should begin when:
   (a) finance costs are being incurred;
   (b) expenditures for the asset are being incurred; and
   (c) activities that are necessary to get the asset ready for use are in progress. Necessary activities can, in fact, start before the physical construction of the asset, for example technical and administrative costs such as obtaining permits.
9. Capitalisation must cease when the asset's physical construction is complete and ready for use, even if it has not yet been brought into use.

Stopping companies from continuing to capitalise interest after completion closes a loophole used widely in the past whenever properties have proved harder to let than was originally expected.

LAND SECURITIES *Accounting policies 2003*

Investment properties

Capitalisation of interest
Gross interest associated with direct expenditure on
properties under development or undergoing major
refurbishments is capitalised . . .
    Interest is capitalised as from the commencement
of the development work until the date of practical
completion.
    The capitalisation of finance costs is suspended,
however, if there are prolonged periods when
development activity is interrupted.

Under IFRS, capitalisation was until recently, an option
subject to certain conditions being satisfied. However,
IASB has issued a revised version of IAS 23 which will
make capitalisation mandatory if certain conditions are
satisfied. IAS 23 (revised) will become mandatory in
2009.

Investment income

Investment income may comprise dividends received from
companies or interest received or receivable.

Taxation

The basis of the tax charge in the profit and loss account is
dealt with in Chapter 20, which covers deferred tax and tax
in the balance sheet.

Segment reporting

SSAP 25, Segmental reporting, requires companies that
have two or more classes of business or that operate in
two more geographical segments, to report turnover, profits
and net assets for each class of business and for each geographical segment.
    This standard is dealt with in Chapter 10, which covers
particular issues relating to analysis of accounts, as well as
IFRS implications and developments.

Group issues

Parent company profit and loss account

If, at the end of a financial year, a company is a parent
company, group accounts have to be prepared as well as individual accounts for the parent company (CA 1985, s. 227).
    As will be explained in Chapter 28, group accounts
comprise a consolidated balance sheet and profit and loss
account dealing with the parent company and its subsidiary undertakings.
    Under s. 230 (3) of the Companies Act 1985, the parent
company's profit and loss account may be omitted from
the consolidated accounts providing the parent company's
balance sheet shows the parent company's profit or loss
for the year. Since most listed companies are holding
companies, i.e. have subsidiaries, in practice one seldom
if ever sees the parent company's own profit and loss
account; one sees only the profit and loss account of the
group.

Subsidiaries and groups

FRS 2 Accounting for subsidiary undertakings, FRS 6
Acquisitions and mergers, FRS 7 Fair values in acquisition
accounting, FRS 10 Goodwill and intangible assets, and
FRS 11 Impairment of fixed assets and goodwill, all affect
the P & L account in one way or another; see Chapters 14
and 28.

Associated undertakings

'Income from interests in associated undertakings' and
'Income from other participating interests' both appear in
the formats but FRS 9 Associates and joint ventures calls
for additional disclosures as explained in Chapter 29.

CHAPTER 10

The profit and loss account: interpretation, ratio analysis, segmental analysis and earnings per share

Interpretation and ratio analysis

Introduction

Most well-run companies of any size make extensive use of ratios internally, to monitor and ensure the efficient running of each division or activity.

In addition to the published report and accounts of a group, resort can be made to Companies House for accounts filed by subsidiaries, although these can be misleading

- if goods and services have been transferred within the group at unrealistic prices; or
- if major adjustments have been made on consolidation.

In any case, the accounts of subsidiaries are often not filed at Companies House until some time after the group accounts have been published.

Horizontal analysis

The simplest method of comparing one year's figures with another involves working out the percentage change from the previous year of each main component of the accounts, as with BRANDON HIRE, a company that employs the single-column format to display the effects of acquisitions in its profit and loss account.

Percentage changes in themselves may reveal a certain amount about a company's performance but, like many ratios, they are of most value in prompting further enquiry. For example: What did Brandon Hire acquire in 1999? Why was the 23.0% margin so much higher than Brandon's own 13.5%?

Are they in areas where Brandon could expand?

BRANDON HIRE *Extract from 1999 P & L account*

	1999 £000	1998 £000
Turnover		
Tool hire – Continuing operations	21,907	16,859
Acquisitions	1,596	3,465
	23,503	20,324
Catering hire – Discontinued operations	–	7,381
	23,503	27,705
Operating profit		
Continuing operations	2,947	2,252
Acquisitions	367	596
Total operating profit	3,314	2,848

BRANDON HIRE *Year-on-Year analysis*

Continuing operations

Turnover 1999/1998	21,907/20,324	=	+7.8%
Operating profit	2,848/2,947	=	+3.5%
Margins 1998	2,252/16,859	=	13.4%
1999	2,947/21,907	=	13.5%

Acquisitions

Margins 1998	596/3,465	=	17.2%
1999	367/1,596	=	23.0%

Comment
The company is making some high margin acquisitions, but they are relatively small, and will have little impact unless they can be expanded.

Vertical analysis

Year-on-year comparisons can be thought of as working across the page, comparing each item with the previous year to get the percentage change, or looking at several years to see the trend of an item.

If we work vertically, calling the total 100, we can construct what are termed 'common size' statements giving a percentage breakdown of an account item.

The advantages of this method are, firstly, that the items are reduced to a common scale for inter-company comparisons and, secondly, that changes in the financial structure of a company stand out more clearly.

Vertical analysis can be used over several years to show how the sales/profitability pattern or financial structure of a company is changing.

Operating ratios

The three main operating ratios are:

1. profit margin,
2. return on capital employed,
3. sales to capital employed.

1. Profit margin $= \dfrac{\text{Trading profit}}{\text{Sales}}$ as a percentage

Where:

Trading profit = profit before interest charges and tax. Investment income and the company's share of the profits of associated undertakings are not included.

Sales (Turnover) = Sales (excluding VAT and excluding transactions within the group).

This ratio gives what analysts term the profit margin on sales; a normal figure for a manufacturing industry would be between 8% and 10%, while high-volume/low-margin activities like food retailing can run satisfactorily at around 3%. This profit margin is not the same thing as the gross profit margin (the difference between selling price and the cost of sales, expressed as a percentage of selling price), which can be obtained only if the company reports cost of sales (as BRANDON HIRE does, in a note to the acounts).

Unusually low margins can be set deliberately by management to increase market share or can be caused by expansion costs (e.g. new product launching), but in general depressed margins suggest poor performance.

Somewhat better than average margins are normally a sign of good management, but unusually high margins

may mean that the company is 'making a packet' and will attract competition unless there are barriers to entry (e.g. huge initial capital costs, high technology, patents or other special advantages enjoyed by the company).

The converse also applies: if a company has lower margins than others in the same sector, there is scope for improvement. For example, between 1985 and 1993 TESCO managed to more than double its margins as it shifted away from the 'pile it high and sell it cheap' philosophy of its founder, the late Sir Jack Cohen, towards SAINSBURY's quality image and better margins. As the table below shows, neither is now finding it easy to maintain margins, let alone to continue to increase them, and SAINSBURY's have tumbled.

Example 10.1 Comparison of margins

Year ended	1985	1993	1997	2002
TESCO	2.7%	6.5%	5.6%	5.6%
SAINSBURY	5.1%	8.1%	5.2%	4.1%

Trading profit margins are also important in that both management and investment analysts usually base their forecasts of future profitability on projected turnover figures multiplied by estimated future margins.

An alternative definition of trading profit, used by Datastream and some analysts, is before deducting depreciation, the argument being that different depreciation policies distort inter-company comparisons. If this approach is used, then trading profit should also be before deducting rental charges, to bring a company that leases rather than owns plant and premises on to a comparable basis. Our view is that depreciation is a cost and should be deducted in any calculation of profit; we therefore prefer to deal with cases where a company's depreciation charge seems unduly low (or high) by making an adjustment, rather than by adding back every company's depreciation charge. Datastream also excludes exceptional items.

2. Return on Capital employed $= \dfrac{\text{Trading profit}}{\text{Capital employed}}$

Return on capital employed (ROCE), expressed as a percentage, is a traditional measure of profitability for several reasons:

- a low return on capital employed can easily be wiped out in a downturn;
- if the figure is lower than the cost of borrowing, increased borrowings will reduce earnings per share (e.p.s.) unless the extra money can be used in areas where the ROCE is higher than the cost of borrowing;
- it serves as a guide to the company in assessing possible acquisitions and in starting up new activities – if their *potential* ROCE isn't attractive, they should be avoided;
- similarly, a persistently low ROCE for any part of the business suggests it could be a candidate for disposal if it isn't an integral part of the business.

ROCE can be calculated either for the company overall or for its trading activities:

Capital employed (in trading) = Share capital + Reserves + All borrowing including obligations under finance leases, bank overdraft + Minority interests + Provisions – Associates and investments. Government grants are not included.

Capital employed (overall) Associates and investments are not deducted, while the overall profit figure includes income from investments and the company's share of the profits of associated companies, in addition to trading profit.

However, ROCE can be seriously distorted by intangible fixed assets and by purchased goodwill that has been written off directly to reserves under previous accounting rules (immediate write-off). Ideally, purchased goodwill that was written off direct to reserves should be added back in calculating ROCE, but FRS 10 does not require this in the accounts; and information which would allow analysts to do this for themselves is not always available.

We suggest that intangible items shown in the balance sheet should be included in capital employed at their cost less any subsequent amortisation; for example, patents, newspaper titles and brand names that have been purchased, but not newspaper titles and brand names that have been built up internally. As Sir Adrian Cadbury said, after RHM had put £678m of brands at valuation in its balance sheet: 'The market value of a company's brands can only be established objectively when their ownership is transferred. Any other form of valuation is by definition subjective.'

The figure for capital employed should, strictly speaking, be the average capital employed during the year, but for simplicity's sake it is normally satisfactory to use the capital employed at the end of the year unless there have been major changes. Some companies label the total at the bottom of their balance sheet as 'capital employed'

(BRANDON HIRE shows equity shareholders' funds). But using the balance sheet total can be deceptive, in that bank overdrafts and loans repayable within 12 months are netted out against current assets, giving a company that has perhaps an embarrassingly large short-term debt a better ROCE than a company whose debt is more prudently funded long-term.

Another variation used by some analysts is to deduct any cash from the overdraft or, where a company has a net cash position, to deduct net cash in calculating capital employed. Netting out cash against overdraft can be justified where cash and overdraft are both with the same bank and the bank is known to calculate interest on the net figure (Overdraft – Cash), but in general we accept the figures used for the purposes of FRS 5 Reporting the substance of transactions and FRS 1 Cash flow statements.

If a company feels it prudent to operate with a large cash margin it should be measured accordingly, and if the company's cash is locked up somewhere (e.g. if it has arisen from retaining profits overseas to avoid UK taxation) the situation should be reflected in the ratio.

Any upward revaluation of property is likely to reduce ROCE in two ways:

1. it will increase capital employed (the surplus on revaluation being credited to capital reserve), and
2. it will probably increase the depreciation charge, and thus reduce profits.

See Chapter 13 regarding valuations under FRS 15 Tangible fixed assets.

3. $$\dfrac{\text{Sales}}{\text{Capital employed in trading}}$$

Expressed as a multiple.

Improving the return on capital employed

A rising sales/capital employed ratio usually indicates an improvement in performance, i.e. the amount of business being done is increasing in relation to the capital base, but beware of an improvement in the ratio achieved when a company fails to keep its plant and machinery up to date; depreciation will steadily reduce the capital base and improve the ratio without any improvement in sales. Beware, too, of any rapid increase in the ratio, which may well be a warning signal of *overtrading*, i.e. trying to do too much business with too little capital.

In inter-company comparisons care should be taken to compare like with like: the ratio can be misleading unless the operations of the companies concerned are similar in their activities as well as in their products. For example, a television manufacturing group which is vertically integrated (makes the tubes, electronic circuits and the cabinets and then puts them together) will have much more capital employed than a company which merely assembles bought-in components.

A better measure of performance might be that of value added compared with capital employed, but value added is rarely included in published information.

The three ratios are, of course, interrelated:

$$\frac{\text{Trading profit}}{\text{Sales}} \times \frac{\text{Sales}}{\text{Capital employed}} = \frac{\text{Trading profit}}{\text{Capital employed}}$$

as seen from BRANDON HIRE:

BRANDON HIRE *Extracts from 1999 accounts*

	1999 £000	1998 £000
Sales (Turnover)	23,503	20,324
Operating profit	3,314	2,848
Capital employed	20,592	20,948
BRANDON HIRE *Ratios*		
Profit margin	14.1%	14.0%
Return on capital employed	16.1%	13.6%
Sales/capital employed	1.14	0.97

In 1999 BRANDON HIRE managed to do more business than in 1998 on slightly less capital employed, with maintained margins.

The ratio trading profit/capital employed helps to illustrate the four ways in which management can improve this ratio:

1. by increasing the first factor by:
   (a) reducing costs or
   (b) raising prices,
   to produce higher profit margins;
2. by increasing the second factor by:
   (a) increasing sales or
   (b) reducing capital employed,
   so raising volume of output per £1 of capital.

A healthy way of improving profitability is to dispose of low profitability/high capital parts of the business, provided this can be done without adversely affecting the remainder.

Segment analysis

Accounting standard

SSAP 25 Segmental reporting requires companies that have two or more classes of business or which operate in two or more geographical segments to report turnover, profit and net assets for each class of business and for each geographical segment: e.g. DIAGEO (see below).

Analysis of profitability

The analyst can work on a segmental analysis, calculating various ratios and using them to compare performance between classes of business and between geographical areas.

Return on capital employed (ROCE) is widely used internally for management decisions, but for the external analyst the ratio can have serious problems because of:

- The different ways in which companies define capital employed.
- The huge amounts of purchased goodwill that companies wrote off under earlier accounting rules (see Chapter 14).
- The differences in the ways companies allocate central overheads and finance costs.

For these reasons many analysts no longer use ROCE, focusing instead on margins.

For example DIAGEO's margins (operating profit/turnover), using the figures in the table below, show:

DIAGEO *Margins in 2002 and 2003*

	2003	2002	*Change*
Class of business			
Premium drinks	20.2%	15.3%	13.2%
Discontinued operations			
Packaged food	–	12.6%	–
Quick service restaurants	11.1%	12.0%	(7.5%)
Geographical area			
Great Britain	10.7%	9.4%	13.8%
Rest of Europe	16.8%	19.6%	(14.3%)
North America	22.6%	9.0%	151.1%
Asia Pacific	24.1%	22.9%	5.2%
Latin America	28.1%	29.4%	(4.4%)
OVERALL	19.7%	14.6%	34.0%

At the same time note should be taken of the chairman's statement, the chief executive's report or review of operations and/or financial review as, in a good set of accounts, these will contain comment on marked changes, they may indicate strategy, and they may give further details: e.g. DIAGEO.

DIAGEO *Extract from a note to the accounts for the year ended 30 June 2003*

Segmental information by class of business

	Premium drinks £million	Other £million	Discontinued operations Packaged food £million	Quick service restaurants £million	Total £million
2003					
Turnover	8,961	–	–	479	9,440
Operating profit before exceptional items	1,976	–	–	53	2,029
Exceptional items charged to operating profit	(168)	–	–	–	(168)
Operating profit	1,808	–	–	53	1,861
. . .					
2002					
Turnover	8,704	–	1,455	1,123	11,282
Operating profit before exceptional items	1,766	–	184	156	2,106
Exceptional items charged to operating profit	(432)	–	–	(21)	(453)
Operating profit	1,334	–	184	135	1,653

Geographical information

	Great Britain £million	Rest of Europe £million	North America £million	Asia Pacific £million	Latin America £million	Rest of World £million	Total £million
2003							
Turnover	1,472	2,568	3,159	1,008	481	752	9,440
Operating profit	158	431	713	243	135	181	1,861
. . .							
2002							
Turnover	1,601	2,603	4,717	1,001	639	721	11,282
Operating profit	151	511	426	229	188	148	1,653

DIAGEO *Extracts from 2003 report*

Chairman's statement
. . . there are signs of returning consumer confidence in North America. US consumers are the engine which drives the economy for consumer goods. If they are confident then we have cause to be so.

Chief Executive's review
. . . we completed our exit from food by the sale of Burger King. Our determination to acquire Seagram's spirits and win brands has been well rewarded. That transaction has generated significant value for Diageo, and is already delivering very high quality returns in an industry where further consolidation is widely anticipated.

Non-disclosure

Segmental information need not be disclosed if doing so is considered by the directors to be seriously prejudicial to the interests of the company:

WATERMARK *Note to the 2000 accounts*

Segmental analysis
In the opinion of the directors the segmental reporting of results would be seriously prejudicial to the business and accordingly it has not been disclosed.

International Financial Reporting Standards

IAS 14 identifies business segments and geographical segments, and requires entities to identify one as primary (requiring a higher level of disclosure) and one as secondary (requiring a lower level of disclosure).

For accounting periods commencing on or after 1 January 2009, IAS 14 Segment reporting is replaced by IFRS 8 Operating segments.

IFRS 8 requires operating segments to be identified on the basis of internal reports that are regularly reviewed by the entity's chief operating decision maker in order to allocate resources and assess performance. The extract below from the accounts of GENMAB gives an overview of the contrasting approaches of the two international segment reporting standards.

In summary, IFRS 8 sets out requirements for disclosure of information regarding:

- the entity's operating segments;
- the entity's products and services;
- the geographical areas in which entity operates;
- the entity's major customers.

GENMAB *Annual Report 2006*

IFRS 8, 'Operating Segments', require an entity to adopt the 'management approach' to reporting on the financial performance of its operating segments. Generally, the information to be reported would be what management uses internally for evaluating segment performance and deciding how to allocate resources to operating segments . . .

As such, information may be different from what is used to prepare the income statement and balance sheet, IFRS 8 requires explanation of the basis on which the segment information is prepared and reconciliations to the amounts recognised in the income statement and balance sheet. The standard, which replaces IAS 14, 'Segment Reporting', is effective for periods beginning on or January 1, 2009. No significant impact is expected on the company's financial reporting from this new Standard.

Earnings per share

Introduction

> Earnings per share (e.p.s.) – a key measure, but open to abuse

Earnings per share (e.p.s.) is a key measure of a company's profitability each year. It is a measure of its ability to pay dividends, and is the most widely used measure of 'growth'. But it is open to abuse.

Definition

FRS 22 Earnings per share, requiring the total profit attributable to ordinary shareholders to be used in the calculation of basic e.p.s.:

$$\frac{\textit{Profit attributable to ordinary equity holders}}{\textit{Weighted average number of ordinary shares outstanding during the period}}$$

Discontinued operations

An entity that reports a discontinued operation must disclose both basic and diluted e.p.s. for the discontinued operation.

Company's own figure for e.p.s. (adjusted e.p.s.)

Companies are free to show their own version of earnings per share but, if they do so, they must provide a reconciliation to the 'basic e.p.s.' figure (FRS 14, paragraph 74).

The ASB took the view that, if everything was included, then companies could make whatever adjustments they wished, to produce the *'Company's own e.p.s.'*.

Given the details of the adjustments, analysts would be able to judge whether the company's own e.p.s. was a fair 'normalised' figure and, if not, to make their own adjustments.

Let's look at an example, KINGFISHER, where one or two of the adjustments are questionable:

KINGFISHER *Note on e.p.s. in the 2003 accounts*

	Earnings £millions	Per share amount pence
Basic earnings per share	169.7	8.0
Effect of exceptionals		
Operating exceptional items	51.6	2.4
Demerger costs	11.8	0.6
Loss on sale of operations	228.4	10.8
(Profit) on disposal of fixed assets	(143.0)	(6.7)
Tax impact on exceptional items	24.6	1.2
Minority share of exceptional items	(1.3)	(0.1)
Acquisition goodwill amortisation	11.7	0.5
Basic – adjusted e.p.s.	353.5	16.7

Although the IIMR approach excludes bid defence costs, as the company didn't choose to be bid for, it does not allow the costs of actions a company chooses to make, i.e. costs of a failed merger or takeover bid, to be excluded. Similarly IIMR would not allow start-up costs to be excluded. (**Note:** IIMR is now the UK society of Investment Professionals.)

In addition, companies do not always clearly distinguish basic, FRS 3, earnings per share from their own preferred version. Take, for instance, THE RANK GROUP (see page 81). After the deduction of minority interests [A], and preference dividends [C] and [D] (*Note 7*), Rank's profit and loss account shows three figures for 2003 e.p.s.:

[H]	19.2p	before exceptional items
[I]	(4.9p)	exceptional items per share
[J]	14.3p	after exceptional items.

The basic earnings per share [J] represent actual performance, i.e. how much per share was actually available to pay ordinary dividends and provide some retained earnings to plough back into the company.

In fact Rank's 14.3p was only just enough to pay the ordinary dividends of 13.9p, [E] plus [F], leaving only £1.8m to plough back: [G] to be transferred to reserves.

Had the group *not* incurred exceptional items of (4.9p) per share [I], it would have had 19.2p per share, [H],

enough to pay dividends of 13.9p per share, leaving 5.3p per share of retained earnings.

Note 8 *Earnings per Ordinary share* (see page 81) shows the calculation of [J].

Amortisation

FRS 10 Goodwill and intangible assets complicates matters by allowing two methods of accounting:

(a) to retain the assets in the balance sheet at cost with an annual review for impairment; or
(b) to amortise them over a finite period, usually a maximum of 20 years.

Some companies using method (b), particularly those with a large amount of goodwill from acquisitions on their balance sheet, have taken to showing e.p.s. both before and after amortisation, e.g. WASTE RECYCLING:

WASTE RECYCLING *Earnings per share*

Profit and loss account	1999 £000	1998 £000
. . .		
Profit for the financial year	7,127	6,847
Dividends	(4,100)	(1,404)
Retained profit	3,027	5,443
Earnings per share	6.7p	13.8p
Adjusted earnings per share (note 9)	17.3p	13.8p

Note 9 Earnings per ordinary share
In order to show results from operating activities on a comparable basis an adjusted earnings per ordinary share has been calculated which excludes goodwill amortisation of £11,361,000 (1998 – £nil) from earnings.

Going for growth. . . .

In the fourth edition of this book we gave an interesting example of a company whose pre-tax profits had *grown* by 41.9% p.a. between 1984 and 1988, but whose e.p.s. had *fallen* by 8.3% p.a. The company was MAXWELL COMMUNICATION CORPORATION, and we said: 'chairman Robert Maxwell's stated goal was to become "a global information and communications corporation before the end of the decade with annual revenues of £3–5 billion, with profits growth to match". Maxwell's sales in the period had grown from £266.5m to over £1bn, at an annual rate of 42.9% with profits growth almost to match, but this was achieved by the profligate use of paper, and earnings per share suffered accordingly.'

THE RANK GROUP *Group profit and loss account 2003*

Group Profit and Loss Account for the year ended 31 December 2003

		2003			2002		
		Before exceptional items	*Exceptional items*	*Total*	*Before exceptional items*	*Exceptional items*	*Total*
	Note	£m	£m	£m	£m	£m	£m
. . .							
Profit (loss) on ordinary activities after tax		133.1	(31.9)	101.2	140.5	(1.7)	138.8
Equity minority interests	**[A]**	(2.3)	2.8	0.5	(2.1)	–	(2.1)
Profit (loss) for the financial year	**[B]**	130.8	(29.1)	101.7	138.4	(1.7)	136.7
Dividends and other appropriations							
Preference – non-equity	**[C] and [D]** 7	(17.1)	–	(17.1)	(21.0)	–	(21.0)
Ordinary – equity	**[E] and [F]** 7	(82.8)	–	(82.8)	(78.2)	–	(78.2)
Transfer to (from) reserves		30.9	(29.1)	**[G]** 1.8	39.2	(1.7)	37.5
Earnings (loss) per Ordinary share	8	19.2p **[H]**	(4.9)p **[I]**	14.3p **[J]**	19.9p	(0.3)p	19.6p

As subsequent events confirmed, companies which go for growth regardless of e.p.s. are best avoided. But the fact that an acquisition for paper makes e.p.s. grow at a slower rate than profits does not necessarily mean that acquisitions for paper are bad for e.p.s. It all depends on whether the e.p.s. are higher with the acquisition than they would have been without it (as they are in Example 10.2).

The effect of acquisitions on earnings per share

Buying earnings cheaply enables a company to boost its e.p.s. when its own earnings are static, or even falling.

Suppose in Example 10.2 that the attributable profits of the company were expected to fall the following year to £912,000, despite the recently acquired business performing satisfactorily. The company finds another victim (Example 10.3).

'But,' you may say, 'how did the company in Example 10.3 manage to get the shareholders of the second acquisition to accept 2.4 million shares for attributable earnings of £468,000, which is 19.5p per share, far higher than the e.p.s. of the acquiring company?' And well may you ask – the secret is in 'market rating'.

Example 10.2 Acquisition for paper

	Existing company	*Acquisition*	*Company post-acquisition*
Attributable profit	800,000	200,000	1,000,000
Issued equity (shares)	8,000,000		
Vendor consideration (shares)		1,600,000	
Resulting equity (shares)			9,600,000
e.p.s.	10.0p		10.4p

In this case 1.6m shares are issued for a company bringing in £200,000 at the attributable profit level, or 12.5p for each new share, which is higher than the e.p.s. of the existing company, so the e.p.s. of the company, post-acquisition, are improved. Had the acquiring company paid more than 2m shares for the acquisition, its earnings per share would have fallen.

Example 10.3 Further acquisition

	Present company	Second acquisition	Resulting company
Attributable profits (£)	912,000	468,000	1,380,000
Issued equity (shares)	9,600,000		
Vendor consideration (shares)		2,400,000	
Resulting equity (shares)			12,000,000
e.p.s.	9.5p		11.5p

Market rating – the PER

The measure of a company's market rating is its price earnings ratio (P/E ratio, PE ratio or PER):

$$\text{Price earnings ratio} = \frac{\text{Market price per ordinary share}}{\text{Basic earnings per share}}$$

It is normal to take the previous day's middle market price of the ordinary share divided by the earnings per share. Analysts and newspapers often take not the basic earnings per share but normalised e.p.s. (see below), so watch with care.

The PER one can expect depends mainly on four things:

1. the overall level of the stock market;
2. the industry in which the company operates;
3. the company's record; and
4. the market's view of the company's prospects.

In an average market the PER of the average company in an average sector might be around 12, with high quality 'blue chips' like BOOTS or MARKS & SPENCER standing on a PER of around 15 and small glamour growth stocks on 20 or more, while companies in an unfashionable sector might be on a multiple of only 8.

We say more about PERs in the section 'Investment ratios' on page 85.

Wonder growth by acquisition

There is nothing fundamentally wrong with improving a company's earnings per share by acquisition, and it can be beneficial all round if there is some industrial or commercial logic involved, i.e. if the acquired company's business fits in with the acquiring company's existing activities or employs common skills and technology, or if the acquirer can provide improved management and financial resources. However, the practice was open to abuse, especially in bull markets.

Enter the 'whiz-kid' (known as a 'gunslinger' on the other side of the Atlantic), who might proceed as follows:

1. Acquire control of a company that has a listing on the Stock Exchange, but little else, e.g. the Demised Tea Company, known in the jargon as a 'shell'.
2. Reverse the shell into an unlisted company, thus giving his victim the benefit of a ready market for his shares and himself the benefit of a company with real assets.
3. Sell off some of the assets, particularly property that is ripe for development. He doesn't lose any sleep over the fact that closing a factory throws 200 people out of work, as the office block that will replace it will house twice that number of civil servants in the department recently set up to encourage investment in industry; this 'asset-stripping' process is essential to provide the cash to gain control of his next victim.
4. By now the earnings per share of the Demised Tea Company, since renamed Anglo-Triumph Assets, have shown remarkable growth, albeit from a very low base (it's very easy to double profits of next-to-nothing), the bull market has conveniently started and the press has noticed him.

He projects a suitable image of dynamic young management, talking to them earnestly about the need for

British industry to obtain a fair return on assets, and his photograph appears in the financial sections of the Sunday papers. The 'whiz-kid' has arrived.

5. His share price responds to press comment, putting his 'go-go' company on a PER of 15 or 20; he continues to acquire companies, but now uses shares rather than cash, thus continually boosting his e.p.s., as we have shown.

6. Following press adulation, he broadens out into TV financial panels, seminar platforms, and after-dinner speeches; the bull market is now raging. Anglo-Triumph features regularly as an 'up stock' in the price changes table in the FT as the PER climbs towards 30. Deals follow apace, and Anglo-Triumph thrusts ahead, acquiring a huge conglomeration of businesses in an ever-widening range of mainly unrelated activities – it may be shoes, or ships or sealing-wax, but it's certainly Alice in Wonderland.

7. The moment of truth. The bull market, after a final glorious wave of euphoria, tops out. Profits in Anglo-Triumph's businesses turn down as little or nothing has been done to improve their management. Asset-stripping becomes politically unacceptable, and the word 'conglomerate' is coined to describe hotch potch outfits like Anglo-Triumph.

Down goes Anglo-Triumph's share price, and with it the market rating; without a high Price Earnings Ratio the company can no longer boost profits by acquisition, and the game is up.

Whether the whole edifice of Anglo-Triumph collapses completely or it becomes just another lowly rated ex-glamour stock depends on the financial structure of the company. If it has geared up (i.e. has built up debt, on which interest has to be paid), and hasn't the cash to service the debt, the company will probably be forced into liquidation unless some sympathetic banker (possibly embarrassed by the prospect of disclosing a huge loss if the company goes under) decides to tide things over until 'hopefully' better times.

Two things, both of which are required by FRS 3, do much to prevent this happening today. They are:

(i) the publication of earnings per share; and

(ii) the subdivision of results down to operating profit level into continuing operations, acquisitions and discontinued operations, both of which have made this sort of behaviour much more transparent.

Normalised e.p.s.

As described on pages 70 and 71, the IIMR (which has since become the UK Society of Investment Professionals) developed a standard approach, focusing on the trading activities of a company, to produce *Headline earnings* and, from that figure, *Normalised earnings per share*.

This approach has been followed by the *Financial Times*, using normalised e.p.s. in calculating figures for the P/E column in their London share price pages, and is generally used in the City, though with individual variations.

Investigating trends

It is frequently a worthwhile exercise to set alongside one another, growth in:

(a) turnover;
(b) profit before tax;
(c) earnings per share;
(d) dividend per share.

If they are wildly different, the cause should be investigated. In the sixth edition we looked at MITIE GROUP, a relatively small cleaning and maintenance contractor, saying that it was 'taking advantage of the trend towards outsourcing such services' while at the same time expanding by making a series of small acquisitions.

As we said in the sixth edition, growth (in 1990–1995) had been spectacular:

- turnover increase had averaged 51% per annum;
- profits had almost kept pace at 48% per annum;
- because of acquisitions for paper, e.p.s. had grown at an average of only 22% per annum;
- from a very low base (and covered nine times) dividends had increased at an average of 43% p.a.

So shareholders certainly did not complain.

We decided to follow up the story. As will be seen from Example 10.4, the very rapid growth in turnover slowed down to around 20% p.a., there had been a consolidation in profitability, falling to 34% p.a. between 1995 and 2000, and then to 20%, with e.p.s. and dividend growth also slowing.

MITIE GROUP *Group statistical record 1995 to 2003 (extracts)*

	2003 £000	2002 £000	2001 £000	2000 £000	1999 £000	1998 £000	1997 £000	1996 £000	1995 £000
Turnover	565,840	518,852	415,375	346,514	264,455	236,293	209,425	161,149	125,183
Profit on ordinary activities before taxation	34,113	30,997	25,148	19,758	14,542	11,100	8,210	6,302	4,571
Earnings per share	7.3p	6.8p	5.1p	4.3p	3.3p	2.6p	2.0p	1.6p	1.2p
Dividend per share	1.9p	1.6p	1.25p	1.0p	0.8p	0.6p	0.5p	0.4p	0.3p

Earnings and Dividend per share figures have been restated to reflect the subdivision of shares in 1998 and 2001.
  The results of merger accounted acquisitions are reflected in full in the year of acquisition and subsequent years but only the year prior to acquisition has been restated on a comparable basis.

Example 10.4 **MITIE GROUP** Average growth rate per annum

	Average increase per annum		
	1990–1995	1995–2000	2000–2003
Turnover	51%	22%	18%
Profit on ordinary activities before tax	48%	34%	20%
Earnings per share	22%	29%	19%
Dividend per share	43%	27%	24%

There was also a much greater dependence on partly-owned subsidiaries: minorities as a percentage of equity shareholders' funds increased from 5.4% in 1995 to 26.6% in 2000 (not shown).

However spectacular a company's growth is, it must slow down as the company gets bigger, or management will be in danger of losing control.

Adjustments to basic earnings per share

The number of shares issued during the year may change for a number of reasons, some of which involve the company receiving or paying cash, others with no cash effect. Possible situations include:

- issue of shares for cash including a rights issue;
- share split;
- scrip, bonus or capitalisation issue;
- shares issued as consideration for an acquisition;
- share consolidations;
- repurchase of shares.

Earnings per share calculations may be complex – FRS 22 sets out detailed rules and provides guidance in the form of worked examples (see below).

Diluted earnings per share (diluted e.p.s.)

Companies are required to publish both basic earnings per share (as described above) as well as diluted e.p.s. These e.p.s. numbers are usually presented on the face of the profit and loss account (although they may alternatively be presented in the notes to the accounts).

The standard describes the objective of diluted e.p.s. as consistent with that of basic e.p.s., i.e. to provide a measure of the interest of each ordinary share in the company's performance. The difference between the two measures is that diluted e.p.s. reflects the effect of all 'dilutive potential ordinary shares' outstanding during the period.

Two examples of dilutive potential ordinary shares are:

1. Share options held by employees – in a future account-ing period optionholders who satisfy the necessary qualifying conditions will be entitled to subscribe for shares in the company for cash, at a preferential rate (referred to as the 'exercise price' – see Chapter 24, page 203). If the optionholder exercises his or her rights, the company will receive cash (which will have the opportunity of increasing earnings) whilst additional new shares will be issued.

   Such 'potential ordinary shares' are to be treated as 'dilutive' only if conversion to ordinary shares would decrease (i.e. dilute) e.p.s. or increase loss per share.

2. Convertible loan stock – in a future accounting period loan stock holders may be entitled to convert (i.e. exchange) their loan stock for ordinary shares. From the company's perspective this would increase earnings (because the company would no longer have to pay interest) but the number of ordinary shares would be increased (as a result of the loan stock being replaced by shares).

Again, such 'potential ordinary shares' are to be treated as 'dilutive' only if conversion to ordinary shares would decrease (i.e. dilute) e.p.s. or increase loss per share.

FOCUS SOLUTIONS

9 Earnings per ordinary share
The basic earnings per share is based on attributable profit for the year of £128,000 (FY2005: £26,000) and on 28,629,000 ordinary shares (FY2005: 28,588,000) being the weighted average number of ordinary shares in issue during the year.

The diluted earnings per share is based on attributable profit for the year of £128,000 (FY2005: £26,000) and on 28,852,000 shares (FY2005: 29,150,000) calculated as follows:

	Year ended 31 March 2006 000s	Year ended 31 March 2005 000s
Basic weighted average number of ordinary shares	**28,629**	28,588
Dilutive potential ordinary shares:		
Share Options	**223**	562
	28,852	29,150

Worked examples

Calculations of fully diluted e.p.s. are very detailed and complex – readers who wish to follow these through should refer to the illustrative examples contained in FRS 22: Examples 5 and 5A deal with share options, whilst Example 6 deals with convertible bonds.

In all, FRS 22 contains 12 illustrative examples, which are a useful source of reference.

International Financial Reporting Standards

IAS 33, Earnings per share is identical to its UK equi-valent, FRS 22 which replaced its predecessor FRS 14 as part of the process of converging UK GAAP with IFRS.

Investment ratios

These are the ratios used by investors when deciding whether a share should be bought, sold or held. Most of them relate to the current price of the share, and therefore vary from day to day. The two most popular ones are the price earnings ratio (PER), already mentioned, and the dividend yield.

The price earnings ratio (PER)

$$\text{Price earnings ratio} = \frac{\text{Market price per ordinary share}}{\text{Basic earnings per share}}$$

Where market price = The middle market price, which is the average of the prices at which shares can be sold or bought on an investor's behalf (the market maker's bid and offer prices respectively). The analyst will normally calcu-late two price earnings ratios: the 'historical PER', using last year's e.p.s., and the 'prospective PER', using his estim-ate of e.p.s. for the current year; he may also project his earnings estimates to produce a PER based on possible earnings for the following year.

What the PER represents

One way of looking at the PER is to regard it as the num-ber of years' earnings per share represented by the share price, i.e. x years' purchase of e.p.s., but this assumes static e.p.s., while in practice the PER reflects the market's view of the company's growth potential, the business risks involved and the dividend policy. For example, a company recovering from a break-even situation, with zero e.p.s. last year, will have a historical PER of infinity but may have a prospective PER of 12 based on expectations of modest profits for the current year, falling to 6 next year if a full recovery is achieved.

The PER of a company also depends not only on the company itself, but on the industry in which it operates and, of course, on the level of the stock market, which tends to rise more than reported profits when the business cycle swings up and to fall more than profits in a downturn.

The Actuaries Share Indices table published in the *Financial Times* every day except Mondays also gives the PER for each industry group and subsection, so any historical PER calculated for a company can be compared with its sector and with the market as a whole (see Example 10.5). The result of comparing it with the market as a whole (usually with the FTSE All-Share PER) is called the PER Relative:

$$\text{PER Relative} = \frac{\text{PER of Company}}{\text{PER of Market}}$$

Example 10.5 Historical and prospective PER

Suppose the fully taxed normalised e.p.s. calculated from a company's latest report and accounts, published two to three months after the year has ended, are 8.0p. The analyst is expecting profits to rise by about 27% in the current year, and for there to be a disproportionately higher charge for minorities (because one partly owned subsidiary is making a hefty contribution to the improved profits). He therefore estimates that e.p.s. will rise a little less than profits, to about 10.0p.

The current share price is 120p, so last year's e.p.s. = 8p; current year e.p.s. = 10p; historical PER = 15.0; prospective PER = 12.0.

This provides a quick indication of whether a company is highly or lowly rated, although differences in the treatment of tax by individual companies do cause some distortion here, so most analysts use e.p.s. calculated on a full tax charge to compare PERs within a sector.

In general a high historic PER compared with the industry group suggests either that the company is a leader in its sector or that the share is overvalued, while a low

PER suggests a poor company or an undervalued share. In each case check to see if the prospective PER is moving back into line with the sector, as a historic PER that is out of line may be due to expectations of an above average rise in profits for the current year (in which case the historic PER will be higher than average), or to poor results being expected (which would be consistent with a low PER).

Another useful rule of thumb is to be wary when a PER goes much above 20. The company may well be a glamour stock due for a tumble or, if it is the PER of a very sound high-quality company, the market itself may be in for a fall. One exception here is the property sector, where PERs are normally very high because property companies tend to be highly geared and use most of their rental income to service their debt, leaving tiny e.p.s.; investors normally buy property company shares more for their prospects of capital appreciation than for their current earnings.

Price earnings growth factor (PEG)

The price earnings growth factor (PEG) is a yardstick introduced by Jim Slater in his very readable book *The Zulu Principle*, which is full of useful advice for the private investor. The PEG is a measure of whether a share looks overrated or underrated:

$$\text{PEG} = \frac{\text{Price earnings ratio}}{\text{Prospective growth in e.p.s.}}$$

Where the PER is appreciably higher than the prospective growth rate (i.e. PEG well over 1.0), the shares are likely to be expensive. Conversely a PEG of between 0.5 and 0.7 means that the prospective growth rate isn't fully reflected in the PER, and the shares look attractive.

Dividend policy and the PER

As the price of a share is influenced both by the e.p.s. and the dividend, a company's dividend policy affects the PER.

Some companies pay tiny dividends and plough back most of their profits to finance further growth. Shares in these companies may enjoy a glamour rating while everything is going well, but the rating is vulnerable to any serious setback in profits, as there is little yield to support the price.

Blue chip companies like to pay a reasonable dividend and to increase it each year to counteract the effects of inflation and reflect long-term growth; and that is what the shareholders expect, particularly those who are retired and need income from their investments. This means that major companies usually pay out between 30% and 40% of attributable profits, retaining a substantial amount to reinvest for future growth and to avoid having to cut the dividend in lean years. For example BRITISH AIRWAYS maintained its dividend in 1991, when profits had more than halved, but the dividend was still covered.

If a company pays out much more than 50% in dividends it suggests it has gone ex-growth; it also runs a higher risk of having to cut its dividend in hard times (which tends to be very unpopular with investors) and, in times of high inflation, a company distributing a large proportion of its reported profits (calculated on a historical cost basis) will tend to lose credibility.

Dividend yield

Dividend yields are now generally based on the net amount received.

$$\frac{\text{Dividend}}{\text{yield (\%)}} = \frac{\text{Net dividend in pence per share} \times 100}{\text{Ordinary share price in pence}}$$

Dividend cover

$$\text{Cover} = \frac{\text{e.p.s.}}{\text{Net dividends per share}}$$

(See Example 10.6.)

Example 10.6 Calculation of dividend cover

In year 2000 Cover plc had profits attributable to ordinary of £1.240m. 20m ordinary shares of £1 each were in issue throughout the year. The company paid total ordinary dividends of 2.3p per share net.

Basic earnings per share will be £1.240m ÷ 20m = 6.2p. Cover = 6.2 ÷ 2.3 = 2.7.

Payout ratio

The payout ratio is the reciprocal of the dividend cover. It indicates the extent to which the attributable profits are distributed to ordinary shareholders. An equally valid measure is the amount retained by the company as a percentage of the attributable profit (Example 10.7).

Example 10.7 Calculation of payout ratio

Basic earnings per share will be £1.240m ÷ 20m = 6.2p. Cover = 6.2 ÷ 2.3 = 2.7.

Payout ratio = 1 ÷ Cover = 1 ÷ 2.70 = 0.37 or 37%.

The payout ratio could equally well be computed:

(20m × 2.3p) ÷ 1.240m = 0.37 or 37%.

CHAPTER 11

Equity statements, dividends and prior period adjustments

Introduction

In Chapter 1, we referred to the four main primary statements under UK GAAP, namely:

1. the profit and loss account,
2. the statement of total recognised gains and losses (STRGL),
3. the balance sheet,
4. the cash flow statement.

This chapter deals with STRGL and a further statement, the movement in shareholders funds. Equity dividends are also dealt with in this chapter – current accounting practice does not allow equity dividends to be passed through the profit and loss account. We refer also to an additional equity statement required by IFRS.

The statement of total recognised gains and losses (STRGL)

STRGL is a primary statement required by FRS 3, Reporting Financial Performance. The purpose of STRGL is to bring together in a single statement all gains and losses, including those which UK GAAP does not allow to be included in the profit and loss account. STRGL effectively shows the extent to which shareholders' funds have increased or decreased from all gains and losses recognised in the period.

STRGL will usually contain the following elements:

- profit or loss for the financial year (this is the number taken from the final line in the profit and loss account);

- surpluses and deficits on the revaluation of fixed assets (see Chapter 13);
- foreign currency translation differences (see Chapter 29);
- prior period adjustments (see later in this chapter).

The need for such an equity statement was illustrated by the celebrated case of POLLY PECK: the company took an adverse exchange rate variance of £170.3m on net investment overseas direct to reserves in 1988, a year in which it only made an operating profit of £156.9m. The exchange variance was due largely to borrowing in Deutschmarks (DM) and Swiss francs (SFr), where interest rates were low, while keeping money on deposit in very soft Turkish lira. The very high interest received on the soft currency deposits was credited to the profit and loss account, while the capital loss was taken straight to reserves, together with the increase in the sterling value of DM and SFr borrowings. This portent of disaster was missed by some analysts and by most shareholders, but would have been obvious from a STRGL.

STRGL normally appears immediately after the profit and loss account. The following examples show the types of items which might appear in a STRGL.

Examples of STRGLs

Statement of total recognised gains and losses for the year ended 31 December 2007

	2007 £	2006 £
Profit for the period	455,000	421,500
Other recognised gains – surpluses on revaluation of fixed assets	450,000	300,000
Total recognised gains and losses relating to the period	905,000	721,500

EMI GROUP *Interim statement 2003*

**Statement of total recognised gains and losses
for the six months ended 30 September 2003
(unaudited)**

	Six months ended 30 Sep 2003		Six months ended 30 Sep 2002	
	£m	£m	£m	£m
Profit for the period:		8.8		138.4
Currency retranslation – Group	11.1		7.1	
Currency retranslation – Joint venture and associates	(0.2)		(0.2)	
Other recognised gains		10.9		6.9
Total recognised gains and losses relating to the period		19.7		145.3

Reconciliation of movement in shareholders' funds

FRS 3 also requires (paragraph 28) companies to provide a note reconciling the opening and closing totals of shareholders' funds for the period. Often this follows the statement of total recognised gains and losses but sometimes it is found in the note on reserves.

Typically the change in shareholders' funds which it discloses represents:

(a) transfer from profit and loss account, i.e.
  (i) profit attributable to shareholders, less
  (ii) dividends;
(b) unrealised profit (deficit) on revaluation of fixed assets (normally properties);
(c) currency translation differences;
(d) new share capital subscribed (net);
(e) purchase of own shares;
(f) prior year adjustments.

A basic example follows:

Example 11.1 Reconciliation of movements in shareholders' funds statement

	2007 £	2006 £
Shareholders funds at 1 January	3,186,500	3,016,500
Profit for the financial year	455,000	421,500
Dividends paid	(185,000)	(130,000)
Other recognised gains and losses relating to the year – surplus on revaluation of property	450,000	300,000
Shareholders' funds at 31 December	3,906,500	3,186,500

Prior period adjustments

Definition

The term prior period adjustment(s) (frequently referred to by the older term 'prior year adjustment') is defined as a material prior period item(s) which is (are) the result of:

- changes in accounting policies, or
- the correction of fundamental errors.

Changes in accounting policies

In Chapter 3 we referred to the fundamental principle of *comparability* (sometimes referred to as *consistency*) and referred to FRS 18 which basically says that: 'Users need to be able to able to compare an entity's financial information over time in order to identify trends in its financial performance and financial position. They also need to be able to compare the financial information of different entities in order to evaluate their relative financial performance and financial position.'

When companies change their accounting policies, figures for the previous year should be restated in line with the new policy so that current and previous year figures are comparable. Comparability between companies can be distorted by companies adopting different accounting policies.

NETCALL below gives disclosure of the impact of the policy change on individual line items. This disclosure is more detailed than that normally required by UK GAAP and was based on extensive disclosures of IFRS (paragraph 28 of IAS 8, Accounting policies, changes in accounting estimates and errors).

NETCALL *Extract from the Annual Report 2003*

Note 1 (Extract)

1. **Accounting policies**
   The financial statements are prepared in accordance with applicable accounting standards. The particular accounting policies adopted are described below. They have all been consistently applied throughout the year and the preceding year with the exception of the policy for recognising maintenance and support revenue for the first year of a supply agreement (refer to note 3).
   ...

3. **Prior year adjustment**
   During the year the group changed its accounting policy for maintenance and support income for the first year of a supply agreement. Previously this income had been recognised in full upon installation of the system. The current policy is to spread the first year support and maintenance revenue over the year rather than in full upon installation. As a consequence of the company changing its accounting policy in this regard, a prior year adjustment has resulted and the prior year results restated accordingly.

The effect of the prior year adjustment is as follows:

	2002
Turnover	£
Turnover as previously stated	861,231
Effect of prior year adjustment	(53,667)
Turnover as restated	807,564
Increase in loss for the financial year	(53,667)

	2002
Accruals and deferred income	£
Accruals and deferred income as previously stated	148,667
Effect of prior year adjustment	53,667
Accruals and deferred income as restated	202,334
Decrease in net assets	(53,667)

The correction of fundamental errors

FRS 3 paragraph 63 explains the above term:

'In exceptional circumstances it may be found that the financial statements of prior periods have been issued containing errors which are of such significance as to destroy the true and fair view and hence the validity of those financial statements. The corrections of such fundamental errors and the cumulative adjustments applicable to prior periods have no bearing on the results of the current period and they are therefore not included in arriving at the profit or loss for the current period. They are accounted for by restating prior periods, with the result that the opening balance of retained profits will be adjusted accordingly, and highlighted in the reconciliation of movements in shareholders' funds. As the cumulative adjustments are recognised in the current period, they should also be noted at the foot of the statement of total recognised gains and losses of the current period.'

Two disclosure examples follow (Examples 11.2 and 11.3):

Example 11.2 Note 5 – Prior year adjustment

As referred to in the Directors' Report, an accounting irregularity was discovered at Bromsgrove which was announced to shareholders on 10 April 2007. Accordingly, the group has made an adjustment of £425,000 to reduce the 2006 profit and loss account to correct the effect of this irregularity.

The effect of these adjustments on the 2006 group profit and loss account are summarised below:

	2006
	£000
Turnover overstated	4
Cost of sales understated	581
Administration expenses understated	5
	590
Corporation tax charge overstated	(165)
	425

The effect on the group balance sheet at 31 March 2006 was as follows:

	2006
	£000
Stocks overstated	556
Trade debtors overstated	4
Other debtors overstated	25
Other taxes and social security costs	
understated	5
Corporation tax creditor overstated	(165)
	425

Example 11.3 Note 2 – Accounting errors

Credit notes of £1.5m accounted for in the year ended 27 April 2006 and related invoices subsequently received were incorrectly recorded in the profit and loss account. In the light of new information made available to the Board these entries have been reversed. The impact of these adjustments is to increase the profit before tax for the year ended 26 April 2007 by £0.4m (see note . . .). The impact on the balance sheet as at 26 April 2007 is to reduce net assets by £1.1m before tax (see note . . .). £0.8m relates to the year ended 27 April 2007 and is accounted for as a prior year adjustment (see note . . .).

Equity dividends

Accounting treatment

FRS 25, Finance instruments – Presentation and Disclosure, brought in a change to the long-standing treatment of equity dividends. Prior to FRS 25, equity dividends were presented in the profit and loss account as a deduction in arriving at retained profit. Furthermore, in accordance with accounting standards and Companies Act 1985, proposed equity dividends (recommended by the directors for approval by shareholders in annual general meeting) were included in the balance sheet as a liability.

This all changed with effect from accounting periods starting on or after 1 January 2005. Current accounting standards and law require equity dividends paid to be shown as a movement on profit and loss reserves. Effectively equity dividends are regarding as a transaction with the shareholders, and not a finance cost to be charged to the profit and loss account (the special case of preference dividends is referred to below).

Proposed final dividends are a memorandum disclosure and not entered in the accounting records until approved by the shareholders. So dividends proposed in relation to the current period will not be entered in the company's accounting records until the following period.

Example 11.4 Profit and loss reserves note

	£
Profit and loss account at 1 July 2006	550,000
Profit for the financial year	350,000
Dividends paid	(100,000)
Profit and loss account at 30 June 2007	800,000

Equity dividends proposed

Equity dividends proposed are dealt with by memorandum disclosures. They do not become a legal liability until approved by the shareholders at the annual general meeting after the year end. The Companies Act 1985 requires the proposed dividend to be disclosed in a memorandum note as shown in the example below.

Note 10 – Dividends

	£
Dividends paid:	
Final dividend in respect of the year	
ended 31 March 2005 (. . . pence	
per share)	105,000
Interim dividend in respect of the year	
ended 31 March 2007 (. . . pence	
per share)	80,000
	185,000

The Directors have proposed a final dividend in respect of 2007 amounting to £120,000. This will be recommended to the shareholders at the company's annual general meeting.

(The dividend of £120,000 will be recorded, when it is paid, in the accounts for the year to 31 March 2008, and will be shown as a movement on profit and loss reserves.)

Change of accounting policy

The following example relates to a change of accounting policy relating to the treatment of proposed equity dividends:

Note 1 – Accounting policies (extract): Prior year adjustment

During the year, the company adopted FRS 21, Events after the balance sheet date and FRS 25, Financial instruments: Disclosure and presentation.

In previous years, equity dividends proposed by the Board of Directors were recorded in the financial statements and accrued as liabilities at the balance sheet date, and equity dividends paid and proposed were recorded in the profit and loss account.

This policy has been changed, and equity dividends proposed by the Board are not recorded in the financial statements until they have been approved by the shareholders at the Annual General Meeting. Equity dividends paid are dealt with as a movement on retained profits.

The change in accounting policy has been dealt with by way of prior year adjustment, and comparative accounts have been restated.

What to consider when paying a dividend

In deciding what profits to distribute the directors of a company should have in mind:

- the company's cash position;
- what is prudent;
- what is legally permissible.

Ideally, directors should choose the lowest of these three figures.

What is prudent?

In deciding what would be prudent, directors should weigh up the cost of raising capital in various ways. Is it, for instance, better to borrow (i.e. increase the gearing) rather than ask equity shareholders to contribute more towards the net assets of the company? And, if equity shareholders are to be called upon to provide more, should they be asked to do so by means of a rights issue, in which case each shareholder has the choice of whether to take up, or sell, his or her rights; or should profits be 'retained', in which case the individual shareholder has no choice?

Unfortunately, the picture is confused by inflation and the present, historical cost, method of accounting. With no inflation (or an inflation accounting system recognised for tax purposes) a company would, in theory, be able to distribute its earnings and still maintain its assets in real terms. With inflation most companies need to retain a proportion of their earnings as calculated by historical cost accounting in order to maintain their assets in real terms (but more of that in Chapter 31).

Having decided how much it is necessary to retain in order to continue the existing scale of operations, and how much should be retained out of profits in order to expand the scale of operations, the directors should look at what remains.

Ideally, a company should pay a regular, but somewhat increasing, dividend. For example, from a market point of view, it is preferable to pay: 8.0p; 9.0p; 9.0p; 9.0p; 9.5p; 10.0p; rather than 8.0p; 12.0p; 10.5p; 4.0p; 10.0p; 10.0p – though both represent the same total sum in dividends over the six years – because investors who need steady income will avoid companies which are erratic dividend payers, and because a cut in dividend undermines confidence in the company's future. In other words, the directors of a company should think twice before paying a dividend this year which they may not be able to maintain, or setting a pattern of growth in the rate of dividend which could not reasonably be continued for the foreseeable future. For if they do either of these things, they are liable to disappoint shareholder expectations, to damage their market rating and to see their share price slashed if their dividend has to be cut or the rate of dividend growth cannot be sustained.

What is legally permissible?

Companies are allowed to distribute only the aggregate of accumulated realised profits not previously distributed or capitalised less accumulated realised losses not previously written off in a reduction or reorganisation of capital (CA 1985, s. 263). The word 'realised' is not defined in the Act, but FRS 18 says that profits should be included in the profit and loss account 'only when realised in the form either of cash or of other assets the ultimate cash realisation of which can be assessed with reasonable certainty'.

In addition, a public company may pay a dividend only if the net assets of the company after payment of the dividend are not less than the aggregate of its called up share capital and undistributable reserves (s. 264(1)). Undistributable reserves are defined in s. 264(3) as:

- share premium account;
- capital redemption reserve;
- accumulated unrealised profits not capitalised less accumulated unrealised losses not previously written off in a capital reduction or reorganisation;
- any reserve which the company's memorandum or articles prohibits being distributed.

This requirement means that public companies now have to cover net losses (whether realised or not) from realised profits before paying a dividend.

Where the company's audit report has been qualified, the auditor must provide a statement in writing as to whether the qualification is material in deciding whether the distribution would be a breach of the Act, before any distribution can be made.

Recent guidance

- ICAEW/ICAS Technical Circular 02/07 on Distributable profits: Implications of IFRS;
- www.icaew.co.uk – click on Technical and Business Topics, then Technical Releases.

Preference dividends

Preference dividends that the company is required to pay (i.e. dividend payments over which directors have no discretion) must be shown as a finance cost in the profit and loss account. Note the following:

- preference shares carry a fixed rate of dividend, normally payable half-yearly;
- preference shareholders have no legal redress if the board of directors decides to recommend that no preference dividends should be paid;
- if no preference dividend is declared for an accounting period, no dividend can be declared on any other type of share for the period concerned, and the preference shareholders usually become entitled to vote at shareholders' general meetings;
- if the dividend on a cumulative preference share is not paid on time, payment is postponed rather than omitted

and the preference dividend is said to be 'in arrears', and these arrears have to be paid before any other dividend can be declared. Arrears of cumulative preference dividends must be shown in a note to the accounts.

(See also Chapter 22.)

Equity statements under IFRS

IAS 1, Presentation of financial statements, requires the following to be shown on the face of the equity statement:

- the profit or loss for the period;
- each item of income or expense that, as required by the other Standards, is *recognised directly in equity*, and the total of these items; and
- the cumulative effect of changes in accounting policy and the correction of errors recognised under IAS 8.

In addition, the following must be presented within *either* the statement of changes in equity *or* in the notes:

- the amounts of capital transactions with equity holders and distributions to equity holders (i.e. equity dividends paid);
- the balance of retained earnings at the beginning of the period and at the balance sheet date, and the movements for the period; and
- a reconciliation between the carrying amount of each class of equity share capital, share premium and each reserve at the beginning and the end of the period, separately disclosing each movement.

Format alternatives

The above requirements may be satisfied by adopting either of two formats:

- **format 1** – a columnar format that reconciles opening and closing balances for *each* element within equity (Example 11.5);
- **format 2** – to present only the items specified in IAS 1.96 above (the statement using this format is usually referred to as the 'Statement of recognised income and expense'). If this format is used, the movement on share capital and each reserve category must be disclosed in the notes to the financial statements (Example 11.6).

Example 11.5 Format 1 – Statement of changes in equity for the year 31 July 2007

	Share capital £	Fair value reserve[1] £	Retained earnings £	Total equity £
Balance at 1 July 2006 brought forward	450,250	12,768	434,022	897,040
Available for sale investments:				
Valuation gains on investments taken to equity[1]		6,760		6,760
Tax on items taken directly to or transferred from equity		(2,028)		(2,028)
Net income recognised directly in equity	–	4,732	–	4,732
Profit for the period	–	–	403,272	403,272
Total recognised income and expense for the period	–	4,732	403,272	408,004
Ordinary dividends paid	–	–	(80,000)	(80,000)
Balance at 30 June 2007	450,250	17,500	757,294	1,225,044

Note: Comparatives must be shown covering equivalent information for the year ended 31 July 2006.

1. See Chapter 15 for the treatment of available-for-sale financial assets and the fair value reserve.

Example 11.6 Format 2 – Statement of recognised income and expense for the year ended 31 July 2007

	2007 £	2006 £
Available for sale investments:		
Valuation gains taken to equity	6,760	10,000
Tax on valuation gains	(2,028)	(3,000)
Net income recognised directly in equity	4,732	7,000
Profit for the period	403,272	340,000
Total recognised income and expense for the period	408,004	347,000

Notes:
1. Companies with defined benefit schemes (see Chapter 9) who wish actuarial gains and losses to be dealt with outside the income statement must use the above format. The actuarial gains and losses will then be shown as a separate line item in arriving at 'net income recognised directly in equity'.
2. If format 2 is used, a separate reconciliation of the movement on each component of equity must be provided.

CHAPTER 12

The balance sheet: an introduction

Introduction

This chapter provides an introduction to the format and content of the balance sheet under UK GAAP. It also contrasts the position under UK GAAP with the alternatives available (and used in practice) under IFRS.

The format of the balance sheet under UK GAAP

Although the Companies Act 1985 offers UK companies a choice of two balance sheet formats, in practice almost all companies use the format shown in Example 12.1. In this format, the total of creditors due within one year is deducted from the total of current assets to give a subtotal of 'net current assets'. This latter is sometimes referred to as 'working capital' (although this term is not used on the face of the balance sheet).

International Financial Reporting Standards

Comparison with UK GAAP

Under UK GAAP format rules set out in Sch. 4 of the Companies Act 1985 are rigid and prescriptive. By contrast IAS 1, Presentation of financial statements, does not prescribe a particular balance sheet format. The format example in the appendix to IAS 1 is for guidance and is not mandatory.

IAS 1.51 requires an entity to 'present current and non-current assets, and current and non-current liabilities, as separate classifications on the face of its balance sheet . . . except when a presentation based on liquidity provides information that is reliable and is more relevant. When that exception applies, all assets and liabilities shall be presented broadly in order of liquidity . . .'.

Format possibilities and examples

In practice, UK companies have chosen a variety of formats – these fall into four broad categories (with variations within each):

Formats	Companies that have adopted the format
1. Non-current assets + (current assets – current liabilities) – non-current liabilities = B/S total Equity = B/S total	Axis Shield SR Pharma Kingfisher AWG Workspace Group
2. Non-current assets + current assets = B/S total Equity + non-current liabilities + current liabilities = B/S total	Smith & Nephew Rok Property Solutions Royalblue Mears Group BAT
3. (Non-current assets + current assets) – (current liabilities + non-current liabilities) = B/S total Equity = B/S total	Northern Foods Marks & Spencer Severfield Rowan plc G.Wimpey
4. Assets in order of liquidity = B/S total Liabilities and equity in order of liquidity	Lloyds TSB Group

Format possibilities 1 and 2 are illustrated below in Examples 12.2 and 12.3 with their notes after Example 12.3.

Example 12.1 UK GAAP Balance sheet as at 31 March 2007

	2007		2006	
	£	£	£	£
Fixed assets				
Intangible assets[1]		90,500		96,500
Tangible assets[2]		613,128		658,228
Investment properties[2]		389,000		312,500
Investments[3]		41,000		16,000
		1,133,628		1,083,228
Current assets				
Stocks[4]	169,286		141,070	
Debtors[5]	548,106		496,755	
Cash at bank and in hand[6]	989,513		75,000	
	1,706,905		712,825	
Creditors due within one year				
Trade and other creditors[7]	104,824		98,275	
Current tax[8]	286,425		24,200	
	391,249		122,475	
Net current assets		1,315,656		590,350
Total assets less current liabilities		2,449,284		1,673,578
Creditors due after more than one year				
Bank loans[9]	250,000		300,000	
Deferred tax[10]	235,490		128,460	
Preference shares[11]	250,000	735,490	250,000	678,460
		1,713,794		995,118
Capital and reserves				
Equity share capital[12]		450,250		450,250
Investment property revaluation reserve[13]		199,000		122,500
Retained earnings[14]		1,064,544		422,368
		1,713,794		995,118

The above topics are covered in the following chapters:

1 – Chapter 14
2 – Chapter 13
3 – Chapter 15
4 – Chapter 16
5 – Chapter 17
6 – Chapter 18
7 – Chapter 19
8 – Chapter 20
9 – Chapter 21
10 – Chapter 20
11 – Chapters 22 and 24
12 – Chapter 24
13 – Chapters 13 and 24
14 – Chapters 11 and 24.

Example 12.2 Illustration of format 1 (traditional UK approach)

	2007 £	2007 £	2006 £	2006 £
Non-current assets				
Property, plant and equipment[2]		613,128		658,228
Investment properties[2]		389,000		312,500
Goodwill[1]		96,500		96,500
Available for sale financial assets[3]		53,760		22,000
		1,152,388		1,089,228
Current assets				
Inventories[4]	169,286		141,070	
Trade and other receivables[5]	548,106		496,755	
Investments held for trading[6]	53,600		122,450	
Derivative financial instruments[15]	28,450		23,472	
Cash and cash equivalents[6]	431,357		75,000	
	1,230,799		858,747	
Current liabilities				
Trade and other payables[7]	104,824		98,275	
Current tax payable[8]	126,628		24,200	
	231,452		122,475	
Net current assets		999,347		736,272
Total assets less current liabilities		2,151,735		1,825,500
Non-current liabilities				
Long-term borrowings[9]	250,000		300,000	
Preference shares[11]	500,000		500,000	
Deferred tax[8]	176,691	926,691	128,460	928,460
		1,225,044		897,040
Equity				
Share capital[12]		450,250		450,250
Fair value reserve[14]		17,500		12,768
Retained earnings[14]		757,294		434,022
		1,225,044		897,040

Example 12.3 Illustration of format 2 (traditional European approach)

	2007 £	2006 £
ASSETS		
Non-current assets		
Property, plant and equipment[2]	613,128	658,228
Investment properties[2]	389,000	312,500
Goodwill[1]	96,500	96,500
Available for sale financial assets[3]	53,760	22,000
Total non-current assets	1,152,388	1,089,228

▶

Current assets

Inventories[4]	169,286	141,070
Trade and other receivables[5]	548,106	496,755
Investments held for trading[6]	53,600	122,450
Derivative financial instruments[15]	28,450	23,472
Cash and cash equivalents[6]	431,357	75,000
Total current assets	1,230,799	858,747
Total assets	2,383,187	1,947,975

EQUITY AND LIABILITIES
Equity

Share capital[12]	450,250	450,250
Fair value reserve[14]	17,500	12,768
Retained earnings[14]	757,294	434,022
Total equity	1,225,044	897,040

Non-current liabilities

Long-term borrowings[9]	250,000	300,000
Preference shares[11]	500,000	500,000
Deferred tax[8]	176,691	128,460
Total non-current liabilities	926,691	928,460

Current liabilities

Trade and other payables[7]	104,824	98,275
Current tax payable[8]	126,628	24,200
Total current liabilities	231,452	122,475
Total liabilities	1,158,143	1,050,935
Total equity and liabilities	2,383,187	1,947,975

The above topics are covered in the following chapters:

1 – Chapter 14
2 – Chapter 13
3 – Chapter 15
4 – Chapter 16
5 – Chapter 17
6 – Chapter 18
7 – Chapter 19
8 – Chapter 20
9 – Chapter 21
10 – Chapter 20
11 – Chapters 22 and 24
12 – Chapter 24
13 – Chapters 13 and 24
14 – Chapters 11 and 24
15 – Chapter 23.

Tangible fixed assets

Tangible fixed asset categories

Introduction

Tangible fixed assets are items used in a company to earn revenue. They may include:

- land and buildings,
- plant and machinery,
- fixtures, fittings and tools,
- vehicles,
- office and computer equipment.

Investments properties are separately referred to later in this chapter.

Depreciation

Definition

FRS 15 defines depreciation as the measure of the cost or revalued amount of the economic benefits of the tangible fixed assets that have been consumed during the period. Consumption includes the wearing out, using up or other reduction in the useful economic life of a tangible fixed asset whether arising from use, effluxion of time or obsolescence through either changes in technology or demand for the goods and services produced by the asset.

Illustration

Consider this example from BLUE CIRCLE:

BLUE CIRCLE INDUSTRIES *Accounting policies 2000*

Depreciation
Depreciation is provided from the date of original use or subsequent valuation by equal annual amounts over the estimated lives of the assets, except for freehold and leasehold mineral lands where it is provided on the basis of tonnage extracted.

Traditionally fixed assets are shown in the balance sheet at cost less accumulated depreciation to date (i.e. at net book value). This book value is not, and does not purport to be in any sense, a valuation, though fixed assets, particularly land and buildings, are often revalued. In UK practice, sometimes, but by no means always, the valuation is taken into the books.

Companies Act requirements

The requirements of the Companies Act 1985 with regard to fixed assets are complex. In summary:

COMPANIES ACT REQUIREMENTS

Tangible fixed assets

Accounting bases
Fixed assets may be shown on

- a historical cost basis, *or*
- at valuation.

Historical cost

Assets are stated in the balance sheet at depreciated actual cost. Amounts must be shown under the following headings:

- cost;
- cumulative provision for depreciation;
- book (or carrying) value (i minus ii).

At valuation

The amount included must be shown, together with the years and amounts of the valuations. If valued during the year, the names of the valuers and the basis of valuation must be given (see page 105 on QUEENS MOAT HOUSES). Historical cost details must also be given.

Modified historical cost

In practice, UK companies frequently adopt the **modified historical cost convention**, under which historical cost is employed, but certain assets are revalued.

Under all bases

- Assets should be classified under headings appropriate to the business.
- Land must be analysed into freehold, long (over 50 years unexpired) and short leaseholds.
- Details must be given of *acquisitions* and *disposals* made during the year.

FRS 15 requires companies to disclose the method of depreciation used for each category of asset, together with the effective useful lives assumed.

Rates of depreciation

The following are typical rates (using the straight line method of depreciation, described below):

Freehold land	Nil
Freehold buildings	2% = 50-year life
Leasehold property:	
Long leases (over 50 years)	2% = 50 years
Short leases	Over life of the lease
Tenants' improvements	Over life of the lease
Plant and machinery	10% = 10 years
Vehicles	20% = 5 years
Ships, according to type	4–10% = 10–25 years
Furniture and equipment	10% = 10 years

Where there is a wide range of estimated useful lives within a single classification, some companies also show an *average life*, which is much more informative. An example is CABLE & WIRELESS:

CABLE & WIRELESS *Accounting policies 2003*

Tangible fixed assets and depreciation

	Lives	Average
Cables	Up to 20 years	15 years
Network equipment	3 to 25 years	8 years
Ducting	40 years	40 years

Useful economic life

Determination of useful economic life (the period over which the present owner expects to derive economic benefit from the asset's use) is a matter for management and depends on business circumstances. For example, the chairman's statement of THE JERSEY ELECTRICITY COMPANY refers to a site redevelopment that will allow relocation of the company's head office and provision of commercial retail and other office space. A note to the accounts discloses that the site has been examined in relation to FRS 11, Impairment of fixed assets and goodwill. As a result of this examination, depreciation has been accelerated to ensure that the assets will be written off during the development period. As a consequence, additional depreciation of £0.7m has been charged in 1998. It seems that this charge relates principally to buildings which will be demolished to allow completion of the development.

Where depreciation is shown in the accounts

Depreciation appears in several places. HALMA, in the extracts shown below, provides an example of what a good set of accounts shows:

- the note on *Accounting policies*;
- Note 3 and Note 22: the depreciation charge for the year;
- Note 11: disposals and the cumulative amount of depreciation to date;
- Note 11 also illustrates several other requirements of the Companies Act 1985, e.g. the analysis of land into freehold, long leasehold and short leasehold.

HALMA *Extracts from the 2003 accounts*

Accounting policies:
Tangible fixed assets and depreciation
Tangible fixed assets are stated at cost less provisions for impairment and depreciation which, with the exception of freehold land which is not depreciated, is provided on all tangible fixed assets on the straight line method, each item being written off over its estimated life.

The principal annual rates used for this purpose are:

Freehold buildings	2%
Leasehold properties	
more than 50 years unexpired	2%
less than 50 years unexpired	Period of lease
Plant, machinery and equipment	8% to 20%
Motor vehicles	20%
Short-life tooling	$33^{1}/_{3}\%$

Note 3 to the profit and loss account:

	2003 £000	2002 £000
Operating profit is arrived at after charging:		
Depreciation	7,554	7,371

Note 22 Reconciliation of operating profit to net cash inflow from operating activities:

Operating profit	42,865	45,721
. . .		
Depreciation	7,554	7,371

Note 11
Fixed assets – tangible assets

Group		Land and buildings			Plant,	
		Freehold	*Long*	*Short*	*equipment*	
Cost		*properties*	*leases*	*leases*	*& vehicles*	*Total*
At 30 March 2002		21,449	1,355	2,478	60,915	86,197
Assets of businesses acquired		4,713	–	51	3,217	7,981
Additions at cost		2,401	93	305	8,458	11,257
Disposals		(1,246)	–	(178)	(4,694)	(6,118)
Exchange adjustments		186	–	(33)	(806)	(653)
At 29 March 2003	(a)	27,503	1,448	2,623	67,090	98,664
Accumulated depreciation						
. . .						
At 29 March 2003	(b)	4,420	319	1,357	42,685	48,781
Net book amounts						
At 29 March 2003	(a – b)	23,083	1,129	1,266	24,405	49,883

Depreciation methods

The most common method or basis of depreciation is the straight line (or fixed instalment) method.

Other methods include:

- the reducing balance method;
- the renewals method;
- the production unit method (see BLUE CIRCLE INDUSTRIES, above).

The straight line (or fixed instalment) method

Depreciation under the straight line method is computed as follows (see also Example 13.1 below):

Annual depreciation

$$= \frac{\text{Cost} - \text{Residual value}}{\text{Useful economic life}}$$

Example 13.1 Straight line depreciation

If a machine having a useful economic life of five years is purchased for £10,000, and is expected to have a residual value of £1,000 at the end of that life, depreciation will be:

$$\frac{£10,000 - £1,000}{5} = \frac{£9,000}{5} = £1,800 \text{ per annum}$$

and the accounts will show:

End of year	Depreciation for the year (shown in the P & L account)	Cost	Provision for depreciation to date	Net book value
		← shown in the balance sheet →		
	£	£	£	£
1	1,800	10,000	1,800	8,200
2	1,800	10,000	3,600	6,400
3	1,800	10,000	5,400	4,600
4	1,800	10,000	7,200	2,800
5	1,800	10,000	9,000	1,000

TERMINOLOGY

Tangible fixed assets

Tangible fixed assets are long-lived assets held for the purpose, directly or indirectly, of earning revenue. They include not only items like **plant and machinery**, which are actually used to provide the product, but assets used to house or support operations, such as **land, buildings, furniture, computer equipment and motor vehicles**.

They may be owned by the company or financed by finance leases.

Depreciation is the measure of the cost or revalued amount of the economic benefits of the asset that have been *consumed* during the period.

Consumption includes the wearing out, using up or other reduction in the useful economic life of a tangible fixed asset whether arising from use, effluxion of time or obsolescence through changes either in technology or in demand for the goods and services produced by the asset.

Useful economic life of a tangible fixed asset is the period over which the company expects to derive economic benefit from that asset.

Residual value is the realisable value of an asset at the end of its useful economic life.

The straight line method is ideal where the service provided by the asset continues unabated throughout its useful economic life, as might be the case with a 21-year lease of a building. It is the method generally used wherever the equal allocation of cost provides a reasonably fair measure of the asset's service (e.g., for buildings, plant, machinery, equipment, vehicles and patents). A key advantage is that it is easy to calculate, and conceptually simple to understand.

The reducing balance method

The reducing balance method used to be the most popular method of depreciation; but, except for tax purposes, it has largely been supplanted in recent years by the straight line method.

Under the reducing balance method, the annual depreciation charge represents a fixed percentage of the net book value brought forward (i.e. cost less accumulated depreciation). The calculation of the annual charge is simple enough once the appropriate percentage has been determined, but this requires the use of tables or a calculator:

Depreciation rate $= 1 - (\text{Residual value} \div \text{Cost})^{1/n}$

where n = useful economic life in years and depreciation rate is a decimal.

Among the disadvantages of the reducing balance method are these:

- most users do not calculate the rate appropriate to each particular item of plant, but use standard percentages, which tend to be too low rather than too high;
- unless notional adjustments are made to cost and residual value, it is impossible to calculate satisfactorily a reducing balance rate if the residual value is nil: the net book value can never get to nil, as it can only be reduced by a proportion each year;
- even if the asset is assigned a nominal scrap value (say £1 so that it is not overlooked in the books) or if there is some residual value but it is small in relation to cost, the method is unlikely to be satisfactory without notional adjustments, because it leads to such high charges in the early years.

The renewals method

Definable major assets or components within an infrastructure or network with determinable finite lives should be treated separately and depreciated over their useful economic lives.

For the remaining tangible fixed assets within the system or network, renewals accounting may be used as a method of estimating depreciation (FRS 15, paragraph 97).

Where renewals accounting is adopted, the level of annual expenditure required to maintain the operating capacity of the infrastructure asset is treated as the depreciation charged for the period (FRS 15, paragraph 98). For example the SOUTH STAFFORDSHIRE GROUP:

SOUTH STAFFORDSHIRE GROUP *Accounting policies 2000*

Infrastructure assets
Infrastructure assets comprise a network of systems that, as a whole, is intended to be maintained in perpetuity at a specified level of service by the continuing replacement and refurbishment of its components . . .

The depreciation charge for infrastructure assets is the level of annual expenditure required to maintain the operating capability of the network . . .

Change in expected useful life

The useful economic life of a tangible fixed asset is reviewed as part of the normal end of period reporting procedures. If it is revised, the carrying amount of the tangible fixed asset at the date of revision should be depreciated over the revised life (FRS 15, paragraph 93).

Changes in useful life can have a significant effect on profits. For example STORM, the cartoon character licensing group, changed its accounting policy on film costs in its 1992 accounts to reflect a change in group strategy, as the chairman explained.

STORM GROUP *Extract from Chairman's statement*

It was decided that Storm would no longer utilise its own funds to invest in animated cartoon film productions . . . all production work would be funded from commissions, external funding or pre-sales revenue.

As a result of this change in strategic focus, the Board elected to adopt a revised accounting policy in respect of film costs and to write them off to the profit and loss account as incurred. The total sum involved was £2.289m, of which £1.538m was charged in 1992 and the balance treated as a prior year item.

The effect of the change in accounting policy was the major cause of the group reporting a pre-tax loss of £2.1m. But the chairman's statement went on to say:

STORM GROUP *Second extract from Chairman's statement*

It is, however, vitally important to emphasise that the write-off of film production costs should not be seen to detract from the inherent value of the animation programmes to which they relate. Animated cartoons have traditionally generated revenues over a long period . . .

STORM claimed that the revised policy had been adopted on the grounds of prudence, but does it necessarily provide 'a true and fair view'? Future profits will be enhanced by hundreds of thousands of pounds per annum for several years, because animation programmes will no longer have to be depreciated.

Impairment

As explained in Chapter 7, FRS 11, Impairment of fixed assets and goodwill calls for the writing down of fixed assets if they are judged to have become permanently impaired. The standard introduced the implication that assets must be stated in the balance sheet at amounts that are expected to earn at least a satisfactory rate of return. Companies earning a poor rate of return, even though profitable, should write down their assets (see page 115 regarding impairment reviews).

The useful economic life of a tangible fixed asset should be reviewed at the end of each reporting period and revised if expectations are significantly different from previous estimates. If a useful economic life is revised, the carrying amount of the tangible fixed asset at the date of revision should be depreciated over the revised remaining useful economic life (FRS 15, paragraph 93).

What is more, where the residual value is material the review has to take account of reasonably expected technological changes based on prices prevailing at the date of acquisition (or revaluation). A change in its estimated residual value should be accounted for prospectively over the asset's remaining useful economic life, except to the extent that the asset has been impaired at the balance sheet date (FRS 15, paragraph 95).

Changing method

A change from one method of providing depreciation to another is permissible only on the grounds that the new method will give a fairer presentation of the results and of the financial position. Such a change does not, however, constitute a change of accounting policy; it does not give rise to an exceptional item: the carrying amount of the tangible fixed asset is depreciated using the revised method over the remaining useful economic life, beginning in the period in which the change is made (FRS 15, paragraph 82).

Freehold land and buildings

Traditionally, neither freehold land nor buildings were depreciated, though the majority of companies had been depreciating freehold buildings in years before accounting standards were introduced.

Under FRS 15 companies are normally required to depreciate freehold and long leasehold buildings.

If, however, no depreciation charge is made on the grounds that it would be immaterial, or on the grounds that the estimated remaining useful life of the asset is over

50 years, tangible fixed assets should be reviewed for impairment at the end of each reporting period.

Revaluation of fixed assets

Background

Under historical cost accounting, assets appear at cost less depreciation, and they are not revalued to show their current worth to the company. But because of the effects of inflation, the practice grew up in the UK of revaluing assets, particularly freehold land and buildings, from time to time.

Indeed, Sch. 7, para. 1 of the Companies Act 1985 requires the difference between the market value of property assets and the balance sheet amount to be disclosed in the directors' report if, in the opinion of the directors, it is significant. UK companies thus face the choice; they must either

- incorporate any revaluation in the accounts, or
- disclose it in the directors' report.

Effects of revaluation

Where assets are revalued and the revaluation is incorporated in the accounts, both 'sides' of the balance sheet are affected, and depreciation from then on is based on the revalued amounts, as the example below illustrates.

Example 13.2 Effects of revaluation

A company has freehold land which cost £1.0m and buildings which cost £4.2m, have a useful life of 50 years and were 10 years old on 31 December 1999. Depreciation to that date would therefore be 2% p.a. for 10 years on £4.2m = £840,000, so the balance sheet would show:

	£m
Freehold land and buildings at cost	5.200
less depreciation to date	0.840
Book value at 31 December 1999	4.360

On 1 January 2000 the land was revalued at £3.8m and the buildings at £8.1m. After the revaluation the

accounts would show freehold land and buildings at the valuation figure of £11.9m, an increase of £7.54m. On the other side of the balance sheet the reserves would normally be increased by £7.54m. (If, however, the company has entered into a binding agreement to sell the buildings, FRS 19, paragraph 14 requires a provision to be made out of the revaluation surplus for the tax which would be payable on disposal, and this would be credited to deferred tax, the remainder of the surplus being credited to reserves.)

The 2000 accounts would be required to disclose the basis of valuation used and the name or qualification of the valuer (CA 1985, Sch. 4, para. 43 (b)).

The revaluation will affect the company in several ways:

1. The annual depreciation charge on the buildings, based on the new value and the current estimate of the remaining useful life (40 years), will increase from £84,000 to £202,500 ($2\frac{1}{2}$% p.a. on £8.1m), thus directly reducing the pre-tax profits by £118,500 in each future year.
2. The overall profitability of the company, as measured by the ratio return on capital employed (ROCE, described in Chapter 10), will also appear to deteriorate because the capital employed will have increased by £7.54m. For instance, if the company in our example went on to make £3m before interest and tax in 2000, and had £20m capital employed before the revaluation, the 2000 return on capital employed would be:

No revaluation   *Revaluation*

$$\frac{3,118,500}{20,000,000} = 15.6\% \qquad \frac{3,000,000}{27,540,000} = 10.9\%$$

3. The borrowing powers of most companies are expressed as a multiple of share capital and reserves, so the increase in reserves will raise the borrowing limits, and improve the capital cover of existing lenders.
4. The higher property value may give more scope for borrowing on mortgage.
5. The increase in reserves will also increase the net asset value per share.

The arguments for and against revaluations

On the one hand, valuations can produce figures that fluctuate wildly, and a lot may depend on the valuer, and whether he thinks his client wants a 'very full' valuation or a parsimonious one. He who pays the valuer calls the tune.

For example, at the end of 1991 the hotel group QUEENS MOAT HOUSES had its properties independently valued by a well-known firm of chartered surveyors at a figure of £2,000m.

At the end of the following year a different but equally reputable firm of chartered surveyors valued the same portfolio of hotels at £861m.

The *new* chairman explained what had happened:

QUEENS MOAT HOUSES *Extract from chairman's statement*

At 31 December 1991, the group's properties were valued by Weatherall Green & Smith (WGS) at £2.0 billion, a valuation which was incorporated in the 1991 audited balance sheet . . .

In June the previous board appointed Jones Lang Wootton (JLW) to value the group's hotel portfolio in place of WGS. They have valued the portfolio of properties as at 31 December 1992 at £861 million . . .

After careful consideration the board accepted the JLW valuation and it has been incorporated into the group's balance sheet at 31 December 1992. In the UK and Continental Europe there was considerable hotel expansion in the late 1980s fuelled by the abundant availability of capital. Circumstances have changed materially over the past few years and the recent market place for hotels in the UK has been dominated by distressed sale values. On the continent, the declining profitability has lagged the UK but the market place has shown similar adverse developments. It is this adverse context of declining profitability and limited purchasers' interest in hotels in which the valuation has been prepared . . .

On the other hand, as the former chairman of the ASB, Sir David Tweedie, has pointed out, it is nonsense to have a property shown in the balance sheet at £10m if the bank, valuing it at £50m, has accepted it as security for a £40m loan.

We rather agree with Sir Adrian Cadbury, who said at his last AGM as chairman of CADBURY SCHWEPPES that the only time the real value of a brand (or any other asset) is known is when it changes hands.

FRS 15, Tangible fixed assets

The ASB has grasped the nettle somewhat cautiously. Under FRS 15, revaluing tangible fixed assets remains optional as is also the case under IFRS.

But, where a policy of revaluation is adopted, it must be applied to a whole class of assets and the valuations kept up to date. This will generally be achieved by a five-yearly full valuation of an asset with a qualified external valuer, and an interim valuation in year 3. Valuations in the intervening years are only required where there is likely to have been a material change in value.

Revaluation gains should be recognised in the profit and loss account only to the extent that they reverse valuation losses on the same asset that were previously recognised in the profit and loss account. All other revaluation gains should be recognised in the statement of total recognised gains and losses (FRS 15, paragraph 63).

Revaluation losses caused by a clear loss of economic benefit should be recognised in the profit and loss account. Other revaluation losses should normally be recognised in the statement of total recognised gains and losses until the carrying amount reaches its depreciated historical cost (FRS 15, paragraph 65).

Sales and other disposals of fixed assets

Where fixed assets are disposed of for an amount which is greater (or less) than their book value, the profit or loss on disposal should be shown separately on the face of the profit and loss account after operating profit and before interest, and attributed to continuing or discontinued operations (FRS 3, paragraphs 19 and 20), for example, TESCO:

TESCO *Extract from profit and loss account 2003*

	2003 £m	2002 £m
Operating profit	1,484	1,322
Share of operating profit of joint ventures and associates	70	42
Net loss on disposal of fixed assets	(13)	(10)
Profit on ordinary activities before interest and taxation	1,541	1,354
Net interest payable	(180)	(153)
Profit on ordinary activities before taxation	1,361	1,201

Where assets which have been revalued are subsequently disposed of, the gains or losses are to be calculated against the carrying value (valuation amount less any subsequent depreciation).

Investment properties

UK GAAP

Currently, while FRS 15 requires annual depreciation charges to be made on fixed assets, and makes it clear that an increase in the value of a fixed asset does not remove the necessity to charge depreciation, a different treatment is applied to fixed assets held as disposable investments.

Under SSAP 19, 'investment properties' (i.e. properties held as investments rather than for use in a manufacturing or commercial process) are not depreciated, but are revalued each year at their open market value, and the valuation is reflected in the balance sheet. Changes in the value of investment properties should be treated as a movement on an 'investment property revaluation reserve'. The cumulative amounts credited to reserve can be very large. If, however, there is a fall in value that exceeds the balance in the investment property revaluation reserve, the excess should be charged to the profit and loss account; i.e. the reserve cannot 'go negative'.

International Financial Reporting Standards

IFRS adopts a markedly different approach allowing investment properties to be accounted for in one of two ways.

1 The fair value method

Like SSAP 19, investments properties are included in the balance sheet at what is effectively a market value. But there are two differences:

1. Changes in fair value are taken direct to the income statement and are effectively reflected in operating profit;
2. Deferred tax must be provided in accordance with IAS 12.

2 The cost method

Under this alternative, investment properties would be stated in the balance sheet at cost and depreciated over their useful lives.

Government grants

Capital-based grants

Capital-based grants are grants made as a contribution towards specific expenditure on fixed assets. SSAP 4 requires capital-based grants to be credited to revenue (i.e. to the profit and loss account) over the expected useful life of the asset concerned.

Revenue-based grants

These include grants to finance the general activities of an enterprise over a specific period, which SSAP 4 requires to be credited to the profit and loss account in the period in which they are paid.

RMC GROUP *Extract from accounting policies 2003*

Grants
Grants received from governments and other agencies, where they relate to expenditure on fixed assets or are to finance the activities of the group over a number of years, are recognised in the profit and loss account over the expected useful economic lives of the related assets or over that number of years, and to the extent not so recognised are treated as deferred income.

Grants which are intended to give immediate financial support or assistance or which are made to reimburse costs incurred are included in the profit and loss account so as to match with those costs in the period in which they become receivable.

Where the amounts involved are material, grants will appear:

- separately in the profit and loss account or notes as a contribution to profit; and
- in the balance note on creditors and deferred income.

Hybrid grants

With some grants (e.g. Regional Selective Investment Grants) that are made to help generate jobs in Assisted Areas, it is debatable whether they should be treated as capital grants or as revenue grants.

Ratios

Ratios may be useful in looking at a manufacturing company's *tangible fixed assets*. For example, on plant and machinery:

Question 1: **Is it being kept well renewed?**

$$\text{Ratio 1} = \frac{\text{Additions each year}}{\text{Annual depreciation charge}}$$

Question 2: **Is it reasonably up to date?**

$$\text{Ratio 2} = \frac{\text{Cumulative depreciation}}{\text{Cumulative cost}}$$

For example LOCKER GROUP (see below).

LOCKER GROUP *Plant and equipment*

	Year to 31 Mar:	1996 £000	1997 £000	1998 £000	1999 £000	2000 £000
	Cost					
(a)	At beginning of year	8,256	18,983	19,653	19,627	21,633
(b)	Exchange differences	272	(808)	(948)	21	(346)
(c)	Subsidiary acquired	10,078	–	–	760	–
(d)	Additions	611	1,855	1,543	1,847	2,307
(e)	Disposals	(234)	(377)	(621)	(622)	(975)
(f)	At end of year	18,983	19,653	19,627	21,633	22,619

	Depreciation					
(g)	At beginning of year	5,100	9,917	10,755	11,162	12,637
(h)	Exchange differences	149	(439)	(545)	9	(226)
(j)	Subsidiary acquired	3,966	–	–	436	–
(k)	Depreciation charge for year	880	1,573	1,490	1,587	1,736
(l)	Disposals	(178)	(296)	(538)	(557)	(666)
(m)	At end of year	9,917	10,755	11,162	12,637	13,481
	Ratios					
(d/k)	Additions / Depreciation charge	69.4%	117.9%	103.6%	116.4%	132.9%
(m/f)	Cu. depreciation / Cu. Cost	52.2%	54.7%	56.9%	58.4%	59.6%
(l/e)	Disposals: Depreciation / Cost	76.1%	78.5%	86.6%	89.5%	68.3%

Ratio 1, line (d) / line (k)

This shows an increasing amount being spent each year on additions, compared with the annual depreciation charge.

Ratio 2, line (m) / line (f)

This shows that cumulative depreciation is becoming a larger percentage of cumulative cost.

But ratios can be much more interesting if looked at in the context of what's happening in the company. For example, the 1996 column of the table shows that the LOCKER GROUP made a very large acquisition in that year.

The company acquired was called PENTRE, and it was, in fact, a reverse takeover, in which the chairman and the chief executive of Pentre (both founder directors of Pentre, aged 44 and 48 respectively) replaced Locker's elderly chairman and its chief executive.

It is interesting to look at Ratio 2 of PENTRE when acquired, and of LOCKER at the beginning of 1996:

£000		Pentre	Locker
$\dfrac{\text{Cu. Depreciation}}{\text{Cumulative cost}}$	=	$\dfrac{3,966}{10,078}$	$\dfrac{5,100}{8,256}$
Ratio 2		39.4%	61.8%

In other words, Pentre's plant and equipment was pretty up to date, while Locker's was getting a bit old, like the previous chairman.

Many companies in the service sectors have no significant amount of tangible fixed assets but where they do, for example with hotels, these ratios may be useful. For example, take the case of the London restaurant chain GROUPE CHEZ GERARD:

GROUPE CHEZ GERARD *Fixtures and fittings*

Year end	Cumulative cost £000	Cumulative depreciation £000	Percentage depreciated
1994	1,323	944	71.4%
1995	1,533	1,085	70.8%
1996	1,980	1,271	64.2%
1997	3,049	1,586	52.0%
1998	4,050	2,031	50.1%

The improving trend was due partly to the opening of new restaurants, with brand new fixtures and fittings.

CHAPTER 14

Intangible fixed assets

Intangible fixed asset categories

Introduction

The balance sheet heading 'intangible fixed assets' may comprise a diverse range of assets including:

- purchased goodwill;
- capitalised developments costs;
- software which is an integral part of a computer's operating system;
- capitalised development costs;
- licences, concessions, patents and trademarks ('rights');
- customer lists;
- brands.

Internally-generated or purchased

Some of the above intangible assets may have been created or developed by the company itself. In practice, restrictive rules in accounting standards make it extremely difficult for companies to bring such assets into the balance sheet.

Other intangible assets may be purchased individually, for example, a famous brand name. Some are acquired when a company buys another business, which includes a mixture of tangible and intangible assets.

UK GAAP and IFRS requirements

Accounting for intangibles is an intricate area, and one where the detailed rules in International Financial Reporting Standards (IAS 38, Intangible assets, and IFRS 3, Business combinations) differ from those in UK GAAP

(FRS 10, Goodwill and intangible assets, and SSAP 13, Accounting for research and development).

Goodwill

Introduction

Goodwill may only be included as an intangible fixed asset if it arises as a result of a purchase of a company, division of a company or an unincorporated business. Such goodwill is often referred to as *purchased goodwill* to distinguish it from the goodwill category that cannot be recognised on the balance sheet, namely *internally-generated goodwill*.

UK GAAP

FRS 10, Goodwill and intangible assets presumes that purchased goodwill has an economic life not exceeding 20 years. The standard requires that goodwill is amortised over this period.

As is the case in Example 14.1, purchased goodwill is usually a positive amount, i.e. an asset in the balance sheet. However occasionally the amount turns out to be negative. Suppose that in the Example 14.1, the numbers had been the other way round and the purchase had resulted in negative goodwill of £400,000.

Under FRS 10, the credit of £400,000 would have been shown under fixed assets as a negative amount (presented in the balance sheet with brackets around it). It would have then been released to the profit and loss account over a number of years (in accordance with the rules in FRS 10

Example 14.1

A company purchases a business for cash and pays £1.5m. The fair value of the assets of the business (see Chapter 28) are assessed at £1.1m and the directors consider the useful life of the goodwill to be 20 years. The goodwill is £400,000 (£1.5m – £1.1m). The annual amortisation charged is £400,000/20 = £20,000. Each year the profit and loss account will be charged with £400,000 in arriving at operating profit. In the balance sheet, the goodwill will presented at cost less accumulated amortisation, i.e. it will appear in succeeding balance sheet at £400,000; £380,000; £360,000 and so on.

this usually turned out to be a short period of say three or five years).

Suppose that the directors determined that the negative goodwill was to written back over five years. Each year the profit and loss account would be credited with £100,000 (in arriving at operating profit) and the balance sheet amount would be reduced by £100,000.

The 'true and fair override'

A small minority of UK companies took advantage of a limited 'window' in FRS 10 that permitted them to include goodwill in the balance sheet each year at cost, without any amortisation charge to the profit and loss account. The price to be paid for overriding the companies' requirement to amortise goodwill was that such companies had to carry out each year an annual valuation of goodwill, referred to as an *impairment review*. If such a review comprising detailed and extensive calculations revealed that goodwill was effectively worth less than its current carrying value, the goodwill was deemed to be 'impaired'. This resulted in the goodwill being written down in the balance sheet at this lower amount. The amount of the reduction (usually referred to as an *impairment charge*) was charged to the profit and loss account in determining the operating profit for the year.

'Old' goodwill

Under UK GAAP, any purchase goodwill arising on acquisitions which occurred before 1 January 1998 was

usually charged immediately against reserves (one of the alternative permitted accounting treatments at that time under a former, and now discredited, standard – SSAP 22). Such goodwill was not charged to the profit and loss account unless and until the part of the business to which it related to was sold.

Under the Companies Act 1985 companies were required to disclose in a memorandum note the cumulative amount of goodwill resulting from acquisitions that has been written off to reserves in earlier years (i.e. without charge to the profit and loss account). This disclosure is not required under IFRS and therefore this information will no longer be available to analysts.

This old accounting treatment continues to be referred to in some IFRS accounts (see, for example, DAILY MAIL AND GENERAL TRUST 2006 Annual Report, below).

DAILY MAIL AND GENERAL TRUST *Annual Report 2006*

Accounting policies extract
Goodwill written off to reserves under UK GAAP prior to 1998 has not been reinstated and is not included in determining any subsequent profit on disposal.

International Financial Reporting Standards

The accounting treatment of goodwill under IFRS is set out in IFRS 3, Business combinations. IFRS 3 requires a radically different approach from FRS 10 and prohibits the systematic annual amortisation of goodwill. The accounting treatment differs according to whether the goodwill is 'positive' or 'negative'.

Positive goodwill

Purchased goodwill is stated in the balance sheet under the caption 'Intangible fixed assets' initially at its cost. This figure must be reviewed each year for impairment. The detailed tests are set out in IAS 38, Impairment of assets: this is essentially a complex valuation exercise. If the test reveals that the goodwill is not impaired, goodwill remains at its cost figure. On the other hand, if the test reveals actual impairment, the goodwill must be written down to a lower amount, with an impairment charge taken to the profit and loss account.

Note that IFRS prohibits the systematic amortisation of goodwill – this is an important difference compared with UK GAAP.

Negative goodwill

Accounting for negative goodwill is far simpler. When the negative goodwill first arises (as a result of the purchase of a business), the standard requires the calculations to be carefully rechecked. If the result is the same, the negative goodwill should be immediately credited to the income statement.

The example below relates to the 31 October 2006 accounts of FIRST CHOICE HOLIDAYS PLC. The note is long and accordingly we have annotated it:

FIRST CHOICE HOLIDAYS *Annual Report 2006*

Extract from accounting policies – Intangible assets
Goodwill represents amounts arising on acquisition of subsidiaries[1], associates and jointly controlled entities[2]. In respect of business acquisitions that have occurred since 1 November 2004[3], goodwill represents the difference between the fair value of consideration paid and the fair value of the net identifiable assets and contingent liabilities acquired[1]. Identifiable intangibles are those which can be sold separately or which arise from legal rights regardless of whether those rights are separable.

Goodwill is stated at cost less any accumulated impairment losses. Goodwill is allocated to cash generating units[4] and is not amortised but is tested annually for impairment. In respect of joint ventures and associates, the carrying amount of goodwill is included in the carrying amount of the investment in the associate[2].

In respect of acquisitions prior to 1 November 2004, goodwill is included at 1 November 2004 on the basis of its deemed cost[3] which represents the amount recorded under UK GAAP which was broadly comparable save that only separable intangibles were recognised and goodwill was amortised. Amortisation of goodwill ceased on 1 November 2004[3]. This goodwill is tested annually for impairment.

Purchased goodwill in respect of acquisitions before 1 January 1998 was written off to reserves in the year of acquisition, in accordance with the accounting standard then in force[5].

. . .
Negative goodwill arising on an acquisition is recognised in the income statement.
. . .
Goodwill is not amortised but is systematically tested for impairment at each balance sheet date.
. . .

1. Acquisitions are covered in Chapter 28.
2. Associates and joint ventures are covered inn Chapter 29.
3. Special rules dealing with transition from UK GAAP to IFRS are covered in Chapter 34.
4. IAS 36, Impairment of assets, requires a business to identify 'cash-generating units' (CGUs). These are parts of the business which generate cash flows that are largely independent from cash flows from other parts of the business. The total goodwill number has to be allocated to each CGU. Each allocated part of goodwill is then tested for impairment.
5. See comments above re lack of disclosure relating to the amount of goodwill written off to reserves under a former accounting policy.

Additional example

Rok plc, Annual Report 2006, Note 13 on intangible assets (www.rokgroup.com)

ENODIS *Annual Report 2006*

Extract from accounting policies – Goodwill
In the case of acquisitions that arose prior to 1998, goodwill was written off directly to equity. Prior to the Group's transition to IFRS on 3 October 2004, goodwill previously written-off to equity was charged to the consolidated income statement when the related business was sold. Following the Group's transition to IFRS, goodwill remaining in equity is no longer charged to the consolidated income statement when the related business is sold.

Capitalised development costs

UK GAAP

SSAP 13, Accounting for research and development, regards expenditure incurred on pure and applied research as part of a continuing operation required to maintain a company's business and competitive position, and so no one particular accounting period rather than another is expected to benefit. Such expenditure should be charged to the profit and loss account in the period in which it is incurred.

However, SSAP 13, paragraph 9, distinguishes the above expenditure from that relating to the development of new products or services where expenditure is normally undertaken with 'a reasonable expectation of specific commercial success and of future benefits arising from the work, either from increased revenue and related profits or from reduced costs'. Where development expenditure is for clearly defined projects on which expenditure is separately identifiable and for which commercial success is reasonably certain, companies *may* if they wish defer charging development expenditure 'to the extent that its recovery can reasonably be regarded as assured'. Subject to satisfying criteria laid down in SSAP 13, a company effectively has a choice between:

- expensing development costs (i.e. charging to profit and loss account in the period in which the expenditure is incurred); or
- capitalising development costs as an intangible fixed asset and amortising the expenditure over a number of years, with amortisation charged to the profit and loss account.

Until recently the more popular option under UK GAAP has been the first, but this trend may change in the future as more companies adopt IFRS and as UK GAAP itself converges with IFRS.

International Financial Reporting Standards

IAS 38, Intangible assets, requires research expenditure (including expenditure relating to the research phase of a project) to be recognised as an expense when it is incurred. However, an intangible asset arising from development (or from the development phase of an internal project) shall be recognised if, and only if, an entity can demonstrate all of the following conditions:

- the technical feasibility of completing the intangible asset so that it will be available for use or sale;
- its intention to complete the intangible asset and use it or sell it;
- its ability to use or sell the intangible asset;
- how the intangible asset will generate probable future economic benefits (among other things, the entity can demonstrate the existence of a market for the output of the intangible asset or the intangible asset itself or, if it is to be used internally, the usefulness of the intangible asset);
- the availability of adequate technical, financial and other resources to complete the development and to use or sell the intangible asset;
- its ability to measure reliably the expenditure attributable to the intangible asset during its development.

ROYALBLUE GROUP below is an example of a company that chose to expense development costs under UK GAAP but which is required to capitalise them under IFRS. ENODIS below acknowledge the requirements of IAS 38 but disclose the fact that the necessary criteria to justify capitalisation cannot be demonstrated.

ROYALBLUE GROUP *Annual Report 2006*

Accounting policies extract – Research and development
Research expenditure is recognised as an expense as incurred. Costs incurred on product development (relating to the design, programming and testing of new or enhanced products) are capitalised as intangible assets when it is probable that the development will provide economic benefits, considering its commercial and technological feasibility, resources are available for the development, and costs can be measured reliably. The expenditure capitalised is the direct labour costs and is managed and controlled centrally. Other development expenditures are recognised as an expense is incurred. Product development costs previously recognised as an expense are not recognised as an asset in a subsequent period.

Capitalised product development expenditure is stated at cost less accumulated amortisation and impairment losses. Product development costs that have been capitalised are amortised from the time of development on a straight line basis over three years.

ENODIS *Annual Report 2006*

Accounting policies extract
Expenditure on research activities is charged to the income statement in the period in which it is incurred.

Development expenditure on new or substantially improved products is capitalised only once the criteria specified under IAS 38, Intangible assets have been met which among other requirements, requires the technical feasibility of the developed product having been proven.

Prior to and during the 52 weeks ending on 30 September 2006, no development expenditure satisfied the necessary conditions of IAS 38.

Computer software

UK GAAP

Not all purchased computer software is classed as an intangible fixed asset. FRS 10 states:

'Software costs that are directly attributable to bringing a computer system or other computer-operated machinery into working condition for its intended use within the business are treated as part of the cost of the related hardware (i.e. as a tangible fixed asset) rather than as a separate intangible asset.'

International Financial Reporting Standards

Several companies have reviewed their classification of computer software on transition from UK GAAP to IFRS, as MANAGEMENT CONSULTING GROUP shows:

MANAGEMENT CONSULTING GROUP *Interim Report 2005*

Extract from note 11 – Transition to IFRS

IAS 38 Intangible assets
IAS 38 requires computer software costs, including development costs, to be classified as intangible assets. Capitalised software of £0.4m is reclassified at 30 June 2004 as intangible assets, which continue to be amortised over three years or the life of the software contract if shorter.

FIRST CHOICE HOLIDAYS *Annual Report 2006*

Accounting policies extract – computer software
Computer software consists of all software that is not an integral part of the related computer hardware and is stated at cost less accumulated amortisation and impairment losses.

DAILY MAIL AND GENERAL TRUST *Annual Report 2006*

Accounting policies extract – Intangible assets
Costs that are directly associated with the production of identifiable and unique software products controlled by the Group, and that are expected to generate economic benefits exceeding costs and directly attributable overheads are capitalised as intangibles. Computer software which is integral to a related item of hardware equipment is accounted for as property, plant and equipment.

Other intangibles

Purchase intangibles

Purchase intangibles (whether purchased individually or as part of a business) may include:

- Copyright and similar publishing rights which provide the holder with the exclusive rights to produce copies of, and control over, an original musical, artistic or literary work.
- Licences which relate to agreements entered into by a company with government or third parties and which enable the company to carry out certain trading functions (e.g. brewers operating licensed premises; bookmakers required to obtain a licence for each bookmaking shop; licences purchased by companies allowing them to use software or technology developed by third parties; licences from government authorities).
- Patents which assure an inventor of the sole right to make, use and sell his or her invention for a determined period.
- Trademarks which provide legal protection to the name or symbol used to differentiate the products sold by a manufacturer or distributor from those of competing manufacturers and dealers.

UK GAAP

FRS 10, Goodwill and intangible assets, requires that intangible assets purchased separately from a business should be capitalised at cost. Intangible assets acquired as part of a business acquisition should be capitalised separately from goodwill, provided their value can be measured reliably.

International Financial Reporting Standards

IFRS is far more demanding than UK GAAP in its review of assets acquired as a result of a business purchase. Consequently, under IFRS, companies are identifying a far wider range of intangibles, for example, customer lists. Under UK GAAP some of these intangibles may have been subsumed within the overall goodwill figure.

Under UK GAAP, when all intangibles and goodwill are being amortised, this blurring of goodwill and intangibles may make little difference to profit as goodwill is being amortised anyway. This is certainly not the case under IFRS where some intangibles are amortised over 20 years, other such as customer lists over far shorter periods, and goodwill where amortisation is prohibited altogether.

An illustration of customer lists is shown by AWG:

AWG Annual Report 2006

Accounting policy extract – Intangible assets: customer lists
The fair value attributable to customer lists or portfolios at the point of acquisition is determined by discounting the expected future cash flows to be generated from that asset. . . . Amortisation periods are currently 10 years but will be dependent on the business. Separate values are not attributed to internally-generated customer lists or relationships.

Residual goodwill

IFRS also requires more information regarding intangibles which are not separately recognised but which are subsumed within the overall heading of goodwill. IFRS 3 contains an overriding disclosure requirement to disclose 'information that enables users of its financial statements to evaluate the nature and financial effect of business combinations . . .'.

One specific disclosure aspect required by the standard is 'a description of the factors that contributed to a cost that results in the recognition of goodwill'. For each intangible asset that is not recognised separately from goodwill, this requires an explanation of why the intangible's fair value could not be measured reliably. FIRST CHOICE HOLIDAYS provides an illustration of this new disclosure requirement.

FIRST CHOICE HOLIDAYS Annual Report 2006

Extract from Note 13, Investments
. . .

(c) Residual goodwill
A consistent process is undertaken at each acquisition to identify the fair value of separable assets and liabilities acquired, including the fair value of intangible assets, being brands, order books and customer databases. The residual goodwill on acquisition represents the value of assets and earnings that do not form separable assets under IFRS 3 but nevertheless are expected to contribute to the future results of the Group.

At 31 October 2006, the residual goodwill represents mainly:

- Market knowledge of particular geographic areas such as the Americas and the Far East;
- Knowledge of particular market segments, for example escorted tours;
- Involvement of existing management and employees and transfer of their knowledge of the operation of the business model;
- Integration synergies, particularly cost optimisation in our yacht holidays business;
- The ability to sell acquired product through existing channels and existing products through acquired channels.

Internally-developed intangibles

IAS 38 contains a prohibition on the recognition of the following internally-generated intangibles:

- brands,
- mastheads,
- publishing titles,
- customer lists,
- items similar in substance.

Impairment

UK GAAP

FRS 11, Impairment of fixed assets and goodwill, requires assets not to be recorded in the balance sheet at more than their *recoverable amount*, which is the higher of:

- net realisable value – what an asset could be sold for; or
- value in use – the present value of the cash flows which the asset is expected to generate.

FRS 11 only requires assets to be reviewed for impairment, that is for a reduction in their recoverable amount below book value, in specific circumstances. For goodwill and intangibles these circumstances are:

- when goodwill or intangibles appear in the balance sheet and are not amortised at all or are amortised over a period greater than 20 years;
- where there are indicators of impairment which suggest that the asset's book value may not be fully recoverable – these indicators include: persistent operating losses; negative operating cash flows; a significant fall in an asset's market value; a significant change in the competitive or regulatory environment;
- when an acquisition of a business took place in the previous year, an impairment review should take place at the end of the first full year following acquisition.

The impairment rules in FRS 11 apply also to tangible fixed assets and fixed asset investments.

International Financial Reporting Standards

Under IFRS, annual impairment reviews are automatic for goodwill, and for intangibles which are not being amortised or which are being amortised over more than 20 years.

For intangibles being amortised over 20 years or less, an impairment review is only required as a result of significant indicators of impairment being identified.

Revaluation

Both UK GAAP and IFRS place considerable restrictions on the opportunity to revalue intangibles. In practice, very few companies find they can satisfy the extremely demanding conditions set.

The conditions are very detailed but essentially intangibles can only be revalued if they are traded in an 'active market' and the fair value is identified by reference to an 'active market'.

IFRS specifically states that intangibles such as brands, newspaper mastheads, music rights, publishing titles, patents, etc. cannot be revalued because 'each such asset is unique'.

CHAPTER 15

Fixed asset investments

Fixed asset investment categories

Investments may be fixed assets or current assets. This chapter considers only investments which are fixed assets, i.e. held long-term, rather than for resale or as a temporary store of value.

Fixed asset investments fall into four categories:

1. investment in subsidiaries,
2. investment in associates,
3. investment in joint ventures,
4. other investments.

Under IFRS, other investments could include 'available for sale financial assets' and 'Held to maturity investments' (see below). Current assets investments could include those described as 'held for trading' (see Chapter 18).

UK GAAP

Investments in subsidiaries

In simple terms, a subsidiary undertaking is a company, partnership or unincorporated association, where the company owning the investment (the parent company) is able to control the board of directors, either by virtue of its voting power or in some other way. A parent company is required by law to produce group accounts, in which the profits, assets and liabilities of the subsidiary are combined with those of the parent company, as described in Chapter 28.

A company which is a parent company thus publishes two balance sheets: one for the company itself and a group balance sheet. This is demonstrated in the extract from the accounts of RMC shown below. The figures in the columns headed Parent are for investments owned directly by RMC itself.

RMC *Note to the 2003 accounts*

Note 13 Fixed asset investments

	Parent		Group	
	2003	2002	2003	2002
	£m	£m	£m	£m
Group undertakings	2,796.9	2,832.3	–	–
Joint ventures	0.9	3.6	61.1	77.5
Associated undertakings	–	–	38.5	70.9
Other investments	1.7	1.7	6.4	4.8
Total	2,799.5	2,837.6	106.0	153.2

Investments in associates

Where an investing company or group holds a *participating interest* in a company *and exercises significant influence*, that company is deemed to be an **associate**.

A *participating interest* is an interest held by the investor on a long-term basis to secure a contribution to its activities by the exercise of control or influence. A holding of 20% or more is presumed to be a participating interest unless shown to the contrary.

To *exercise significant influence* the investor must be actively involved and influential in the making of policy decisions on strategic issues: for example, on the expansion or contraction of the business, and on dividend policy.

Associates are covered in Chapter 29.

Investments in joint ventures

Where the investor holds a long-term interest in a company and shares control under a contractual arrangement, that company is deemed to be a **joint venture**.

Joint ventures are covered in Chapter 29.

Fixed asset investments

Whereas at first sight it may seem that these will consist entirely of investments of less than 20% this is not always the case. However, where a company has a holding of 20% or more in another undertaking, but does not treat it as an associated undertaking or as a participating interest, it should explain why. For example:

TT ELECTRONICS *Extract from note to 2003 accounts*

Fixed asset investments
TT electronics plc owns 24.4% of the equity share capital of Pressac plc. In 2003 TT electronics plc did not exercise significant influence over the financial or operating policies of Pressac plc and this holding was accounted for as an investment.

Other investments may include works of art (as with CORDIANT, formerly SAATCHI & SAATCHI). Investments in works of art, other than by art dealers, should be viewed with distinct suspicion; directors should not indulge their artistic tastes with shareholders' money. In the past this has sometimes been a warning sign of an arrogant top management.

They may also include life assurance policies and the company's own shares held for employee share option schemes (e.g. DIAGEO):

DIAGEO *Extracts from the notes to the 2003 accounts*

14. Fixed assets – investments
Investment in associates comprises the cost of shares, less goodwill written off on acquisitions prior to 1 July 1998, of £2,619 million plus the group's share of acquisition reserves of £415 million.

(a) **General Mills Inc** included in associates is the group's 79 million shares . . . valuing the group's interest at $3,745 million (£2,270 million).
(b) **Moet Hennessy** . . .
(c) **Investment in other associates** . . .
(d) **Investment in own shares** At 30 June 2003 investment in own shares comprised 42.8 million in respect of long term incentive plans . . . and 2.2 million in respect of savings-related share option schemes. The market value of these shares at 30 June 2003 was £291 million.

Other investments should be shown separately:

KINGFISHER *Extract from note to 2003 accounts*

Fixed asset investments

Other Investments	Listed in the UK £m	Listed Overseas £m	Unlisted £m
At 2 February 2002	0.4	4.0	6.1
Additions	–	–	3.4
Disposals and write-off	(0.2)	–	(0.4)
Effect of foreign exchange rate changes	. . .	0.2	0.3
At 1 February 2003	0.2	4.2	9.4

The aggregate market value should also be shown where it differs from cost (CA 1985, Sch. 4, para. 45). Unlisted investments should be shown at cost or valuation.

Disclosures on significant holdings

Where *either* a company holds 20% or more of any class of share in another company, *or* the book value of the holding is more than one-fifth of the other company's assets, the accounts must show

- the name of the other company;
- country of incorporation if not Great Britain;
- if unincorporated, the address of the business;
- identity of each class of share held;
- the proportion held.

Balance sheet presentation under UK GAAP

The Companies Act 1985 requires that where investments are shown as fixed assets, a further breakdown should be given, if individual amounts are material, either in the balance sheet itself or in notes:

(a) shares in group undertakings;
(b) loans to group undertakings;
(c) interests in associated undertakings;
(d) other participating interests;
(e) loans to undertakings at (c) and (d);
(f) other investments other than loans;
(g) other loans;
(h) own shares.

Points to watch

A holding may indicate

- the possibility of an eventual bid, particularly if the holder is predatory by nature;
- a blocking position taken by the holder to protect its trade interests from the risk of the company concerned being taken over by some (larger) competitor.

There is no hard and fast rule about which is which, and a holding could indicate a blocking position pending a possible bid in the distant future.

In this context it is worth checking whether directors have substantial holdings and, if so, whether any are nearing retirement age.

If the holding is of *20% or more* and the company is not treated as an associate, the chances are probably more in favour of a bid than a blocking position – the unwelcome holder of a substantial stake being unlikely to be given a seat on the board.

If the holding is of *25% or more* the holder is in the strong position of being able to block any arrangements and reconstructions that the company might wish to make

with creditors and members under s. 425 of the Companies Act 1985, which requires three-fourths to vote in favour.

Interlocking holdings

Where a number of companies under the same management have substantial holdings in each other or in another company, the holdings may be entirely innocent; but interlocking holdings can give scope for manipulation to the detriment of outside shareholders and should be viewed with caution.

A classic illustration of the dangers of interlocking holdings was provided by the affairs of several companies in the LOWSON GROUP, which came under investigation by the Department of Trade in 1973.

The appointed inspectors found that a number of defaults in the management 'were knowingly committed by Sir Denys [Lowson] and constituted grave mismanagement of the affairs of the companies concerned' and that in some transactions 'his motive was to obtain a very substantial gain for himself and his family'.

> **Take care where a chairman or chief executive's private interests seem difficult to distinguish from those of the group he or she manages.**

As Robert Maxwell showed in connection with PERGAMON and MAXWELL COMMUNICATION CORPORATION, danger lies in wait for shareholders, employees and pensioners, and for the reputations and profits of city institutions and auditors alike, once private and public interests become intertwined.

We have more to say about related party transactions in Chapter 25.

International Financial Reporting Standards

Subsidiaries, associates and joint ventures

The accounting treatment under IFRS of investments in subsidiaries, associates and joint ventures is dealt with in Chapters 28 and 29.

Other investments

The accounting treatment under IFRS of other investments is dealt in IAS 39, Financial instruments: recognition and measurement.

IAS 39 requires financial assets to be categorised under particular headings, which then determines their appropriate accounting treatment. Under IFRS, the term financial assets is very broad and includes other assets as well as investments. The principal categories, and the chapters in which they are dealt, are as follows:

- financial assets at fair value through profit or loss – this includes investments held for trading (see Chapter 18) and derivatives (see Chapter 23);
- held-to-maturity investments (see below);
- loans and receivables (see Chapter 17);
- available-for-sale financial assets (see below).

Held-to-maturity investments

These are essentially financial assets (quoted or unquoted) with the following features:

- fixed or determinable payments;
- fixed maturity;
- the holder of the investment must have positive intention and ability to hold to maturity.

Such investments are held in the balance at their amortised cost, which will reflect the amount repaid to the holder on maturity. The following example illustrates the calculations:

Example 15.1

A company acquired a bond at a cost of £95,000 inclusive of specific transaction costs. The bond will pay interest of £4,000 per annum, over the next five years. Interest will be received on the last day of each year. The issuer is required to redeem the bond on 31.12.X04 at par value of £110,000 so the investor will receive £114,000 (principal £110,000 plus final interest payment of £4,000) at the end of the final period.

The schedule of payments using the amortised cost method is as follows. The effective rate of interest has been determined by a computer program at 6.96% p.a.

Year	Amortised cost at start of year £	Interest income at 6.96% £	Cash flows £	Amortised cost at end of year £
20X0	95,000	6,610	(4,000)	97,610
20X1	97,610	6,790	(4,000)	100,400
20X2	100,400	6,990	(4,000)	103,390
20X3	103,390	7,190	(4,000)	106,580
20X4	106,580	7,420	(114,000)	0

Note that if such investments are sold before maturity, the accounting treatment becomes more complex, involving reclassification of other investments in the 'held to maturity' category – this is not referred to here.

Available for sale (AFS) financial assets

AFS financial assets are initially recorded at cost. At the balance sheet date, the assets will be revalued at fair value. Any increase compared with the previous amount will be recorded in equity in a separate reserve, usually referred to as a fair value reserve. AFS financial assets will usually appear in the balance sheet under the heading of fixed asset investments (but see also page 143).

When the asset is eventually sold, the profit or loss on sale must include any amounts relating to that asset held in the fair value reserve.

Example 15.2

An AFS financial asset is acquired on 15 June 20X4 at a cost of £155,000. At the subsequent balance sheet date of 31 December 20X4, the asset has a fair value of £185,000 as so £30,000 is included in the fair value reserve. At 31 December 20X5 the asset is still held and has a fair value of £225,000 so a further £40,000 is transferred to the fair value reserve

▶

making a cumulative total of £70,000. The asset is eventually sold on 12 March 20X6 for proceeds of £230,000.

Ignoring taxation, the profit on sale recorded in the income statement for the year ended 31 December 20X6 is £75,000 (i.e. £5,000 (= £230,000 – £225,000) + £70,000). This is the same amount that would have been arrived at had the asset never been revalued (£230,000 – £155,000).

The following are examples of accounting policy wordings:

ROYALBLUE GROUP *Annual Report 2005*

Accounting policy extract – Available for sale financial assets
The Group's investment in equity securities and certain debt securities are classified as available for sale financial assets. Subsequent to initial recognition, they are measured at fair value and changes therein . . . are recognised directly in equity. When an asset is derecognised, the cumulative gain or loss in equity is transferred to profit or loss.

CATTLES *Annual Report 2006*

Accounting policy extract – Financial assets
Management determines the classification of the group's financial assets at initial recognition into one of the following categories and re-evaluates this classification at each reporting date:

Loans and receivables
[See Chapter 17.]

Financial assets at fair value through profit or loss
This category has two sub-categories: financial assets held for trading; and those designated at fair value through profit or loss at inception. A financial asset is classified at fair value through profit or loss if acquired principally for the purpose of selling it in the short-term or if so designated by management. Derivatives (refer to the accounting policy entitled 'Derivative financial instruments and hedging activities') are also categorised as held for trading unless they are designated as hedges. [See Chapter 23.]

Held-to-maturity
Held-to-maturity investments are non-derivative financial assets with fixed or determinable payments and fixed maturities that the group has a positive intention and ability to hold to maturity.

Were the group to sell a significant amount of held-to-maturity assets the entire category would be tainted and reclassified as available-for-sale.

Available-for-sale
Available-for-sale investments are those intended to be held for an indefinite period of time, which may be sold in response to needs for liquidity or changes in interest rates, exchange rates or equity prices.

The group has not held any held-to-maturity or available-for-sale financial assets at any point during the period.

. . .

Financial assets are derecognised when the rights to receive cash flows from the financial assets have expired or where the group has transferred substantially all the risks and rewards of ownership.

Unlisted equity investments

IFRS contains a specific rule for investments which are unquoted *and* for which a reliable fair value cannot be obtained. IAS 39 requires that such investments shall be measured at cost.

Note that where a reliable fair value can be obtained, the investment *must* be measured and accounted for at fair value at each subsequent balance sheet date (see, for example, the HOME RETAIL GROUP and DAILY MAIL & GENERAL TRUST extracts below).

How fair value is determined

Companies usually explain in their accounting policies how they determine fair value for the various categories of investments. A typical wording is:

'Fair value is the amount for which a financial asset, liability or instrument could be exchanged between knowledgeable and willing parties in an arm's length transaction. It is determined by reference to quoted market prices adjusted for estimated transaction costs that would be incurred in an actual transaction, or by the use of established estimation techniques. The fair values at the balance sheet date are approximately in line with their reported carrying values unless specifically mentioned in the notes to the financial statements.'

HOME RETAIL GROUP and DAILY MAIL & GENERAL TRUST give details as to how they arrive at fair values, as shown in the illustrations below.

HOME RETAIL GROUP *Annual Report 2007*

Accounting policy extract

Fair value estimation
The quoted market price for assets held by the Group is the current bid price . . . The fair value of financial instruments for which there is no quoted price is determined by a variety of methods incorporating assumptions that are based on market conditions existing at each balance sheet date.

DAILY MAIL & GENERAL TRUST *Annual Report 2006*

Accounting policy extract – Investments
The fair value of listed securities is determined based on quoted market prices, and of unlisted securities on management's estimate of fair values determined by discounting future cash flows to net present value using market interest rates prevailing at the year-end.

CHAPTER 16

Stocks and long-term contracts

Different classes of stock

The three main classes for manufacturing companies

Most manufacturing companies have traditionally shown stocks as a single figure under current assets, described either as 'stocks', as 'inventories' or as 'stocks and work in progress', but these terms cover three very different classes of asset:

- items in the state in which they were purchased; these include raw materials to be used in manufacture, components to be incorporated in the product and consumable stores (such as paint and oil) which will be used in making it;
- items in an intermediate stage of completion ('work in progress');
- finished goods.

For wholesalers and retailers, stocks are almost entirely goods purchased for resale.

Sub-classification

The balance sheet formats in Sch. 4 of the Companies Act 1985 require stocks to be analysed under the following subheadings:

- raw materials and consumables;
- work in progress;
- finished goods and goods for resale;
- payments on account (for items of stock not yet received).

SSAP 9, Stocks and long-term contract, calls for the accounts to show the subclassification of stocks and work in progress 'in a manner which is appropriate to the business and so as to indicate the amounts held in each of the main categories'. For example, GLENMORANGIE's stock is mostly whisky:

GLENMORANGIE *Note to the 2003 accounts*		
15 Stocks		
	2003	2002
	£000	£000
Group		
Whisky	74,034	69,520
Other stocks	3,291	2,589
	77,325	72,109

UK GAAP

The matching principle

Expenditure on stocks which remain unsold or unconsumed at the balance sheet date (or upon work in progress which is incomplete) is carried forward into the following period and set against the revenue from the stocks when it arises. This is an application of what accountants term the matching principle, i.e. matching cost and revenue in the year in which the revenue arises rather than charging the cost in the year in which it is incurred.

Dead stock

Stocks and work in progress should be valued at the lower of cost and net realisable value, and any irrecoverable cost (e.g. due to deterioration or obsolescence) should be charged to revenue.

Allowing 'dead' stock to be carried forward at cost is a classic way of boosting profits.

Consistency

The method of valuing stock should be consistent and sets of accounts include a statement in the notes on how stocks have been valued:

THE BODY SHOP *Extract from accounting policies 2003*

Stocks are valued at the lower of cost and net realisable value. Cost is calculated as follows:

Raw materials	Cost of purchase on a first-in first-out basis.
Work in progress and finished goods	Cost of raw materials and labour together with attributable overheads.

Net realisable value is based on estimated selling price less further costs to completion and disposal.

DIAGEO *Extract from accounting policies 2003*

Stocks are stated at the lower of cost and net realisable value. Cost includes raw materials, direct labour and expenses, and an appropriate proportion of production and other overheads.

A particular point to look for is any statement of a change in the basis between year ends and, when one is made, why, and whether any indication is given of how much difference the change has made to the year-end stock figure and, hence, to profits.

The importance of stock valuation

The accurate valuation of stock on a consistent basis is important, because quite small percentage variations can very significantly affect profits (see Example 16.1).

Problems in valuing stock

Three main problems arise in valuing stock:

1. the price to be used if an item has been supplied at varying prices;
2. the value added in manufacture both to incomplete items (work in progress) and to completed items (finished goods);
3. the assessment of net realisable value.

Example 16.1 Stock valuation

	£000	£000
Sales		2,000
Cost of goods sold:		
Opening stock	600	
Purchases in period	1,500	
	2,100	
Closing stock	400	
		1,700
		300
Wages, overheads, etc.		200
Operating profit		100

Had the opening stock been overstated by 10% (at £660,000) and the closing stock undervalued by 10% (at £360,000), the cost of goods sold would appear £100,000 higher and the operating profit would have been wiped out.

Stocks in a large retail business

Having defined the main principles and problems, let us now look at stocks in practice, beginning with the control of stocks in a large retail business, where virtually all stocks are goods purchased for resale and the complications of work in progress (WIP) and finished goods do not arise.

The central management of most supermarkets controls the efficiency and honesty of local stores by charging goods out to those stores at selling price, and by maintaining overall stock control accounts in terms of selling price by broad product groups. By suitably analysing takings it will then be possible, for each of these product groups, to compare theoretical stock with actual stock:

$$\begin{array}{c}\text{Operating} \\ \text{stock at} \\ \text{selling} \\ \text{price}\end{array} + \begin{array}{c}\text{Deliveries} \\ \text{at selling} \\ \text{price}\end{array} - \text{Takings} = \begin{array}{c}\text{Theoretical} \\ \text{closing stock} \\ \text{at selling price}\end{array}$$

With this sort of operation, it is usual for the purpose of monthly, quarterly, half-yearly and annual accounts to deduct from the value of stock at selling price the normal gross profit margin:

> **TESCO *Extract from accounting policies 2003***
>
> Stocks comprise goods held for resale and properties held for, or in the course of, development and are valued at the lower of cost and net realisable value. Stocks in stores are calculated at retail prices and reduced by appropriate margins to the lower of cost and net realisable value.

SSAP 9 requires that before such a figure is used for the purposes of the annual accounts, it is tested to ensure that it gives a 'reasonable approximation of the actual cost'.

Stocks in a manufacturing business

Most manufacturing businesses employ a system of cost accounting. They do so:

- as an aid to price fixing, so that they can charge the customer with the materials used and the time actually taken to complete the job – as is the case with a motor repair garage or jobbing builder;
- in order to provide the estimating department with information on which to base future estimates or tenders; and/or
- as a means of controlling operating efficiency.

The type of record employed varies widely, from a few scribblings on the back of an envelope, to a cost system parallel to the normal financial system, reconciled with it but not part of it, right up to a completely integral cost and financial accounting system. In all but the first of these there is normally some form of stock record.

Methods of pricing issues from stock

A number of methods of pricing issues from stock are commonly employed and are acceptable today under UK GAAP. These methods include:

- First-in-first-out (FIFO): good storekeeping demands that goods should, as far as possible, be used in the order in which they are received. FIFO merely assumes for accounting purposes that the normal rules of good housekeeping have been followed.
- Average cost or weighted average price (AVCO): when an organisation receives a number of deliveries during an accounting period at a series of different prices, it is reasonable to take the average price (or, for more accuracy, the weighted average price).

Two other commonly-used methods are:

- standard cost;
- selling price less margin (see above, including the extract from TESCO).

The inclusion of overheads in stock

Companies are required to value work in progress and finished goods at the full cost of purchase plus the cost of conversion (inclusive of fixed overheads).

Costs of general management, as distinct from functional management, are excluded unless directly related to current production (as they may be to some extent in smaller companies), but the Companies Act 1985 does allow a reasonable proportion of interest on capital borrowed to finance production costs to be included in the value of stock; however, if this is done the amount must be disclosed.

Net realisable value

Net realisable value is:

> 'the actual or estimated selling price (net of trade but before settlement discounts) less:
>
> (a) all further costs to completion; and
> (b) all costs to be incurred in marketing, selling and distributing'.

Consignment stocks

Consignment stocks are stocks held by one party, *the dealer*, but legally owned by another party, *the manufacturer*. The terms of the agreement between them give the dealer the right to sell the stock in the normal course of his or her business or, at *his or her* option, to return it unsold to the legal owner.

FRS 5, Reporting the substance of transactions requires the agreement to be analysed to decide how it actually works in practice.

If it can be shown that the benefits and risks remain with the manufacturer until transfer of legal title; the stock will not be included in the dealer's balance sheet. For example CAFFYNS:

CAFFYNS *Note to the 2003 accounts*

Note 14 Stocks

	2003 £000	2002 £000
Group		
Vehicles	11,229	12,557
...		
Vehicles on consignment	5,510	6,756
...		
	19,725	23,629

In addition, non-interest bearing consignment vehicles excluded from the company balance sheet at 31 March 2003 had a cost of £772,000 (in 2000, £1,003,000).

The danger of rising stocks

Although SSAP 9's requirement to include production overheads in arriving at the cost of finished goods gives a fair picture when stocks are being maintained at prudent levels in relation to demand, when a manufacturer leaves production unchanged in periods of lower demand their inclusion can produce unduly optimistic profits (see Example 16.2). In practice, the profit from full production would be likely to be reduced by interest charges to finance carrying increased stock, but even so management may try to bolster profits in the short term by continuing high production in the face of falling demand. Rising stocks unmatched by rising turnover may give some warning here, and this can be monitored by the ratio stocks/turnover.

TERMINOLOGY

Stocks

Cost, in relation to stocks, is expenditure which is incurred in the normal course of business in bringing the product or service to its present location and condition. It includes, in addition to cost of purchase, costs of conversion that are appropriate to that location and condition.

Cost of purchase comprises purchase price including import duties, transport and handling costs and any other directly attributable costs, less trade discounts, rebates and subsidies.

Cost of conversion comprises:

- costs which are specifically attributable to units of production, e.g. direct labour, direct expenses and sub-contracted work;
- production overheads;
- other overheads, if any, attributable in the particular circumstances of the business to bringing the product or service to its present location and condition.

Production overheads are overheads incurred in respect of materials, labour or services for production, based on the normal level of activity, taking one year with another.

Net realisable value is the actual or estimated selling price (net of trade but before settlement discounts) less:

- all further costs to completion; and
- all costs to be incurred in marketing, selling and distributing.

Unit cost is the cost of purchasing or manufacturing identifiable units of stock.

Average price is the price computed by dividing the total cost of the item by the total number of units.

This average price may be arrived at by means of continuous calculation, a periodic calculation or a moving periodic calculation.

FIFO (first in, first out) represents the calculation of the cost of stocks on the basis that quantities in hand represent the latest purchases or production.

Example 16.2 Rising stocks

A company with a single-product factory faces a year in which demand is forecast to fall by 30% due to an economic recession.

Production overheads (rent of factory, etc.) = £1m
Production capacity = 100,000 units per annum
Variable costs = £10 per unit
Selling price = £25 per unit
Sales last year = 100,000 units

The management is faced with the decision of whether

(a) to continue at full production, hoping that demand will pick up sharply the following year if not sooner, and that it possibly won't fall quite as sharply as forecast; or

(b) to cut production by up to 30%.

Under SSAP 9, assuming demand does fall by 30%, the figures that will be reported at the end of the year under these two choices will be:

	(a) Full production	(b) Production cut by 30%
	Units	Units
Opening stock	20,000	20,000
Units manufactured	100,000	70,000
	120,000	90,000
Units sold	70,000	70,000
Closing stock	50,000	20,000
Fixed costs	1,000,000	1,000,000
Variable costs (£10 per unit)	1,000,000	700,000
Total costs	2,000,000	1,700,000
Costs per unit manufactured	£20	£24.285

Profit and loss account

	£	£
Sales (£25 per unit)	1,750,000	1,750,000
Cost of goods sold:		
Opening stock (£20 per unit)	400,000	400,000
Cost of units manufactured	2,000,000	1,700,000
less Closing stock by FIFO method	1,000,000 (£20)	485,700 (£24.285)
Cost of goods sold	1,400,000	1,614,300
Gross (or trading) profit	350,000	135,700

NOTE: A watchful auditor would require to be satisfied (i) as to the net realisable value of the closing stock under (a); and (ii) that the requirements of SSAP 9 regarding spreading of overheads on the basis of 'normal production' were met.

SPRING RAM *Extract from chairman's statement 1991*

A most satisfying result was achieved for the year under review, despite a generally very difficult economic climate. Group profits before tax advanced to a record £37.6m (1990 £30.1m), an increase of 25% on the previous year. Consolidated turnover of £194.2m (1990 £145.3m) . . . Earnings per share were 7.1p (1990 5.4p).

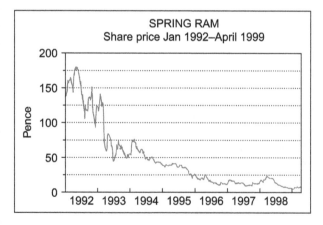

The example below is of a rising stocks/turnover ratio giving warning of trouble. It illustrates two key points. See if you can spot them.

But in market conditions described by the chief executive of one housebuilder, BELLWINCH, as 'certainly the worst in post-war years', SPRING RAM's results seemed too good to be true. The sharp rise in the ratio 'finished goods and goods for resale/turnover', to the unprecedented level of 13.5%, was a warning signal (see below).

SPRING RAM *Extracts from 1987–1991 accounts*

	1987 £000	1988 £000	1989 £000	1990 £000	1991 £000
Turnover	60,785	85,173	121,017	145,285	194,173
Stocks					
Raw materials	3,296	6,386	8,035	8,813	12,984
Work in progress	297	927	1,160	1,277	1,787
Finished goods and goods for resale	4,508	10,041	10,984	15,019	26,255
Total stocks	8,101	17,354	20,179	25,109	41,026
Ratios (%)					
Raw materials/turnover	5.4	7.5	6.6	6.1	6.7
WIP/turnover	0.5	1.1	1.0	0.9	0.9
Finished goods and goods for resale/turnover	7.4	11.8	9.1	10.3	13.5
Total stocks/turnover	13.3	20.4	16.7	17.3	21.1

The 1992 interim results showed further growth in turnover, profits and earnings per share. It wasn't until the week before the 1992 final figures were due to be announced that SPRING RAM issued a profit warning and asked for its shares to be suspended.

Profits at a bathroom manufacturing subsidiary had been overstated by £5.6m, mainly through the inflation of stock values and sales.

Key point 1

When a sector of the market is going through hard times, and the management of a company in that sector tells you 'we are going to buck the trend', be highly sceptical. Our experience is that they are about to run into very serious trouble.

Key point 2

If a company's results seem too good to be true, don't believe them.

Long-term contracts

Definition

A long-term contract is defined by SSAP 9 as 'a contract entered into for manufacture or building of a single substantial entity or the provision of a service where the time taken to manufacture, build or provide is such that a substantial proportion of all such contract work will extend for a period exceeding one year'.

Shipbuilders, constructional engineers and the like frequently engage in long-term contracts. Because of the length of time such contracts take to complete, to defer taking profit into account until completion would result in the profit and loss account reflecting not a true and fair view of the activity of the company during the year, but rather the results of those contracts which, by the accident of time, were completed by the year end.

SSAP 9 requirements on long-term contracts

In the past, accounting treatment of long-term contracts has varied enormously from company to company. BOVIS, for example, in its 1972 accounts noted that 'no provision is made for anticipated future losses' and a year later had to be rescued by P&O. At the other end of the scale companies like JOHN LAING pursued policies of extreme prudence: all losses were taken when they were foreseen, but no account was taken of profits on contracts unfinished at the end of the year.

SSAP 9 requires that 'The amount at which long-term contract work in progress is stated in periodic financial statements should be cost plus any attributable profit, less any foreseeable losses and progress payments received and receivable', and the amount of attributable profit included should be disclosed. Attributable profits on contracts are, however, only required to be taken up when 'it is considered that their outcome can be assessed with reasonable certainty before their conclusion'; if the outcome cannot be reasonably assessed, 'it is prudent not to take up any profit', so management is still left with a certain latitude, and the key point to watch for is undue anticipation of profits.

SSAP 9 also requires balance sheets to show how the amount included for long-term contracts is reached by stating:

- the amount of work in progress at cost plus attributable profit (i.e. profit or loss taken to date), less foreseeable losses;
- cash received and receivable at the accounting date as progress payments on account of contracts in progress.

KBC ADVANCED TECHNOLOGIES, which provides profit improvement services to the hydrocarbon and energy industries world-wide, provides an actual example:

KBC ADVANCED TECHNOLOGIES *Extracts from 2002 accounts*

Accounting policies

Long-term contracts
Turnover on long-term contracts is recognised using the percentage-of-completion method. Under this method revenues recorded represent the aggregate of costs incurred during the year and a portion of estimated profit . . .

Anticipated losses on contracts are charged to income in their entirety when the losses become evident.

Note 12 Work in progress

	2002	2001
This comprises:	£000	£000
Revenue recognized	21,142	17,209
Less: amounts invoiced	(17,681)	(13,572)
	3,461	3,637

In the accounts, work in progress is included under debtors and creditors under the following headings:

Amounts recoverable on contracts	4,465	4,302
Payments on account	(1,004)	(665)
	3,461	3,637

A further accounting policy example is as follows:

Example 16.3 Construction contracts

Revenue from construction contracts, including long-term service provision contracts, is recognised by reference to the stage of completion of contract activity at the balance sheet date. This is normally determined by the proportion that contract costs incurred to date bear to the estimated total contract costs, except where this would not be representative of the stage of completion. If the nature of a particular contract means that costs incurred do not accurately reflect the progress of contract activity, an alternative approach is used such as the achievement of pre-determined contract milestones.

Profit attributable to contract activity is recognised if the final outcome of such contracts can be reliably assessed. On all contracts, full provision is made for any losses in the year in which they are first foreseen.

Stock ratios

Introduction

Except when stocks are built up in anticipation of sharp price rises, well-run companies usually try to carry the minimum stock needed for the satisfactory running of their business. They do so:

- to minimise interest charges on the money tied up in stocks;
- to save unnecessary storage costs (including pilferage); and
- to reduce the risk of being left with goods that can't be sold due to deterioration, becoming obsolete or going out of fashion.

Although some distortion can occur with accelerating growth, because stock is a year-end figure while sales occur throughout the year (on average several months earlier), a rising stock ratio without any special reason is regarded as bad news, reflecting lack of demand for goods and/or poor stock control.

Stocks/turnover ratio

The most generally used stock ratio (as shown in our SPRING RAM example on page 127) is

$$\frac{\text{Stocks}}{\text{Turnover}} = \text{expressed as a percentage}$$

Stocks/turnover ratios vary enormously with the nature of a business. At one end of the scale, and apart from advertising agencies and other service industries, ready-mixed concrete companies probably have one of the lowest stocks/turnover figures of any industry: aggregates are extracted from the ground when required and the product is delivered the same day, so all that is needed in stock is a supply of fresh cement and fuel, giving a typical stocks/turnover figure of 5%. At the other end of the scale, a company that maintains depots of finished goods and replacement parts world-wide, such as a power transmission and mechanical handling systems manufacturer, can reasonably be expected to have a ratio as high as 35% in order to maintain a first-class service to its customers all over the world. Nevertheless, a high ratio in comparison to similar companies is undesirable.

For an average manufacturing company a stocks/turnover ratio of around 15–20% would be reasonable, increasing as the larger and more complex the goods made; for instance, an aircraft manufacturer might have stocks and work in progress representing 30–35% of turnover and this level could be subject to sharp fluctuations, depending on whether completed aircraft had been delivered to clients just before or just after the end of the year; in contrast, a company making a limited range of

nuts and bolts could probably run on a few weeks' stock, though if supplies were subject to interruption and/or shortages it might be prudent to carry more raw materials, and if orders tended to be erratic a higher stock of finished goods would be needed.

Stocks/cost of sales ratio

P&L accounts using Format 1 (see page 52) show the *cost of sales*. Where this is available it can be used to compute the average amount of stock held during the year, which can be expressed as so many months' stock, or so many days' stock. Many analysts take the average of the opening and closing stocks, which has a smoothing effect, and dampens the effect of a major change in stocks over the period.

Stock (months)

$$= \frac{(\text{Opening stock} + \text{Closing stock}) \div 2}{\text{Cost of sales}} \times 12$$

Stock (days)

$$= \frac{(\text{Opening stock} + \text{Closing stock}) \div 2}{\text{Cost of sales}} \times 365$$

Cost of sales/stock ratio

The previous ratio can be inverted, cost of sales/stock, to give the number of times the stock has been turned over in the year, the **stockturn**:

$$\text{Stockturn} = \frac{\text{Cost of sales}}{(\text{Opening stock} + \text{Closing stock}) \div 2}$$

Example 16.4 Calculation of stock ratios

Extracted from accounts:

	1998 £m	1999 £m	2000 £m
Year-end stock	2.10	2.20	3.00
Sales		10.00	12.00
Cost of sales		7.50	8.00
Ratios:			
Stocks/sales		22.0%	25.0%
Stock (days)		104.6 days	118.6 days
Stockturn		3.49×	3.08×

International Financial Reporting Standards

IAS 2, Inventories

IAS 2 uses the terms 'inventories' but apart from that is similar in measurement terms to SSAP 9. IAS 2 requires that inventories are measured at the lower of cost and net realisable value.

Where the standards differ is disclosure – IAS 2 requires more detailed disclosure than SSAP 9. Additional disclosures required by IAS 2, paragraph 36, include:

- the carrying amount of inventories carried at fair value less costs to sell (i.e. how much stock in the balance sheet is carried at expected selling price rather than cost, because it is expected to be sold at a loss);

- the amount of any inventories recognised as an expense in the period.

IAS 11, Construction contracts

As regards profit measurement, IAS 11 adopts a similar approach to SSAP 9 – both require the percentage of completion method. Revenue and expenses should be recognised by reference to the stage of completion of the contract activity at the balance sheet date. So the two standards should result in the same figures for the year's reported profit and for shareholders' funds in the balance sheet.

Where the standards differ is the requirements for disclosure of information in the notes to the accounts. IAS 11 contains an appendix with illustrative examples of disclosure.

CHAPTER 17

Debtors and other receivables

Categories of trade debtors and other debtors

Introduction

Debtors (also known as 'receivables') are a current asset, representing amounts owing to the business.

The Companies Act 1985 requires debtors to be sub-divided into:

- trade debtors – those arising from the sale of goods on credit;
- amounts owed by group undertakings – see Chapter 28;
- amounts owed by undertakings in which the company has a participating interest – see Chapter 29;
- other debtors (e.g. debts due from the sale of fixed assets or investments); and
- prepayments and accrued income (e.g. rent or rates paid in advance).

The amount falling due after more than one year should be shown separately for each item included under debtors. Other items which may be found shown separately under debtors (and which are not trade debtors for the purpose of computing collection ratios) include

- corporation tax recoverable (see Chapter 20);
- deferred taxation (see Chapter 20);
- loan notes (see Chapter 21).

Most companies show a single figure for debtors in their balance sheet, and give the required details in a note, as illustrated here.

THE BODY SHOP *Extract from note to the accounts*

Debtors	2003 £m	2002 £m
Amounts receivable within one year		
Trade debtors	25.5	28.0
Other debtors	5.8	12.1
Prepayments	5.5	6.8
	36.8	46.9
Amounts receivable after more than one year		
Other debtors*	7.1	6.6
	43.9	53.5

* Included in 'Other debtors' is £6.0 million relating to the deferred payment arrangement on the sale of the manufacturing division to Creative Outsourcing Solutions International Ltd.

Bad and doubtful debtors

The granting of credit inevitably involves some risk that the debtor will fail to pay, that is, will become a bad debt. When a business recognises that a debt is bad, the debt is written off to the profit and loss account. That is to say, the balance appearing as 'debtors' falls by the amount of the debt, and 'bad debts' appears as an expense. But this expense is shown separately in the published accounts only if the amount is material.

In addition, it is normal to set up a 'provision for doubtful debtors'. To do so a charge is made to the profit and loss account and, in the balance sheet, the cumulative provision for doubtful debtors is deducted from the total debtors. It is disclosed separately in the published accounts only if it is material. A provision for doubtful debtors may be specific, that is to say where management estimate the probable loss, studying each debt in turn; for instance, there is a 10% probability that Tin Pott plc will fail to pay its debt of £121,000, and they must therefore provide £12,100; or it may be general, for example, $2^1/2$% of total debtors; or a combination of the two.

The importance of debtors

Companies such as supermarket chains, whose turnover is almost entirely cash, will have very few debtors; the figure appearing in the balance sheet is likely to be largely prepayments and non-trade debtors. Trade debtors may have little significance. SAINSBURY, for example, with sales excluding VAT of £17,430m, showed trade debtors of a mere £116m in its 2003 accounts. At the other extreme are companies whose entire turnover is on credit terms, in which case very large amounts of working capital may be tied up in debtors. Here the efficiency with which credit accounts are handled, and the timing of the taking of profit where payments are by instalment, are of considerable interest to the analyst.

Debt collection period

The ratio trade debtors/sales can be used to monitor a company's credit control. Logically it should be sales including VAT, because the debtors include VAT, but the VAT inclusive figure is not usually available.

Analysts often feel that a more meaningful measure is that expressed in terms of time, as the debt collection period (or, simply, the collection period) in days or months:

$$\text{Debt collection period (days)} = \frac{\text{Trade debtors}}{\text{Sales}} \times 365$$

$$\text{Debt collection period} = \frac{\text{Trade debtors}}{\text{Sales}} \times 12$$

But it may be expressed simply as a percentage of sales:

$$\frac{\text{Trade debtors}}{\text{Sales}} \times 100$$

For example, given trade debtors of £8.219m and sales of £50m:

$$\text{Collection period} = \frac{£8.219m}{£50m} \times 365 = 60 \text{ days}$$

$$\text{Collection period} = \frac{£8.219m}{£50m} \times 12 = 1.97 \text{ months}$$

$$\frac{\text{Trade debtors}}{\text{Sales}} = \frac{£8.219m}{£50m} \times 100 = 16.4\%$$

Trade debtors/sales has the advantage of stating the percentage of the year's sales which were outstanding at the balance sheet date (which is correct) rather than suggesting that the business's debtors represent 60 days' sales (which we cannot say).

Apart from 'strictly cash' businesses like supermarkets, with virtually zero debtors, normal terms tend to be payment at the end of the month following delivery, so with 100% prompt payment the average credit given would be between six and seven weeks, making debtors about 12% of turnover. In practice, a figure of 15–20% is quite normal although some companies may, as a matter of policy, give more generous credit in order to give themselves a competitive edge, while others may factor their debts (see page 135) and so possibly show abnormally low debtors.

A falling collection period is generally a good sign – an indication of effective financial control – but it could reflect a desperate need for cash, involving extra discounts for cash and undue pressure on customers.

On the other hand, a marked rise in the ratio can be a warning signal. For example BOOSEY & HAWKES:

BOOSEY & HAWKES *Extracts from 1999 accounts*		
	1999	1998
	£000	£000
Profit and loss account		
Turnover	96,766	98,895
Note on debtors		
Trade debtors	25,568	20,699
Ratio (calculated)		
$\dfrac{\text{Trade debtors}}{\text{Turnover}} =$	26.4%	20.9%

The huge jump in the ratio suggested that there might be 'something nasty in the woodshed'. And so there was:

BOOSEY & HAWKES *Extracts from 2000 interim report*

CHAIRMAN'S STATEMENT

North American bad debt provision
Earlier this year the Board made a decision to investigate possible securitisation of trade debt. . . . As part of this process, we instigated a review of the sales ledger of our Chicago-based distribution company, Boosey & Hawkes Musical Instruments Inc. The results of this review indicated that, for the past two years, the level of bad debt provisioning was significantly inadequate and that some of these debts are irrecoverable.
. . . the directors have made a provision of £3.52m which has been fully charged as an exceptional item. Further investigations are being conducted into the levels of stock . . .

The Chairman commented: 'Having regard to the underlying trading performance of the Group and our confidence for the remainder of the year the directors have declared an interim dividend of 2.395p (1999: 2.395p)'.

But his confidence was misplaced. There was worse to come:

BOOSEY & HAWKES *Extracts from trading statement November 2000*

These investigations [conducted by Ernst & Young, the Group's auditors] are now nearing completion. A write-down of a further £10m will be required, which has arisen mainly in the areas of stock and prepayments as a result of a long series of misleading and incorrect accounting entries . . . The personnel responsible have been dismissed and the evidence supporting a legal action against them is being evaluated . . . A final dividend is therefore unlikely to be paid.

What we would like to know

The analyst can tell comparatively little about debtors unless a significant proportion of debtors are due after more than one year or unless the company discloses more than the minimum information required by law. Among the things which one would like to find out (and should be on the look out for any hint about in the chairman's statement or financial review) are the following:

- Is an undue proportion due from one major customer, or from customers in one industry?
- Would failure of one or two customers have a material effect upon the company's future?
- What is the age pattern of debtors? Are some unduly old?
- Is there adequate provision for bad and doubtful debts?
- Are any of the debts which fall due after more than one year very long-term in nature? In the UK debtors appear at their face value regardless of when they are due. In the USA, if a debt is not due within one year, it is usually necessary to discount it, i.e. to take account of imputed interest. Thus, a debt of $1m due three years hence might appear, taking interest into account at 10%, as $751,300.

Factors affecting the debt collection period

A short debt collection period is, other things being equal, preferable to a longer one; but as with many ratios one has to qualify this general principle. For by restricting credit and selling entirely for cash, a business can have a zero debt collection period; but if this drives its customers into the arms of competitors it is scarcely an improvement so far as the business as a whole is concerned. Subject to that qualification, any improvement in collection period, since it represents a reduction in overall debtors, means that more capital is available for other purposes, or that there is less need to borrow money from the bank.

At first sight it may seem that an increase in collection period represents a fall in the efficiency of the debt collection section. This is likely to be the case, but it is not necessarily so. The debt collection period may increase (decrease) between one period and another for a number of reasons:

1. if there is a policy change with regard to:
   (a) credit terms to existing customers; if, for example, the board of directors, to obtain a valuable order from a major customer, offers two months' credit instead of one;
   (b) the granting of credit; for instance, if potential customers whose credit ratings were formerly insufficient for them to be granted credit, are

granted credit – for such customers are unlikely to be among the fastest payers;
2. where there is poor credit management or accounts administration, for example:
   (a) if credit is given to unsatisfactory customers;
   (b) if the invoicing section falls behind; customers will not pay until they receive an invoice and, in general, pay at a fixed time determined by the date on which they receive it (e.g. at the end of the month in which they receive the invoice);
   (c) if statements are late – while some businesses ignore statements, others wait until they receive one;
   (d) if there is no consistent follow-up of overdue debts, by letter and/or telephone, or as a last resort in person;
3. if a subsidiary with an atypical debt collection period is disposed of or acquired (e.g. BASS's sale of the CORAL betting business and over 300 managed pubs in 1998 increased the group's debt collection period by several days);
4. if factoring or invoice discounting is introduced or discontinued (see pages 135–137).

Although it is necessary for most businesses to offer some credit, any unnecessary credit is bad management because it ties up money which (normally) earns no return, and which is subject to increased risk. Customers who are short of money, and who find that they can order things from a company without having to pay for them at the end of the month, tend to place more and more of their orders with that company; if they later go into liquidation, they may do so owing a hefty amount.

Debtors due after more than one year

Traditionally, liabilities were regarded as current if they were expected to fall due within one year. Similarly, assets were treated as current if it was expected that they would be turned into cash within one year. The Companies Act 1985 changed that. Debtors are shown under current assets whenever they fall due, though the amount falling due after more than one year is required to be shown separately for each item. The inconsistency is clearly evident in the accounts of MARKS & SPENCER (below) where the figure of £1,610.2m for net current assets in 2003 included as a current asset the item 'Debtors: Receivable after more than one year £1.547.5m':

MARKS & SPENCER *Group balance sheet 2003*

	2003 £m	2002 £m
Current assets		
Stocks	361.8	325.3
Debtors		
Receivable within one year	907.9	952.1
Receivable after more than a year	1,547.5	1,667.2
Investments	304.0	272.7
Cash at bank and in hand	167.9	543.4
	3,289.1	3,760.7
Current liabilities		
Creditors: due within one year	(1,678.9)	(1,750.8)
Net current assets/(liabilities)	1,610.2	2,009.9

The Act does not require the breakdown of debtors to be shown on the face of the balance sheet (as M&S does), but UITF Abstract 4 requires this where the amount is material in the context of net current assets. However, the misdescription 'net current assets' usually remains, leading the unwary to compute a false current ratio (see page 148). Presentation under IFRS is quite different (see below).

Hire purchase and credit sale transactions

Definitions

A *hire-purchase transaction* is a transaction in which the hirer agrees to hire goods from their owner in return for paying (usually) a deposit and a series of weekly, monthly, quarterly or yearly payments. The intention is that when the hiring period comes to an end, the ownership of the goods will pass to the hirer, sometimes on the payment of a nominal sum, sometimes with the final instalment; ownership, therefore, does not pass to the hirer until all payments have been made.

A *credit sale* is an outright sale (usually by a retailer) where payment by instalments is agreed in writing as a condition of the sale. Under a credit sale arrangement the property in the goods passes immediately to the purchaser, who becomes the owner of the goods, but payment is required to be made over a period.

Interest is normally charged by the seller both in credit sale and hire-purchase arrangements; the great difference between them is that in a credit sale the 'purchaser' owns the goods from the outset, whereas in the case of a hire-purchase sale, they do not become his or hers until the final payment is made. Thus the seller cannot reclaim the goods in the case of a credit sale if the purchaser defaults, whereas, subject to the terms of the agreement and the law on hire purchase, he or she can in the case of a hire-purchase transaction.

Amounts due under credit sale transactions are debtors, and normally appear with other trade debtors, though they may be shown separately. In the case of a hire-purchase transaction, there has, strictly speaking, been no sale, and the goods involved are still an asset of the seller; but, adopting the principle of 'substance over form' (FRS 5) most companies refer to 'hire-purchase debtors' or 'instalments due under hire-purchase agreements'.

Timing of profit taking

Although the legal form of the above arrangements clearly differ, in substance they are the same. The transaction is effectively a sale but with credit terms for the purchase consideration. There are therefore two elements of profit:

1. the profit on the sale of the goods themselves – this profit will be recognised at the point of sale;
2. interest on the amounts outstanding – this should be spread over the life of the agreement using the actuarial or effective interest rate method, so that the allocation

of interest reflects the balance outstanding period-by-period.

GUS *Annual Report 2000*

Accounting policies extract – Instalment and hire purchase debtors
The gross margin from sales on extended credit terms is recognised at the time of sale. The finance charges relating to these sales are included in the profit and loss account as and when instalments are received. The income in the Finance Division under instalment agreements is credited to the profit and loss account in proportion to the reducing balances outstanding.

Factoring and invoice discounting

Factoring

Factoring involves the sale of a company's trade debtors to a factoring house. Factoring houses offer three facilities:

1. the provision of finance for working capital;
2. a credit management and sales accounting service;
3. bad debt protection.

GUS *Information on hire purchase*

Note 18. Debtors	2003 Due within one year £m	2003 Due after more than one year £m	2002 Due within one year £m	2002 Due after more than one year £m
Trade debtors:				
Instalment and hire purchase debtors	198	53	129	39
Provision for unearned finance charges	(26)	(6)	(21)	(6)
	172	47	108	33
Instalment debtors	842	153	862	148
Other trade debtors	528	52	462	6
Total trade debtors	1,542	252	1,432	187

The provision of finance

This is the main reason why companies use factoring. The factor assesses the client's trade debtors and agrees the level of 'prepayment' that he or she will provide; this is normally between 70% and 80% of the value of the invoices. The client may then sell his or her existing trade debts to the factor and receive prepayment immediately; the debtors are informed that the debts have been factored, and are asked to make payment direct to the factor.

All new invoices then carry an assignment notice, asking the debtors to make payment direct to the factor. Copies of all invoices are sent to the factor, who will make the agreed prepayment. If the agreed level of finance is 75%, the client will receive the balance of 25%, less the factor's charges, as his or her debtors settle each invoice. The factor provides credit advice and runs the sales ledger, sending statements and reminders.

Service charge

A service charge is made, usually between 1% and 3%, depending on the number of customers and invoices involved. The factor also makes a finance charge on any funds drawn under the prepayment arrangement, usually at rates similar to bank overdraft rates of interest. Because factoring finance is based on the trade debtors, it fluctuates automatically with the level of business, and is thus more flexible than an overdraft.

Bad debt protection

There are two types of factoring agreement: 'with recourse' and 'without recourse' to the client. Under a with recourse agreement, the client takes the risk of bad debts, and the factor will pass the debt back to his or her client if the debtor has not paid within 90 or 120 days.

Most factors offer bad debt protection as an optional extra, providing cover on all *approved* invoices. The cover is for 100%, which compares favourably with the 80% offered by most credit insurance companies. Factors usually add between $1/4$% and $3/4$% to their service charge for bad debt protection, depending on the industry involved.

International factoring

An increasing proportion of British goods go to Western Europe, North America and other markets. Many exporters use factors primarily to obtain credit advice and bad debt protection, although prepayment finance is available.

Factors handling exports send correspondence and make telephone calls in the language of overseas customers, and know the local business practices; this usually enables them to obtain faster collection of export debts.

Invoice discounting

This is similar to factoring except that, under an invoice discounting arrangement, the client continues to run his or her sales ledger and collect the payments, which he or she banks to the account of the discounting company. When each debtor's payment is banked, the discounter deducts the prepayment already made to the client, plus charges, and pays the balance into the client's bank account.

Most invoice discounting agreements are with recourse, i.e. the client takes the risk of bad debts. Because the client goes on running the ledger and collecting payments, it is sometimes called *confidential invoice discounting*.

Factoring in the accounts

In the past it has not always been possible to tell from the accounts whether a company was using factoring or invoice discounting. However, under FRS 5, Reporting the substance of transactions, companies are normally required to disclose factoring and invoice discounting and the degree of debt protection.

Debt factoring is considered in Application Note C of FRS 5, which also covers invoice discounting. Accounting treatment depends upon the precise terms of the contract. If the debts are sold at a fixed price, with no recourse, the seller has no further interest in the debts which no longer appear in the balance sheet; but an interest charge will normally appear in the profit and loss account. See, for instance, PIC INTERNATIONAL:

PIC INTERNATIONAL *Extract from 1998 accounts*

Note 4 Interest

	1998	1997
	£m	£m
Interest payable and similar charges:		
On bank loans and overdrafts	15.2	20.6
Non recourse finance	1.4	2.0

In respect of the prior year non recourse finance, the Group was not obliged to support any losses and did not intend to do so. The providers of this finance . . . confirmed that they would not seek recourse from the Group.

However, when the factor or invoice discounter has full recourse in the event of bad debts, the substance of the transaction is that the company is taking all the risk, and the factor or invoice discounter is merely providing finance. The company's accounts would therefore show (where £80m was advanced by a factor, with full recourse, on debtors of £100m):

	£m
Current assets:	
Debtors	100
Current liabilities:	
Finance from factor	80

rather than debtors of £20m, as was long the case.

Loans receivable

Classification and presentation

FRS 25, Financial instruments: disclosure and presentation, defines a financial asset as including any asset that has a contractual right to receive cash. This includes trade debtors (trade accounts receivable) and loans receivable.

Under UK GAAP, trade debtors are stated at original cost (based on fair value of goods or services provided – see Chapter 8) less provision for impairment or doubtful debts.

Example

Cattles plc (www.cattles.co.uk) is a financial services company that includes the following divisions:

- a consumer credit division, which includes unsecured and secured personal loans, and hire-purchase credit facilities sold to consumer credit customers;
- a debt collection division, which provides a full debt recovery service for external clients and the consumer credit division;
- a corporate services division, which provides working capital finance to small and medium-sized enterprises in the business community.

The extracts below relate to the 2004 financial statements prepared on the basis of UK GAAP.

(Extracts from the 2006 financial statements prepared on an IFRS basis appear later in the chapter.)

CATTLES *Annual Report 2004*

The Balance sheet shows 'Customers' accounts receivable' amounting to £1,871m. Under UK GAAP this appears under the caption of 'Current assets' split between amounts falling due after more than one year of £1,143m and due within one year of £728m (see reference to UITF Abstract 4 above). Under IFRS, these amounts would be separately presented under non-current and current assets respectively (see CATTLES Annual Report 2006, below).

Accounting policies (extract)

Instalment credit agreements (part of note)
Interest receivable on secured and unsecured interest-bearing personal loan agreements is recognised on the accruals basis. In the case of hire purchase agreements, interest receivable is computed at the inception of the loan, added to the customer's

---

balance and released to profit on the 'sum of the digits'[1] basis. . . .

Customers' accounts receivable (part of note)
Customers' accounts receivable consist of amounts outstanding under instalment credit agreements, finance leases and factoring agreements including repayments not yet due at the year-end, less appropriate provision for bad and doubtful debts based upon the individual assessment of accounts and formulae related to past experience. . . .

1. This method is sometimes used as an acceptable approximation to the more precise actuarial method (as illustrated in Example 17.1 below). Suppose a finance agreement requires repayment over a one-year period by 12 monthly instalments. The so-called sum of the digits is $1 + 2 + 3 + 4 \ldots + 11 + 12 = 78$. If the total finance income on the agreement was, say, £15,600 then 1/78 (= £200) would be allocated to the first instalment, 2/78 (= £400) to the second instalment, and 12/78 (= £2,400) to the final instalment.

Loans receivable that include a premium on final settlement

Accounting for loans receivable may, in some cases, be more complex. Apart from entitlement to interest payments, say, every six months, the loan holder may also be entitled to a premium at the end of the term of the loan. Example 17.1 illustrates the actuarial or amortised cost (as is it is now frequently referred to) method of allocating finance income.

International Financial Reporting Standards

Overview

IAS 39 requires financial assets to be categorised under particular headings, which then determines their appropriate accounting treatment (see Chapter 15). Under IFRS, the term 'financial assets' is very broad and includes assets

---

Example 17.1

A Limited lends £100,000 to B Limited. The loan carries an interest coupon of 4.7% per annum (fixed) and has a term of five years, At the end of this period, the principal amount of the loan will be repaid with a premium of £25,000 (i.e. total repayment of £125,000). The fixed interest of 4.7% amounts to £59,000 per annum and is paid at the end of each year (4.7% × £125,000 = £5,900).

Under the amortised cost method, the schedule of interest income and cash flows will be as follows. The effective rate of interest is 10% per annum:

Year	Amortised cost at start of year £	Profit and loss account[1,2] – interest income at 10.0% £	Cash flows £	Balance sheet[3] – amortised cost at end of year £
20X0	100,000	10,000	5,900	104,100
20X1	104,100	10,400	5,900	108,600
20X2	108,600	10,900	5,900	113,600
20X3	113,600	11,300	5,900	119,000
20X4	119,000	11,900	130,900*	–

*£125,000 + £5,900

1. The interest income column shows how much interest received is credited to the profit and loss account each period.
2. The effective interest rate (10% in this example) would normally be calculated using a computer program – it is the rate which effectively equates the present value of the cash receipts with the initial amount of £100,000. In the first year, the closing balance is £100,000 + 10% of £100,000 – £5,900 = £104,100 and so on.
3. The amortised cost at the year end represents the balance sheet asset for loans receivable.

other than investments. The principal categories, and the chapters in which they are dealt, are as follows:

- financial assets at fair value through profit or loss – this includes investments held for trading (see Chapter 18) and derivatives (see Chapter 23);
- held-to-maturity investments (see Chapter 15);
- loans and receivables (see below);
- available-for-sale financial assets (see Chapters 15 and 18).

IAS 1 requires all asset categories, including trade and other receivables, to be grouped under the subheadings of either current or non-current assets. For an asset to be classified as current it must be 'expected to be realised within twelve months after the balance sheet date'.

Trade and loan receivables

IAS 39 defines loans and receivables as financial assets with fixed or determinable payments and requires them to be measured at amortised cost using the effective interest method (see under UK GAAP above).

IFRS refers to 'trade receivables' as opposed to 'trade debtors' under UK GAAP. The carrying amount in the balance sheet must be assessed for impairment (see below).

Any element of the receivable not due within 12 months of the balance sheet date must be separately disclosed under 'non-current assets' in accordance with IAS 1. Contrast this with UK GAAP, which requires all debtors to be classified under current assets, with separate disclosure of non-current element. IFRS make for more logical ratio analysis!

The extracts below refers to revenue recognition (see Chapter 8) as well as classification and a carrying amount in the balance sheet.

HOME RETAIL GROUP *Annual Report 2007*

Accounting policy extract – trade receivables
Trade receivables are recognised and carried at original invoice amount less provision for impairment. The gross margin from the sale of a product on extended credit terms is recognised at the time of sale of the retail product. The finance charges relating to the sale of financial services are included in the income statement as and when instalments are received[1]. Income under instalment agreements is

---

credited to the income statement using the effective interest method[2].

A provision for impairment of trade receivables is established when there is objective evidence that the Group will not be able to collect all amounts due according to the original terms of receivables. The amount of the provision is recognised in the balance sheet[3], with the cost of unrecoverable trade receivables recognised in the income statement immediately.

Accounting policy extract – revenue recognition
[part of the note referring to interest income]
Interest income on customer store card accounts and loans is recognised as revenue on a time-proportion basis using the effective interest method. When a receivable is impaired, the Group reduces the carrying amount to its recoverable amount being the estimated future cash flow discounted at the original effective interest rate, and continues to recognise the unwinding of the discount as interest income[4].

1. See discussion above under UK GAAP, Hire purchase and credit sales transactions.
2. See Example 17.1 above, which illustrates the calculations in the effective interest rate (EIR) method.
3. IAS 39 paragraph 58 requires the entity to assess at each balance sheet date whether there is any objective evidence that a financial asset or group of financial assets is impaired.
4. IAS 39 paragraph 63 requires impairment to be determined on the basis of the present value of the estimated future cash flows (discounting is not explicitly required under UK GAAP).

Example 17.2

A finance company has a loan receivable with a carrying amount of £200,000. No further interest will be received on this loan owing to the borrower's financial situation and it has been agreed that £150,000 will be received in one year's time.

Under UK GAAP, the impairment provision would normally be calculated on an undiscounted basis at £50,000 (£200,000 – £150,000).

Under IFRS, the provision must be calculated on a discounted basis. Using a discount rate of 8% for the purposes of illustration, the recoverable amount of the loan receivable is £150,000 divided by 1.08 = £138,889. The loan receivable would be presented in the balance sheet at £138,889 and the income

▶

statement charged with an impairment loss amounting to £61,111 (£200,000 – £138,889).

Assuming the amount received turns out to be £150,000, the difference between the carrying amount of £138,889 and the cash of £150,000 (= £11,111) would be credited to the income statement as finance income over the remaining period of the lease (sometimes referred to as 'unwinding of discount').

CATTLES *Annual Report 2006*

Accounting policy extract – financial assets
Management determines the classification of the group's financial assets at initial recognition into one of the following categories and re-evaluates this classification at each reporting date:

Loans and receivables
Loans and receivables are non-derivative financial instruments with fixed or determinable payments that are not quoted in an active market. They arise when the group provides money directly to a customer with no intention of trading the receivable. This classification includes advances made to

customers under hire purchase agreements and acquired debt. . . .

[The reminder of the policy note refers to: financial assets at fair value through profit or loss; held-to-maturity; available-for-sale – see Chapter 15.]

Accounting policy extract – revenue recognition

Interest income
Interest income is recognised in the income statement for all financial assets measured at amortised cost using the effective interest method. The effective interest method is a method of calculating the amortised cost of a financial asset and allocating the interest income over the relevant period. The effective interest rate (EIR) is the rate that exactly discounts estimated future cash flows through the expected life, or contractual term if shorter, of the financial asset to the net carrying amount of the financial asset[1]. When calculating the EIR, the group estimates cash flows considering all contractual terms of the financial instruments, such as early settlement options, but does not include an expectation for future credit losses. The calculation includes all fees charged to customers, such as acceptance or similar fees, and direct and incremental transaction costs, such as brokers' commissions and certain agents' remuneration . . .

1. See example calculations in Example 17.1 above.

CHAPTER 18

Current asset investments; cash at bank and in hand

Current asset investments – UK GAAP

Introduction

As explained in Chapter 15, investments may be held as fixed assets or as current assets. This chapter considers only investments which are current assets – i.e. held short-term, either for resale or as a temporary store of value – and not intended for use on a continuing basis in the company's activities.

Types of current asset investments

Current asset investments include:

1. Short-term government and other listed securities:
   (a) intended to be held to maturity;
   (b) not intended to be held to maturity (but for trading).
2. Certificates of deposit.
3. Certificates of tax deposit.
4. Commercial paper.
5. Short-term deposits, e.g. money market deposits.
6. Short-term local authority bonds.
7. Options and warrants.
8. Other unlisted investments.

Accounting for current asset investments

A current asset investment is initially recorded at its purchase cost, including expenses, and is normally included in the balance sheet at the lower of cost and net realisable value. It must be written down to its net realisable value at the balance sheet date if that is less than its cost, and the loss taken to the P&L account. If at a subsequent balance sheet date the net realisable value has increased again, that higher value (up to the purchase cost) must be taken as the balance sheet value and any increase credited to the P&L account.

Under the Companies Act 1985 historical cost principles can be replaced by alternative accounting rules to allow for revaluations. The provisions allow investments of any description to be shown either at market value determined at the date of their last valuation or at a value ('fair value') determined on any basis which appears to the directors to be appropriate in the circumstances of the company. The method of valuation and the reasons for adopting it must be shown in the notes to the accounts.

In theory this makes a variety of treatments possible, including the occasionally used practice known as *marking to market*, where investments are written up to market value and the profit taken to the profit and loss account. So any note in the accounting policies on current asset investments should be read carefully. For example GLAXOSMITHKLINE:

GLAXOSMITHKLINE *Extract from the note on accounting policies in the 2003 accounts*

Current asset investments
Current asset investments are stated at the lower of cost and net realisable value.

In the case of securities acquired at a significant premium or discount to maturity value, and intended to be held to redemption, cost is adjusted to amortise the premium or discount over the life to maturity of the security. Floating rate bonds are stated at cost . . .

Equity investments are included as current assets when regarded as available for sale.

Current asset investments in practice

Many listed companies only have cash and short-term deposits. Some, like THE BODY SHOP, seem to prefer to hold cash. But there are groups which do have very large amounts of current asset investments, e.g.:

GLAXOSMITHKLINE *Extracts from the 2003 accounts*

Note 25 Net debt

	2003 £m	2002 £m
Liquid investments	2,493	1,256
Cash at bank	962	1,052
	3,455	2,308

At the balance sheet date the Group's liquid investments had an aggregate market value of £2,509 million (2002 – £1,264 million).

Some companies, like REUTERS, draw a distinction between government securities and other listed investments and, within unlisted securities, between CDs (certificates of deposit), term deposits and other investments:

REUTERS GROUP *Extract from the notes to the 2003 accounts*

Note 19. Short-term investments

		2003 £m	2002 £m
Listed			
Government securities:	UK	10	23
	Overseas	18	29
Other deposits:	Overseas	109	329
		137	381
Unlisted			
Certificates of deposit		1	2
Term deposits:	UK	47	47
	Overseas	32	29
Other deposits:	UK	24	4
	Overseas	381	107
		485	189
Total short-term investments		622	570

Significance of short-term investments

Cash rich companies like GLAXOSMITHKLINE and REUTERS have a significant part of their assets in short-term investments, but they are not central to the operation of the company. However, in a few companies they are. For example C.H. BAILEY:

C.H. BAILEY *Extracts from 2000 accounts*

Group balance sheet	2000 £	1999 £
Fixed assets . . .		
Current assets:		
Stocks and WIP	75,279	165,443
Debtors	794,737	762,625
Current investments	7,821,838	7,816,789
Cash at bank and in hand	748,407	859,950
	9,440,261	9,604,807
. . .		
Net assets	15,789,974	15,821,829

In 2000 the Group made a pre-tax loss of £265,661, while income from current asset investments was reported as £351,754, and profit from sale of investments £673,521.

As we pointed out earlier, the controlling shareholder of a company can do very much what he likes within his own personal feifdom. Many do, though some less patently than others.

Availability of short-term investments

Do not assume that current asset investments are necessarily available to meet current liabilities; read the small print (e.g. TATE & LYLE):

TATE & LYLE *Note from 2003 accounts*

Current asset investments	2003 £m	2002 £m
Listed on overseas exchanges	30	31
Loans, short-term deposits and unlisted fixed interest securities	97	32
	127	63

Cash at bank and in hand

The last item among current assets in the standard formats is cash at bank and in hand. Apart from this, the Companies Acts contain no specific requirements on cash balances; and while the sums involved can be considerable, most companies do not explain the amount shown either by way of note or in their accounting policies:

DIAGEO *Extract from the consolidated balance sheet as at 30 June 2003*

	2003 £million	2002 £million
. . .		
Cash at bank and liquid resources	1,191	1,596
. . .		

Cash at bank and in hand forms part of Cash as defined in FRS 1. It is closely related to current asset investments; indeed while many companies previously treated deposits as current asset investments, others treated them as bank balances.

Cash at bank and in hand is shown on the face of the balance sheet, but the formats are inconsistent: loans and overdrafts, as we shall see in Chapter 19, are relegated to a note.

Where a group has both credit balances and overdrafts with the same bank, the question arises as to the extent to which one can be set off against the other (and how this should be reflected in the accounts). Many groups have cash pooling arrangements with their bank.

Guidance on offsetting is provided by FRS 5, Reporting the substance of transactions.

Disclosure requirements

Disclosure requirements, which are the same whether an investment is a fixed asset or a current asset, are as follows:

1. the amount relating to listed investments;
2. the aggregate market value of listed investments must be shown if different from the book value, and the stock exchange value if it is less than the market value;

3. various details must be provided where the investment is 'significant', i.e. where:
   either it is 20% or more of the nominal value of the shares of that class in the investee,
   or it represents more than 20% of the investor's own assets; the details to be disclosed are:
   (a) the name of the investee;
   (b) its country of incorporation (if outside Great Britain); and
   (c) a description of the investment and the proportion of each class of share held.

Current asset investments – IFRS

Under IFRS all investments must first of all be classified in accordance with IAS 39, Financial instruments: recognition and measurement.

Fixed asset investments are dealt with in Chapter 15 and, subject to satisfying the relevant criteria may be classified as:

- investments in subsidiaries;
- investments in associates;
- investments in joint ventures;
- held to maturity investments;
- available for sale investments.

Current asset investments may be classed as either 'held for trading', providing the demanding criteria of IAS 39 can be satisfied, or as 'available for sale'.

Held for trading (HFT)

The IAS 39 definition of held for trading is complex, but the relevant condition here is that the asset was acquired principally for the purpose of selling in the near term. IAS 39 contains Application Guidance which states that 'trading generally reflects active and frequent buying and selling, and financial instruments held for trading generally are used with the objective of generating a profit from short-term fluctuations in price or dealer's margin'.

In the situations envisaged in this chapter, the category is likely to apply mainly to businesses which trade partly or wholly in investments on a regular basis as one of their main business activities.

HFT investments should be stated in the balance sheet at fair value, with changes in fair value dealt with through the income statement.

Available for sale (AFS)

AFS investments should also be stated in the balance sheet at fair value. However changes in fair value should be dealt with in equity (usually presented as a movement on a separately designated reserve, a 'fair value reserve'). Gains held in fair value reserve will not usually be included in the Income statement until the year in which the investment is sold, as the extract below shows.

DAILY MAIL & GENERAL TRUST *Annual Report 2006*

Accounting policies (extract)
Investments are classified as either held-for-trading or available-for-sale.

Where securities are held-for-trading purposes, gains and losses arising from changes in fair value are included in net profit or loss for the period.

For available-for-sale investments gains and losses arising from changes in fair value are recognised directly in equity, until the security is disposed of or is determined to be impaired, at which time the cumulative gain or loss previously recognised in equity is included in the net profit or loss for the period. The fair value of listed securities is determined based on quoted market prices, and of unlisted securities on management's estimate of fair value determined by discounting future cash flows to net present value using market interest rates prevailing at the year end.

Companies usually explain in their accounting policies how they determine fair value for the various categories of investments, as the following example shows:

HOME RETAIL GROUP *Annual Report 2007*

Accounting policy extract

Fair value estimation
The fair value of financial instruments traded in organised active financial markets is based on quoted market prices at the close of business on the balance sheet date. The quoted market price for assets held by the Group is the current bid price.

Cash at bank and in hand – IFRS

Under IFRS, the above should be presented in the balance sheet, under the sub-heading of current assets, and described as 'cash and cash equivalents'.

This also links in with the cash flow statement under IAS 7 (see Chapter 26), where the standard requires the cash and cash equivalent at the foot of the cash flow statement to be reconciled to the relevant heading(s) in the balance sheet.

The term 'cash and cash equivalents' is usually explained in the accounting policies note, as the following example shows:

DAILY MAIL & GENERAL TRUST *Annual Report 2006*

Accounting policies (extract)

Cash and cash equivalents
Cash and cash equivalents comprise cash in hand, short-term deposits and other short-term highly liquid investments that are readily convertible to a known amount of cash and are subject to an insignificant risk of changes in value.

CHAPTER 19

Creditors and provisions

Creditors

Presentation

Most companies use balance sheet Format 1 (set out in the Companies Act 1985), which nets out creditors falling due within one year (also known as current liabilities) against current assets to produce net current assets (liabilities).

Amounts falling due after one year are then deducted from total assets less current liabilities to give net assets; see the example from THE BODY SHOP below.

Types of creditor

The following items are required to be shown, if material:

- debenture loans (see Chapter 22);
- bank loans and overdrafts (see Chapter 21);
- payments received on account;
- trade creditors;
- amounts owed to group undertakings (see Chapter 28);
- amounts owed to undertakings in which the company has a participating interest (see Chapter 29);
- other creditors, including taxation and social security;
- accruals and deferred income.

Details of creditors are usually given in the notes rather than in the balance sheet itself.

THE BODY SHOP *Extract from 2003 Group balance sheet*

	Note	2003 £m	2002 £m
Fixed assets			
Intangible assets		34.7	37.7
Tangible assets		67.8	74.4
Investments		4.7	4.7
		107.2	116.8
Current assets			
Stocks		49.1	52.2
Debtors		36.8	46.9
Debts due after more than one year		7.1	6.6
Cash at bank and in hand		25.9	5.5
		118.9	111.2
Creditors: amounts falling due within one year	16	(96.9)	(99.5)
Redeemable convertible loan notes		–	(1.4)
		96.9	100.9
Net current assets		22.0	10.3
Total assets less current liabilities		129.2	127.1
Creditors, amounts falling due after more than one year	17	(1.6)	(1.8)
Provisions for liabilities and charges		(1.6)	(1.3)
[Net assets]		126.0	124.0

THE BODY SHOP *Extract from 2003 accounts*

16. Creditors: Amounts falling due within one year

	2003 £m	2002 £m
USA loans	0.3	0.2
Bank loan	45.6	44.9
Bank overdraft	0.4	0.3
Obligations under finance leases	0.2	–
Trade creditors	12.2	16.3
Corporation tax	5.0	4.7
Other taxes, social security costs	5.6	3.4
. . .	. . .	. . .
Other creditors	5.7	5.8
Accruals	14.2	16.3
	96.9	99.5

Note 17 (not shown) is mainly concerned with bank and other loans falling due after more than one year.

Trade creditors represent money owed for goods supplied. The size of trade creditors shows the extent to which suppliers are financing a company's business. For example, TESCO's suppliers finance not only its stock and debtors, but also its money market investments, earning interest for TESCO, not for its suppliers:

TESCO *Extracts from 2003 accounts*

	2003 £m	2002 £m
Current assets		
Stocks	1,140	929
Debtors	662	454
Investments	239	225
Cash at bank and in hand	399	445
	2,440	2,053
Creditors: Amounts falling due within one year		
. . .		
Trade creditors	2,196	1,830

Taxation and social security are each shown separately. Taxation due within 12 months will normally include one year's corporation tax and any foreign tax due.

An *accrual* is an apportionment of a known or determinable future liability in respect of a service already partly received. Thus, a business paying rent of £60,000 half-yearly in arrears on 30 June and 31 December would, if it had an accounting year ending 30 November, show an accrual of £50,000 (the five months' rent from 1 July to 30 November unpaid at the end of its accounting year).

Also under creditors may appear various items that are not in the example from THE BODY SHOP.

Deferred income is money received by or due to the company but not yet earned. Companies like VODAFONE GROUP (see below), which take a month's rental in advance, may well have greater accruals and deferred income than trade creditors.

VODAFONE GROUP *Note to the 2003 accounts*

18. Creditors:
Amounts falling due within one year

	2003 £m	2002 £m
Bank loans and overdrafts	1,078	1,219
Commercial paper	245	–
Finance leases	107	100
Trade creditors	2,497	3,335
Amounts owed to associated undertakings	13	10
Taxation	4,137	3,107
Other taxes and social security costs	855	509
Other creditors	1,342	1,485
Accruals and deferred income	3,407	3,179
. . .	. . .	. . .
	14,293	13,455

Deposits: in addition to deposits in respect of a contemplated purchase (included under payments received on account), deposits may have been charged where goods have been despatched in containers, drums, barrels or boxes, to ensure their return. The container, etc., remains part of the stock of the despatching company until it becomes apparent that it will not be returned (e.g. when the return period has elapsed), when it is treated as having been sold.

In financial companies, where deposits are a major item, representing money deposited to earn interest, they are shown as a separate heading.

Payments received on account arise where a *customer* is asked as a sign of good faith to deposit money in respect of a contemplated purchase. If the purchase goes through, the deposit becomes a part payment and ceases to appear under creditors. Should the sale not be consummated, the deposit would normally be returned, though it could conceivably be forfeited in certain circumstances.

the TESCO example we showed above. In contrast, in a sector like building materials, you may find the company *has* to keep large stocks in order to provide a really good service to its customers world-wide, and to give them plenty of credit to be competitive. For example the printing group ST IVES:

Working capital and liquidity ratios

Working capital ratios

Now that we have described stocks, debtors and creditors, this may be a good place to deal with working capital, the working capital ratio, and liquidity ratios.

 Watch the working capital ratio.

The working capital ratio is important for two reasons:

- Firstly, if it is high, expansion of the business, especially rapid expansion, is going to gobble up cash like crazy.
- Secondly, if it is not kept under control, the business will eat up more cash than it should.

Some types of business are well placed with working capital. Supermarkets do particularly well, as illustrated by

ST IVES *Working capital ratio 2002*

	2002 £m	2001 £m
Stocks	15.444	21.134
+ Trade debtors	61.952	77.974
– Trade creditors	(32.630)	(38.830)
Working capital	44.766	60.278
Turnover	466.806	498.154
Working capital ratio	**9.6%**	**12.1%**

Had the working capital ratio remained at the 2001 level in 2002, the amount tied up in working capital would have been £466.806m × 0.121 = £56.483m, rather than £44.766m. Having £11.717m less tied up has saved over £0.5m interest on borrowings.

Let's see how well THE BODY SHOP has controlled its figure over the last eight years:

THE BODY SHOP *Working capital 1996 to 2003*

Year end	1996 £m	1997 £m	1998 £m	1999 £m	2000 £m	2001 £m	2002 £m	2003 £m
Stocks	37.6	34.8	47.7	38.6	44.7	51.3	52.2	49.1
+ Trade debtors	27.5	31.7	31.3	27.8	30.3	30.3	28.0	25.5
– Trade creditors	7.7	10.2	11.0	13.0	20.5	10.7	16.3	12.2
Working capital	57.4	56.3	68.0	53.4	54.5	70.9	63.9	62.4
Turnover (Sales)	256.5	270.8	293.1	303.7	330.1	374.1	379.6	378.2
RATIOS								
Stocks/Sales	14.7%	12.9%	16.3%	12.7%	13.5%	13.7%	13.8%	13.0%
Trade debtors/Sales	10.7%	11.7%	10.7%	9.2%	9.2%	8.1%	7.4%	6.7%
Trade creditors/Sales	3.0%	3.8%	3.8%	4.3%	6.2%	2.9%	4.3%	3.2%
Working capital/Sales	22.4%	20.8%	23.2%	17.6%	16.5%	19.0%	16.8%	16.5%

Comment on The Body Shop's ratios

Stocks/sales In 1998 the ratio jumped sharply to 16.3%. If stocks had increased in 1998 in line with the increase in sales, they would have been £37.7m at the 1998 year end, instead of £47.7m.

The company had plenty of cash at the year end, so the £10m extra stock wasn't increasing the overdraft. But even so it could have earned a useful £0.5m on deposit. Stock levels returned to a more normal level in the following years.

Trade creditors/sales This ratio is small, suggesting that THE BODY SHOP pays its suppliers more quickly than most.

Working capital/sales After peaking at 23.2% in 1998, this overall ratio was brought well below 20% by new management.

Liquidity ratios

The two ratios most commonly used in assessing a company's liquidity are concerned with current assets (stocks and WIP, debtors and cash) and current liabilities (creditors, bank overdraft and any debts due to be settled within the next 12 months):

1. Current ratio

$$= \frac{\text{Current assets}}{\text{Current liabilities}}$$

2. Quick or liquidity ratio

$$= \frac{\text{Current assets} - \text{Stock}}{\text{Current liabilities}}$$

The Companies Act 1985 requires all amounts owing by the company to be included under creditors, with amounts due within one year and after one year being shown separately. When they can be identified, provisions for amounts due within one year should be included in current liabilities.

Current ratio

The current ratio is a broad indicator of a company's short-term financial position: a ratio of more than 1 indicates a surplus of current assets over current liabilities. A current ratio of 2 or more used to be regarded as prudent in order to maintain creditworthiness, but in recent years a figure of about 1.5 has become quite normal, and a higher figure isn't necessarily a good sign: it may be due to excessive stocks or debtors, or it may mean that the directors are sitting on an unduly large amount of cash which could be more profitably invested.

When looking at an individual company's current ratio, there is no simple rule of thumb on what the company's ratio 'ought' to be, because it so much depends on a number of different factors, including the following:

1. *The nature of the company's business.* If large stocks and the giving of generous credit terms are normal to the business, the current ratio needs to be higher than the general average, whereas a retail business with only cash sales, no work in progress and stocks financed mainly by suppliers (i.e. with creditors being a large item) may be expected to have a lower than average current ratio.
2. *The quality of the current assets.* Stocks, for example, may be readily saleable (e.g. gold) or virtually unsaleable (e.g. half-completed houses in a property slump).
3. *The imminence of current liabilities.* A large loan due for repayment very soon could be embarrassing. It would be acutely embarrassing if gearing was already very high, there was no scope for an equity issue and neither cash nor further overdraft facilities were available. Even that is not perhaps as embarrassing as being unable to pay the wages next week, and next week's wages do not, of course, appear in the balance sheet.

   The key factor is whether a company has scope for further borrowings or is right up against its limits.
4. *The volatility of working capital requirements.* A company with a highly seasonal business pattern, for instance a Christmas card manufacturer or a UK holiday camp operator, may well make use of a much higher average level of borrowings during the year than the balance sheet shows, particularly as companies usually arrange their year end to coincide with low stocks and/or a low level of activity. When the interest charge in the P&L account is disproportionately large

in comparison to the borrowings shown in the balance sheet, this is a clear indication that borrowings during the year have been significantly higher than at the year end.

Because of these individual factors, the most informative feature of a current ratio is its normal level and any trend from year to year. A drop below normal levels is worth investigating, and a continuing decline is a warning signal that should not be ignored.

Quick ratio or liquidity ratio or acid test

As we have said, not all current assets are readily convertible into cash to meet debts; in particular stocks and work in progress may be able to be run down a certain amount, but not eliminated if the business is to continue. The quick ratio recognises this by excluding stocks from current assets and applies the 'acid test' of what would happen if the company had to settle up with all its creditors and debtors straight away: if the quick ratio is less than 1 it would be unable to do so.

Some companies whose normal terms of trade allow them to sell goods for cash before paying for them habitually operate with a quick ratio of well under 1 (0.2 is typical for a supermarket); so it is a poorer than average figure compared with other companies in the same industry, coupled with a declining trend, that signals possible trouble ahead. A feature that a low and declining ratio often highlights is a rising overdraft: the question then is, 'Are their bankers happy?' Fears in this direction may be allayed by a statement in the annual report about operating well within the facilities available, or by a statement at the time that new money is raised confirming that working capital will be adequate.

A large difference between the current ratio and the quick ratio is an indication of large stocks:

$$\text{Current ratio} - \text{Quick ratio} = \frac{\text{Stocks}}{\text{Current liabilities}}$$

Bathroom and kitchen unit manufacturer SPRING RAM, which has had a very chequered time over a ten-year period, provides an interesting example:

THE SPRING RAM CORPORATION *Current ratio and Quick ratio*

	1990 £m	1991 £m	1992 £m	1993 £m	1994 £m	1995 £m	1996 £m	1997 £m
Current assets	91.1	128.8	128.0	91.3	109.5	130.1	83.8	72.1
Current liabilities	54.9	79.4	95.1	90.5	65.7	105.1	70.6	72.2
Current ratio	1.66	1.62	1.35	1.01	1.67	1.24	1.20	1.29
Stocks	25.1	41.0	52.4	45.4	47.7	64.7	38.8	33.1
Current assets – Stock	66.0	87.8	75.6	45.9	61.8	65.4	45.0	37.0
Quick ratio	1.20	1.11	0.79	0.51	0.94	0.62	0.64	0.51
See Note	1	2	3	4				

Notes:

1. *Chairman's statement:*
   Bonus issue The strength of the Group's balance sheet is such that, on 26 April 1991, shareholders approved a one for one bonus issue, the fifth since flotation in 1983 . . .
   Management The number and quality of the Corporation's management teams continues to grow. There are now 47 directors managing 16 autonomous operating companies.
2. Stock increased by more than 60%, although Turnover was marginally down from £194m to £191m. Invested £37.1m in buildings and plant. Spent £12.8m on Stag furniture acquisition.
3. *New chairman's statement:* The five months of 1993 since the new team was installed have been used to stabilise the financial position of the company . . . severe recession in the UK housing market. Prompt action was necessary to eliminate the excessive decentralization which had led both to the Group's businesses competing with each other and to the duplication of overheads and stockholdings . . . the number of businesses operated by the company was reduced from 22 to 11.
4. Rescue rights issue; 2 for 9 to raise £42.1m net.

We would like to tell you that, after the rescue rights issue, the company was soon restored to good health. Sadly not. As the ratios continue to indicate, this company is still poorly. Its share price bottomed at 4p, down from 188p in the heyday of the first chairman.

The wounds were deep. Due to the unbounded optimism of the first chairman in the face of a recession, the company had gone from cash at bank of £45.8m at the beginning of 1992 into net bank borrowings of £37.8m by the end of August 1993.

But worse still was the damage done to the integrity of the company by some serious creative accounting. As the *Investors Chronicle* wisely warned its readers:

INVESTORS CHRONICLE *Extract from 26 March 1993*

Battered Ram
Cautious investors would be right to avoid Spring Ram shares until credibility is restored.
   Investors have good reason to be angry with the former market darling Spring Ram . . .
   First there was last November's debacle at Balterley Bathrooms. The problem is believed to have been the result of huge pressure on the divisional finance director to perform. He apparently overvalued stocks to produce the figures that head office wanted to see.
   Although the group sought to reassure shareholders that this was an isolated incident this week's shocks have undermined its attempt.
   Last week, trading in its shares was suspended ahead of a profit warning. Management blamed more stringent accounting policies.

Provisions

Background

Before FRS 12, Provisions, contingent liabilities and contingent assets, the making of provisions gave imaginative companies enormous scope for enhancing profits. All you had to do was this:

- Year 1 make a huge provision, so large that analysts would ignore it in their calculation of that year's earnings per share, and forget about it in subsequent years.
- Year 2 and in subsequent years, offset against the provision costs that you would prefer not to hit the profit and loss account, until such times as the 'kitty' is used up.
- Then scratch around for another suitable provision.

The two classics were ICI's provision of several hundred million for 'Restructuring' and UNILEVER's £800m for 'Entry into Europe'.

We are sure that both these companies were scrupulous in choosing what costs to offset against these jumbo provisions, but the scope for creative accountancy was enormous. FRS 12 severely curtails the scope for this particular dodge.

Definition

A *provision* is a liability that is of uncertain timing or amount. A provision should be recognised when a company has an obligation which it will probably be required to settle, and a reliable estimate can be made of the amount of the obligation. Unless these conditions can be met, no provision should be recognised.

A 'provision' (as defined by CA 1985) is either:

(a) any amount written off by way of providing for depreciation or diminution in the value of assets (in which case it is deducted from the fixed asset); or
(b) any amount retained to provide for any liability or loss which is either likely to be incurred, or certain to be incurred but uncertain as to the amount or as to the date on which it will arise (it then appears among provisions for liabilities and charges).

FRS 12 (see below) sets out more demanding conditions than those in (b) above, and it is those in FRS 12 which have to be applied in practice.

Provisions for liabilities and charges are frequently made for:

- pensions and similar obligations (see page 64);
- taxation, including deferred taxation (see Chapter 20); and
- other provisions.

The item 'Taxation' will normally only include deferred taxation (see Chapter 20), as other taxation will be shown under creditors, unless the amount is uncertain.

When to make provisions

Under FRS 12 a provision – a liability that is of uncertain timing or amount – should *only* be recognised when:

- a company has an *obligation* which it will probably be required to settle; and
- a *reliable estimate* can be made of the amount of the obligation.

Unless these conditions can be met, no provision should be recognised. A provision should be *used* only for expenditure for which the provision was originally recognised.

Annual review and disclosure

Provisions should be reviewed at each balance sheet date and adjusted to reflect the current best estimate.

If it is no longer probable that a transfer of economic benefits will be required to settle the obligation, i.e. if it looks as though the company is no longer likely to have to cough up, the provision should be reversed.

As SMITHS GROUP (see below) illustrates, the company's annual report should disclose:

- the carrying amount at the beginning and end of the period;
- additional provisions made in the period, including increases to existing provisions;
- amounts used (i.e. incurred and charged against the provision) during the period; and unused amounts reversed during the period.

SMITHS GROUP *Extract from notes to the 2003 accounts*

Note 24, Provisions for liabilities and charges

| | At 1/8/02 £m | Exchange adjustments £m | Profit and loss account | | Acquisitions £m | Utilisation £m | Disposals £m | At 31/7/03 £m |
			Provisions £m	Releases £m				
Service guarantees and product liability[1]	34.7	0.5	28.2	[5.0]	11.9	[19.2]	(2.0)	49.1
Reorganisation[2]	37.1	0.1	–	[1.9]		[20.9]	(0.4)	14.0
Property[3]	20.0	–	5.8	[5.5]		[2.9]	(0.3)	17.1
Litigation[4]	18.3	0.2	6.9	[2.6]	2.1	[2.7]	–	22.2
	110.1	0.8	40.9	[15.0]	14.0	[45.7]	(2.7)	102.4
Deferred taxation	3.7							13.6
Total provisions	113.8							116.0

1. **Service guarantees and product liability** Service guarantees and warranties over the company's products typically cover periods of between one and three years. Provision is made for the likely cost of after-sales support based on the recent past experience of individual businesses.
2. **Reorganisation** Significant parts of the company's operations, especially in Aerospace and Sealing Solutions, have been undergoing a phased restructuring programme. Full provision is made for reorganisation approved and committed by the end of each financial year. This year's residual balance relates mainly to Aerospace.
3. **Property** As stated in the Accounting Policies . . . where a property is vacant, or sub-let under terms such that rental income is insufficient to meet all outgoings, the company provides for the expected future shortfall up to termination of the lease. Provision is also made for the cost of reinstatement work on leased properties where there is an obligation under the lease, and the costs can be reasonably estimated. Where evidence of contamination is found on property in the company's occupation, provision is made for estimated remedial costs pending action on the affected site. Provisions totalling £5.5m were released following a reassessment of certain future obligations.
4. **Litigation** The company has on occasion been required to take legal action to protect its patents and other business intellectual property rights against infringement, and to similarly defend itself against proceedings brought by other parties. Provision is made for the expected fees and associated costs, based on professional advice as to the likely duration of each case. Provisions totalling £2.6m were released relating to litigation settled at less than the expected cost.

Provisioning – the main areas

Provisions can involve huge sums of money. The main areas are:

- Environmental (SHELL, $5.2 billion)
- Restructuring (UNILEVER, €445m)
- Litigation (GKN, £266m).

SHELL *Note to the 2002 accounts*

Decommissioning and restoration costs
For the purpose of calculating provisions for decommissioning and restoration costs, estimated total ultimate liabilities of $5.2 billion at December 31 2002 (2001: $4.4 billion) were used. Such estimates are subject to various regulatory and technological developments.

UNILEVER *Note to the 2003 accounts*

19. Restructuring and other provisions
Provisions are recognised when either a legal or a constructive obligation, as a result of a past event, exists at the balance sheet date and where the amount of the obligation can be reasonably estimated.

	€ million 2003	€ million 2002
Restructuring provisions	**445**	633
Other provisions . . .		

Restructuring provisions at the end of 2003 relate to the Path to Growth initiative described in Note 4 on page 86. These amounted to €0.4 billion, the cash impact of which is expected to be . . .

GKN *Note to the 1997 accounts*

Provisions for liabilities and charges

	1997 £m	1996 £m
Deferred taxation	2	7
Post-retirement and other provisions	174	173
Meineke litigation	266	270
	442	450

Meineke litigation
In the interests of prudence an exceptional litigation provision of $270m was made in the 1996 accounts following a judgment of the US District Court, Charlotte, North Carolina in respect of claims brought by certain of its franchisees against Meineke Discount Muffler Shops Inc. (owned by one of GKN's subsidiaries) alleging breach of contract and fiduciary duty . . . by Meineke . . . appeal with the US Court of Appeal . . .

   The movement on the provision represents legal costs incurred in the year.

So GKN's lawyers took a cool $4m off the company in 1997. Litigation is a serious hazard in doing business in the USA.

Other areas include:

- warranties;
- onerous leases;
- dilapidation provisions on property leases;
- a restructuring provision should include only the direct expenditures arising from the restructuring, which are those that are necessarily entailed by the restructuring;
- a restructuring provision does not include such costs as: (a) retraining or relocating continuing staff; (b) marketing; or (c) investment in new systems and new distribution networks;
- no obligation arises for the sale of an operation until the company is committed to the sale i.e. there is a binding sale agreement.

Other accounting standards on provisions

Where another FRS or an SSAP deals with a more specific type of provision, that standard applies, rather than FRS 12. These include:

- long-term contracts (SSAP 9, see page 127);
- deferred tax (FRS 19, see page 157);
- leases (SSAP 21, see pages 153);
- pension costs (FRS 17, see pages 65).

Other uses of the term provision

The term 'provision' may also be used in the context of items such as depreciation, impairment of assets and doubtful debts: these are adjustments to the carrying amounts of assets, and are not covered by FRS 12.

What does this all mean to the investor?

Prior to FRS 12 the recognition (making) of a provision was based on management's intention, or possible intention, of making expenditures, rather than on any legal or moral obligation to do so.

In particular, as we have mentioned, there was the use of what Sir David Tweedie, when chairman of the ASB, called *'big bath' accounting*. Several years of future expenditure, including items related to continuing operations, and possibly a sum to cover unforeseen costs, would be heaped together into one large provision, which would be reported as an exceptional item.

This gave enormous scope for earnings to be *'smoothed'*: large fluctuations in reported earnings being avoided by provisions being released in lean years.

The new rules should make management much more accountable. The hope is that companies will keep shareholders more closely informed about provisions and exceptional expenditure. Companies which haven't already adopted the Operational and Financial Review (see page 35) should do so to help achieve this better communication.

The danger is that management will become less inclined to 'grasp nettles' in continuing operations, for fear of causing a 'blip' in reported profits.

Leases

Finance leases and operating leases

SSAP 21, Accounting for leases and hire purchase contracts, divides leases into two types:

1. finance leases,
2. operating leases.

A *finance lease* is defined as a lease which transfers substantially all the risks and rewards of ownership of an asset to the lessee. All leases other than finance leases are classified as *operating leases*.

SSAP 21 requires quite differing accounting treatments for each type. Finance leases are treated as though the related asset had been bought on credit terms using a loan. The related asset is shown on the balance sheet under tangible fixed assets, and the related liability or obligation under creditors (see Example 19.1). Operating lease commitments are not shown as creditors but instead are presented as an 'off-balance sheet' memorandum disclosure (see Chapter 25).

Accounting for finance leases

Prior to SSAP 21 a company could enter into a finance lease instead of borrowing the money to purchase an asset, and neither the asset nor the commitment to pay leasing charges would appear in the balance sheet. This was an example of what was known as 'off balance sheet financing', which produced 'hidden gearing', as the company had effectively geared itself up just as much as if it had borrowed the money to purchase the asset, except that it had to pay leasing charges rather than paying interest and bearing depreciation charges.

SSAP 21 requires a finance lease to be recorded in the balance sheet of the lessee as an asset and as an obligation to pay future rentals. The initial sum to be recorded both as an asset and as a liability is the present value of the minimum lease payments, which is derived by discounting them at the interest rate implicit in the lease. The method of accounting is illustrated in Example 19.1.

Example 19.1 Accounting for a finance lease

A company acquires a small computer system on a finance lease. Lease payments are £10,000 p.a. for 5 years, with an option to continue the lease for a further 5 years at £1,000 p.a. Payments are made annually in advance, i.e. the first payment is made on taking delivery of the computer. The interest rate implicit in the lease is 10%, and the estimated useful life of the system is 5 years.

The present value of the minimum lease payments discounted at 10% p.a. can be calculated using the table *Annuity table: Present value of 1 in n years' time* in Appendix 4:

Payment date	Present value of 1 (from table)	Present value of £10,000 payment £
On delivery	1.000	10,000
In 1 year	0.909	9,090
In 2 years	0.826	8,260
In 3 years	0.751	7,510
In 4 years	0.683	6,830
Present value of minimum lease payments		£41,690

The computer system will thus be recorded as an asset of £41,690 and the liability for future rental payments will also be recorded as £41,690. After the first year:

(a) The asset will be depreciated over the shorter of the lease term (the initial period plus any further option period, i.e. a total of 10 years in this case), and its expected useful life (5 years). Annual depreciation charge on a straight line basis is therefore one-fifth of £41,690 = £8,338, reducing the asset value to £33,352.

(b) The present value of the remaining minimum lease payments is recomputed. There is no longer a payment due in 4 years' time (£6,830 in our table above), so the present value of future payments is now £41,690 – 6,830 = £34,860. £6,830 is deducted from the future liability and the remaining £3,170 of the £10,000 payment made on delivery is shown as interest paid.

These calculations would then be repeated each subsequent year as shown in Example 19.2.

Example 19.2 Accounting for a finance lease – subsequent years

| End of year | Balance sheet | | P & L account | |
| | Asset value | Remaining payments | Interest charge | Depreciation charge |
	£	£	£	£
1	33,352	34,860	3,170	8,338
2	25,014	27,350	2,490	8,338
3	16,676	19,090	1,740	8,338
4	8,338	10,000	910	8,338
5	Nil	Nil	Nil	8,338

IFRS

Creditors

The accounting is the same as under UK GAAP but trade creditors are described in the balance sheet as 'trade payables'.

Provisions

The accounting is the same as under UK GAAP (IAS 37, Provisions, contingent liabilities and contingent assets). Balance sheet presentation differs from UK GAAP. Under IFRS, the total provision balance must be analysed between current liabilities and non-current liabilities and the two totals separately disclosed under the appropriate balance sheet heading.

Leases

Under IFRS, finance leases are treated in a similar way to UK GAAP (see above). However, IAS 17, on leases, approaches operating leases in a different and more complex way although for most companies the practical impact of this is not likely to be significant.

CHAPTER 20

Tax in the balance sheet

Introduction

The purpose of this chapter is to explain the basis of the tax charge in the profit and loss account, and tax liabilities and assets in the balance sheet. We explain what deferred tax is and how it is calculated. We also explain why the tax charge might not be 'normal', i.e. why the charge might differ from what you would expect by applying the applicable corporation tax rate to the profit shown in the profit and loss account, calculated on the basis of accounting principles.

Company tax is a complex area and this chapter is intended to give an explanation of the basics.

A UK resident company is liable to corporation tax (CT) on its income and capital gains. If it has income taxable abroad, it will also suffer overseas tax. All this appears in the profit and loss account under the heading 'Taxation'.

VAT, excise duty, employee PAYE and other forms of tax that the company may bear, or be involved in as an unpaid tax collector, are not normally shown.

Disclosure requirements for company taxation appear in three places:

1. Companies Act 1985;
2. FRS 16, Current tax;
3. FRS 19, Deferred tax.

There are a number of differences in the accounting treatment of taxation between UK GAAP and IFRS. These are dealt with at the end of the chapter.

UK GAAP – current taxation

Introduction

Whilst companies pay corporation tax on their profits, the amount of tax unfortunately cannot simply be calculated by applying a corporation tax rate to the accounting profit shown in the profit and loss account. There are a number of reasons for this, including the following:

(a) The company receives tax relief capital allowances on its fixed assets, in place of the depreciation charged in the profit and loss account (see Example 20.1).
(b) Some of the expenditure charged in the profit and loss account may not be allowable for tax purposes.
(c) Some of the income included in the profit and loss account may not be liable for tax.
(d) The company may be able to claim tax relief in the current period because it has suffered trading losses in previous accounting periods.

Depreciation and capital allowances

Different classes of asset have long been treated quite differently for accounting and tax purposes. The annual *depreciation charge* on an asset is determined by the accounting policy, particularly as regards estimation techniques such as asset lives and residual values. The annual *capital allowance* on an asset is determined by the government and is applied by HMRC (Her Majesty's Revenue and Customs). The two are seldom the same size.

The impact of capital allowances on the tax a company pays is illustrated in Example 20.1.

Example 20.1 Depreciation and capital allowances

If a large company invested £1m in plant and machinery in 2001 and used straight line depreciation spread over an expected ten-year life, the capital allowances and depreciation would be:

	Capital allowances £	Depreciation £
2001	250,000	100,000
2002	187,500	100,000
2003	140,625	100,000
2004	105,469	100,000
2005	79,102	100,000
2006	59,326	100,000
2007	44,495	100,000
2008	33,371	100,000
2009	25,028	100,000
2010	75,084	100,000
	1,000,000	1,000,000

Note: This assumes that trading ceased in 2010 and that the plant and machinery had no residual value. If the company continued trading, the allowances would continue ad infinitum at 25% a year on the declining balance, i.e. £18,771 in 2010, £14,078 in 2011 . . . £334 in the year 2024, and so on.

The advantage of the reducing balance method is that it simplifies calculations.

If the company made taxable trading profits before capital allowances of £2m in each of the ten years and we ignore all other allowances for the purpose of illustration, the corporation tax payable, assuming a 30% rate throughout, would be:

	Taxable profit £		Corporation tax liability £
2001	1,750,000		525,000
2002	1,812,500		543,750
2003	1,859,375		557,813
2004	1,894,531		568,359
2005	1,920,898		576,269
2006	1,940,674		582,202
2007	1,955,505		586,651
2008	1,966,629		589,989
2009	1,974,972		592,492
2010	1,924,916	(Note 1)	577,475
	19,000,000	(Note 2)	5,700,000

Notes:
1. Assuming trading ceases in 2010 and the plant and machinery has no residual value, to give capital allowances of £75,084 that year.
2. The reported profit before tax each year would be £1,900,000 (£2m less £100,000 depreciation), so the total taxable profit over the ten years would be the same as the total reported profit, and the total tax payable would be the same as a tax charge of 30% each year on reported profit.

The total tax charge in the profit and loss account

Whilst the above tax charge is a starting point, it does not fully represent the total charge shown in the profit and loss account. The reason is that accounting standards require companies to take account of *deferred tax* (see below). This takes account of the fact that certain gains and losses are recorded in the financial statements in different accounting periods compared with when they are recognised in the relevant corporation tax computation. These are usually referred to as '*timing differences*' – for example:

- a company obtains tax relief on capital expenditure according to rules laid down in the tax legislation, but charge depreciation in accordance with the company's own accounting policy;
- accounting losses are recognised in the period in which they occur but tax relief may not be available until a future year when profits are available to offset the tax losses against.

What deferred tax cannot deal with are differences between a company's taxable profits and its accounting profits, as shown in the profit and loss account, that arise because certain types of income and expenditure are non-taxable or disallowable (see (b) and (c) above). These differences are referred to as *permanent differences* and help to explain some of the reasons why the company's tax charge is not 'normal' (see UK GAAP – the tax reconciliation note, below).

The calculation of the total tax charge (current tax plus deferred tax) is dealt with later in the chapter (see UK GAAP – the tax charge in the profit and loss account, below).

UK GAAP – deferred tax

Definition

The purpose of deferred tax is to remove the effect that any timing differences would otherwise have on the annual tax charge.

The formal definition of deferred tax (in paragraph 2 of FRS 19) is 'the estimated future tax consequences of transactions and events recognised in the financial statements of the current and previous periods'. For example, a company may incur developments costs amounting to £100,000 and obtain tax relief on all the expenditure in the current period, but may choose under SSAP 13 (see Chapter 14) to defer the expenditure over a period of five years.

Without taking account of deferred tax, a company's tax charge could fluctuate wildly from year to year even thought its accounting profit was fairly stable. In the above example, the tax charge (if deferred tax were ignored) would be very low in the first period but then jump to a much higher level in the following four years. Deferred tax reflects the consequences of timing differences.

Timing differences

These are defined in FRS 19 as 'differences between an entity's taxable profits and its results as stated in the financial statements that arise because certain types of income and expenditure are non-taxable or disallowable, or because certain tax charges or allowances have no corresponding amount in the financial statements'.

One of the most important examples of a timing difference is capital expenditure, where capital allowances are allowed for tax purposes, but where depreciation is charged for accounts purposes on the basis of the company's accounting policies.

Calculating and presenting deferred tax

Example 20.2 shows how deferred tax is calculated and how appears in the financial statements.

Example 20.2 Deferred tax in the accounts

An engineering company buys £2m of plant and machinery at the beginning of its first year.

Accounting – depreciation charges in the profit and loss account
The company depreciates the plant and machinery on a straight line basis over ten years, i.e. £200,000 per annum.

Tax allowances – deductions in the annual corporation tax computation
For corporation tax purposes the company is entitled to a writing down allowance of 25% per annum on a reducing balance basis, i.e. £500,000 (= 25% of £2m) in year 1, £375,000 (= 25% × [£2m − £500,000]) in year 2, £281,250 (= 25% × [£2m − £500,000 − £375,000]) in year 3, and so on.

Corporation tax calculations
Suppose the company's profit before charging depreciation is £1.4m (i.e. accounting profit shown in the profit and loss account is £1.4m less depreciation of £200,000 = £1.2m).

Taxable profit of £900,000 in this simple case equals profit before charging depreciation of £1,400,000, less the tax writing down allowance of £500,000. Tax payable at a rate of 30% is £270,000. This will be payable in the following period and included in the balance sheet under 'Creditors'.

Deferred tax calculations
The originating timing difference in year 1 is £300,000 (= £500,000 tax allowance less £200,000 depreciation charge). With a tax rate of 30%, the deferred tax charge is 30% × £300,000 = £90,000. As this is the company's first year, the deferred tax balance at the beginning of the year is zero, so the year end balance is £90,000 (i.e. £0 + £90,000).

(In the following year, the deferred tax charge will be worked out in a similar way. The deferred tax provision in the balance sheet at the end of the second year will be calculated by adding this charge to the provision at the beginning of the second year of £90,000.)

Tax charge in the profit and loss account
The total charge of £360,000 will consist of two separate elements:

- **Current tax** £270,000
- **Deferred tax** £90,000.

(See below under 'UK GAAP – the tax charge in the profit and loss account' for examples of presentation.)

As there are no permanent differences (see above for definition) the total tax charge of £360,000 equals 30% of the profit on ordinary activities before tax in the profit and loss account of £1.2m.

Tax provisions in the balance sheet
At the end of year 1 these will be:

- **Corporation tax payable** £270,000
- **Deferred tax provision** £90,000.

Deferred tax assets

The following may give rise to deferred tax assets (as opposed to provisions in the examples above):

- Defined benefit pension schemes (FRS 17) where the pension obligations exceed the fund assets and there is a net obligation: the deferred tax asset is calculated by multiplying the net liability by the rate of corporation tax. Under UK GAAP, the deferred tax asset must be offset against the net pension obligation and a single figure shown in the balance sheet.
- Tax losses (FRS 19): the deferred tax asset is the tax value of the losses but this is not necessarily included in the balance sheet as an asset in view of uncertainty about its recoverability. In most cases this will be disclosed as a memorandum item, not included in the balance sheet as an asset.
- Share-based payment charge (FRS 20): the accounting charge will be made in the current period but tax relief may not be obtainable until a later period (e.g. in the case of share options this will be when the optionholder pays cash to the company as consideration for new shares issued). Deferred tax for the period will be assessed on the timing difference (accounting charge in the profit and loss account compared with tax relief, which may be zero in the current period). Any deferred tax will need to be assessed for recoverability.

UK GAAP – the tax charge in the profit and loss account

As mentioned above, the tax charge in the profit and loss account comprises current tax (the corporation tax assessed on the company's taxable profits) and the deferred tax.

Presentation of tax in the profit and loss account under UK GAAP

The tax charge may contain the following elements:

UK corporation tax:

Current tax	x
Tax over or under provided in prior periods	x
	x
Double tax relief	(x)
Foreign tax	x
Current tax	x
Deferred tax	x
Total tax charge	x

IDEAL SHOPPING DIRECT *Annual Report 2005*

Note 5 – Taxation on profit on ordinary activities

Ideal Shopping Annual Report 2005
5. TAXATION ON PROFIT ON ORDINARY ACTIVITIES
The tax charge represents:

	2005 £000	2004 £000
Corporation tax at 30% (2004: 30%)	1,694	45
Total current tax	1,694	45
Deferred tax:		
Origination and reversal of timing differences	556	1,304
Total deferred tax	556	1,304
Tax on profit on ordinary activities	2,250	1,349

The deferred tax charge of £556,000 represents release of the deferred tax asset established in respect of trading losses in prior years under FRS 19 and other timing differences. The tax assessed for the period is lower (2004: lower) than the standard rate of corporation tax in the UK of 30% (2004: 30%). The differences are explained as follows:

▶

	2005 £000	2004 £000
Profit on ordinary activities before tax	**7,404**	4,105
Profit on ordinary activities multiplied by standard rate of corporation tax in the UK of 30% (2004: 30%)	**2,221**	1,231
Effect of:		
Expenses not deductible for tax purposes	9	98
Differences between capital allowances and depreciation	3	63
Marginal relief	–	(26)
Utilisation of tax losses	(294)	(1,305)
Other timing differences	(245)	(16)
Current tax charge for the period (see note below on page 160)	**1,694**	45

UK GAAP – accounting policies

The following are examples of typical accounting policy disclosures under UK GAAP:

CHARTERIS *Annual Report 2006*

Extract from accounting policies – deferred taxation
Deferred tax is recognised in respect of all timing differences that have originated but not reversed at the balance sheet date where transactions or events that result in an obligation to pay more tax in the future or a right to pay less tax in the future have occurred at the balance sheet date. Timing differences are differences between the Group's taxable profits and its results as stated in the financial statements that arise from the inclusion of gains and losses in tax assessments in periods different from those in which they are recognised in the financial statements.

Deferred tax is measured at the average tax rates that are expected to apply in the periods in which timing differences are expected to reverse, based on tax rates and laws that have been enacted or substantially enacted by the balance sheet date.

CI TRADERS *Annual Report 2006*

Extract from accounting policies – taxation
The charge for current tax (including UK and foreign tax) is based on the profit for the year as adjusted for tax purposes.

Deferred tax is recognised in respect of all timing differences that have originated but not reversed at the balance sheet date where transactions or events that result in an obligation to pay more tax in the future or a right to pay less tax in the future have occurred at the balance sheet date. Timing differences are differences between the Group's taxable profits and its results as stated in the accounts that arise from the inclusion of gains and losses in tax assessments in periods different from those in which they are recognised in the accounts. A net deferred tax asset is regarded as recoverable and therefore recognised only when, on the basis of all available evidence, it can be regarded as more likely than not that there will be suitable taxable profits from which the reversal of the underlying timing differences can be deducted.

Deferred tax is not recognised when fixed assets are revalued unless by the balance sheet date there is a binding obligation to sell the revalued assets and the gain or loss expected to arise on the sale has been recognised in the accounts. Neither is deferred tax recognised when fixed assets are sold and it is more likely than not that the taxable gain will be rolled over, being charged to tax only if and when the replacement assets are sold. . . .

Deferred tax is measured at the average tax rates that are expected to apply in the periods in which the timing differences are expected to reverse, based on tax rates and laws that have been enacted or substantially enacted by the balance sheet date. . . .

UK GAAP – the tax reconciliation note

Is the tax charge 'normal'? If not, WHY NOT?

The tax charge shown in the profit and loss account is unlikely to be 'normal', i.e. what the layperson might expect, namely, pre-tax profits times average rate of corporation tax during the company's accounting year. It is important to understand why this is the case.

The amount of corporation tax payable does not depend purely on the company's pre-tax profit figure. The tax charge varies not only because of differences that arise between the taxable profit and the profit shown in the company's accounts (the 'book profit'), but because of differences in the rate charged on particular types of income.

As discussed earlier in the chapter, the differences fall into two categories:

1. *Timing differences*, where the company may be liable to pay the full rate of tax at some time, but not in the year being reported.
2. *Permanent differences* where expenses are disallowed or income is tax-free.

One of the most important examples of a *timing* difference is capital expenditure, where capital allowances are allowed for tax purposes, but depreciation is charged for accounts purposes (see Example 20.2 above for a numerical example).

The tax reconciliation disclosure

FRS 19 requires disclosure of a reconciliation of the current tax charge reported in the profit and loss account, with the charge which would result from applying the relevant standard rate of tax to the reported profit. The reconciliation will highlight reasons for abnormal tax charges.

The reconciliation may be presented in monetary terms or in percentage terms. In practice, most companies present the reconciliation in monetary terms, as illustrated by IDEAL SHOPPING (see above).

UK GAAP – tax in the balance sheet

In the balance sheet taxation may appear under the following headings:

- *Creditors falling due within one year*: the amount falling due within one year will, typically, include one year's corporation tax, and any foreign tax due.
- *Provisions*: any provision for deferred tax and any other provision for other taxation shown separately.
- *Debtors due in more than one year*: any deferred tax asset.

CHARTERIS *Annual Report 2006*

Note 11 – Debtors
Deferred tax asset of £44,000 recognised in the balance sheet of which the note states 'the deferred tax asset comprises the tax effect of unutilised tax losses of £17,000 (2005: £30,000), other timing differences of £56,000 (2005: £53,000) less accelerated capital allowances of £29,000 (2005: £45,000).'

IFRS

Differences compared with UK GAAP

The most important difference is that IAS 12, Income taxes, is based on a concept of 'temporary differences' (as compared with timing differences under UK GAAP). The area most affected by this is where fixed asset revaluations are incorporated into the accounts. This could relate to a revaluation of a building occupied by the company for its own purposes (IAS 16) or it could relate to a revaluation of a property let out to others (investment property, IAS 40).

Under UK GAAP, this timing difference is not usually reflected in the accounts, it is a memorandum disclosure (see, for example the UK GAAP accounting policy of CI TRADERS, above) which is in accordance with FRS 19 paragraph 15, which prohibits the recognition of deferred tax in the circumstances described in the company's note.

IAS 12 approaches deferred tax from the viewpoint of the asset's carrying amount in the balance sheet (e.g. in accordance with IAS 16 or IAS 40). The carrying amount is compared with the asset's tax base (which is usually historical cost) and deferred tax is based on the difference between the two amounts. The carrying amount will be dependent on the company's accounting policy (e.g. relating to depreciation) whilst the tax basis will be dependent on the applicable tax rules.

For example, suppose a property occupied by the company and which cost £2m is revalued at the year-end at £2.5m. The revaluation is reflected in the balance sheet. Assume the applicable rate of corporation tax is 30%.

Under UK GAAP, the increase of £500,000 would be credited to revaluation reserve. In accordance with FRS 19 paragraph 15, the company is prohibited from making a deferred tax provision. Potential deferred tax of £150,000 would be noted as a memorandum disclosure in accordance with FRS 19 paragraph 64(c).

Under IFRS, the carrying amount (the revaluation number) is £2.5m and the tax base is £2.0m. Deferred tax to be provided in the balance sheet amounts to £150,000. The net credit to revaluation reserve would be £350,000.

Tax reconciliation note

Under IFRS, the hypothetical tax is reconciled to the total tax charge (current tax plus deferred tax) as opposed to current tax under FRS 19 (see above). MANAGEMENT CONSULTING GROUP is an example of a disclosure under IFRS.

Disclosure examples

MANAGEMENT CONSULTING GROUP *Annual Report 2006*

Management Consulting Group Annual Report 2006

Significant accounting policies (extract)

Taxation
The tax expense represents the sum of the tax currently payable and deferred tax. The tax currently payable is based on taxable profit for the year. Taxable profit differs from net profit as reported in the income statement because it excludes items of income and expense that are taxable or deductible in other years or are never taxable or deductible. The Group's liability for current tax is calculated using tax rates that have been enacted or substantively enacted by the balance sheet date.

Deferred tax is recognised on differences between the carrying amounts of assets and liabilities in the financial statements and the corresponding tax bases used in the computation of taxable profit and is accounted for using the balance sheet liability method. Deferred tax liabilities are generally recognised for all taxable temporary differences. Deferred tax assets are generally recognised for all deductible temporary differences to the extent that it is probable that taxable profits will be available against which such differences can be utilised.

The carrying amount of deferred tax assets is reviewed at each balance sheet date and reduced to the extent that it is no longer probable that sufficient taxable profits will be available to allow all or part of the asset to be recovered in the foreseeable future.

Deferred tax is calculated at the tax rates which are expected to apply in the period when the liability is settled or the asset realised. Deferred tax is charged or credited to the income statement, except when it relates to items charged or credited directly to reserves, in which case the deferred tax is also dealt with in reserves.

Deferred tax assets and liabilities are offset when there is a legally enforceable right to set off current tax assets against current tax liabilities and when they relate to income taxes levied by the same taxation authority and the Group intends to settle its current tax assets and liabilities on a net basis.

Tax expense

	2006 £000	2005 £000
Tax in respect of current year		
UK corporation tax	326	500
Foreign tax	5,540	4,899
Deferred tax – acquired intangible assets	(316)	–
Deferred tax – tax losses and other temporary differences	(2,250)	(838)
Deferred tax – US goodwill	813	795
Total deferred tax	(1,753)	(43)
Total current year tax	4,113	5,356
Prior year taxation	485	(1,228)
	4,598	4,128

The deferred tax charged for US goodwill arises from tax deductions in the US for goodwill which is not amortised in the income statement. A deferred tax liability is required to be held for this item in accordance with accounting standards. UK corporation tax is calculated at 30% (2005: 30%) of the estimated assessable profit for the year. Taxation for other jurisdictions is calculated at the rates prevailing in the respective jurisdictions.

The charge for the year can be reconciled to the profit per the income statement as follows:

	2006 £000	2005 £000
Profit before tax	13,348	13,920
Tax at the average tax rate applicable across the Group of 35% (2005: 36%)	4,672	5,011
Net tax effect of unrelieved losses	(1,279)	1,967
Net tax effect of permanent differences and other	720	(1,622)
Relating to prior years	485	(1,228)
Tax expense for the year	4,598	4,128
Effective tax rate for the year	34%	30%

Tax assets and liabilities

		Group		Company
	2006	2005	2006	2005
	£000	£000	£000	£000
Current tax liabilities	5,728	3,959	1,000	394
Non-current tax liabilities				
Tax liabilities	1,859	1,859	–	–
Deferred tax liabilities	5,852	2,815	–	–
	7,711	4,674	–	–
Total tax liabilities	13,439	8,633	1,000	394

The following are the major deferred tax assets and liabilities recognised by the Group and movements thereon during the current year.

Group

Deferred tax assets

	Tax losses	Other	Total
	£000	£000	£000
At 1 January 2006	1,101	257	1,358
Acquisition of subsidiaries	–	1,089	1,089
Charge to income	(1,100)	(97)	(1,197)
Credit to income	2,347	–	2,347
At 31 December 2006	2,348	1,249	3,597

	Profits taxable in future years	Arising on acquisitions	Other	Total
Deferred tax liabilities	£000	£000	£000	£000
At 1 January 2006	1,100	1,715	–	2,815
Transfer to corporation tax creditor	(465)	–	–	(465)
Acquisition of subsidiaries	–	3,005	–	3,005
Charge to income	115	813	85	1,013
Credit to income	(200)	(316)	–	(516)
At 31 December 2006	550	5,217	85	5,852

Additionally the Group has potential unrealised deferred tax assets at the year end of approximately £24 million (2005: £25 million) in respect of tax losses. The tax losses are partly not yet agreed with tax authorities and/or may be subject to adjustment on tax audits. Consequently, they are subject to uncertain and unquantifiable adjustments. Due to these uncertainties, and uncertainty as to the likely jurisdictions of future profits against which the losses can be offset, the deferred tax asset recognised is limited to the amount stated above.

CHAPTER 21

Bank loans and overdrafts

Bank facilities

There are three main methods by which a company can borrow money from a bank:

1. by overdrawing on its current account;
2. by loans; and
3. by the use of acceptance credits.

The bank normally agrees with a company the maximum amount that can be borrowed under each method, and this is called granting a facility. For example, a company that has the bank's permission to run an overdraft of up to £1m has overdraft facilities for that amount.

What is shown in the balance sheet is, however, only the amount actually borrowed from the bank at the balance sheet date, although the average amount overdrawn during the year can be estimated from the interest charged to the profit and loss account.

FRS 13 required borrowing facilities available to a company to be disclosed (e.g. NATIONAL GRID TRANSCO):

NATIONAL GRID TRANSCO *2003 accounts*

Note 21 Financial instruments
At 31 March 2003 the Group had . . .

Undrawn committed borrowing facilities

Expiring:	£m
in one year or less	1,155
in more than 1 year, but not more than 2 years	966
in more than 2 years	980
	3,101

Of the unused facilities, £2,135m were being held as backup to commercial paper and similar borrowings. The remainder was available as additional backup to commercial paper and for other general corporate purposes.

Bank loans and overdrafts fall in the formats under the headings 'Creditors: amounts falling due within one year' and 'Creditors: amounts falling due after more than one year', and are often grouped with finance leases.

Where security has been given (see page 168), the amounts secured and a general indication of the security must be stated (e.g. ICI):

ICI *Extract from note to 2003 accounts*

20. Loans	Repayment dates	2003 £m	2002 £m
Secured loans:			
US dollars	2004	6	98
Other currencies	2004/2006	41	72
Total secured		47	170
Secured by fixed charge – bank loans		23	17
– other		–	1
Secured by floating charge – bank loans		7	132
– other		17	20
		47	170

For each item the following amounts must be shown separately:

- amounts payable otherwise than by instalments five years hence;

- those payable by instalment, any of which are due more than five years hence;
- the total of such instalments.

In addition listed companies must disclose amounts which are payable between one and two years, and those payable between two and five years. ICI more than meet this requirement, disclosing year by year up to five years:

ICI *Extract from note to 2003 accounts*

Loan maturities	2003	2002
...	£m	£m
Total loans		
Loans or instalments thereof repayable:		
After 5 years from balance sheet date	312	44
From 4 to 5 years	287	470
From 3 to 4 years	427	187
From 2 to 3 years	181	135
From 1 to 2 years	146	527
Total due after more than one year	1,353	1,363
Total due within one year	534	500
Total loans	1,887	1,863

Where any part of the debt is repayable after more than five years, the terms of repayment and rates of interest payable should be shown. If the information is excessive, a general indication of terms and rates of interest is permitted.

Overdrafts

The traditional method of clearing bank lending is to allow customers to overdraw on their current accounts. It was originally designed to cover fluctuations in the company's cash during the year and gives the company complete flexibility of drawing within a given limit, which is normally reviewed annually.

Bank advances on overdraft are technically repayable on demand and, although this is seldom enforced, the bank when granting overdraft facilities may expect the customer to produce budgets and cash flow forecasts to show the purposes for which the facilities are intended and the plans for eventual repayment. Bank lending on overdraft is traditionally short-term in character, designed to cover fluctuations in working capital requirements rather than to provide permanent capital for the company.

When long-term interest rates were driven high by inflation, few finance directors were willing to commit their companies to long-term fixed interest rate debt, especially if they expected interest rates to fall in due course. Instead they resorted more and more to borrowing from their banks, where interest on an overdraft is charged at an agreed percentage over the clearing bank's base rate (see below), which they hoped would average less than the long-term rate at the time, and where the company is free to reduce its borrowing whenever it wishes. Although it is now quite common for companies to finance a large part of their working capital in this way, clearing banks are usually reluctant to let companies increase their overdraft ad lib, even against a floating charge, preferring their clients to convert any 'hard-core' borrowing that has built up on overdraft into loans (see under 'Bank facilities' on page 163).

The cost of borrowing on overdraft

The interest a company has to pay on its overdraft is usually set at a given percentage above its bank's base rate, depending on the standing of the customer; a financially stable, medium-sized company might pay a fixed $1^{1}/2\%$ above base.

The base rate, the datum on which the rates of interest are based, is adjusted up and down to reflect fluctuations in short-term interest rates. Each bank sets its own base rate, though in practice the clearing banks' base rates keep very much in line with each other.

Fluctuations in amount

As we have said, the overdraft figure given in the balance sheet is the amount the overdraft facility is being used at the year end. Companies normally choose their year end to fall when business is at its slackest, and the balance sheet figure is most unlikely to be the maximum amount the company has overdrawn during the year.

For example, a company in a seasonal business, with peak sales in the summer, could be expected to build up stocks from early spring and to carry high debtors across the summer. With an annual turnover of, say, £15m, £200,000 in the bank at its year end (31 December) and £120,000 bank interest paid (reflecting an average overdraft of £1.5m during the year, bearing interest on average at 8%), the amount the company was actually overdrawn during the year would be likely to fluctuate with the sales cycle as shown in Example 21.1.

Example 21.1 Annual fluctuation in sales and overdraft

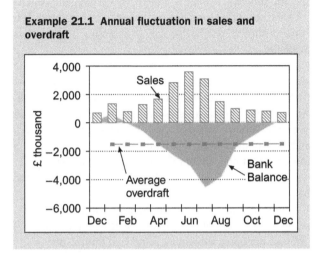

In practice, profit on sales and depreciation on assets would accumulate during the year, steadily improving the overdraft position, but sharp increases would be expected with the payment of dividends and corporation tax, and capital expenditure would also have an immediate effect on the overdraft position.

Vulnerability

Companies which rely heavily on borrowing on overdraft and on floating-rate loans (see below) are vulnerable to rising interest rates, particularly if their profit margins are small, and those which let their overdrafts steadily increase year by year without raising further equity or fixed-interest capital are steadily increasing their interest rate risk. Another hazard of financing on overdraft is that the amount a bank can lend has in the past been subject to Bank of England controls, which were tightened from time to time without much warning.

Banks are also liable to restrict credit on their own account when they find themselves up against their own overall lending limits or having lent too heavily in the particular sector in which the company operates. As credit restrictions often come when conditions are unfavourable for capital raising, a company which is financed extensively by overdraft can all too easily find its operations severely constrained by its immediate cash position.

Bank loans

The simplest type of bank loan is one where the full amount is drawn by the borrower at the outset and is repaid in one lump sum at the end of the period. The duration (or 'term') of the loan is seldom more than seven years but, unlike an overdraft, a bank loan cannot be called in before the end of the term unless the borrower defaults on any condition attached to the loan.

Interest is charged either at a fixed rate or, more frequently, at a floating rate: an agreed percentage over base rate, or over London Inter-Bank Offer Rate (LIBOR). Where LIBOR is used, an interest period is agreed between the borrower and the bank, and the bank then, on the first day of each interest period, determines the rate at which deposits are being offered in the inter-bank market for the relevant period.

For example, if a rate of $1/2\%$ over LIBOR and a three-month interest period have been agreed and the three-month LIBOR rate is 5.7% at the start of the period, the borrower will pay 6.2% for the next three months, and the rate will then be redetermined. Banks frequently allow borrowers to vary their choice of interest period – one month, three months or six months – during the life of a loan.

Where the borrower does not need all the money at once, the bank may allow the loan to be drawn down in tranches (specified instalments). Repayments may also be arranged in instalments, which may often be a stipulation of the lender; banks like to see money coming back gradually to make repayment easier for the borrower and to give early warning of a borrower getting into difficulties over repayment. Details of drawing down and repayment are agreed in advance, together with the rate of interest payable and the security to be given, although any of these features can be altered subsequently by mutual agreement.

Security

Bank loans are sometimes secured on assets acquired by the loan or on other assets of the company, but a floating charge is more usual. If the loan is not secured at all, the company may be required to give a *negative pledge*, i.e. to undertake not to give security to any new or existing creditor or to borrow further amounts under existing security without the bank's prior agreement in writing.

Flexible loan facilities

There is an increasing trend, particularly in European banking, to provide companies with more flexible financing than term loans by granting loan facilities, usually for periods of between three and five years. Drawing down (usually with a minimum limit on any one drawing) can be allowed at any time given a little notice, repayment is flexible, and subsequent redrawing is often allowed, but the borrower will be charged for this flexibility by a commitment commission payable on any unused portion of the facility for as long as the facility is left open. Facilities giving this flexibility are called revolving, and can be single- or multi-currency (e.g. UNIQ):

UNIQ *Extract from note to 2003 accounts*

18. Borrowings and Finance Leases
At 31 March 2003, the Group had revolving credit facilities of £132.7m (2002: £230.0m) of which £28.5m was drawn down, under which it may repay amounts borrowed at its option while retaining the flexibility to re-borrow under the facilities. These facilities expire on 30 June 2004.

The big picture

As we have seen in this chapter, amounts borrowed from the bank do not normally appear on the face of the balance sheet but fall within 'Creditors' as 'Amounts due within one year' or 'Amounts due after more than one year', and are detailed in the notes to the balance sheet.

There is thus no netting of amounts owed by banks and amounts owing to banks; but while this might be important to an economist, as such it is not particularly significant either to the company or to analysts or investors.

The key question is:

Is there enough cash or credit available to meet the debts and obligations of the business when they fall due?

The balance sheet and the notes to it do not answer this question.

This is largely due to the UK system of operating with an overdraft. Although theoretically an overdraft is repayable on demand, in practice a limit is agreed for a specific time and normally adhered to by the bank. But as we have seen, that limit does not have to be disclosed. If it is not disclosed, one has no way of assessing how much is available.

Imagine two companies, A and B, much the same size. Each owes wages and other creditors due tomorrow £1.5m. A has an overdraft of £27m, B has £1m in the bank. At first sight, B looks more solvent than A. But if A has an overdraft limit of £50m, £23m of which remains unused, and B, having a poor reputation for past dealings and a low credit rating, cannot raise an overdraft or borrow elsewhere, we would not normally be able to tell from the balance sheet.

'Going concern' assurances required in the directors' report or the corporate governance statement (see page 49) offer a safeguard, although a somewhat limited one.

Cash flow statements

Chapter 26 is devoted to FRS 1 Cash flow statements. Nevertheless, because of its close relationship to the content of this chapter, it is perhaps right to say a few words here.

Cash is defined in FRS 1 to be:

(a) cash in hand and deposits repayable on demand with any qualifying financial institution (i.e. an entity that as part of its business receives deposits or other repayable funds and grants credits for its own account); less

(b) overdrafts from any qualifying financial institution repayable on demand.

To qualify as 'cash' the deposits must be capable of being withdrawn at any time without notice and without penalty. They count as 'on demand' if a maturity or period of notice of not more than 24 hours or one working day has been agreed. Cash includes cash in hand and deposits denominated in foreign currencies.

It will be seen that the definition of 'cash' for the purposes of FRS 1 is extremely narrow.

IFRS, by contrast, uses the far broader caption heading of 'cash and cash equivalents' (see Chapter 26).

CHAPTER 22

Loan capital

Company borrowings generally

The advantages of borrowing

If a company confidently expects that its return on capital (i.e. the trading profit expressed as a percentage of the capital the company employs) will exceed the cost of borrowing, then borrowing will increase the profit attributable to the ordinary shareholders. There are, however, various limitations on the amount a company can borrow, which we will discuss later in this chapter, and borrowing also increases risk.

The risk of borrowing

The risk of borrowing is twofold: firstly the interest on most borrowings has to be paid promptly when due (unlike dividends on shares, which can be deferred or omitted altogether) and secondly most borrowings have to be repaid by a certain date (unlike most share capital, which is only repayable on liquidation).

In a poor year, interest charges can drastically reduce the pre-tax profits of a heavily borrowing company. Take, for example, two companies that are identical except that one, Company A, is financed entirely by shareholders while the other, Company B, is financed half by shareholders and half by borrowing, which bears a rate of interest of 10% per annum.

The table in Example 22.1 below shows the profitability of the two companies with varying rates of return on capital employed: in an average year Company B earns 15% on money borrowed at 10%, and so gains 5% on £2,000,000, adding £100,000 to pre-tax profits. This extra profit, after tax, adds 3.5p to the earnings attributable to each of the 2,000,000 shares that Company B has issued,

---

Example 22.1 Financing by share capital and by borrowing

	Company A			Company B		
Issued equity (£1 shares)	£4,000,000			£2,000,000		
Borrowings (10% interest)	Nil			£2,000,000		
	Good year	*Average year*	*Poor year*	*Good year*	*Average year*	*Poor year*
Rate of return	25%	15%	5%	25%	15%	5%
	£000	£000	£000	£000	£000	£000
Trading profit	1,000	600	200	1,000	600	200
Interest	–	–	–	200	200	200
Pre-tax profit	1,000	600	200	800	400	0
Taxation (30%)	300	180	60	240	120	0
Profit after tax	700	420	140	560	280	0
Earnings per share	17.5p	10.5p	3.5p	28.0p	14.0p	0p

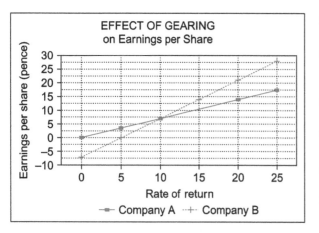

EFFECT OF GEARING
on Earnings per Share

making the earnings per share 14.0p compared with 10.5p for Company A.

In a good year the advantage of borrowing will enhance Company B's earnings per share even more (28p compared with 17.5p for Company A) but in a poor year, as our table shows, all the trading profit is used servicing the borrowings of Company B, while Company A still manages to earn £140,000 after tax for its shareholders.

The point at which the two companies do equally well as far as their shareholders are concerned is shown in the graph above. Their earnings per share are both 6.7p when the return on capital employed is 10% per annum; as one would expect, borrowing at 10% to earn 10% neither adds to nor detracts from Company B's profits. As the graph also shows, borrowing makes a company's profits more volatile and the risk of borrowing is further increased when money is borrowed at a variable rate of interest (e.g. on overdraft). If interest rates had risen above 10% in our example's 'poor year', Company B would have actually made a loss.

We will come back to the effects of borrowing later in this chapter, but let us now look in detail at various types of borrowing.

Types of borrowing

There are many ways in which a company can borrow money, the main characteristics of different types of debt being:

- the length of time for which the money is borrowed;
- the rate of interest paid;

- the security offered to the lender by way of charges on the assets of the company;
- the negotiability of the debt instrument (i.e. does the lender receive a piece of paper which he can sell if he wishes to disinvest before the date of repayment?);
- the flexibility to the company and to the lender in the timing of borrowing and repayment;
- any deferred equity option given to the lender.

A company's borrowings fall broadly into three categories:

1. Debentures and unsecured loan stock, issued on the UK market, and bonds, issued on the Eurobond and other markets. These can be held by the general public, and can be bought and sold in the same way as shares.
2. Loans from banks and other financial institutions.
3. Bank overdrafts (described in Chapter 21).

Categories 1 and 2 are shown separately in the balance sheet, with a note describing the terms on which each loan is repayable and the rate of interest, dividing them into secured and unsecured loans.

An analysis of the maturity of debt should be given, showing amounts falling due:

- in one year or less, or on demand;
- between one and two years;
- between two and five years; and
- in five years or more.

 A loan which is soon due for repayment may significantly weaken a company's position.

This can be a very serious threat to a company that is already short of funds if it is likely to have any difficulty refinancing the loan.

Security given to the lender

When a company wishes to issue loan capital it can offer the lender some specific security on the loan. If it does so, the loan is called a debenture (£100 units) or debenture stock (usually units of £1); if not it is unsecured loan stock (ULS), and these are the two main types of loan capital raised in the UK from the general public (often referred to as corporate bonds).

Debentures, unsecured loan stock and bonds

Debentures

Debentures can be secured by fixed and/or floating charges described below, the most common type of debenture being one that is secured on specific land or buildings, sometimes called a mortgage debenture.

Bonds

A bond is the generic name given to loan capital raised in the Eurobond market and in the US and other domestic markets. Issues in the Eurobond market may be denominated in sterling or in a foreign currency, and are normally of between seven and ten years' duration.

The Eurobond market began with the issue of Eurodollar bonds – US$ denominated securities issued outside the USA. It now encompasses offshore issues in a variety of currencies, but it is still mainly a US$ market. An increasing number of UK companies make use of this market (e.g. PEARSON):

PEARSON *Note to the 2003 accounts*

Borrowings by instrument

Unsecured (£ million)	2003	2002
9.5% Sterling Bonds 2004	108	120
6.125% Eurobonds 2007	343	370
4.625% Euro Bonds	348	338
10.5% Sterling Bonds 2008	100	100
7% Global Dollar Bonds 2011	278	310
7% Sterling Bonds 2014	235	250

. . .

Fixed charge

A fixed charge is similar to a mortgage on a house. The company enters into a debenture deed which places a charge on specific identifiable assets. This gives the debentureholder a legal interest in the assets concerned as security for the loan, and the company cannot then dispose of them unless the debentureholder releases the charge (which he or she is unlikely to do unless offered some equally good alternative security). If the company defaults

or falls into arrears on interest payments or capital repayments, the debentureholder can either:

(a) appoint a receiver to receive any income from the assets (e.g. rents); or
(b) foreclose, i.e. take possession and sell the assets, using the proceeds of the sale to repay the debentureholders in full; any surplus remaining is then paid to the company, but if the proceeds of selling the assets charged are insufficient to repay the debentureholders in full, the debentureholders then rank equally with unsecured creditors for the shortfall.

Floating charge

This is a general charge on the assets of a company. But the debentureholder has no legal interest in the assets unless and until an event specified in the debenture deed occurs; for example, if the company goes into liquidation or ceases trading, or falls behind with interest payments or capital repayments, or exceeds specified borrowing limits. In the event of default the debentureholder can then appoint a receiver, who takes physical possession of the assets of the company. The receiver can also be appointed as the manager or a separate manager can be appointed to continue running the company, or the receiver can sell off the assets; the former course is adopted if possible, because a company can normally be sold as a going concern for more than the break-up value.

The ranking of unsecured loan stock (ULS) and bonds

In a liquidation the holders of unsecured loan stock and bonds rank equally with other unsecured creditors, that is after debentureholders and preferential creditors (tax, rates and certain obligations to employees). In practice trade creditors often restrict a company to 'cash with order' terms if they see it running into difficulties, and to that extent ULS and bonds tend to rank behind suppliers.

Typical characteristics of debentures and ULS

Interest

Most debentures, ULS and bonds carry a fixed annual rate of interest (known loosely as the 'coupon') which is payable (normally half-yearly) regardless of the company's profitability. Interest is deductible before the company is assessed for tax, i.e. it is an allowable expense for tax purposes, and therefore costs the company less than the same amount paid out in dividends on shares.

Redemption

Each issue is normally for a given term, and is repayable at the end of the term (at the redemption date) or, where there is a redemption period (e.g. 2006/08), it is repayable when the company chooses within that period. A few irredeemable stocks do exist, but they are rare, except in the case of water companies.

Liquidation

In the event of liquidation, debentureholders are entitled to repayment in full from the proceeds of disposal of the charged assets. Then the ULS and bond holders and other unsecured creditors, and the fixed charge debentureholders if not already fully satisfied, rank equally after preferential creditors, and have to be repaid before the shareholders are entitled to anything.

The trust deed

Where a debenture, loan stock or bond is to be issued to more than a very small number of holders, and particularly when it is going to be listed, a trustee or trustees are appointed to represent the holders collectively, and the company enters into a trust deed rather than a debenture deed.

For listing, the UK Listing Authority requires that at least one trustee must be a trust corporation which has no interest in or relation to the company which might conflict with the position of the trustee. A large insurance company or the specialist LAW DEBENTURE CORPORATION is often appointed as trustee.

The deed contains all the details of the issue, except the issue price, including:

(a) details of fixed and floating charges, together with provision for substitution (securing further assets to replace secured assets which the company may subsequently wish to dispose of during the term of the loan). Provision may also be made for topping up

(securing further assets if the value of secured assets falls below a given limit);

(b) redemption price and redemption date or period, and details of any sinking fund;

(c) conditions under which the company may repurchase in the market, by tender and from individual holders;

(d) redemption price in the event of liquidation;

(e) conditions for further pari passu (equal ranking) issues, restrictions on prior borrowings and, for ULS and bonds, overall borrowing limits;

(f) minimum transferable unit;

(g) powers to approve modifications to the terms and conditions.

The trust deed may also include restrictive clauses:

(h) to prevent the nature of the company's business being changed; this is known as a 'Tickler' clause, after the celebrated case of the jam manufacturer who was taken to court by the holders of an unsecured loan stock;

(i) to prevent major disposals of the company's assets – a 'disposals' clause;

(j) to restrict the transfer of assets between charging subsidiaries (those within the charging group, i.e. included in the charge on assets) and other subsidiaries – sometimes known as a 'ring fence' clause.

Deep discount issues

Some companies issue loan capital at a substantial discount to par value in order to reduce the coupon, i.e. to reduce the amount of interest they have to pay during the life of the security concerned. The investor is compensated for receiving less interest by getting back appreciably more than he or she paid when the security is redeemed.

For tax purposes, a *deep discount security* is one:

- where the discount on issue represents more than 15% of the capital amount payable on redemption; or
- where the discount is 15% or less but exceeds half the number of complete years between issue and redemption.

The income element is calculated as the percentage rate at which the issue price would have to grow on a compound basis over each income period to equal the redemption price at the date of redemption. The income element is treated as income of the holder and as a deductible expense of the issuer, as AVIVA shows in its accounting policies.

AVIVA *Extract from accounting policies 2003*

Subordinated debt and debenture loans
Subordinated debt and borrowings issued at a discount are included in the balance sheets at their proceeds, net of other expenses, together with amortised discount to the balance sheet date. The discount, amortised on a compound basis, and expenses are charged to loan interest in the profit and loss account over the term of the relevant instrument.

Stepped interest bonds

These are where the interest payable increases by fixed steps over the life of the bond. An example was CANARY WHARF'S £120m stepped fixed interest tranche which was part of a £555m first mortgage debenture, where interest was paid at 5% until October 1999. From October 1999 the interest then increased in steps to 9.53%, which was payable from October 2006.

In such cases, the profit and loss account should be charged at a constant rate computed over the anticipated life of the bond, irrespective of the amount of interest paid each year.

Mezzanine finance

Mezzanine finance is the term used to describe a form of finance that lies between straight debt and share capital. It is used in situations (e.g. management buy-outs (MBOs) and institutional purchases) where the amount of debt that can be raised is limited, and the amount of cash available to subscribe for shares is insufficient to make up the total required.

It is usually in the form of a loan that ranks after the normal debt (the 'senior' debt) and, because of the higher risk, bears a higher rate of interest and either carries an option to convert part of the loan into equity or has a warrant to subscribe for equity.

For example in BBA's sale of its automotive products businesses in the spring of 1995, the purchase by the new company AUTOMOTIVE PRODUCTS GROUP LTD was arranged by leading venture capital company CINVEN, financed as follows:

AUTOMOTIVE PRODUCTS GROUP *Financing of institutional purchase*

	£000	
Senior debt	90,000	(Note 1)
Mezzanine finance	20,000	(Note 2)
Senior management investment	1,244	
Cinven investment	62,956	(Note 3)
Opening revolving credit	4,435	
	£178,635	

Notes:

1. Medium-term loan at 2% over LIBOR, reducing to 1.5% providing certain profit targets are met. Final repayment date December 2001.
2. 8-year term loan at 3.5% over LIBOR. Carries warrants to subscribe for an additional 9% of the ordinary share capital.
3. Equity underwritten by Cinven's clients, who also underwrote a further £1.5m share offer to the remaining employees.

Highly geared (leveraged) deals are high risk; hence the need for the mezzanine debt to have an equity 'sweetener'.

Yields

The yield on an irredeemable security is the gross amount of income received per annum divided by the market price of the security. Redeemable securities have two yields, their running yield and their gross redemption yield.

Running yield

The running yield is the same as the yield on an irredeemable security: it measures income and is concerned purely with the annual gross interest and the price of the stock; for instance, an 8% unsecured loan stock issued at £98% will yield 8% ÷ 0.98 = 8.16% at the issue price, or a $4^1/_2\%$ debenture purchased at £50% will give the purchaser a yield of 9%, ignoring purchase expenses.

Redemption yield

The gross redemption yield is rather more complicated, as it measures 'total return'; i.e. it takes into account both the stream of income and any capital gain (or loss) on redemption. It is not just the sum of the running yield and the capital gain per annum, but is obtained by discounting the future interest payments and the redemption value at a rate that makes their combined *present value* equal to the current price of the stock. (The concept of discounting to obtain present value is explained in Appendix 4.) The rate required to do this is the gross redemption yield (see Example 22.2).

Typical gross redemption yields for a well secured debenture are $3/4\%$ to $1^1/2\%$ above the yield on the equivalent gilt-edged security (i.e. a UK government stock of similar life and coupon), and 1% up to 5% or more for ULS, depending very much on the quality of the company and the amount of prior borrowings (borrowings that would rank ahead in a liquidation).

Net redemption yields (i.e. the yields after tax) vary with the individual holder's rate of income tax payable on the stream of interest payments and the rate of tax on any capital gain on redemption.

Redemption date

When a stock has a final redemption period (e.g. 2006/08) it is assumed in computing redemption yields that the company will choose the earliest date for redemption, 2006, if the stock is currently standing above par, otherwise the latest date, 2008. When there is a sinking fund which allows redemptions only by drawings, the average life can be calculated accurately and should therefore be used as the number of years to redemption in calculating redemption yields. However, if the company is allowed to redeem by purchase in the market or by inviting tenders, the stockholder can no longer be sure that early drawings at par will take place, and the average life is therefore ignored.

Example 22.2 Gross redemption yield

A 6% debenture due for redemption at £105% in four years' time is standing in the market at £90. Interest is payable in the normal manner, half-yearly in arrears (at the end of each six months). The present value of the stock is the sum of the present values of the eight future six-monthly interest payments discounted at $(1 + i)$ per half year (where i expressed as a decimal = gross redemption yield).

$$\frac{3}{(1 + i)^{0.5}} + \frac{3}{(1 + i)^{1.0}} + \cdots + \frac{3}{(1 + i)^{4.0}}$$

plus the present value of the sum received on redemption in four years' time:

$$\frac{105}{(1 + i)}$$

Solving for i by trial and error:

Value of I	Present value of income	Present value of redemption	Total
10% =	19.48 +	71.72 =	£91.20
11% =	19.09 +	69.15 =	£88.24

Inspection suggests that the gross redemption yield on a market price of £90 is about $10^1/2\%$, and a more accurate figure can be obtained by further manual calculation or by computer. Alternatively, the yield can be obtained from bond tables.

The amount a company can borrow

The amount a company can borrow may be limited by the following:

- *Its borrowing powers*. The directors' borrowing powers are normally limited by a company's Articles of Association, and cannot be altered except with the approval of shareholders at a general meeting. Borrowing powers are usually expressed as a multiple of shareholders' funds (issued share capital plus reserves, excluding intangible assets such as goodwill, although some companies, e.g. CADBURY SCHWEPPES, now include purchased goodwill in defining the directors' borrowing powers).
- *Restrictions imposed by existing borrowings*. The terms of the trust deeds of existing loan capital may restrict or preclude the company from further borrowing. In particular the terms of an unsecured loan stock may include a clause preventing the company from issuing loans that rank ahead of the stock concerned, and unduly restrictive clauses are often the reasons for companies redeeming loan capital in advance of the normal redemption date.
- The lender's requirement for *capital and income covers*.
- *The lender's general opinion* of the company and its overall borrowing position.

Example 22.3 Capital cover

Capital	Amount	Cumulative total	Simple cover	Rolled-up cover
	£000	£000		
6% Debenture	15,000	15,000	4.0	4.0
8% ULS	10,000			
10% ULS	5,000	30,000	3.0	2.0
Ordinary shares	12,000			
Reserves (less goodwill)	18,000	60,000		
Total capital		60,000		

Example 22.4 Income cover

A company has £5.76m of earnings before interest and tax, and the following loan capital, with the ULS and the CULS ranking equally:

Nominal value of issue	Annual interest	Cumulative interest	Times covered	Priority percentage
£12m of 6% Debenture	£0.72m	£0.72m	8.0	0–12½%
£10m of 8% ULS	£0.80m			
£8m of 5% CULS	£0.40m	£1.92m	3.0	12½–33⅓%

Capital and income covers

These are two standard measures that the intending purchaser of a debenture or loan stock may use to assess the security of his or her investment.

The *capital* or asset cover can be calculated in two ways, on a simple basis or on a 'rolled-up' basis.

Using the simple basis, the cover is the total capital less all prior-ranking stocks, divided by the issued amount of the stock in question. Using the 'rolled-up' basis, the cover is the total capital divided by the stock in question plus all prior-ranking stocks.

As Example 22.3 above shows, the two equal-ranking ULS issues are three times covered on a simple basis (£60m total capital less £15m prior-ranking debenture, divided by the total of £15m ULS), but only twice covered on a rolled-up basis. The more conservative rolled-up basis is normally used for assessing capital covers.

For a floating charge debenture a rolled-up capital cover of at least 3 or 4 is expected by the lender, and 2½ times is the normal minimum for an unsecured loan stock, but both depend on the quality of the assets, i.e. the likely realisable value of the assets on the open market in the event of a liquidation.

The *income cover* is normally worked out on a rolled-up rather than a simple basis: i.e. it is the number of times the interest on a stock plus the interest on any prior-ranking stocks could be paid out of profits before interest and tax. This cover can also be expressed as a priority percentage, showing the percentile ranking of a stock's interest, with earnings before interest and tax representing 100% (see Example 22.4 above).

Accounting for finance costs

Introduction

There are three elements to finance costs. The first is the interest payable each year. The second and third are the issue expenses and the difference between the issue price and the amount payable on redemption, i.e. the premium or discount on issue if redeemable at par. These two are amortised and charged against profits at a constant rate over the life of the debt instrument.

So the carrying amount, the amount at which the debt instrument is shown in the balance sheet at any time, starts off as the net proceeds of the issue and ends up at the redemption date as the amount payable on redemption.

Example 22.5 illustrates the operation of the effective interest rate method (this method is also referred to in Chapter 17 in connection with the asset category 'loans receivable').

Example 22.5

A company took out a loan of £110,000 on 1 January 20X2. The transaction costs amounted to £10,000 and the loan is repayable on 31 December 20X6 at a premium of £15,000 (i.e. the amount to be repaid is £125,000). The interest coupon on the borrowing is £5,900 and is payable on the last day of each year.

The total finance costs are £29,500 (interest) + £15,000 (debt premium) + £10,000 (transaction costs) = £54,500.

The effective interest rate on the borrowing is approximately 10% per annum as shown in the calculation below:

Year ending 31 December	Opening liability £	P/L charge £	Cash paid £	Closing liability £
20X2	100,000	10,000	5,900	104,100
20X3	104,100	10,410	5,900	108,610
20X4	108,610	10,861	5,900	113,571
20X5	113,571	11,357	5,900	119,028
20X6	119,028	11,872*	5,900	125,000
		54,500	29,500	

* £11,872 is a balancing figure as the effective interest rate was not precisely 10%.

MARKS AND SPENCER GROUP *Annual Report 2006*

Accounting policies extract – Bank borrowings
Interest-bearing bank loans and overdrafts are recorded at the proceeds received, net of direct issue costs. Finance charges, including premiums payable on settlement or redemption, and direct issue costs, are accounted for on an effective interest method and are added to the carrying amount of the instrument to the extent that they are not settled in the period in which they arise.

Repurchase of debt

Where the cost of repurchase or early settlement differs from the carrying amount in the balance sheet, the difference is taken to the profit and loss account in the accounting period of repurchase or early settlement.

Share capital

Background

We talk about share capital in detail in Chapter 24. It is necessary to talk about it in this chapter as well because of a major shift in accounting thinking in recent years. This is a direct result of the convergence process of bringing UK GAAP further into line with International Financial Reporting Standards.

Whilst most companies will continue to present their share capital in the balance sheet as equity share capital (see Chapter 24), some companies with more than one class of share capital may present part of their capital under the balance sheet heading of creditors due in more than one year (UK GAAP) or non-current liabilities (IFRS).

So what should dictate when share capital should be treated for accounting purposes as liabilities? The key point is to determine the rights which the shares confer on individual shareholders. A simple example of a class of shares which should be recognised as liabilities is where the payment of a divided is mandatory, i.e. where payment is *not* at the discretion of the directors, and where the shares must be redeemed at a specified future date or at the request of the shareholders. Further examples are given below.

The rule in FRS 25

FRS 25, Financial instruments: disclosure and presentation, sets out the detailed rules which determine whether shares should be classified as equity or liabilities. FRS 25 uses the term 'instrument' to include financial instruments – a very broad term which encompasses among other things, share capital and loan stock.

On initial recognition of the issue of the shares a company is required to classify the instrument (or its component parts) as a financial liability, financial assets or equity in accordance with the substance of the contractual arrangement. The important point is that it is the financial instrument's substance, rather than its legal form, that governs its classification on the issuer's balance sheet.

The classification rules in FRS 25 are extremely complex, but in practice affect a relatively small proportion of companies.

Example 22.6

The company's preference shares carry a right to a cumulative fixed net dividend per share of 5% of the nominal value with half-yearly dividend payments.

The company must redeem the preference shares by five equal half yearly instalments of £66,666 and one final instalment of £66,670 payable half yearly in each year commencing on 31 December 20X4. On a return of capital, the preference shareholders are entitled to a payment of the subscription price paid, plus a sum equal to arrears and accruals of dividend.

The substance of the contractual arrangements is that the preference shares contain two obligations:

1. The first is a financial liability to pay dividends – the company has no discretion over this (the possible lack of available distributable profits at a future date would make no difference to this analysis).
2. The second is that the company is obliged to repay the shares in accordance with a schedule of payments.

The preference shares should therefore be reclassified as a financial liability. FRS 25 also requires that the dividend payments relating to the above shares should be recognised as a finance cost expense in the profit and loss account.

Example 22.7

The company's non-voting, non-participating redeemable shares do not entitle the shareholder to the payment of a dividend and the shareholder may not vote at any general meeting of the company.

The company *may* redeem all or part of the non-voting, non-participating shares at any time. The redeemable shares are redeemable at par plus a capital redemption premium, which is calculated at a rate of 8% per annum from date of issue up to a maximum of £40,000.

On a winding-up, the non-voting, non-participating redeemable shares in issue carry priority over the ordinary shares to the extent of capital paid up.

The substance of the contractual arrangements is that the preference shares contain no obligations – the company can exercise discretion over dividend payments as well as over redemption of capital.

Under FRS 25 the preference shares would fall to be classified in the balance sheet as equity, and any dividends paid (which would be entirely at the directors' discretion) would have to be debited direct to equity (see Chapter 24).

Convertible loan capital

Introduction

Convertible loan capital, which is usually convertible unsecured loan stock (CULS) or convertible bonds rather than convertible debentures, entitles the holder to convert into ordinary shares of the company if he or she so wishes (see also convertible preference shares, Chapter 24).

The coupon on a convertible is usually much lower than the coupon needed for the issue of a straight unsecured loan stock with no conversion rights. This is because a convertible is normally regarded by the market as deferred equity, valued on the basis of the market value of the shares received on conversion plus the additional income enjoyed before conversion (the coupon on issue being higher than the yield on the ordinary shares).

Because convertibles are a form of deferred equity, listed companies can issue them without shareholders' prior approval only as a rights issue or as part or all of the consideration in an acquisition. In a takeover situation the bidder can use a suitably pitched convertible to provide the shareholders of the company being acquired with a higher initial income than they would receive from an equivalent offer of the bidder's ordinary shares. This is particularly useful when a bidder with low-yielding shares wants to avoid the shareholders of the company he wishes to acquire suffering a fall in income if they accept his offer.

CULS is attractive to investors seeking higher income, for example, to an income unit trust, and it also provides greater security than ordinary shares for both income and capital. From a company's point of view, CULS is cheaper to service than convertible preference shares, as the interest on the former is deducted in the assessment of corporation tax, but this advantage has been considerably eroded by the reduction in the rate of corporation tax. Most companies now prefer to issue convertible preference shares rather than CULS in order to reduce rather than increase their gearing.

Terms of a convertible loan

The holder has the option of converting into ordinary shares during a given period in the life of the loan stock or bond (the conversion period), at a given conversion price per share, expressed as so many shares per £100 of stock, or as so much nominal stock per ordinary share (see Example 22.8).

The period between issue and the first date for conversion is sometimes called the 'rest period', and the period from the last date for conversion to the final redemption date the 'stub'. Diagrammatically the GREAT PORTLAND convertible can be shown as:

		Stub
Rest period	Conversion period	
1988	1992	2002

A rest period of two or three years is normal, and most conversion periods run for at least four or five years. Some convertibles have a stub of several years, which is more prudent because if convertible holders decide not to exercise their conversion rights the company concerned is probably not doing very well and would not want to be faced with having to redeem the stock almost as soon as the conversion rights lapsed.

To protect investors the terms of some convertible debt (and some convertible preference shares) include what is known as *bid protection*, a fairly recent innovation. This protection can be either an enhancement of the conversion terms, or compensation based on the average premium over the preceding year, in the event of a takeover.

Another piece of convertible jargon is the *conversion premium*. This is the premium one pays by buying the ordinary

Example 22.8 Convertible loan: GREAT PORTLAND ESTATES

In January 1988 GREAT PORTLAND ESTATES made a rights issue of a 9½% convertible loan stock 2002 at par, on the basis of £1 nominal of CULS for every 4 ordinary 50p shares held. The stock, when issued, was convertible into 30.303 ordinary shares per £100 stock (equivalent to a price of 330p per share when issued at par) in the August of any year between 1992 and 2002 inclusive; these conversion terms will be adjusted for any scrip issues to the ordinary shareholders in the meantime. The terms were subsequently adjusted twice, to give a conversion price of 273p.

Any rights issues to ordinary shareholders will *either* be made to the holders of the convertible as if they had been converted, *or* an adjustment will be made to the conversion terms (most CULSs specify only one method).

In the event of a bid the company will endeavour to ensure that a like offer is made to the CULS holders as if they had converted; they would, however, lose any income advantage they enjoyed over the ordinary shareholders. This is a risk you have to take if you buy the CULS rather than the ordinary shares.

If more than 75% of the stock is converted, GREAT PORTLAND has the right to force remaining stockholders to convert or redeem straight away; this is a fairly standard condition, enabling the company to clear a convertible off its balance sheet once most of it has been converted. Stock that remains unconverted at the end of the conversion period will be redeemed by GREAT PORTLAND at par on 1 December 2002.

shares via the convertible rather than buying them direct. For example, if the GREAT PORTLAND convertible in Example 22.8 was standing at 120% (per £100 nominal) and the ordinary shares were standing at 300p, the cost of getting into the ordinary shares through the convertible would be £120 ÷ 36.63 (£30.303 adjusted for subsequent scrip issues) = 327.6p, a conversion premium of just over 9%.

A good indication of the likely market price of a convertible can be obtained by discounting the future income advantage to present value and adding it to the market value of the underlying equity. One caveat to this method is that if the price of the ordinary shares is very depressed, the price of the convertible in the market can become mainly dependent on its value as a fixed-interest security, particularly if the conversion period has not long to run.

A good indication of the likely market price of a convertible can be obtained by discounting the future income advantage to present value and adding it to the market value of the underlying equity. One caveat to this method is that if the price of the ordinary shares is very depressed, the price of the convertible in the market can become mainly dependent on its value as a fixed-interest security, particularly if the conversion period has not long to run.

Convertibles with put options

In the euphoria before the market fall in October 1987, several companies were so confident that their share price was going on up for ever that they agreed to the innovation suggested by fee-hungry US investment banks to include a 'put' option in the terms of their convertibles. This 'put' option gave the convertible bond holders the option to redeem after four or five years at a substantial premium, which was calculated to give a specified gross redemption yield.

From an investor's point of view, an early 'put' option is a 'heads I win, tails I can't lose' situation (unless the company goes bust). But from a company's point of view it is asking for trouble: if the ordinary share price is depressed when the date for exercising the 'put' option approaches, it is unlikely to be a good time for the company to have to redeem the convertible.

In addition, the market may become worried about whether the company has the financial resources to meet the repayment; this may further depress the share price, increasing the likelihood of investors exercising their 'put' options (e.g. the fashion retailer NEXT).

Next had one £50m and one £100m convertible with conversion prices of 286p and 430p respectively, and 'put' options to redeem in 1992. Next's share price peaked in 1987 at 378p, but fell to under 100p in 1989 as the company was hit by the recession and moved into loss. By this time the market became anxious about whether Next could fund redemption, and the share price tumbled to $6^1/_2$p at one point.

Next did survive, but only by selling off its mail order subsidiary Grattan in 1991 to pay for the 'put' options which were, of course, exercised. As the result of Next and several other companies burning their fingers badly, the drawbacks of 'put' options are now well appreciated, and companies issuing convertibles have stopped giving them. However, they may appear again in the euphoria of the next roaring bull market; if they do – beware.

Convertibles with warrants

A warrant gives the holder the right to subscribe at a fixed price for shares in a company at some future date. Where a company is reluctant to raise loan capital, for example, when very high long-term interest rates prevail, or investors are reluctant to commit themselves to purely fixed-interest securities, loan capital can be raised with a lower coupon by attaching warrants to issues of stock.

Warrants issued in this way are normally detachable and exercisable as soon as the stock to which they are attached is fully paid, and in some issues stock can be surrendered at its nominal value as an alternative to cash payment when the warrants are exercised.

For accounting purposes, when a debt instrument is issued with warrants attached, the proceeds of the issue should be allocated between the debt and the warrants (FRS 4, paragraph 22).

In a takeover situation, warrants can provide a more flexible way for the bidder to give loan stock an equity interest than convertibles, because the number of warrants, sometimes called the equity 'kicker', can be varied as the company wishes, while the quantity of ordinary shares to which convertible holders are entitled is defined within a narrow range by the limit the market will accept on the conversion premium.

On the other hand, a drawback to warrants is that they will seldom be exercised until close to the final exercise date, because they are bought by investors who want the gearing they provide, so the future flow of money into the company's equity is more chancy than with a convertible.

Accounting for convertible loan stock (CLS)

FRS 25 requirement

The section on share capital (see above) referred to the requirement in FRS 25 requiring a company to classify a 'financial instrument (*or its component parts*) as a financial liability, financial assets or equity . . .'.

So when a company issues convertible loan stock, FRS 25 requires it to evaluate the terms of the CLS to determine whether it contains both a liability and an equity component. The component parts of the CLS shall be classified separately as financial liabilities, financial assets or equity instruments in accordance with the substance of the contractual arrangement and the respective definitions.

CLS example

A convertible bond may be converted by the holder into a fixed number of ordinary shares of the issuer. The conversion rate, for example, 125 shares in exchange for each £100 of bond, is fixed and does not change in relation to changes in the value of the company's shares. If holders do not exercide their right to convert to shares, the bonds will be redeemed at par on a specified date.

From the issuer's perspective, such an instrument comprises two components:

1. **a financial liability** – a contractual arrangement to deliver cash or other financial assets, and
2. **an equity instrument** – a call option granting the holder the right, for a specified period of time, to convert into a fixed number of ordinary shares of the issuer.

The split accounting treatment required in this situation, is illustrated in Example 22.9.

Example 22.9 Split accounting for CLS

FRS 25 describes the two stages required to determine the initial carrying amounts of the separate components of the bond convertible into equity shares:

1. The issuer first determines the carrying amount of the liability component by measuring the fair value of a similar liability.
2. The carrying amount of the equity instrument represented by the option to convert the instrument into common shares is calculated by deducting the carrying amount of the financial liability from the amount of the compound instrument as a whole.

An entity issues 2,000 convertible bonds at the start of year 1. The bonds have a three-year term, and are issued at par with a face value of £1,000 per bond, giving total proceeds of £2m. Interest is payable annually in arrears at a nominal annual interest rate of 6%. Each bond is convertible at any time up to maturity into 250 equity shares.

When the bonds are issued, the prevailing market interest rate for similar debt without conversion options is 9%.

The liability component is measured first, and the difference between the proceeds of the bond issue and the fair value of the liability is assigned to the equity component. The present value of the liability component is calculated using a discount rate of 9%, the market interest rate for similar bonds having no conversion rights, as shown below.

	£
Present value of the principal – £2,000,000 payable at the end of three years	1,544,367
Present value of the interest – £120,000 payable annually in arrears for three years	303,755
Total liability component	1,848,122
Equity component (by deduction)	151,878
Proceeds of the bond issue	2,000,000

The numbers for the three years are as follows:

	Principal £	Interest £	Income statement £
Balance 1 January 20X1	1,544,367	303,755	
Income statement unwinding of discount (9%)[1]	138,993	27,338	[166,331]
Cash paid		(120,000)	
Balance 31 December 20X1[2]	1,683,360	211,093	
Income statement unwinding of discount (9%)	151,502	18,998	[170,500]
Cash paid		(120,000)	
Balance 31 December 20X2	1,834,862	110,091	
Income statement unwinding of discount (9%)	165,138	9,909	[175,047]
Cash paid		(120,000)	
Balance 31 December 20X3	2,000,000	–	[511,878]

1. This is the finance cost charged to the profit and loss account for 20X1.
2. This is the total liability in the balance sheet at 31/12/X1.

For some CLS, the conversion rate is variable and changes in line with changes in the value of the underlying shares. For example, if the share price halved, the conversion rate would automatically double, effectively protecting the holder's conversion rights. Such CLS is a liability throughout, as it represents an obligation of the issuing company. It does not contain an equity element and the split accounting treatment illustrated below would not be appropriate.

Financial instrument disclosure issues

FRS 25 contains several disclosure requirements but under UK GAAP these are mandatory only for restricted categories of companies (those who adopt the measurement standard FRS 26). This is unlikely to affect many private companies.

Fully listed and AIM-listed companies are referred to under IFRS.

Reporting the substance of transactions, FRS 5

Introduction

We cover FRS 5 in this chapter, on the ground that it is largely concerned with borrowing, but it applies to all transactions or arrangements of a reporting entity whose financial statements are intended to give a true and fair view except:

- forward contracts and futures (such as the use of foreign currencies or commodities);
- foreign exchange and interest rate swaps;
- contracts where a net amount will be paid or received based on the movement in a price or an index (called 'contracts for differences');
- expenditure commitments (such as purchase commitments) and orders placed, until the earlier of delivery or payment;
- employment contracts.

Essentially the Standard is very simple:

'A reporting entity's financial statements should report the substance of the transactions into which it has entered. In determining the substance of a transaction, all its aspects and implications should be identified and greater weight given to those more likely to have commercial effect in practice.'

Quasi-subsidiaries

Under FRS 5 a quasi-subsidiary is:

'a company, trust, partnership or other vehicle that, though not fulfilling the definition of a subsidiary, is directly or indirectly controlled by the reporting entity and gives benefits for that entity that are in substance no different from those that would arise were the vehicle a subsidiary . . .

'Where the entity has a quasi-subsidiary, the substance of the transactions entered into by the quasi-subsidiary should be reported in the consolidated financial statements.'

BRITISH AIRWAYS accounts explain the position in a note:

BRITISH AIRWAYS *Note on Accounting Policies 2003*

Basis of consolidation
Where an entity, though not fulfilling the legal definition of a subsidiary, gives rise to benefits for the Group that are, in substance, no different than those that would arise were that entity a subsidiary, that entity is classified as a quasi-subsidiary.

In determining whether the Group has the ability to enjoy the benefits arising . . . regard is given as to which party is exposed to the risks inherent in the benefits and which party, in practice, carries substantially all the risks and rewards of ownership. The group currently accounts for its investment in the London Eye Company Ltd. as a quasi-subsidiary.

Sale and leaseback

Sale and leaseback is an arrangement where the owner of an asset, typically a property, sells the asset and then leases it back. Under FRS 5, the accounting treatment of the transaction will depend on its substance:

- If the '*seller*' retains the risks and rewards of ownership (e.g. would benefit/suffer from any subsequent increase/

decrease in the value of the property) *the transaction is treated as a financing transaction.*

The property would remain on the seller's balance sheet, and the cash received would be regarded as a loan.

- On the other hand, if the *'purchaser'* benefits from any subsequent increase in value, and the seller pays rentals subject to periodic review, *the transaction is treated as a sale.*

The property would be removed from the seller's balance sheet, and the profit/loss on sale would be taken to the seller's profit and loss account.

Gearing ratios

Introduction

Financial ratios fall into two broad groups, gearing ratios and liquidity ratios.

Gearing is concerned with the proportion of capital employed that is borrowed, the proportion provided by shareholders' funds and the relationship between the two, while liquidity ratios (see page 148) are concerned with the company's cash position.

Financial gearing

Financial gearing can be defined in a multiplicity of ways, the two most common being:

1. the debt/equity ratio, shown as borrowings/shareholders' funds in the *Investors Chronicle*, and called 'leverage' in the USA and elsewhere; and
2. the percentage of capital employed represented by borrowings.

Whatever method is used to compute gearing, a company with 'low gearing' is one financed predominantly by equity, whereas a 'highly geared' company is one which relies on borrowings for a significant proportion of its capital.

To illustrate (see Example 22.10), let us take the bottom half of three different companies' balance sheets, adjusting them to include bank overdraft and any other borrowings falling due within one year (these are normally netted off against current assets in a company's balance sheet, but are just as much a part of capital employed as long-term

borrowings are). As you can see, debt/equity ratio is a more sensitive measurement of gearing than debt/capital employed, and it also gives a better indication of the effect of gearing on equity income, known across the Atlantic as the 'leverage effect'.

Example 22.10 Calculation of gearing and debt/equity ratios

		Company A £000	B £000	C £000
Ordinary share capital		600	500	250
Reserves		850	550	300
Ordinary shareholders' funds	[A]	1,450	1,050	550
Redeemable preference share capital (3.5%)	[B]	–	100	–
Minorities	[C]	150	150	150
Provisions		400	400	400
Loan stock (10%)	[D]	–	150	400
Overdraft (currently 12%)	[E]	–	150	500
Capital employed	[F]	2,000	2,000	2,000

	A	B	C
Debt/Equity (Leverage) $=\left(\dfrac{B+D+E}{A+C}\right)$	0%	33%	128%
Debt/Capital Employed $=\left(\dfrac{B+D+E}{F}\right)$	0%	20%	45%
Gearing	None	Low	High

[B] The treatment of preference shares is a problem: although they are not debt they do carry a *fixed* rate of dividend that is payable ahead of ordinary dividends. On balance we favour treating them as debt if redeemable in the reasonably near future, say in less than 10 years, but otherwise as equity when looking at capital (because it would be misleading to ascribe the same Debt/Equity ratio to a company with, say, 60 debt/40 equity as one with 60 pref./40 equity).

[C] Minorities have been included as equity in the calculation of Debt/Equity ratios, on the assumption that minority interests in subsidiaries are all pure (non-redeemable) equity.

Leverage effect

The effect of leverage can be expressed as a ratio: percentage change in earnings available to ordinary shareholders brought about by a 1% change in earnings before interest and tax (EBIT).

Suppose each of the three companies in Example 22.11 has a return on capital employed (ROCE) of 10%, and that the rate of corporation tax is 30%; then earnings before interest and tax (EBIT) will be as shown in Example 22.11.

Leverage, of course, works both ways; if EBIT fell by 50% then earnings available to ordinary shareholders would fall to £70,000 (Company A) and to £43,400 (Company B); and Company C would be on the point of making a loss.

Example 22.11 Calculation of leverage effect

		Company	
	A	B	C
	£000	£000	£000
EBIT	200.00	200.00	200.00
Less			
Loan stock interest	–	(15.00)	(40.00)
Interest on overdraft	–	(18.00)	(60.00)
Pre-tax profits	200.00	167.00	100.00
Tax at 30%	(60.00)	(50.10)	(30.00)
Profits after tax	140.00	116.90	70.00
Preference dividends	–	(3.50)	–
Available for minorities and ordinary shareholders [G]	140.00	113.40	70.00
1% change in EBIT	2.00	2.00	2.00
Tax	0.60	0.60	0.60
Available for minorities and ordinary shareholders [H]	+ 1.40	+ 1.40	+ 1.40
Leverage ratio			
$\dfrac{H}{G} \times 100$	1.00	1.23	2.00

Interest rate sensitivity

A simple calculation can be made to see the sensitivity of a company's profits to interest rates: if, in Example 22.11, the rate charged on overdrafts rose to 16% (or fell to 8%), Company C's pre-tax profit would be reduced (or increased) by 20%.

Operational gearing

In assessing what level of financial gearing might be reasonable for a company, we must first look at the volatility of profits. This depends to a large extent on the sensitivity of profits to turnover, which we will call operational gearing (although the term 'operational gearing' is sometimes used in the sense of overall gearing to include the effects of financial gearing as well).

The operational gearing of a company can be described as the ratio of the percentage change of trading profit which results from 1% change in turnover, and depends on the relationship between fixed costs, variable costs and net profit, where fixed costs are costs that are incurred regardless of turnover, and variable costs are directly proportional to turnover:

Operational gearing
= (Turnover – Fixed costs) + Trading profit

or

(Trading profit + Fixed costs) + Trading profit

Example 22.12 overleaf demonstrates this.

Profit/volume chart

The effect of gearing can also be illustrated graphically on a 'profit/volume chart', as shown in Example 22.13 overleaf. A profit/volume chart is constructed by plotting two points:

1. trading profit against actual turnover;
2. fixed costs against zero turnover;

and joining the two points together. The point where this line crosses the horizontal 'zero profit' line represents the level of turnover at which the company 'breaks even', i.e. makes neither a profit nor a loss. The steeper the gradient of the line the higher the operational gearing of the company.

Aggravating the problem

It is fairly obvious that a company with high operational gearing aggravates the problem by gearing up financially. Suppose, for instance, that Company E has borrowings that incurred interest charges of £3m p.a.; Example 22.14 shows the effect on profits.

Example 22.12 Effects of operational gearing

	Turnover £m	Fixed costs £m	Variable costs £m	Trading profit £m	Operational gearing
Company D	100	20	70	10	3:1 ((100 − 70):10)
Company E	100	70	20	10	8:1 ((100 − 20):10)

If turnover increases by 10%:

	£m	£m	£m	£m	Change in profits
Company D	110	20	77	13	+30%
Company E	110	70	22	18	+80%

This is fine for both D and E, especially for E, which is much more highly geared operationally than D. But, as with high financial gearing, high operational gearing works against a company when turnover falls. Assume a 10% fall in turnover:

	£m	£m	£m	£m	Change in profits
Company D	90	20	63	7	−30%
Company E	90	70	18	2	−80%

Example 22.13 Profit/volume chart

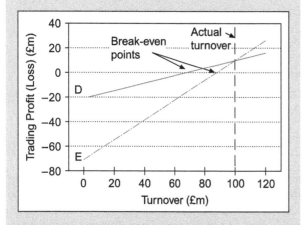

The break-even point can also be calculated:

Break-even turnover

$$= \text{Fixed costs} \times \frac{\text{Turnover}}{\text{Turnover} - \text{Variable costs}}$$

e.g., Company D $= 20 \times \dfrac{100}{100 - 70} = £66.67\text{m}$

Company E $= 70 \times \dfrac{100}{100 - 20} = £87.50\text{m}$

Example 22.14 Effect of high financial gearing coupled with high operational gearing

Turnover £m	Net trading profit £m	Interest charges £m	Pre-tax profits £m
100	10	3	7
110	18	3	15
90	2	3	−1

But the directors of a property company with mainly completed developments let to substantial clients will know that they have an assured rental income coming in each quarter, and they would not be considered imprudent to borrow heavily (i.e. gear up) provided the level of interest payments plus running expenses could not exceed the stream of rental income. We say 'could not exceed', because one of the ways property companies get into trouble is by borrowing short-term with a variable interest rate (e.g. on bank overdraft), rather than at a fixed rate; they then get caught out when interest rates go up faster than rental income.

Fixed charges cover

This is a very useful ratio, not often shown in company reports and accounts. An exception is W H SMITH.

W H SMITH *Extracts from financial review 2003 and from notes to the 2003 accounts*

Fixed charges cover
A key measure of financial strength for the businesses is fixed charges cover. The fixed charges cover. The fixed charges comprise operating leases, property taxes, other property costs and interest. They were covered 1.4 times by profits before fixed charges (2002; 1.5 times).

Note 11 Fixed charges cover

	2003 £m	2002 £m
Interest expense (income)	4	(8)
Operating lease rentals	206	207
Property taxes	36	36
Other property costs	13	15
Total fixed charges	**259**	**250**
Profit before tax	**102**	**117**
Profit before tax and fixed charges	**361**	**367**
Fixed charges cover	**1.4**	**1.5**

Fixed charges cover is calculated by dividing profit before tax and fixed charges by total fixed charges.

International Financial Reporting Standards

The measurement, accounting and presentation rules in UK GAAP and IFRS are almost identical, with exceptions referred to below. The key differences relate to disclosures.

Measurement

Apart from terminology differences, UK GAAP and IFRS are identical. Differences relating to fair value measurements do not impact upon the areas covered in this chapter.

Accounting

Under UK GAAP, all companies except for the minority who adopt FRS 26, Financial instruments: recognition and measurement, will continue to adopt those parts of FRS 4, Capital instruments, which have not been superseded by FRS 25.

Under IFRS, companies must follow IAS 32 and IAS 39.

Presentation

The rules in FRS 25 and IAS 32 are identical.

Disclosure

Fully listed groups are required to adopt the disclosure requirements of IAS 32, although extended requirements in IFRS 7 become mandatory for accounts periods beginning on or after 1 January 2007.

Many AIM-listed companies adopted IFRS at the same time as fully listed groups, and the same applies as above. AIM-listed companies who have until recently adopted UK GAAP must adopt IFRS for periods no later than those starting on or after 1 January 2007.

The requirements of IFRS 7 are extremely detailed and are not reproduced in this chapter. FIRST CHOICE provides a good practical example of the extent to which disclosure requirements will be stepped up as a result of IFRS 7.

FIRST CHOICE *Annual Report 2006*

First Choice Holidays PLC first adopted IFRS for the year ended 31 October 2006. Note 25, Financial instruments, states:

As set out in note 1, the Group has adopted IFRS 7, IAS 32, and IAS 39, only with effect from 1 November 2005. The comparative financial information in these financial statements does not therefore comply with IFRS 7, IAS 32, and IAS 39 as the Group has elected to apply the transitional rules permitted by IFRS 1 and has not restated prior years. Comparative disclosures for the year ended 31 October 2005 have been prepared under UK GAAP FRS 13 and are set out in part (ii) of this note.

Comment

For the year ended 31 October 2005, FIRST CHOICE was required to adopt UK GAAP, and provided financial instruments disclosures on the basis of FRS 13 (FRS 25 was not mandatory for that period).

The following year the group was required to adopt IFRS and could have moved over to IAS 32 (the equivalent of FRS 25). Instead the group decided to adopt the extended requirements of IFRS 7 early, before its mandatory date. Because of special transitional provisions, the 2006 disclosures are on the basis of IFRS 7, whilst the comparatives are those presented in the previous year under FRS 13. The comparison between the 2006 and 2005 disclosures provides users of accounts with a useful insight into the extent to which IFRS 7 will provide additional information.

Readers who wish to see the lengthy and detailed note (almost eight pages) should visit the Investor Relations part of the First Choice website (www.firstchoiceholidaysplc.com) and look for the 2006 Annual Report page 55, note 25, Financial Instruments.

Further examples include DIAGEO 2007, NATIONAL GRID 2007 and VODAFONE 2007.

CHAPTER 23

Derivatives and other financial instruments

Introduction

Most of the business done by companies in the derivative market is for the prudent reduction of risk, primarily interest rate risk, currency risk and commodity risk. For example, SSL INTERNATIONAL include the following note:

SSL INTERNATIONAL *Annual report 2007*

Company accounting policies (extract)
[UK GAAP]

(f) Derivative financial instruments
The Company uses derivative financial instruments to avoid exposure to foreign exchange risk and interest rate movements.

The Company does not hold or issue derivative financial instruments for speculative purposes.

However, there is the other side of derivative business where much is sheer speculation: the unacceptable face of capitalism, doubled and redoubled. This is where derivatives can seriously damage your wealth.

Let us be quite clear about two things:

1. In business school parlance, derivatives are a 'zero sum game'. If anybody is going to 'make a bomb', someone else is going to 'lose a bomb'. The overall outcome is zero.
2. This is cowboy country. As the *Daily Telegraph* reported on 6 October 1995:

DAILY TELEGRAPH *Extracts from article by Banking correspondent*

P & G accuses Bankers Trust of racketeering
Procter & Gamble . . . alleges . . . that 'a culture of greed and duplicity', permeated through Bankers Trust. 'Fraud was so pervasive Bankers Trust employees used the acronym ROF – short for rip-off factor – to describe one method of fleecing clients.'

Procter & Gamble highlights one taped conversation in which a Bankers Trust employee describes a deal he has just concluded with the company as 'a massive future gravy train' . . .

Another tape related to massive profits made by Bankers Trust on a leveraged derivatives transaction sold to Procter & Gamble. 'They would never know,' said one saleswoman. 'They would never be able to know how much money was taken out of that.' A colleague replied: 'Never, no way. That's the beauty of Bankers Trust.' . . .

'Funny business, you know,' said one salesman in a taped conversation. 'Lure people into that calm and then just totally f*** them.' . . .

In the first part of this chapter we will concentrate mainly on the disclosures required by non-financial institutions under UK GAAP. We will also highlight cases involving speculative activity.

In the later part of the chapter, we will consider the impact of the changes introduced by International Financial Reporting Standards, particularly as regards the measurement of derivatives for balance sheet purposes.

UK GAAP

Measurement

Until recently, derivatives such as forward exchange contracts have been accounted for on a historical cost basis. In practice this meant derivatives were included in the balance sheet at a nil amount as historical cost was effectively zero.

International convergence developments are trying to change all this and to require derivatives to be included in the balance sheet at fair value (effectively a market value).

Under UK GAAP the requirement to fair value derivatives is only mandatory for companies that have adopted FRS 26, Financial instruments: recognition and measurement. For unlisted companies, FRS 26 is optional and is only likely to be adopted by those who wish to have investments and derivatives included in the balance sheet at fair value. This could include, for example, market-making or proprietary trading firms whose assets such as investments are held for trading purposes.

Companies adopting IFRS are required to comply with IAS 39 (which is identical to FRS 26) and this requires derivatives to be included in the balance sheet at fair value. We refer to the impact of IAS 39 on derivatives later in this chapter.

Presentation

Companies who adopt FRS 26 are required to comply with the presentation requirements of FRS 25. Under traditional historical cost accounting, many derivatives have a cost of nil and this standard therefore has no impact on them. Derivatives which do have a cost (e.g. warrants in listed companies) would be presented as current assets and measured under UK GAAP at the lower of cost and net realisable value (see Chapter 12).

Disclosure

FRS 13, Derivatives and other financial instruments, until recently was mandatory for companies whose share were publicly traded. FRS 13 was subsequently superseded by FRS 25 and now by FRS 29. In practice, comparatively few unlisted companies come within the scope of these standards (but see the reference to market-making and proprietary traders, above). Most of the companies which

would otherwise be affected are adopting International Financial Reporting Standards (see the IFRS section at the end of this chapter).

Disclosures required fall broadly into two categories:

1. *narrative disclosures*, usually contained in the operating and financial review or the directors' report; and
2. *numerical disclosures* in the notes to the accounts.

Definition of a derivative

Derivatives include futures, options, forward contracts, interest rate and currency swaps, interest rate caps, collars and floors, forward interest rate agreements, and commitments to purchase shares or bonds.

In more formal terms, a derivative is defined as a financial instrument which has all three of the following characteristics.

Firstly, its value changes in response to a change in an underlying item such as a change in interest rates, foreign exchange rates, commodity prices, share prices, stock exchange indices, etc.

For example, consider a company with a loan which has five years to run and which carries a variable rate of interest payable six-monthly. The company may enter into an interest rate swap contract with a third party (a bank) under which the company is committed to make fixed interest payments for, say, a five-year period in exchange for the bank making interest payments to the company at whatever variable interest rate happens to be at payment date. The company has effectively 'hedged' the interest rate risk, as its overall interest payments each period will remain fixed irrespective of any interest rate changes over the period of the swap.

Secondly, it requires no initial net investment (as would be the case with a forward exchange contract or interest rate swap) or an initial net investment that is smaller than would be required for other types of contracts that would be expected to have a similar response to changes in market factors.

An example of the latter would be an option contract such as warrants in the shares of a listed company. An investor may have the choice of either buying shares in ABC plc at the current market price of 130p or buying warrants at a cost of 15p, which entitle the holder to buy shares during a specified future period at a fixed price of, say, 250p. The warrant is a derivative – the cost of the warrant of 15p (which is the price paid to have the option of buying shares or not buying shares at a fixed price of 250p during a specified period) is significantly less than the cost of buying the shares outright (130p). Furthermore, if the quoted share price suddenly increased by, say, 80% because of takeover speculation, the warrant's fair value would increase proportionately.

Thirdly, the contract is settled at a future date – for example, in the case of a forward exchange contract involving the purchase of €30,000, this would be the date when the company had to make the necessary payment in £ sterling.

Risk management and derivative trading

Most large companies, and particularly multinationals, use derivatives to reduce exposure to various types of risk. This is a perfectly normal and usually fairly safe activity, providing you choose your counterparties carefully; i.e. don't deal with cowboys.

Other companies also *trade* in derivatives; this can be a very dangerous activity unless it is

- run by experienced and responsible staff, and
- tightly controlled.

Narrative disclosures

Companies that fall within the scope of the relevant accounting standards on disclosures (see above) must provide both narrative and numerical disclosures on the use of financial instruments. The following accounting policy note refers to a variety of derivative financial instruments.

GLAXOSMITHKLINE makes it clear that it wouldn't touch derivatives trading with a bargepole:

GLAXOSMITHKLINE *2003 accounting policies*

Derivative financial instruments

- The group does not hold or issue derivative financial instruments for trading purposes.

- Derivative financial instruments are used to manage exposure to market risks from treasury operations. The derivative contracts are treated from inception as an economic hedge . . .
- Currency swaps and forward exchange contracts are used to fix the value of the related asset or liability in the contract currency . . .
- Interest differentials under interest swap agreements are recognised . . . by adjustment of interest expense over the life of the agreement.

SHELL, on the other hand, has always been in the business of trading in oil, as its full name, Shell Transport & Trading implies, and has a huge depth of experience in the management of trading:

SHELL TRANSPORT AND TRADING *Extract from 2002 Operational and financial review*

Treasury and trading risks
. . . Apart from forward foreign exchange contracts to meet known commitments, the use of derivative financial instruments by most Group companies is not permitted by their treasury policy.

Some Group companies operate as *traders* in crude oil, natural gas, oil products and other energy-related products, using commodity swaps, options and futures as a means of managing price and timing risks . . . the use of derivative instruments is generally confined to specialist oil and gas trading and central treasury organisations which have appropriate skills, experience . . .

Numerical disclosures show how the company's objectives and policies were implemented in the period and provide supplementary information for evaluating significant or potentially significant exposures: see page 191.

Common types of derivatives

Introduction

The most common types of derivative that the ordinary investor is likely to come across are:

- options;
- futures and forward contracts; and
- currency and interest rate swaps.

An *options contract* is a contract giving the holder the right, but not the obligation, to buy ('call'), or sell ('put') a specified underlying asset at a pre-agreed price, at either a fixed point in the future (European-style), or a time chosen by the holder up to maturity (American-style). Options are available in exchange-traded (e.g. on LIFFE, the London International Financial Futures Exchange) and over-the-counter (OTC) markets (shorthand for anywhere else, between any two parties).

A *futures contract* on the other hand is an agreement (obligation) to buy or sell a given quantity of a particular asset, at a specified future date, at a pre-agreed price. Futures contracts have standard delivery dates, trading units, terms and conditions.

In a *forward contract* the purchaser and its counterparty are obligated to trade a security or other asset at a specified date in the future. The price paid for the security or asset is either agreed upon at the time the contract is entered into, or determined at delivery. Forward contracts are generally traded over-the-counter.

In a *currency swap* a company borrows foreign currency for a given period, and lends the equivalent sterling for the same period. In an *interest rate swap* the company swaps a fixed rate of interest with a bank for a floating rate, or vice versa.

While these are the most common types of derivative that ordinary investors are likely to come across, the range of derivatives possible is limited only by the imagination of investment banks. New types of derivative are being created all the time.

It is convenient to classify derivatives as either

- commodity related, or
- financial.

Commodity-related derivatives

Manufacturers whose business depends upon a particular key commodity (like sugar or cocoa) may well 'hedge', i.e. buy or sell options or futures contracts or employ forward contracts to fix the price of the underlying raw material, or the sales proceeds of a product.

TATE & LYLE discloses its policy on commodity derivatives in its OFR:

TATE & LYLE *Extract from 2003 Operating and financial review*

Commodities
Derivatives are used to hedge movements in the future prices of commodities in those domestic and international markets where the Group buys and sells sugar and maize.

Commodity futures and options are used to hedge inventories and the costs of raw materials for unpriced and prospective contracts not covered by forward product sales.

The options and futures hedging contracts generally mature within one year and are all with organised exchanges.

TATE & LYLE added in a note to the accounts: 'Changes in the fair value of instruments used as hedges are not recognised in the financial statements until the hedged position matures.' This is known as *hedge accounting* (FRS 13, paragraph 58).

In other words, whatever the total cost of acquiring the raw material this way, that is its 'cost'; and whatever the net sales proceeds are as a result of the future, those are the sales proceeds.

Providing the management lays down limits to the amount of hedging, and has control systems in place to ensure that these limits are not exceeded without permission, then hedging is a perfectly normal and reasonable business activity.

Where things go wrong is when you get a *rogue trader*. This happened some years ago in a chocolate manufacturer, where a commodity dealer started to gamble on cocoa futures and went way beyond the company's requirement for cocoa, thinking he could make a lot of money for the company.

When it was noticed that he was over the limits set for him, management stood over him while he closed all his positions. The moment they were out of the room, he opened them all up again.

When he was finally rumbled, a very substantial loss was incurred covering all his positions. In the aftermath of this débâcle the company's share price fell by more than 80%.

Reducing the risk of trading in derivatives

One secret of good management with any trading or dealing in derivatives is to ensure that the functions of confirmation and of settlement are kept entirely separate from the dealing department. In the celebrated case of currency swaps that brought down BARINGS, all these functions in Barings' Singapore office came under one person: Leeson.

Investors should also be wary when a company's dealers are 'earning' huge bonuses. Greed comes before a fall.

Financial derivatives

Companies have traditionally borrowed in foreign currencies to help finance overseas investment and reduce exposure to currency risk. In this modern day and age the mobility of capital in most of the developed countries of the world (exchange controls are still prevalent in Less Developed Countries (LDCs)), along with the increasing sophistication of the financial markets, has led to the development of a wide range of financial instruments to hedge against both currency and interest rate risk.

It no longer follows that you borrow French francs long-term at fixed rates of interest to finance long-term investment in France; it may be advantageous to borrow variable rate in sterling and do a currency swap and an interest rate swap.

Currency swaps

A currency swap is, in effect, the same as a reciprocating or back-to-back loan: the company borrows foreign currency for a given period and, in the same transaction, lends an equivalent amount of sterling for the same period.

For example, a UK company wants to borrow US dollars, but also wants to avoid the currency risk on the principal amount borrowed, i.e. it wants to hedge the currency risk. So it raises, say, £100m by a seven-year 10% Eurobond issue and swaps it for seven years with a bank for, say, $160m at $7^1/2$%. During the seven years the company pays interest to the bank in dollars at $7^1/2$% per annum on the $160m and the bank pays interest to the company in sterling at 10% per annum on the £100m. At the end of the seven years the swap is reversed, so the company gets its £100m back regardless of the sterling/US$ exchange rate and in time to redeem the Eurobond issue.

Currency swaps normally appear either in a note to the accounts or in the financial review (e.g. BP):

BP *Extract from financial review 2003*

Financial risk management

. . .

The main underlying economic currency of the group's cash flows is the US dollar. BP's foreign exchange management policy is to minimise economic and material transactional exposures arising from currency movements against the US dollar . . . In addition, most group borrowings are in US dollars.

Interest rate swaps

An interest rate swap can be used by a company to protect itself against the impact of adverse fluctuations in interest rates on the interest charge it has to pay on its floating rate debt. The company agrees a fixed rate with the bank on a nominal sum for a given period; the company then pays the bank the fixed rate and the bank pays the company the floating rate; as, for example, GLAXOSMITHKLINE:

GLAXOSMITHKLINE *Extract from note to the 2003 accounts*

32. Financial instruments and related disclosures

Interest rate risk management
To manage the fixed/floating interest rate profile of debt, the Group had several interest rate swaps outstanding with commercial banks at 31 December 2003.

When used in conjunction with a currency swap, an interest rate swap enables a company to lock in at a fixed rate of interest in one currency to cover floating-rate interest charges in another currency.

Companies may also use interest rate swaps in the reverse direction to reduce the proportion of their fixed-rate interest charges if they take the view that interest rates will fall. In neither case is there any transfer of principal.

The swap market has grown in recent years for another reason: to exploit the differences that exist between the fixed rate and the extremely competitive floating-rate credit markets in order to reduce the cost of borrowing, as illustrated in Example 23.1.

Example 23.1 Use of swaps to reduce the cost of borrowing

Two companies both want to borrow money for five years. One has an AAA Standard & Poor's credit rating and wants to borrow floating rate, while the other, rated BBB, wants to borrow fixed. Market conditions are:

	AAA	BBB
Company rating	AAA	BBB
Cost of 5-year fixed rate bond	10%	$11^1/_2$%
Cost of 5-year bank loan	LIBOR + $^1/_8$%	LIBOR + $^5/_8$%
Cost of a swap:		
Company pays	LIBOR	$10^1/_2$%
Company receives	$10^3/_8$%	LIBOR

The AAA company, wanting to borrow floating, would issue five-year bonds at 10% and swap; cost of borrowing floating = 10% + LIBOR – $10^3/_8$% = LIBOR – $^3/_8$% compared with the 5-year bank loan's cost of LIBOR + $^1/_8$%.

Similarly the BBB company, wanting to borrow at a fixed rate, would take out a bank loan at LIBOR + $^5/_8$% and swap; cost of borrowing fixed = LIBOR + $^5/_8$% – LIBOR + $10^1/_2$% = $11^1/_8$%, which is cheaper than issuing bonds at $11^1/_2$%.

Interest rate caps

Another way for a company with floating-rate debt to hedge against increases in interest rates is to buy a *cap*. A cap is a contract in which a counterparty, in exchange for a one-time premium, agrees to pay the bond issuer if an interest rate index rises above a certain percentage rate, known as the cap or *strike rate*. It is also called a *ceiling*.

The advantage of a cap over an interest rate swap from floating to fixed is that a cap not only protects the company from the effect of rising interest rates, but allows it to benefit from any fall in interest rates.

A *collar* is the simultaneous purchase of a cap and sale of a floor by the issuer, in which it trades any benefits from a potential fall in the interest rate index for protection against an excessive rise. Under a collar agreement, the issuer defines a specific range for its interest rate payments.

Caps and collars protect issuers from having to pay higher interest rates on variable rate debt if market rates increase beyond the cap rate.

A *floor* is the mirror image of a ceiling. With a floor contract, the bond issuer receives an upfront fee from a counterparty. If the interest rate index falls below the floor or strike level, the issuer makes payments to the counterparty. Similarly to a cap agreement, if the floating index rate does not fall below the strike level, the issuer pays nothing.

One company that uses a mixture of swaps, options, futures and forward rate agreements is SHELL:

SHELL *Note to the 2002 accounts*

28. Financial instruments

. . .

Some Group companies enter into derivatives such as interest rate swaps/forward rate agreements to manage interest rate exposure. . . .

Foreign exchange derivatives, such as forward exchange contracts, and currency swaps/options are used by some Group companies to manage foreign exchange risks. Commodity swaps, options and futures are used . . .

The estimated fair value and carrying amount of derivatives held by Group companies at 31 December is as follows:

	$million
Interest rate swaps/forward rate agreements	169
Fwd exch. contracts, currency swaps/options	(88)
Commodity swaps, options and futures	119
	200

Numerical disclosures

These give an overall picture of a company's currency and interest rate exposure, as TATE & LYLE's accounts illustrate.

TATE & LYLE *Note to the 2003 accounts*

34. Currency and interest rate exposure of financial assets and liabilities
After taking into account the various interest rate and cross currency interest rate swaps entered into by the Group, the currency and interest rate exposure of the financial liabilities of the Group was:

At 31 March 2003	Fixed rate £m	Floating rate £m	Non-interest bearing £m	Total £m
Sterling	50	2	2	54
US Dollars	294	(168)	–	126
Canadian Dollars	–	1	–	1
Euro	155	308	1	464
Others	–	–	–	–
Total	499	143	3	645
of which – gross borrowings	499	143	1	643
– non-equity shares	–	–	2	2
Total	499	143	3	645

Interest rates

	Average interest rate of fixed rate liabilities	Average years to maturity of fixed rate liabilities	Average years to maturity of non-interest bearing liabilities
Sterling	6.5%	9.2	–
US Dollars	4.9%	2.6	
Euro	5.7%	3.4	2.2
Average	5.6%	4.8	2.2

Counterparty risk

Companies which use derivatives are subject to *counterparty risk*, i.e. the risk that the counterparty defaults. The counterparty is simply the party with which one does the transaction.

Some companies with large exposure to derivatives, like REUTERS, describe the risk:

REUTERS *Note to the 2003 accounts*

12. Derivatives and other financial instruments
Hedging
All derivative instruments are unsecured. However, Reuters does not anticipate non-performance by the counterparties who are all banks with recognised long-term credit ratings of 'A3/A' or higher.

Concern about derivatives

What is disturbing about derivatives is that:

1. It is likely that anyone who today has funds invested will, usually unwittingly, be indirectly exposed to derivatives. Many major companies use them in one way or another; investment trusts, unit trusts and pension funds employ them in an effort either to protect themselves or to boost returns; so do some local authorities.

2. The sums involved are astronomical. For instance, BARCLAYS alone reported that at the end of 2003 it held or had issued:

	Contract or underlying principal amount £m
Foreign exchange derivatives	482,712
Interest rate derivatives	3,477,444
Equity and stock index derivatives	65,431
Commodity derivatives	44,402

3. Dealings are international and controls have yet to be agreed internationally.

There has been a series of derivative-based disasters in various countries – BARINGS was no isolated case – which have alerted management to the risks, but there is still plenty of ignorance around.

How can you blame the ignorant when a team of 'big hitters', as they call them in the USA, including the winner of a Nobel Prize for his research work on derivatives, set up an outfit called LTCM, Long Term Credit Management, got backing to the tune of $600bn, turned out in practice to be Short-term Catastrophic Asset Mismanagement (SCAM), but a scam of such gigantic proportions that it had to be rescued by the Fed (the US Federal Reserve Bank).

But why bother with derivatives?

You may well ask 'Why do companies go to all this trouble to complicate matters, when they would probably do just as well in the long run to carry the risk themselves?' Good question. Plenty of companies would agree with you (e.g. RIO TINTO):

RIO TINTO Extract from 2003 financial review

Exchange rates, reporting currencies and currency exposure
. . . the Group does not generally believe that active currency hedging would provide long term benefits to shareholders . . .
     . . . the Group does not generally believe a commodity price hedging programme would provide long term benefit to shareholders.

We can think of three reasons why companies and others use derivatives:

1. The real professionals, like SHELL and TATE & LYLE, have an enormous amount of in-house expertise and long experience of making profits on trading.
2. Although year-on-year currency risk and interest rate risk would probably be a case of swings and roundabouts, companies prefer to minimise the risk of a big hiccough in their reported profits. Investors don't like them, and in a bad year a sharp drop in profits due to adverse movements in currencies and/or interest rates could leave a company open to predators.
3. There is much international competition in banking these days and the traditional business of taking deposits and lending is much less profitable than it used to be. So bankers turn to other means of earning a crust and *some* aren't too particular how they do it.

Benefits of disclosure

There is a great deal of work involved in collecting and disclosing the information required by FRS 13, and the information is likely to be beyond the average investor. But the very process of collecting and reviewing the required information brings to the attention of directors and managers the nature and amount of risk which the company is running, and helps them meet their responsibilities. And most of the problems we have seen over derivatives, whether financial or commodity-based, have been due to weakness of controls and lack of higher management attention.

International Financial Reporting Standards

Introduction

The financial instrument standards relevant to derivatives are:

- IAS 32, Financial instruments: Presentation[1];
- IFRS 7, Financial instruments: Disclosure[2];
- IAS 39, Financial instruments: Recognition and measurement[3].

1. FRS 25 is identical to IAS 32.
2. FRS 29 is identical to IFRS 7.
3. FRS 26 is identical to IAS 39.

It is hardly a well-kept secret that IAS 39 has proved to be a deeply unpopular standard. One reason is its sheer complexity. Another is the potential volatility introduced into the annual profit figure resulting from fluctuations in interest rates and exchange rates, etc.

Classification and measurement

All derivatives (whether assets or liabilities) must be classified as 'financial asset or financial liability at fair value through profit or loss'. This is subject to one exception – this is where the derivative is an effective hedging instrument and where the company chooses to adopt hedge accounting (see the separate section below).

Apart from this exception, derivatives must be accounted for as follows:

- in the balance sheet, measured at fair value and classified as either a financial asset or financial liability;
- gains and losses arising from a change in fair value must be recognised in profit or loss (i.e. included in the income statement under the heading 'Finance costs').

Wherever possible, fair value should be arrived at using, or determined from, published prices in an active market. However this is not always feasible and an alternative approach is to use a valuation technique based on discounted cash flows.

CATTLES sets out classification and accounting treatment of its financial instruments. The parts relevant to derivatives are reproduced in the extract below, which also cross-refers to aspects dealt with in other chapters.

CATTLES *Annual Report 2006*

Accounting policy extract – Financial assets
Management determines the classification of the group's financial assets at initial recognition into one of the following categories and re-evaluates this classification at each reporting date:

Loans and receivables
Loans and receivables . . . [see Chapter 17]

Financial assets at fair value through profit or loss
This category has two sub-categories: financial assets held for trading; [see also Chapter 18] and those designated at fair value through profit or loss at inception. A financial asset is classified at fair value through profit or loss if acquired principally for the purpose of selling it in the short-term or if so designated by management. Derivatives are also categorised as held for trading unless they are designated as hedges.

[This part of the note also cross-refers to a separate accounting policy note dealing with 'Derivative financial instruments and hedging activities' – see below.]
. . .

Held-to-maturity
Held-to-maturity investments . . . [see Chapter 15]

Available-for-sale
Available-for-sale investments . . . [see Chapter 15]
. . .

Purchases and sales of financial assets at fair value through profit or loss are recognised on the trade to date, the date on which the group commits to purchase or sell the asset. Financial assets at fair value through profit or loss are initially recognised, and subsequently, carried at fair value. Gains and losses arising from changes in the fair value of these financial assets are included in the income statement in the period in which they arise. The group's financial assets at fair value through profit or loss relate solely to derivative instruments which cannot be designated as hedges. [Hedge accounting is referred to below.] Consequently they are classified as derivative financial instruments in the balance sheet within assets or liabilities dependent on the individual instrument's fair value at the reporting date.

Financial assets are derecognised when the rights to receive cash flows from the financial assets have expired or where the group has transferred substantially all the risks and rewards of ownership.

Disclosures

Until recently, disclosures given have been based on the requirements of IAS 32 but for accounts periods starting on or after 1 January 2007, disclosures will need to be based on the more stringent and extensive requirements of IFRS 7.

We referred to the 2006 disclosures of FIRST CHOICE HOLIDAYS at the end of Chapter 22 (page 184). The relevant extracts relating to the use of derivatives are reproduced below.

FIRST CHOICE HOLIDAYS *Annual report 2006*

Note 25 – Financial instruments [extracts from a seven and a half page note]

. . .

(a) Treasury risk analysis
The Group has exposure to the following risks from its use of financial instruments: market risk (in respect of changes in foreign exchange rates, fuel prices and interest rates), liquidity risk (in respect of the Group's ability to meet its liabilities) and credit risk (in respect of recovery of amounts owing to the Group).

The Group faces significant financial risks mainly due to the substantial cross-border element of its trading.

Currency risk arises on sales, purchases and borrowings that are denominated in a currency other than the functional currencies of individual Group entities. It is managed by the use of foreign exchange forward, swap and option contracts.

Interest rate risk is split into two separate exposures, namely US dollar interest rates on variable rate aircraft leases and loans, and sterling rates on Group loan and cash balances. Both exposures are managed using interest rate derivatives.

Finally, the Group's exposure to jet fuel prices is managed using energy swaps and options.

(b) Currency risk management
The Group is exposed to currency risks on sales, purchases and borrowings that are denominated in a currency other than the functional currencies of individual Group entities (which are principally Sterling, Canadian dollars, Euros and US dollars).

. . .

The Group hedges its foreign currency exposures season-by-season, with each season comprising a six-month period. At the start of a season the Group will have hedged substantially all of its currency exposure (forecast sales and purchases and related assets and liabilities) for that season, using forward exchange contracts, mostly with a maturity of less than one year from the reporting date.

Derivative financial instruments and hedging activities

 Economic hedge and hedge accounting are not the same

It is important to make a clear distinction between:

- the decisions whether to hedge a particular risk, and
- whether to apply hedge accounting.

The commercial practice of hedging risk (sometimes referred to as an 'economic hedge') and the accounting practice of 'hedge accounting' are not the same. A company may hedge risk exposures but may either choose not to adopt the option of hedge accounting or not even be permitted to adopt hedge accounting because the company is unable to satisfy the demanding criteria in IAS 39 (these criteria are referred to below).

Why do some companies choose to adopt hedge accounting?

The most quoted reason is the desire to avoid the volatility of earnings as between one accounting period and another which would result from the 'normal' treatment of derivatives referred to above, i.e. the rule in IAS 39 which requires gains and losses arising from a change in fair value to be recognised in profit or loss.

In some cases, the rule above may result in gains and losses on assets and liabilities that are managed together being recognised in profit or loss in different periods.

For example, a holiday company may enter into a foreign currency contract to manage the foreign exchange risk related to *committed* foreign purchases (cost of hotel rooms, etc.) which will take place in the following period.

Without hedge accounting, the gain or loss on the derivative would be recognised in the income statement of the current period, whilst the foreign exchange gain or loss on the purchases would not be recognised in the company's income statement until the following period.

What do companies have to do if they want to use hedge accounting?

The short answer is to set up sophisticated systems so that they can demonstrate the evidence required by IAS 39 on an ongoing basis. The criteria are complex but in brief summary are:

- At the inception of the hedge there must be formal designation and documentation of the hedging relationship and the entity's risk management objective and strategy for undertaking the hedge.
- The hedge must be expected to be highly effective and effectiveness must be capable of reliable measurement.
- The hedge must be assessed on an ongoing basis and determined actually to have been highly effective throughout the financial reporting periods for which the hedge was designated.

Types of hedge accounting

IAS 39 has no fewer than three types of hedge accounting:

1. cash flow hedge accounting;
2. fair value hedge accounting;
3. hedge of a net investment in a foreign operation.

A detailed review of each of these is outside the scope of this text – there are many leading accounting manuals that provide much information on hedge accounting, coverage varying from 100 to 160 pages on this topic alone! However, we do refer briefly to one form of hedge accounting – cash flow hedge accounting.

Cash flow hedge accounting

The definition of a cash flow hedge is somewhat long-winded:

A cash flow hedge is defined as a hedge of the **exposure to variability in cash flows** that

- is attributable to a particular risk associated with a recognised asset or liability (such as some or all future interest payments on variable rate debt) or a highly probable forecast transaction; and
- could affect profit or loss.

This covers two quite different situations:

1. recognised assets and liabilities (already entered in the accounting records); and
2. a highly probably forecast transaction (which has not yet happened).

Examples of cash flow hedges include:

- A company expecting to sell goods or services denominated in a foreign currency enters into an option contract giving it the right to sell foreign currency at a specified rate as a hedge of the risk that the domestic currency amount of the sales will fall due to declines in foreign exchange rates.
- A company with fixed-rate debt denominated in a foreign currency enters into a cross-currency swap as a hedge of the risk that debt payments in the domestic currency will change due to fluctuations in foreign exchange rates.
- A company is concerned that future transactions such as purchases denominated in a foreign currency may result in variable cash flows as a result of changes in foreign exchange rates. The company enters into a forward currency derivative to manage the risk. If foreign exchange rates move in an unfavourable manner relative to the purchases, unfavourable cash flows on those transactions will be compensated for by favourable cash flows on the derivative financial instrument.
- A UK company with a 31 December 20X6 year-end is intending to purchase a major item of machinery from a supplier in Germany for a cost of €3m. The equipment will be delivered on 26 February 20X7. As at 3 October 20X6 management regard the purchase as 'highly probable' and so enter into a forward purchase contract for €3m to be settled on 10 April 20X7 (agreed date for payment).

  The company has hedged against the risk that exchange rates will vary between 3 October and 10 April.

  Without hedge accounting, the gain or loss on the fair value of the derivative (the 'hedging instrument') would be recognised in the 20X6 profit or loss figure, even though the depreciation charge on the fixed asset ('the hedged item') would not affect profits until 20X7 – a mis-match between the two periods.

  With hedge accounting, any gain or loss on the derivative up to 31 December 20X6 would be held in a hedging reserve and deferred. The gain or loss would not affect the profit or loss until 20X7 and subsequent years according to the period over which the asset will be depreciated.

CATTLES, below, refers to both cash flow hedge accounting and fair value hedge accounting.

CATTLES *Annual report*

Accounting policies – Derivative financial instruments and hedging activities [extracts]

Derivatives are initially recognised at fair value on the date the derivative contract is entered into and are subsequently re-measured at fair value. The fair value of derivatives is determined by using a valuation model and is primarily based on observable market data. The method of recognising the resulting gain or loss from the re-measurement depends on whether the derivative is designated as a hedging instrument, and if so the nature of the item being hedged.

The group's policy is to designate on the date that the derivative contract is committed to. The group designates derivatives as:

- A hedge of the fair value of a liability ('fair value hedging instrument') or
- A hedge of the cost of a highly probable forecast transaction or commitment ('cash flow hedging instrument').

To qualify for hedge accounting, the group is required, at inception, to document in advance the relationship between the item being hedged and the hedging instrument. The group is also required to document and demonstrate an assessment of the relationship between the hedged item and the hedging instrument, which shows that the hedge will be highly effective in offsetting changes in fair values or cash flows of the hedged item on an ongoing basis. This effectiveness test is re-performed at each reporting date to ensure that the hedge remains highly effective.

. . .

Changes in the fair value of derivatives designated as highly effective fair value hedging instruments are recorded in the income statement within finance costs, together with changes in the fair value of the hedged item attributable to the hedged risk.

The effective portion of changes in the fair value of derivatives designated as cash flow hedging instruments is recognised in equity within the hedging reserve.

Conclusions

Given the demanding nature of the above conditions, together with the theoretical complexity of hedge accounting, it is not surprising that many companies choose not to adopt it even though it might be potentially useful in mitigating volatile earnings trends. On this latter point, IFRS has probably not been in operation in the UK for a sufficiently long enough period for the impact of IAS 39 to be assessed on a retrospective basis.

Looking at IAS 39 overall, it is not a question of whether it will be changed but when. Change will not happen quickly given the complex nature of the topic and the variety of opinions held by experts. It is perhaps worth bearing in mind one of the most quoted comments of the Chairman of the International Accounting Standards Board in relation to IAS 39:

'Those who tell me they understand it haven't read it properly'.

CHAPTER 24

Equity share capital and reserves

Introduction

This chapter deals primarily with equity share capital and reserves but also deals with:

- equity dividends (also referred to in Chapter 11)
- share-based payment (also referred to in Chapter 9).

We refer to classification of share capital between equity and liabilities in Chapter 22.

Share capital

A key point to check is whether shares in a company are widely held or whether the company is under the control of one person, or of a number of people, for example, family controlled.

The normal means of control is to have at least 50% of the votes. This is simple if there is only one class of share, and each share carries one vote. But there are complications when there is more than one class, with different voting rights, or there is a 'golden share' which carries an all powerful vote in certain circumstances.

Control

If a company is under the control of one person or group of persons, the other investors can be on a hiding to nothing. Check directors' holdings and look out for any note on substantial shareholdings.

The following is a good example:

MAXWELL COMMUNICATION CORPORATION *Paragraph in the 1990 Report of the Directors*

Substantial shareholdings
As at the date of this report, pursuant to Section 198 of the Companies Act 1985, the Company had been advised of the following interests of 3% or more in the ordinary share capital of the company:

Name	Number of shares	% of issued share capital
Maxwell Foundation and its subsidiaries	202,558,076	31.34%
Robert Maxwell, his family and companies controlled by him and his family	155,912,928	24.14%

In 1990 MAXWELL COMMUNICATION CORPORATION was one of the world's top ten publishers, capitalised at about £1.4 billion. But the tyrannical management style of the controlling shareholder drove the company into administrative receivership less than two years later.

Authorised and issued share capital

When a company is formed, the authorised share capital and the nominal value of the shares are established and written into the company's memorandum of association, and the procedure for increasing the authorised share capital is included in the company's articles of association. This usually requires the approval of the shareholders.

Thereafter the directors of the company cannot issue new shares in excess of the authorised number, nor can they issue securities carrying rights to new shares that would exceed that number (e.g. convertibles and warrants: see below).

Both the authorised and the issued share capital are shown in the company's accounts, divided into equity and non-equity shares, for example:

BELLWAY *Extract from 2003 Group balance sheet*		
	2003	2002
Capital and reserves	£000	£000
Equity share capital		
Ordinary shares	13,926	13,775
Non-equity capital		
Preference shares	20,000	20,000
Called up share capital	33,926	33,775

Details of the authorised share capital are normally shown in a note to the accounts.

 The concept of authorised share capital is being abolished in the Companies Act 2006.

Types of share capital

Although all shares are referred to generally as 'risk capital', as the shareholders are the first investors to lose if the company fails, the degree of risk can vary within the same company from hardly any more than that of an unsecured lender to highly speculative, with prospects of reward usually varying accordingly.

The main types of share, in increasing order of risk, the order in which they would rank for distribution in the event of liquidation, are:

(a) preference shares,
(b) ordinary shares,
(c) deferred shares,
(d) warrants to subscribe for shares.

Unlike interest paid on loan capital, distributions of profits to shareholders are not an 'allowable expense' for company taxation purposes; i.e. dividends have to be paid out of profits *after* corporation tax has been deducted.

We referred in Chapter 22 to the impact of FRS 25 regarding classification of share capital between equity and liabilities.

Preference shares

Preference shares carry a fixed rate of dividend, normally payable half-yearly but, unlike the holders of loan capital, who can take action against a company in default of interest payments, preference shareholders have no legal redress if the board of directors decides to recommend that no preference dividends should be paid. However, if no preference dividend is declared for an accounting period, no dividend can be declared on any other type of share for the period concerned, and the preference shareholders usually become entitled to vote at shareholders' general meetings. (Provided their dividends are paid, preference shares do not normally carry a vote.)

Varieties of preference shares can include one or a combination of the following features:

- *Cumulative*. If the dividend on a cumulative preference share is not paid on time, payment is postponed rather than omitted. When this happens, the preference dividend is said to be 'in arrears', and these arrears have to be paid by the company before any other dividend can be declared. Arrears of cumulative preference dividends must be shown in a note to the accounts.
- *Redeemable*. The shares are repayable, normally at their nominal (par) value, in a given year (e.g. 2002) or when the company chooses within a given period (e.g. 2001/04).
- *Participating*. In addition to receiving a fixed dividend, shareholders participate in an additional dividend, usually a proportion of any ordinary dividend declared.
- *Convertible*. Shareholders have the option of converting their preference shares into ordinary shares within a given period of time, the conversion period.

Where a company has a large proportion of non-equity shares, it is important to check whether a significant number are due for redemption in the near future.

Chapter 22 page includes examples of different types of preference shares and explains how these should be treated in line with FRS 25.

Ordinary shares

Ordinary shares usually form the bulk of the share capital of a company. Ordinary shareholders are normally entitled to all the profits remaining after tax and preference dividends have been deducted although, as explained later, not all these attributable profits are likely to be distributed. Ordinary shareholders are entitled to vote at general meetings, giving them control over the election of directors.

However some companies put a clause in their articles of association to allow them to disenfranchise a shareholder where the shares are held in a nominee name and the nominee holder fails to respond to a request for information on the underlying holder. This protects the company against the building up of anonymous holdings prior to a possible bid.

Under the Companies Act 1985 companies are allowed to issue redeemable ordinary shares, provided they also have shares in issue which are not redeemable; i.e. the share capital of a company cannot consist solely of redeemable shares. A company may now also purchase its own shares, subject to a large number of conditions, including the prior approval of its shareholders.

The term 'ordinary stock' is rarely used today, but is effectively synonymous with ordinary shares.

Non-voting shares

A number of companies have more than one class of share (other than preference shares), with differing rights on voting and/or dividends and/or on liquidation. The most common variation is in voting rights, where a second class of share, identical in all other respects to the ordinary class, either carries no voting rights (usually called N/V or A shares), or carries restricted voting rights (R/V shares).

The trend over the last few years has, however, been towards the abolition of non-voting shares, and it is becoming increasingly difficult (if not actually impossible) to raise new money by the issue of non-voting shares.

Deferred shares

Another class is the deferred share, where no dividend is payable either:

- until ordinary shareholders' dividends have reached a certain level; or
- until conversion into ordinary shares.

In the 1970s and 1980s, when the top rate of income tax was much higher than the rate of capital gains tax (CGT), there were a number of issues.

For example, in 1989 LONDON MERCHANT SECURITIES made a scrip (capitalisation) issue of 1 Deferred Ordinary share for every 3 Ordinary shares held. The Deferred Ordinary shares do not rank for any dividend but they will be converted automatically into Ordinary shares after the AGM held in 2004.

While the current top rate of UK income tax remains at 40%, the same as CGT, further issues of deferred shares seem unlikely.

Further information on shares

Details of shares and debentures issued during the year should be given in a note to the balance sheet. The terms for redemption for all redeemable shares and the details of all outstanding rights to acquire shares either by subscription or conversion should also be given.

Issue of further shares

Further shares may be issued as a result of:

- rights issues;
- placing and open offer;
- scrip issues;
- share splits;
- scrip dividends;
- exercise of warrants;
- exercise of share options (see below);
- conversion of convertible loan stock (see Chapter 22).

Rights issues

A rights issue is an issue of new shares offered to shareholders in proportion to their existing holdings at a discount to the current market price. Shareholders who do not wish to subscribe can sell their rights 'nil paid'. The discount varies according to the 'weight' of the rights issue; 1 new share offered for every 8 or 10 shares already held would be regarded as a 'light' issue, probably requiring a discount of not more than 15%, while more than 1-for-4 would be 'heavy' and likely to need nearer 20% discount, or more if the company is in poor health. At these discounts underwriting would be arranged to ensure buyers for any shares not taken up by shareholders, but companies occasionally choose to make a rights issue at very much below the market price, the lowest price normally permitted being the par value of the shares.

The effect on the balance sheet of an issue at par is to add the total nominal value of the shares being issued to the issued share capital, and to show the cash received on the assets side. The expenses of the issue would normally be written off against the share premium account.

If the new shares are issued above par, the nominal value of the shares issued is added to the issued share capital and the difference between the issue price and the nominal price of each new share, i.e. the premium at which the shares were issued, is added to the share premium account.

For example, in 2002 KINGFISHER made a 1 for 1 rights issue of 1,293,642,792 Ordinary 13.75p shares at 155p. The issue added £177.9m to its ordinary share capital (1,293.6m × 13.75p) and £1,827.2m (1,293.6m × 141.25p) less £43.9m issue expenses to the share premium account, as illustrated below.

KINGFISHER *Rights issue*		
	Pre-rights £m	*Post-rights* £m
Issued share capital		
Ordinary share capital	177.9	355.8
Share premium		
Pre-rights	371.9	371.9
Premium on shares issued		1,827.2
Expenses of rights issue	_____	(43.9)
	549.8	2,511.0

There are two methods of dealing with convertible stock in a rights issue. Either the holders are offered new shares on the basis of the number of ordinary shares they would hold on full conversion, or the stock has its conversion terms adjusted to allow for the rights issue, whichever method is laid down in the convertible's trust deed (see Chapter 22). Similarly, either warrantholders are offered new shares or the warrant's terms are adjusted.

Placing and open offer

This method, colloquially known as a placing with clawback, is an alternative to a rights issue, and is usually done in conjunction with an acquisition. For example, in November 2003, REGENT INNS raised £13m by an open offer to fund the acquisition of further sites with existing late night licences.

One new ordinary 5p share was offered at 83p on the basis of 1 new share for every 6 ordinary shares held. The issue was underpinned by Panmure, and there was only a 39% take-up.

The main advantage of a placing with open offer is that it either is done at a much tighter discount than a rights issue, under 10%, or can be done when a rights issue would have been difficult if not impossible to underwrite.

The disadvantage is that shareholders who do not want to subscribe cannot sell their rights nil paid.

Scrip issues

A scrip issue, also known as a bonus or capitalisation issue, is a free issue of additional new shares to existing shareholders, made by capitalising reserves. For example, HALMA made a 1-for-3 scrip issue in August 1997. The effect on the balance sheet is shown below.

HALMA *Effect of 1-for-3 scrip issue*		
	Pre-scrip £000	*Post-scrip* £000
Ordinary share capital	26,919	35,905
Share premium account	2,479	614
Profit and loss account	52,283	45,136
Shareholders' funds	81,681	81,655*

* Fall in shareholders' funds due to £26,000 scrip issue costs, which were charged to the share premium account.

As a scrip issue is basically a bookkeeping transaction, the share price would normally be expected to adjust accordingly (e.g. would fall from 240p to 180p with a 1-for-3), and it is open to debate as to whether scrip issues serve any useful purpose.

The main arguments in favour of scrip issues are the following:

- Scrip issues are popular with the investing public, and therefore enhance share prices. Research shows that shares tend to outperform the market after the announcement of a scrip issue, but that companies make scrip issues only when they are doing well, i.e. when their share price would be expected to outperform just as much without the scrip issue.
- A 'heavy' share price in the market, say over £2, tends to make the shares harder to trade and artificially depresses the price. Scrip issues can be used to scale the price down.
- A scrip issue, being 'paid for' out of reserves, enables retained profits and/or the increased value of assets to be reflected by an increased share capital.
- The rate of dividends, expressed as a percentage of an unrealistically small share capital, can look excessive.
- An issued share capital of at least £1m is needed for trustee status.

The last argument appears to be the only factual one in favour of scrip issues; the remainder are psychological, although only a sound and flourishing company is likely to be able to make substantial scrip issues every few years. HALMA's record illustrates this well: the company also made a 1-for-3 scrip issue in 1985, 1-for-2 scrip issues in 1987 and 1989, and 1-for-3 scrip issues in 1991, 1993 and 1995. Thus an investor who purchased 1,000 Halma shares in 1984 would now have a holding of 9,473 ordinary shares.

The arguments against scrip issues are firstly the administrative costs incurred and secondly the increased risk of the share price subsequently falling close to or below par, thus precluding a rights issue. The cost is small, but reducing the market price can cause serious embarrassment if the company wants, at a later date, to make a rights issue only to find that its share price is too low to do so.

Share splits

Where a company feels its share price is 'heavy' but does not want to capitalise reserves – i.e. it does not want to make a scrip issue – it can split its shares into shares with a smaller par value. For example, in 2001 MITIE GROUP split its 5p shares, which were standing at around 280p at the time, into $2^{1}/_{2}$p shares, and the share price adjusted to around 140p.

Scrip dividends

The company allows shareholders to elect to receive new shares, i.e. a *scrip dividend*, in lieu of a cash dividend.

Each shareholder is sent a form of election in advance of each dividend payment, giving them the opportunity to opt for a scrip dividend, although some companies also pay a nominal cash dividend at least once each year in order to preserve 'wider range' investment status under the Trustee Investment Act 1961. The number of shares is calculated to give the same value as the net dividend payable, and counts as income, so there is no tax advantage.

Scrip dividends are popular with private shareholders, because they can add to their holding at middle market price without paying stock brokers' commission.

From the company's point of view, it is able to raise additional equity capital from its existing shareholders without the expense of a rights issue.

Warrants

Warrants are transferable options granted by the company to purchase new shares from the company at a given price, called the 'exercise price'. The warrant is normally exercisable only during a given time period, the exercise period, although one or two perpetual warrants have been issued.

Warrants can be issued on their own, for example HANSON used warrants plus cash in its acquisition of Kidde Inc. in 1987, of Consolidated Goldfields in 1989 and of Beazer in 1991.

They can also be issued attached to new issues of loan stock or bonds to give the holder an opportunity of subsequently participating in the equity of the company; the warrant element makes the issue more attractive and is sometimes referred to as the 'sweetener' (see Chapter 22).

Warrants provide a high risk/high reward form of equity investment. For example, if the ordinary shares of a company stood at 100p, warrants with an exercise price of 75p would then be worth a minimum of 25p. If the ordinary shares doubled to 200p then the warrants would be worth a minimum of 125p, a fivefold increase. In practice warrants command a premium over the ordinary price minus exercise price, although this premium tends to fall over the life of the warrant, reaching zero at the end of the exercise period.

Warrants are comparatively rare in the UK. Most recent issues have been made by investment trusts, which have attached them to issues of ordinary shares.

Details of a warrant's exercise rights should be shown in the report and accounts. For example:

SCHRODER ASIA PACIFIC FUND *Note to 2000 accounts*

Share capital
There were 27,994,495 warrants remaining in issue at 30 September 2000. Each warrant entitles the holder to subscribe for one ordinary share of 10p at a price of 100p, on 31 January in any of the years from 2001 to 2006 inclusive.

The net proceeds from the issue of warrants should be credited to shareholders' funds.

Dividends

Equity dividends

Equity dividends paid should be debited direct to equity and shown as a movement on profit and loss reserves (see Chapter 11).

Preference dividends

Preference dividends where payment is at the discretion of the company should be accounted for as though they were equity dividends and shown as a movement on profit and loss reserves.

Where the payment of the dividend is obligatory, the dividend paid should be charged to the profit and loss account as a finance cost (see Chapter 22).

Distributable profits

Distributable profits are dealt with in Chapter 11.

Reserves

Where reserves come from

Reserves can arise in several ways:

- by the accumulation of profits, either by retained profits from the profit and loss account or from the sale of assets;
- by the issue of shares at a premium, i.e. at more than their nominal value: the issue can be either for cash or as consideration (payment) in an acquisition;
- by the issue of warrants;
- by upward revaluation of assets (see pages 104–106);
- by the acquisition of assets at below their balance sheet value.

They can be reduced by losses, share issue and share redemption expenses, revaluation deficits and the writing off of goodwill. In addition, foreign currency translation differences are taken direct to reserves (see Chapter 29).

The balance sheet formats in Sch. 4 Companies Act 1985 require reserves to be shown in three main subdivisions:

1. share premium account,
2. revaluation reserve, and
3. other reserves.

Capital and revenue reserves

Under s. 264 (2) of the Companies Act 1985, a company's *undistributable reserves* are:

- the share premium account;
- the capital redemption reserve;
- unrealised profits (i.e. the revaluation reserve);
- any other reserve that a company is prohibited from distributing by its memorandum or articles.

Share premium account

Reference: Companies Act 1985, s. 130.

When shares are issued at a premium over their nominal value, the premium element must, by law, be credited to the share premium account, unless the rules of merger accounting apply (see page 241).

The share premium account has to be shown separately on the balance sheet and no part may be paid out to shareholders except on liquidation or under a capital reduction scheme authorised by the court.

It is permissible, however:

(a) to capitalise the share premium account to pay up unissued shares for distribution to shareholders as a scrip issue (otherwise known as a bonus or capitalisation issue), for instance:

	£
Ordinary share capital	100,000
Share premium account	85,000
Company makes 1-for-2 scrip issue:	
Ordinary share capital	150,000
Share premium account	35,000

(b) to charge to the share premium account:
 (i) the preliminary expenses of forming a company,
 (ii) the expenses and commissions incurred in any issue of shares.

Revaluation reserves

The surplus (or shortfall) on the revaluation of assets should be credited (or debited) to a separate reserve, the revaluation reserve. The amount of the revaluation reserve shall be shown 'under a separate sub-heading in the position given for the item "revaluation reserve" in the balance sheet formats, *but need not be shown under that name*' (our italics; CA 1985, Sch. 4, para. 34).

Capital redemption reserve

Shares may only be redeemed or purchased by the company out of distributable profits or out of the proceeds of a new issue of shares. Where redemption or purchase is out of distributable profits, an amount equal to the amount by which the company's issued share capital is diminished must, by law, be transferred to a reserve, called the capital redemption reserve. This reserve is shown separately under 'Other reserves'. The idea behind the law is to prevent a company's overall share capital plus non-distributable reserves from being reduced when share capital is repaid:

the reserve can never be distributed except upon liquidation or in a capital reduction scheme, but it can be capitalised by a bonus issue, as in Example 24.1.

Example 24.1 Capital redemption reserve

1. **Initial position:**

Issued share capital	£
30,000 £1 Redeemable preference shares	30,000
100,000 £1 Ordinary shares	100,000
	130,000

Reserves	
Revenue reserve (retained profits)	75,000

2. **Company then uses retained profits to redeem all the preference shares:**

Issued share capital	£
100,000 £1 Ordinary shares	100,000
	100,000

Reserves	
Capital redemption reserve	30,000
Revenue reserve (retained profits)	45,000

3. **Company then decides to make a 3-for-10 scrip issue, which brings the issued share capital back to £130,000.**

Issued share capital	£
130,000 £1 Ordinary shares	130,000
	130,000

Reserves	
Revenue reserve (retained profits)	45,000

Share-based payment arrangements including share options

Types of schemes

Current share incentive arrangements fall into three categories:

1. the granting of options
2. the award of shares
3. phantom share schemes.

Granting of options

Employers grant their employees share options (the right to acquire shares) at a given price, the exercise price, at a given future date or period, the *exercise period*.

At the exercise date or during the exercise period, the employees may exercise their options if the exercise price is *below* the share price at the time, but may let the options lapse if the share price in the market is *below* the exercise price.

Options may be granted in various schemes:

- executive share option schemes
- unapproved share option schemes
- Enterprise Management Incentives
- Save-As-You-Earn (SAYE) schemes.

CARE UK has five share-based payment schemes as shown below:

CARE UK *Annual report 2006*

Note 21 Share-based payments (extract)
The group has the following share-based payment schemes:

- No.2 Executive Scheme;
- SAYE Scheme;
- Performance Related Option Scheme;
- Long Term Investment Plan; and
- Employee Share Option Scheme.

. . .

These are further referred to below, but full details of the group's disclosure are contained in its Annual Report for 2006 in the Remuneration Report on page 24 and Note 21 on page 61 (www.careuk.com). Although this company adopts IFRS, the disclosures would have been identical under UK GAAP as there are no differences between FRS 20 and IFRS 2.

Sharesave (Save-as-you-earn (SAYE) schemes)

SAYE schemes, which require Revenue & Customs approval, enable share options to be offered to all employees.

To provide the sum required to exercise their options (exercise price set when the options are granted × number of shares under option), regular deductions are made monthly from the employee's net pay. The monthly contribution must be at least £5 and not more than £250 and deductions must be made for between three and five years.

At the end of the period, employees can choose between exercising their option *or* taking the cash in their SAYE account. Heads they win; tails they can't lose.

CARE UK *Annual report 2006*

Note 21 Share-based payments (extract)
. . .

b) SAYE Scheme
Options are granted with a fixed exercise price. The exercise price is based on the average of middle market quotations of the shares under option for three days preceding the grant date less a discount of up to 20 per cent. The options granted under this scheme generally become exercisable on the third anniversary of the commencement of the related savings contract. All employees who work more than fifteen hours per week for any group company are eligible to participate in this scheme. The company anticipates making annual awards under this scheme. An employee generally has six months after leaving employment of the group to exercise any unlapsed options that have vested.

Performance share plans

In this type of plan, also known as LTIPs (long term incentive plans), selected executives are granted the right to receive a fixed number of shares in the company at some future date, subject to one or more criteria.

For example, SCHRODERS has a plan in which the number of shares issued at the end of a five-year period depends on where the total shareholder return (TSR) of Schroders' shares rank in the FT-SE 100 Index:

Below 50th place	no shares issued
41st to 50th	40% of the shares issued
31st to 40th	60%
21st to 30th	80%
20th or above	100%.

The issue is also subject to a minimum average post-tax real return on equity of 7.5% per annum.

Employees are liable to income tax on shares received.

LTIPs have been open to criticism firstly because they are complicated and, more importantly, because research has shown that they do little or nothing to enhance the share price. In contrast, with share options, the interests of executives and shareholders coincide.

CARE UK, referred to above, has several performance – related schemes:

CARE UK *Annual report 2006*

Note 21 Share-based payments (extract)

. . .

c) *Performance Related Share Option Scheme*
None of the Performance Related Share Option Scheme options are accounted for under IFRS 2 as they were granted before 7 November 2002.

All of these options initially became exercisable in three equal tranches in the three years following grant. They may then be exercised up to seven years from the date of grant. The performance targets for each tranche normally require that earnings per share for the previous three years must not be less than those for the base year increased by RPI + 5% with yearly rests.

d) *Long Term Investment Plan*
Options have been granted as nil cost options under the scheme. The options granted under this scheme are generally exercisable at the end of the performance period and for six months thereafter. Awards under this scheme are reserved for employees at senior management level and above. If an employee leaves the employment of the group, a proportion of their award may be deemed to have vested, subject to satisfying any performance conditions and at the discretion of the Remuneration Committee. The company anticipates making annual awards under this scheme.

Awards under the LTIP scheme are subject to two performance criteria, the scales relating to which will be determined annually by the Remuneration Committee. Details of the performance criteria are further discussed in the Remuneration Report on pages 23 to 28 [not reproduced here].

e) *Employee Share Option Scheme*
The options granted were granted with a fixed exercise price being not less than the market price of the shares under option on the date of grant. The options granted will lapse on the third anniversary of the date of grant if the performance conditions have not been met. For the whole of the option to be capable of exercise the growth in the EPS of the company over the performance period must equal or exceed the growth in RPI by 12% per annum. If the growth in the EPS of the company over the performance period does not equal or exceed the growth in RPI by 12% per annum then that option will not be exercisable.

UK GAAP (FRS 20) illustrations

TANGENT COMMUNICATIONS Annual Report 2006, Note 22 on Share options (www.tangentuk.com);
C I TRADERS Annual Report 2006, Note 19 on Called up Share Capital (www.citraders.com);
PANMURE GORDON Annual Report 2006, Note 6 on FRS 20 Option Charges.

Accounting for share option schemes

We referred to share option charges in Chapter 9 and included a simple numerical example. A further example is set out below – this is based on one of the illustrative examples contained in the standard FRS 20.

Example 24.2

A company grants 100 share options to each of its 500 employees and vesting is conditional upon completion of three years' service.

The fair value of each share option is £15 – this is determined by a professional valuer using an option pricing model such as binomial or Black-Scholes.

At the beginning of year 1 the company estimates that 20% of employees will lose their rights to options as a result of failure to complete three years' service.

20 employees leave during year 1. At the end of year 1, the estimate of total employee departures over the three-year period is revised from 100 employees (20%) to 75 employees (15%).

A further 22 employees leave during year 2. At the end of year 2 the estimate of total employee departures over the three-year period is revised from 75 employees (15%) to 60 employees (12%).

A further 15 employees leave during year 3, so total departures over the three years are 57 employees (20 + 22 + 15). These employees forfeit their share option rights, leaving 443 employees entitled.

The company will recognise the following amounts in the accounts:

Year 1 profit and loss account charge
As at the end of year 1, the best *estimate* of the number of options likely to vest is 85% of the

▶

500 employees multiplied by 100 options each, i.e. 42,500 options. Each option is valued at £15 so total value is 42,500 × £15 equals £637,500. This total charge is spread over three years so the year 1 charge is one-third, which equals £212,500.

Note that the option charge is based on the valuer's assessment of the value of each option (£15) calculated as on the first day of the three-year period. This figure of £15 is not revised whatever happens to the company's share price during the three-year period. Because the vesting period is three years, a third of the option value is charged each year.

Year 2 profit and loss account charge

As at the end of year 2, the best *estimate* (which cannot be determined and finalised until the end of year 3 when the company knows *exactly* how many options vest) of the number of options expected to vest is revised to 88% of 500 multiplied by 100 which equals 44,000 options. This is multiplied by £15 to calculate the revised value of the option package which comes to £660,000.

The proportion of this which relates to years 1 and 2 in total is two-thirds of £660,000 i.e. £440,000. Of this, £212,500 has already been charged in year 1 so the amount to be charged in year 2 is £440,000 minus £212,500, which equals £227,500.

Year 3 profit and loss account charge

The number of employees actually entitled is 443 and each has 100 options i.e. 44,300 options. Over the three years the actual total (as opposed to estimated) charge is 44,300 × £15 = £664,500. As the profit and loss account has already been charged with £440,000 in the previous two years, the year 3 charge is £664,500 minus £440,000 = £224,500.

Do you want more complicated examples? If so, there are plenty in FRS 20 (see Appendix on Implementation Guidance) dealing with all types of situations such as share awards, cancellations and complex performance conditions.

Phantom share schemes

These are cash bonus schemes where the performance of the share price determines the amount of the bonus. For example ELECO:

ELECO *Extract from Report and Accounts 2000, Remuneration Committee Report*

Note 6 Phantom Share Option Scheme

The scheme was devised for J.H.B. Ketteley in connection with his appointment as Executive Chairman . . . An option was granted over a maximum of 1,500,000 notional shares of the Company . . . The exercise of the option gives rise to the payment of a bonus based upon the number of shares notionally acquired, multiplied by the amount by which the market value of one ordinary share exceeds 10 pence.

Summary of schemes

Type (see Note)	Current limit on value of shares awarded per employee
Executive share option	£30,000
Unapproved share option	None
EMI (Options)	£100,000
SAYE share option	£22,968
AESOP (Shares)	£7,500
LTIP (shares)	None

Note: Schemes in italics benefit from tax breaks.

The investor's viewpoint

Companies that encourage employee share participation on favourable terms are generally regarded as more likely to prosper than those which do not. In particular, companies that grant options to executive directors and key senior staff, on whose efforts the success of a company largely depends, can expect better than average performance. In short, giving the directors and employees a 'slice of the action' should be regarded as a plus point for investing in a company, providing the directors aren't being too greedy. Avoid companies where the boardroom's total rewards are high in comparison with pre-tax profits.

Effect of inflation

At times of high inflation there is a serious flaw in share schemes for directors and employees:

Purchase and reduction of shares

Company purchasing its own shares

Under s. 162 to 169 of the Companies Act 1985, a company may purchase its own shares, providing it doesn't
buy in all its non-redeemable shares. General authority
may be given for market purchases up to a maximum
number of shares, within a given price range and within a
maximum of 18 months from the date the resolution is
passed.

Most companies pass a resolution each year at their
AGM giving the directors authority, until the next AGM,
to purchase the company's shares, normally up to a maximum of 10% of the shares issued at up to 5% above the
middle market price.

Where a company wishes to purchase shares outside the
market, the transaction must be authorised in advance
by a special resolution. For example in December 1992
FROGMORE ESTATES called an EGM to authorise the purchase of 13.1% of its issued share capital from another
property company at a discount of around 7% to the market
price. The EGM was required firstly because the purchase was by private treaty, i.e. 'off-market', and secondly
because the purchase was of more than 10% of its issued
share capital, the maximum of the general authority
approved at the previous AGM.

To protect investors, Chapter 15 of the UK Listing
Authority's 'Purple Book' lays down various rules about
the purchase of own securities.

Several property companies, including FROGMORE, took
advantage of the 1985 Act to purchase their ordinary
shares at a price below asset value, thus increasing the
asset value of the remaining shares. More recently there

has been a spate of companies falling over themselves to
return 'spare cash' to their shareholders. This can be done

(a) *either* by a company buying its own shares. (Prior to
1 December 2003, shares purchased in this way had to
be cancelled. However, from that date, listed companies may buy their own shares and hold them in Treasury
without cancelling them. These shares may then be
issued or sold at a later date.); *or*
(b) by, in effect, giving cash back to shareholders. In
order to avoid the returned cash being treated as a distribution for tax purposes, the return is achieved by a
bonus issue of B shares, which are then redeemed by
the company; *or*
(c) by a combination of (a) and (b), which is what
W.H. SMITH did:

Reduction of share capital

Under s. 135 of the Companies Act 1985 a company may,
with court approval, reduce its share capital in any way
and, in particular, may:

- reduce or extinguish liability on share capital not fully
  paid up;
- cancel any paid-up share capital which is lost or unrep-
  resented by available assets; and
- repay any paid-up share capital in excess of its
  requirements.

Where the net assets no longer exceed the paid-up value of
the issued share capital, the reserves will appear negative
in the balance sheet.

Take, for example, a company which has 1 million £1 ordinary shares in issue and negative reserves of £831,000. It might, with court approval, reduce its capital to $1^1/_2$ million 25p shares and eliminate share premium account to remove the accumulated losses (see Example 24.3).

Example 24.3 Effect of share capital reduction on the balance sheet

	Before reduction £000	After reduction £000
Issued share capital	1,000	375
Share premium account	206	–
Other reserves	(831)	–
Shareholders' funds	375	375

The Companies Act 2006 (when fully implemented) will simplify procedures for reduction of capital.

International Financial Reporting Standards

Terminology differences

The main difference is that UK GAAP refers to the profit and loss account, whereas IFRS refers to the income statement.

There are also some categories of reserves that may be relevant under IFRS but not under UK GAAP. These include:

- Fair value reserve – see, for example, Chapter 15 on fixed asset investments regarding 'available-for-sale investments';
- Hedging reserve: see Chapter 23 on derivatives and other financial instruments which refers to a 'hedging reserve'.

Share-based payment

The good news is that UK GAAP (FRS 20) and IFRS (IFRS 2) are identical. We referred above to UK GAAP disclosure examples.

Two further examples based on IFRS accounts are:

ROK Annual Report 2006, Remuneration Report on page 66 and Note 26 on Equity Compensation Benefits on page 59 (www.rokgroup.com)

WILMINGTON Annual Report 2007, Remuneration Report on page 21 and Note 24 on Share based payments on page 50 (www.wilmington.co.uk)

CHAPTER 25

Balance sheet disclosures

Introduction

Some of the most interesting (and often crucial) pieces of information available to analysts are tucked away in memorandum notes to the accounts, often towards the end of the annual report. These merit careful reading. Some reviewers of accounts even go as far as recommending reading the annual report backwards!

The areas we will consider in this chapter are:

- related party disclosures;
- operating leases;
- contingencies and commitments;
- events after the balance sheet date (these used to be referred to as post balance sheet events).

Related party disclosures

ASB warning

To quote the Press Notice released by the Accounting Standards Board on the publication of FRED 8 (subsequently superseded by FRS 8, *Related party disclosures*):

'Related party transactions have been a feature of a number of financial scandals in recent years, many of which have had in common *the dominance of the company by a powerful chief executive* who was also involved with the related party.'

The italics are ours. Analysts should be particularly wary of companies where the posts of chairman and of chief executive are held by one person (see page 45).

Disclosure rules

Schedule 5 of the Companies Act 1985 contains requirements for the disclosure of related undertakings, and Chapters 11 and 12 of the UK Listing Authority's *Listing Rules* define related party transactions and lay down requirements on disclosure.

FRS 8, Related party disclosures, extends the definition of related parties and increases the disclosure requirement.

It requires a company to disclose all material transactions with related parties, i.e. parties having a relationship (control or influence) that affects the independence of either the reporting entity or the other party and could have a significant effect on the financial position and operating results of the reporting entity. There are a number of exceptions, for example, pension contributions paid to a pension fund.

Ultimate controlling party

Regardless of whether or not there have been transactions during the year, financial statements must disclose the name of the company's ultimate controlling party. For companies within widely-held public groups, this will be the holding company.

For all other companies, the directors must look beyond the corporate structure to name the controlling interests. There may even be cases where the ultimate controlling party cannot be identified: if so, that fact must be disclosed.

Who is a related party?

The definition of related parties in the FRS is widely drawn. It includes, in addition to the more obvious relationships, such as ultimate and intermediate parent undertakings, subsidiaries and fellow subsidiaries, associates and joint ventures, directors of the reporting entity, pension funds, key management, members of the close family of any party in this list, and partnerships, companies, trusts and other entities in which any individual in the list or their close family has a controlling interest. Entities managed by the reporting entity under management contracts come within the definition of related parties. 'Close family' includes family members, or members of the same household, 'who may be expected to influence or be influenced . . .'. This clearly includes adult children as well as minors and *would have made the late Robert Maxwell's children related parties.*

Subject to certain exemptions, transactions with related parties have to be disclosed even if no consideration passes.

Related parties are considered in two groups:

1. those that are deemed to be related; and
2. those where a related party relationship is presumed.

The existence of '*deemed*' related party relationships cannot be rebutted; all material transactions with directors, group members, associates and joint ventures must normally be disclosed.

The existence of a '*presumed*' relationship can be rebutted (and transactions need not therefore be disclosed) if it can be demonstrated that the relevant party does not exercise significant influence over the entity's financial and operating policies.

Disclosures

Not only are related parties potentially numerous, the required disclosures are also lengthy:

- names of the transacting related parties;
- description of the relationship and the transactions;
- amounts involved;
- balances with the related parties at the balance sheet date, including provisions made and amounts written off such balances; and
- any other elements necessary for an understanding of the financial statements.

Just how useful disclosures about related parties are to the average investor remains to be seen:

- they are often extremely complicated;
- their significance is difficult to assess;
- nevertheless, they largely remove the excuse 'if only I had known, I would not have bought into the company'.

Consider, for example, TARSUS GROUP, the consolidated profit and loss account of which is shown below. Start by trying to decide what happened to the group in 1997–98. We will comment and then gradually add further information.

TARSUS GROUP *Consolidated profit and loss account for 1998*

Consolidated profit and loss account for the year ended 31 December 1998

	Notes [A]	Before Exceptional Items £000	Exceptional Items £000	1998 12 months Total £000	1997 8 months Total £000
TURNOVER – acquisitions		4,784	–	4,784	–
– discontinued operations	[B]	702	–	702	563
		5,486	–	5,486	563
Operating costs		(4,562)	(402)	(4,964)	(539)
OPERATING PROFIT – acquisitions		1,008	(402)	606	–
– discontinued operations		(84)	–	(84)	24
		924	(402)	522	24
Goodwill amortisation		(180)	–	(180)	–
		744	(402)	342	24
Loss on disposal of discontinued operation . . .		–	(3,404)	(3,404)	–
Profit/(loss) on ordinary activities before interest		744	(3,806)	(3,062)	24

The first thing that strikes one is that 1997 represented an eight-month accounting period [A]. There is always a reason for an odd length period.

The second thing is that turnover in 1997 consisted entirely of discontinued activities [B]; this means that the entire nature of the business changed completely between 1997 and 1998.

We looked at the directors' report for clues.

TARSUS GROUP *Extract from the directors' report 1998*

Principal activities, etc.
The principal activity of the Group since 25 June 1998 has been the ownership, organisation and management of exhibitions, conferences, related trade publications and new media.

Prior to 25 June 1998 the Group was principally engaged in design, publishing, marketing and computer related activities. These businesses were sold on 25 June 1998 to Glowdawn Ltd, a company controlled by Philip O'Donnell, a director of the company.

Since 25 June 1998 the Group has developed new and existing events and publications and has acquired business media companies with growth potential.

The related party mention led us to:

TARSUS GROUP *Extract from the directors' report 1998*

Close company status
The company is a close company within the meaning of the Income and Corporation Taxes Act 1988. There has been no change in this respect since the end of the financial year.

And that in turn led us to:

TARSUS GROUP *Extract from the directors' report 1998*

Substantial shareholdings
At 24 February 1999 the Company had been notified of the following discloseable interests in its issued ordinary share capital pursuant to section 198 Companies Act 1985:

	Number of Ordinary Shares	Percentage
N D Buch	6,229,171	26.7
C A Smith	5,000,000	21.4
P O'Donnell	3,828,159	16.4

We studied the note on related party transactions.

TARSUS GROUP *Note 23 to the 1998 accounts*

23. Related party transactions
During the year the Group disposed of the subsidiary BBB Design Ltd to Glowdawn Ltd, a company controlled by P. O'Donnell, a director of the Company. The consideration was £346,000 satisfied in cash. An adjustment may be made to the consideration depending upon the outcome of certain litigation claims as referred to in note . . .

The Company acquired the Labelex Group of companies in June 1998. One of the Labelex vendors was C. Smith, a director of the Company. The initial combined consideration paid was £4.3m and an estimated deferred consideration of £850,000 in respect of the results for the two years ended 31 December 1998. A further deferred consideration payment may be made in 2000 based on the results of Tarsus Publishing Ltd for the year ended 31 December 1999 capped at £250,000. Lease agreements were entered into, at the time of the Labelex acquisition, between Tarsus Exhibitions Ltd, the Labelex Ltd Retirement and Death Benefit Scheme (C. Smith's pension fund) and C. Smith, for the property situated at 129–131 Southlands Road, Bromley. The term of the lease is for five years with an option to break after three years for a combined annual rental of £34,000.

An acquisition search agreement was entered into between the Company and Mayfield Media Strategies Ltd, a company controlled by S. Monnington, a director of the Company. Under the agreement Mayfield Media Strategies Ltd is entitled to receive fees for acquisition search work and further fees for successful acquisitions introduced. The fees paid under this agreement to S. Monnington in 1998 amounted to £33,510.

The fees paid to N. D. Buch (£12,500), S. A. Monnington (£20,000) and B. T. R. Scruby (£3,750) as Directors of the Company are paid to companies controlled by these Directors namely . . .

We are not criticising these accounts. Far from it: they provide a model of modern disclosure, leaving the individual investor to decide whether this is the right group for him.

The note on acquisitions is lengthy, so we reproduce only part of it. We do so for two reasons: firstly it shows

TARSUS GROUP *Extract from note 4 to the 1998 accounts*

4. Acquisitions

The Group made three acquisitions during the year for a total consideration of £7,761,000, of which £1,216,000 is deferred. These acquisitions resulted in goodwill of £9,413,000 before amortisation. From the date of acquisition to 31 December 1998 the acquisitions contributed £4,784,000 to turnover and £1,008,000 to operating profit before interest, goodwill amortisation, exceptional items and taxation.

All of these purchases have been accounted for as acquisitions. The fair value of the Group's identifiable assets and liabilities at the acquisition date (including goodwill) were:

Labelex Group

	Book value £000	Consistency of accounting [X] policies £000	Other £000	Total £000
Net liabilities acquired				
Goodwill	175	–	(175)	–
Tangible fixed assets	226	(36)	–	190
Cash	1,500	–	–	1,500
Debtors	2,702	28	–	2,730
Creditors	(5,501)	(20)	(20)	(5,541)
Provisions	–	–	(485)	(485)
Negative net assets [Y]	(898)	(28)	(680)	(1,606)
Goodwill on acquisition				7,247
				5,641
Satisfied by: Cash				1,450
Shares allotted				2,500
Deferred purchase consideration [Z]				1,100
Costs of acquisition				591
				5,641

just how much information is available on related party transactions; and secondly it demonstrates how acquisition accounting works including:

[X] the accounting adjustments made on an acquisition;
[Y] the calculation of goodwill in a case where the net assets are negative; and
[Z] a business purchase satisfied by a complex structure of consideration including deferred terms.

International Financial Reporting Standards

IAS 24, Related party disclosures, is similar in many ways to FRS 8 referred to above. However, IAS 24 includes a new term 'key management personnel' defined as 'those persons having authority and responsibility for planning, directing and controlling the activities of the entity, directly or indirectly, including any director (whether executive or otherwise) of that entity' and specifies disclosure requirements.

WYEVALE GARDEN CENTRES included the following note in its annual report.

WYEVALE GARDEN CENTRES *Annual report 2006*

Note 30 – Remuneration of Key Management Personnel and Related Party Transactions
The remuneration of the directors, who are the key management personnel of the Group, is set out in aggregate for each of the categories specified in IAS 24 *Related Party Disclosures* in the Directors'

Remuneration Report on pages 13 to 19 [not reproduced here].

Transactions between the company and its subsidiaries, which are related parties, have been eliminated on consolidation and are not disclosed in this note. There are no other related party transactions that require disclosure.

The company received dividends from the other Group undertakings totalling £4,801,000 (2004: £7,850,000). During the year the Company recharged £15,985,000 (2004: £15,609,000) to other Group undertakings for various administrative expenses incurred on their behalf. The Company also received administrative cost recharges of £nil (2004 – £nil) from other Group undertakings. At 1 January 2006 the Company was owed £219,998,000 (2004: £214,692,000) by other Group undertakings and owed £204,000 (2005: £15,000).

Note 31 – Directors' transactions
P H Williamson directly and indirectly controls 43% (2004: 43%) of Wyevale Holdings Limited. During 2005 a subsidiary of Wyevale Holdings Limited, Wyevale Nurseries Limited, supplied 1.1% of all purchases by the Group for resale. The value of these purchases was £1,165,000 in 2005 (2004: £904,000) and the balance outstanding at 1 January 2006 was £32,000 (2004: £84,000). P.H. Williamson resigned as a director of the Group on 27 April 2005.

Operating leases

UK GAAP disclosure requirements

An operating lease is normally for a period substantially shorter than the expected useful life of an asset; i.e. the lessor retains most of the risks and rewards of ownership.

Under an operating lease, the lease rentals are simply charged in the profit and loss account of the lessee as they arise. Leased assets and the liability for future payments do not appear in the balance sheet, even though companies can enter into operating leases of several years' length, as in the extract from SHELL TRANSPORT AND TRADING's accounts illustrated below.

While SSAP 21 sets out the distinction between an operating lease and a finance lease, FRS 5, Reporting the substance of transactions, looks behind the lease at the nature of the underlying transaction.

SHELL TRANSPORT AND TRADING *Note to the 2002 accounts*

16. Commitments
(a) Leasing arrangements
The future minimum lease payments under operating leases and capital leases, and the present value of net minimum capital lease payments at 31 December 2002 were as follows:

	Operating leases	$ million Capital leases
2003	1,906	91
2004	1,192	52
2005	806	51
2006	647	49
2007	512	56
2008 and after	3,553	495
Total minimum payments	8,616	794

. . .

The figures above for operating lease payments represent minimum commitments existing at December 31, 2002 and are not a forecast of future total rental expense.

SSAP 21 requires a lessee to disclose, in addition to the amount charged in the year, the yearly amount of the payments to which he or she is committed at the year end (the annual commitment).

The annual payments to which the lessee is committed should be analysed between those in which the commitment expires within that year, in the second to fifth year inclusive, and over five years from the balance sheet date. Leases of land and buildings are to be shown separately from other operating leases.

International Financial Reporting Standards

IAS 7 goes beyond the requirement to disclose only payments to be made in the following year. It requires companies to disclose the total of future minimum lease payments, under non-cancellable operating leases, analysed between each of the following periods: not later than one year; later than one year and not later than five years; later than five years.

The following is a typical disclosure example under IFRS:

Note 30 – Operating lease commitments
At the balance sheet date, the company had outstanding commitments under non-cancellable operating leases, which fall due as follows:

	2007 £000	2006 £000
Within one year	209	297
In the second to fifth years inclusive	1,320	1,339
After five years	592	830
	2,121	2,466

Operating lease payments represent rentals payable by the company for certain of its office properties. Leases are negotiated for an average term of seven years and rentals are fixed for an average of three years.

Contingent liabilities and contingent assets

Definition

A contingent liability is a potential liability which had not materialised by the date of the balance sheet. By their nature, contingent liabilities are insufficiently concrete to warrant specific provision being made for them in the accounts, and none is in fact made. However, the Companies Act 1985 requires a company to disclose by way of note or otherwise:

- any arrears of cumulative dividends (para. 49);
- particulars of any charge on the assets of the company to secure the liabilities of any other person, including, where practicable, the amount secured (para. 50 (1));
- the legal nature of any other contingent liabilities not provided for, the estimated amount of those liabilities, and any security given (para. 50 (2)).

Examples of contingent liabilities

Typical contingent liabilities include:

- bills of exchange discounted with bankers;
- guarantees given to banks and other parties;
- potential liabilities on claims (whether by court action or otherwise);
- goods sold under warranty or guarantee;
- any uncalled liability on shares held as investments (i.e. the unpaid portion of partly paid shares held).

Contingencies frequently arise in respect of an acquisition as the result of an 'earn-out', where part of the consideration is based on future profits.

Litigation, impending litigation and threatened litigation are popular breeding grounds for contingent liabilities (e.g. BP):

BP *Note to the 2003 accounts*

39. Contingent liabilities
Approximately 200 lawsuits were filed . . . arising out of the Exxon Valdez oil spill in Prince William Sound in March 1989.
    Most of these suits named Exxon, Alyeska Pipeline Service Company (Alyeska), which operates the oil terminal at Valdez, and other oil companies which own Alyeska . . . BP owns a 47% interest in Alyeska . . .
    Exxon has indicated that it may file a claim for contribution against Alyeska for a portion of the costs and damages which it has incurred.

How an oil terminal operator can be held responsible for a tanker running aground is way beyond our comprehension (unless Alyeska provided the pilot), but some people will try anything.

As explained below, companies are also required to disclose 'commitments'. It is often quite difficult to decide just what is a commitment and what a contingent liability; and many groups, like ICI, treat them in a single note.

ICI *Extract from note to the 2003 accounts*

39. Commitments and contingent liabilities
The Group's 50% interest in Teesside Gas Transportation Ltd (TGT) was sold, during 1996, to a subsidiary of its other shareholder Enron Europe Ltd (**Enron**) which is currently in administration.
    TGT contracted with the owners of a distribution network for pipeline capacity for North Sea gas and the commitment is guaranteed severally on a 50:50 basis by ICI and Enron. (The present value of the commitment guaranteed by ICI is estimated at £146m.) . . . (the parent company) Enron Corp. sought Chapter 11 bankruptcy protection in the USA on 2 December 2001.

The significance of contingent liabilities

In many cases notes on contingent liabilities are of no real significance, for no liability is expected to arise, and none does. Occasionally, however, they are very important indeed, and points to watch for are a sharp rise in the total sums involved, and liabilities that may arise outside the normal course of business.

 To guarantee the liabilities of someone, or some company, over which one has no control entails undue risk, and calls into question the management's judgement if the sums involved are significant.

In particular, experience suggests that any contingent liability in respect of a subsidiary that has been disposed of can be extremely dangerous. For example, when COLOROLL took over JOHN CROWTHER it accepted more than £20m of contingent liabilities in order to help the management buy out of Crowther's clothing interests, which it wanted to be shot of.

COLOROLL *Note to the accounts*

Contingent liabilities
At 31 March 1989 the group had contingent liabilities in connection with the following matters:

(a) the sale with recourse of £7,500,000 of redeemable preference shares and £14,250,000 senior and subordinated loan notes in Response Group Ltd which were received as part consideration for the sale of the clothing interests of John Crowther group plc;

(b) the guarantee of borrowings and other bank facilities of . . .

In February 1990 the Response Group called in the receivers, and COLOROLL followed four months later!

Guaranteeing the borrowings of associated undertakings or joint ventures may also be dangerous.

International Financial Reporting Standards

UK GAAP (FRS 12) and IFRS (IAS 37) are identical.

Capital commitments

The Companies Act 1985 requires that, where practicable, the aggregate amounts or estimated amounts, if they are material, of contracts for capital expenditure (not already provided for) be shown by way of note. For example RANK:

RANK *Extract from note to the 2003 accounts*

32. Commitments

Future capital expenditure
At 31 December 2003 commitments for capital expenditure amounted to £35.6m (2002 £24.1m).

Such a note provides some indication of the extent to which the directors plan to expand (or replace) the facilities of the group, and thus of the potential call upon its cash resources. It should be read in conjunction with the directors' report and chairman's statement and any press announcements by the company, but it is not a particularly helpful guide to future cash flows unless it gives some information on timing. Although the sums involved are material, it is impossible to tell from RANK's note how long the various facilities to which it is committed will take to build or deliver, and when payments will fall due.

Events after the balance sheet date

It might be thought that, since a company's report and accounts reflect the state of affairs at the balance sheet date, events arising after that date would be excluded, but this is not entirely the case: post balance sheet events (events occurring between the balance sheet date and the date the accounts are approved by the board) should be reflected or disclosed if they are important.

FRS 21, Events after the balance sheet date, distinguishes between two types of post balance sheet event:

- adjusting events;
- non-adjusting events.

Adjusting events

Adjusting events are post balance sheet events which provide additional evidence of conditions existing at the balance sheet date. The accounts should be adjusted accordingly, but separate disclosure is not normally required.

Typical adjusting events include:

- the subsequent determination of the purchase price of a fixed asset purchased or sold before the year end;
- a property valuation which provides evidence of an impairment in value;
- receipt of the financial statements or other information regarding an unlisted company which provides evidence of a permanent diminution of value of a long-term investment;
- the receipt of evidence that the previous estimate of accrued profit on a long-term contract was materially inaccurate.

Where any subsequent events indicate that the 'going concern' concept should not have been applied to the company or to a material part of it, the accounts should also be adjusted accordingly.

Non-adjusting events

Non-adjusting events are post balance sheet events which concern conditions which did not exist at the balance sheet date. The events should be disclosed together, if practicable, with an estimate of the financial effect (e.g. MEDEVA):

MEDEVA Note 27 to 1998 accounts

27. Post balance sheet events

. . .

On 4 February 1999 Medeva signed an agreement to dispose of the Group's Swiss manufacturing operations to RSP Pharma AG ('RSP'), a company owned by the local management team. Details of this transaction are set out in the Operating and Financial Review on page . . .

Although FRS 21 calls for the disclosure of post balance sheet events in the financial statements:

- there is normally no 'pointer' to any such note in the accounts, i.e. it is 'stand alone', so it is necessary to read the notes in their entirety and not rely on references to them elsewhere in the accounts;
- non-adjusting events tend also to be mentioned or further detail given in the Chairman's Statement, Financial

Review or Review of Operations. For example MEDEVA told more about the RSP deal in its operating and financial review.

MEDEVA Extract from the operating and financial review 1998

On 5 February 1999 the conditional disposal of the Swiss manufacturing operations to RSP Pharma AG ('RSP'), a company owned by the local management team, was announced. The transaction is expected to be effective by 23 April 1999. The assets being disposed of consist of the manufacturing facility and products and certain development projects. In 1998 these assets generated sales of £6.7m (1997: £5.9m) and an operating loss of £0.2m (1997: loss £0.3m). These assets are being sold to RSP at their net asset value of £3.9m and thus no gain or loss will be generated on this disposal. Medeva will receive an initial payment of £1.7m, with the balance payable over a maximum period of 12 years, depending on the profitability of RSP. As part of the deal Medeva will also retain the rights to earn royalties on certain products RSP plan to develop, mainly Purepa, a concentrated, modified fish oil product. Medeva has also entered into an agreement to acquire a 20% investment in RSP at a cost of £0.7m.

Window dressing

One method of improving the appearance of a company's accounts was to borrow short-term money, perhaps just overnight, in order to bump up liquidity at the balance sheet date, a trick that was particularly popular amongst fringe bankers in the early 1970s.

FRS 21 endeavours to preclude this and similar types of cosmetic operation by requiring the disclosure of 'the reversal or maturity after the year end of transactions entered into before the year end, the substance of which was primarily to alter the appearance of the company's balance sheet'.

This requirement does not prevent this type of window dressing, but it certainly discourages auditors from being party to deliberate deception.

International Financial Reporting Standards

UK GAAP (FRS 21) and IFRS (IAS 10) are identical.

CHAPTER 26

Cash flow statements

Overview of the cash flow statement and related notes

A company which runs into heavy losses often makes a recovery. But if it runs out of cash (and credit) it will rarely get a second chance.

The finance director's viewpoint

This is how the FD of a large and successful FTSE 100 company explained it to us:

- **Starting point**: You start off with a kitty of *pre-tax profit* plus *depreciation* (depreciation is added back because it has been deducted in the P&L account, but no cash is paid out).
- **Other money coming in**: *Cash* that may come in from time to time to swell the kitty, like the proceeds of disposals.
- **'No choice' expenditure**: You have to *pay tax* (though increases in deferred tax, charged to the P&L account but not paid to the Revenue, will *add* to the kitty). And you have to *pay interest* on the company's borrowings.
- **Virtually 'no choice' expenditure**: *Dividends*: although there is no legal obligation to declare a dividend, shareholders will normally expect to be paid an at least maintained one, with a modest increase if profits are up. If the company is in good health financially, any board that cuts or passes a dividend without a very good reason does so at its peril, unless the directors have control, or are backed by a controlling shareholder.
- **What's left in the kitty is**: **What the board is free to spend.**

Common sense would tell you that this is the company's *free cash flow (FCF)*, but there are differing opinions on the definition of FCF, which we will discuss later in this chapter.

CASH FLOW STATEMENTS

The requirements of FRS 1

FRS 1 lays down a clearly defined overall format: the cash flow statement should list cash flows for the period, classified under eight standard headings in the following order:

(a) operating activities;
(b) returns on investments and servicing of finance;
(c) taxation;
(d) capital expenditure and financial investment;
(e) acquisitions and disposals;
(f) equity dividends paid;
(g) management of liquid resources;
(h) financing.

The last two headings can be shown in a single section provided a separate subtotal is given for each heading.

Individual categories of inflows and outflows under the standard headings should be disclosed separately either in the cash flow statement or in a note to it unless they are allowed to be shown net.

ABBEYCREST *Extract from 2003 accounts*

Note 23. Reconciliation of operating profit to net cash inflow from operating activities

		Group	
		2003	2002
		£000	£000
Operating profit	[A]	**1,723**	4,124
Depreciation	[B]	**1,961**	1,883
Amortisation of goodwill		**233**	224
Loss (profit) on sale of tangible fixed assets, etc.		**53**	26
(Increase)/decrease in stocks ⎱		**4,077**	(9,558)
(Increase)/decrease in debtors ⎰ Working capital		**1,937**	(1,131)
(Decrease)/increase in creditors ⎰		**(3,858)**	6,245
Net cash inflow from operating activities	[C]	**6,126**	1,813

A real example

Let's look at a real example, ABBEYCREST, a listed company which had been experiencing some difficulties in 2002.

ABBEYCREST *Chairman's Interim Statement*

The results for the half-year have been dominated by the reassessment of various provisions . . . and by events at our manufacturing operation in Thailand . . . substantial loss for the half year.

In addition our supply chain management is currently the subject of review [which] will benefit the company through lower stock requirements next year and consequent lower borrowings.

Begin, as our FTSE 100 FD did, with operating profit **[A]**, and depreciation (and amortisation) **[B]**, which appear at the top of ABBEYCREST's Note 23 on *Reconciliation of operating profit to net cash flow from operating activities*, shown above.

The next thing to notice in Abbeycrest's reconciliation statement is that, in 2002, the *Operating profit* **[A]** plus *Depreciation* **[B]** totalled just over £6m, but the *Net cash inflow from operating activities* **[C]** was only £1.813m. The main reason sticks out like a sore thumb: Stocks up £9.558m – a bit out of control?

In 2003 stocks were reduced by £4.077m, and working capital by £2.156m, compared with an increase in working capital of £4.444m in 2002.

ABBEYCREST *Extract from 2003 accounts*

Consolidated cash flow statement

		2003	2002
		£000	£000
Net cash inflow from operating activities	[D]	**6,126**	1,813
Returns on investment and servicing of finance	[E]	**(2,468)**	(2,080)
Taxation	[F]	**(456)**	(918)
Capital expenditure and financial investment	[G]	**(2,809)**	(1,158)
Acquisitions	[H]	**–**	(723)
Equity dividends paid	[I]	**(1,045)**	(1,627)
Cash (outflow)/inflow before financing		**(652)**	(4,693)
Financing	[J]	**2,437**	(321)
(Decrease)/increase in cash in the year	[L]	**1,785**	(5,014)

ABBEYCREST *Note to the 2003 accounts*

Note 24. Analysis of cash flows

		Group	
		2003	2002
Returns on investment and servicing of finance		£000	£000
Interest received		241	220
Interest paid		(2,556)	(2,298)
Interest element of finance lease rental payments		(2)	(2)
Dividend paid to minority interest		(151)	–
Net cash outflow for returns on investments and servicing of finance	[E]	(2,468)	(2,080)
Capital expenditure and financial investment			
Purchase of tangible fixed assets		(3,080)	(1,291)
Sale of tangible fixed assets		271	133
Net cash outflow for capital expenditure and financial investment	[G]	(2,809)	(1,158)
Acquisitions			
Purchase of shares from minority interests in subsidiaries		–	(1,127)
Cash from sale of investments		–	404
Net cash outflow for acquisitions	[H]	–	(723)
Financing			
Issue of ordinary share capital	[J]	10	3
New secured loan	[K]	6,500	–
Repayment of secured loan	[K]	(650)	(300)
Repayment of loan notes	[K]	(3,399)	–
Capital element of finance lease rental payments	[K]	(24)	(24)
Net cash inflow (outflow) from financing	[M]	2,437	(321)

Watch the working capital. If it isn't kept under firm control it will gobble up the company's cash like a hungry alligator.

To move on, the *bottom line* of the reconciliation statement [C] provides the *top line* of the cash flow statement, [D].

In Abbeycrest's cash flow statement the difference in the top line [D] between 2002 and 2003 is (in £000) 4,313 but the difference in the bottom line [L] is 6,799, which is 2,486 more. Analysts should ask themselves 'Why the difference?'

There were several reasons:

[G] Capex in 2003 was £2.809m v £1,158m in 2002;
[H] No acquisitions in 2003 v £0.723m in 2002;
[I]   Lower dividend in 2003 (no Interim was paid).

But the principal reason was:

[J] the refinancing in 2003, a net £2.437m.

Note 24 gives the details: a new £6.5m secured loan replaced a much smaller secured loan and £3.399m repayment of short-term loan notes – a much more satisfactory longer-term financing.

Reconciliation of net cash flow to net debt

FRS1 requires a note reconciling the movement of cash in the period to the movement in net debt, to be shown either with (but not as part of) the cash flow statement, or in a note. ABBEYCREST shows its reconciliation in Note 26.

ABBEYCREST *Note to the 2003 accounts*

Note 25. Analysis of net debt

	[R] 1 March 2002 £000	[S] Cashflow £000	[T] Exchange movement £000	[U] Non-cash movement £000	[V] 28 February 2003 £000
Cash at bank and in hand	5,286	2,702	(71)	–	7,917
Overdrafts	(25,335)	(917)	–	–	(26,252)
	(20,049)	[L] 1,785	(71)	–	(18,335)
Debt due after one year	–	(4,550)	–	–	(4,550)
Debt due within one year	–	(1,300)	–	–	(1,300)
Loan notes	(3,399)	3,399	–	–	–
Finance leases	(54)	24	–	(28)	(58)
	(3,453)	[M] (2,427)	[O] –	[N] (28)	(5,908)
Net debt	[P] (23,502)	(642)	(71)	(28)	[Q] (24,243)

ABBEYCREST *Note to the 2003 accounts*

Note 26. Reconciliation of net cash flow to movement in net debt

		2003 £000
Increase in cash in the year	[L]	1,785
Cash inflow from increase in debt and lease financing	[M]	(2,427)
		(642)
New finance leases		(28)
Exchange differences		(71)
		(741)
Net debt at beginning of year		(23,502)
Net debt at end of year		(24,243)

Analysis of net debt

FRS1 requires a note analysing the movement in net debt during the period, to be shown separately, either adjoining the cash flow statement, or in a Note. Abbeycrest's analysis, is shown in Note 25.

The changes in net debt should be analysed from the opening **[R]** to the closing component amounts **[V]**, showing separately, where material, changes resulting from:

[S] The cash flows
[T] Exchange movement

[U] Other non-cash changes, and recognition of changes in market value.

TERMINOLOGY

Cash flow statements

Cash is cash in hand and deposits repayable on demand *less* overdrafts repayable on demand; i.e. they can be withdrawn at any time and without penalty. Cash includes cash and deposits denominated in foreign currencies.

Liquid resources are current asset investments held as readily disposable stores of value. To be **readily disposable** an investment must be one that:

(a) is disposable without curtailing or disrupting its company's business; and
(b) is *either* readily convertible into known amounts of cash at or close to its carrying amount, *or* traded in an active market.

Acquisitions and disposals

A note to the cash flow statement should show a summary of the effects of acquisitions and disposals of subsidiary undertakings, indicating how much of the consideration comprised cash (see TT ELECTRONICS below).

27. Acquisitions
(a) The group acquired Optek Technology, a sensor manufacturer, on 3 December 2003

Assets acquired

	Book value £million	Valuation adjust's £million	Fair value £million
Tangible fixed assets	4.9	0.3	5.2
Stocks	3.2	–	3.2
Debtors	4.7	–	4.7
Cash	0.4	–	0.4
Trade and other creditors	(4.7)	–	(4.7)
Deferred tax	1.2	(0.1)	1.1
Total net assets	9.7	0.2	9.9
Goodwill			20.7
Cost of acquisition			30.6

. . .

Satisfied by

	£million
Consideration – cash	30.3
Costs – cash	0.3
	30.6

(b) . . .

Non-cash items and restrictions on transfer

Material transactions which do not result in movements of cash of the reporting company should be disclosed in the notes to the cash flow statement if disclosure is necessary for an understanding of the underlying transactions.

Restrictions on remittability

Where restrictions prevent the transfer of cash from one part of the business or group to another, a note to the cash flow statement should specify the amounts and explain the circumstances.

CADBURY SCHWEPPES, shown below, does not specify the amounts because they have 'no material adverse impact':

Capital structure and resources

. . .

While there are exchange control restrictions which affect the ability of certain of the Group's subsidiaries to transfer funds to the Group, the operations affected by such restrictions are not material to the Group as a whole and the Group does not believe such restrictions have had or will have any material adverse impact on the Group as a whole or the ability of the Group to meet its cash flow requirements.

Limitations of cash flow statements

A cash flow statement is a record of historical facts. It will record expenditure upon additional plant and machinery, but can express no opinion upon whether the expenditure was necessary, or will be profitable.

Similarly it may show an expansion of stocks (or debtors), but it does not tell us whether this was due to

- poor stock or production control;
- inability to sell the finished product; or
- a deliberate act of policy, because of a feared shortage of supply, a potential price rise, or the need to build up stocks of a new model (or product) before it is launched.

Furthermore, in the case of increased debtors, it will not tell us whether it is

- the debtors who are slow to pay; or
- the credit policy which has changed; or
- the accounts department has fallen behind with invoicing; or because
- they merely represent the expansion of turnover.

It will show how new capital was raised, but not whether it was raised in the best way, nor indeed whether it really needed to be raised at all or if the need could have been avoided by better asset control.

When companies have large amounts of cash, the cash flow statement does not tell us where the cash is. Only if it is locked up in an overseas subsidiary, perhaps deposited in an obscure currency in an obscure country (like Turkish Cyprus as was the case with POLLY PECK), where it cannot be remitted to the UK, can we expect to be told – by which time it may well be too late.

Where there are large amounts of both cash and borrowings, the cash flow statement does not tell us why the company does not use the cash to reduce its debts. There may be several reasons:

- It may be better to borrow in the USA, where corporation tax is higher than in the UK, and to keep deposits in the UK.
- The cash may not have been remitted, to avoid having to pay tax on remitting it.
- The company may have borrowed cheaply longer-term or have favourable facilities and be 'round tripping' – borrowing at a lower rate and taking advantage of higher current interest rates to lend money back at a profit.

Borrowing facilities

Some years ago, companies used to be reluctant to disclose details of their *unused* borrowing facilities, for fear, perhaps, that if they subsequently reached the limits, they would not want to disclose 'unused facilities – Nil'.

Nowadays, FRS 13 (see Chapter 23) requires listed companies to disclose details. An example is LONMIN:

LONMIN *Note from the 2003 accounts*

Undrawn committed borrowing facilities

	2003 $m	2002 $m
Expiring in one year or less	178	178
Expiring in more than one year but not more than two years	182	–
Expiring in more than two years	177	87
	537	265

Although it is prudent to have plenty of financial elbow room, *it is not a good idea* for a company to have very large unused facilities in place if it has had to pay its bankers a hefty arrangement fee for setting up the facility and is paying an ongoing annual '*Commitment commission*' on the unused amount.

Take, for example, BOOTS the Chemist:

BOOTS *Extract from 2003 Financial Review*

Liquidity and funding
The company has good access to the capital markets due to its strong credit ratings from Moody's and Standard & Poor's . . .

The group has credit facilities with 7 banks, which mature in 2004, £462m of which remain undrawn. Short-term needs are met from uncommitted bank lines.

It would be helpful to the shareholder to know the underlying strategy; if the undrawn £462m is part of what is known in the City as a '*War chest*' to fund acquisitions being planned, then Boots' reticence is understandable. When a takeover has been announced, a company can be more informative (e.g. RMC the ready mixed concrete group):

RMC *Extract from note to 2003 accounts*

Note 29. Derivatives and other financial instruments
d) Borrowing facilities
The group has undrawn, committed, borrowing facilities at 31 December as follows:

	2003 £m	2002 £m
Expiring in more than one year but not more than two years	–	–
Expiring in more than two years	374.6	539.1
Total	374.6	539.1

A cash flow statement may highlight a deteriorating situation, but does not tell the reader:

- just how close a company is to the limit of its facilities;
- whether it is in danger of breaching any of its borrowing covenants;
- whether the company's bankers are getting nervous, or are still confident of its recovery.

And, of course, it only shows the cash flows for the year which ended some months ago and, as we saw in the recession in the early 1990s, liquidity problems can and do arise very quickly.

Cash requirements

There are three main areas to look at in identifying cash requirements:

1. **Repayment of existing loans** due in the next year or two, including convertible loans whose conversion rights are unlikely to be exercised.
2. **Increase in working capital.** Working capital tends, in an inflationary period and/or when a business expands, to rise roughly in line with turnover. It is useful therefore to use the Working capital/Sales ratio to establish the relationship between working capital and sales.

Working capital to sales

$$= \frac{(\text{Stock} + \text{Trade debtors}) - \text{Trade creditors}}{\text{Sales}}$$

A company with a low working capital ratio should find it easier to grow than a company with a high working capital ratio, like ABBEYCREST. It exercised strict discipline on working capital in 2003: stock was cut by more than £2m, debtors were reduced by £2.5m and trade creditors were increased by nearly £1m.

This cut its working capital/sales ratio from 65% in 2002 to 54% in 2003, reducing working capital by more than £5m.

ABBEYCREST *Working capital ratio*

	2003 £000		2002 £000	
Stock	32,200		36,398	
+ Trade debtors	16,039		18,481	
− Trade creditors	(5,547)		(4,602)	
= *Working capital*	42,692		50,277	
YoY decrease in working capital	(7,585)			
Sales	98,840	[A]	91,475	
YoY increase in sales (£000)	7,365	[B]		
Working capital/Sales ratio (%)	43.19		54.96	[C]
YoY decrease in Wcap ratio (%)	11.77	[D]		
− due to increased sales (£000)	4,048	[B] × [C]		
− due to decrease in ratio (£000)	(11,623)	[A] × [D]		
	(7,585)			

Compare that with TESCO:

TESCO *Working capital ratio*

	2003 £m	2002 £m
Stocks	1,140	929
+ Trade debtors	−	−
− Trade creditors	2,196	1,830
= Negative *Working capital*	(1,056)	(901)
Sales	26,337	23,653
Working capital/Sales ratio (%)	(4.0)	(3.8)

🔑 **Requirements for additional working capital for expansion**

Any business that can sell goods to its customers for cash *before* it has to pay for those goods, won't need any additional working capital for expansion; rather the reverse.

Conversely, companies that have to carry large amounts of stock, work in progress and finished goods at their own expense will need additional working capital if they want to expand; for example the international mining company RIO TINTO:

RIO TINTO *Working capital ratio*

	2003 US$m	2002 US$m
Inventories	1,783	1,502
+ Trade debtors	1,266	1,176
− Trade creditors	(737)	(584)
= Positive *Working capital*	2,312	2,094
Sales	9,228	8,443
Working capital/Sales ratio (%)	25.1	24.8

3. *Capital expenditure requirements.* This is likely to be a rough estimate, unless the company discloses details of both amounts and timing of planned Capex. Points to check:

(a) Note on capital commitments, for example:

ABBEYCREST *2003 accounts*

There was no Note on capital commitments. Capex was cut out to reduce debt.

(b) Cash flow statement, for example:

ABBEYCREST *Note to Group cash flow statement*

	2003 £000	2002 £000
Capital expenditure		
Payments to acquire tangible fixed assets	(3,080)	(1,291)
Receipts from sale of tangible fixed assets	271	133
. . .		

(c) Comments in the annual report, for example:

ABBEYCREST *Chairman's report 2003*

Prospects
. . . The improvements that have been achieved in the operation and control of the Group are already bearing fruit. The commercial advantages and growth potential of Abbeycrest Thailand's new gold jewellery factory will be felt in the current financial year as will the concentration of production . . .

Our comments

If sales increase by, say, 15% in 2004 and the 2003 Working capital/Sales ratio remains unchanged, Abbeycrest will require £53.786 × 0.15 = £8m more working capital.

Cash shortfall

If the net cash flow looks like falling short of the cash requirements we have identified, then the company may have to

(a) increase its overdraft (but is it at the limit of its facilities? – we probably don't know);
(b) borrow longer-term (can it do so within its borrowing limits?);
(c) make a rights issue (is its share price at least 20% above par, is it at least a year and preferably two years since its last rights issue, and are market conditions suitable?);
(d) acquire a more liquid and/or less highly geared company for paper (i.e. bid for another company using shares);
(e) sell some assets (has it any listed investments which could be sold, or has it any activities which could be sold off without seriously affecting the business?);
(f) sell and lease back some of the properties used in the business (has it any unmortgaged properties?);
(g) cut back on capital expenditure that has not already been put out to contract;
(h) tighten credit and stock control;
(i) reduce or omit the ordinary dividend, and possibly even the preference dividend too.

If the company takes none of these steps it will run into an overtrading situation, which is likely to precipitate a cash crisis unless, as a last resort, it:

(j) reduces its level of trading.

Cash flow – definitions and ratios

Free cash flow (FCF)

As discussed at the beginning of this chapter, common sense would suggest that *free cash flow* is 'What the board is *free* to spend' once all obligatory and virtually obligatory payments had been made. And this is how STAGECOACH presented it, as shown below:

STAGECOACH GROUP *Extract from 2003 accounts*

	2003 £m	2002 £m
Consolidated cash flow statement		
Net cash inflow from operating activities	272.2	259.9
Dividends from joint ventures and associates	5.3	5.0
. . .		
Net cash outflow from returns on investments and servicing of finance	(51.9)	(60.9)
Taxation	(7.8)	(16.7)
. . .		
Free cash flow	**217.8**	**184.3**

Free cash flow comprises net cash inflow from operating activities, dividends from joint ventures and associates, net cash outflow from returns on investments and servicing of finance, and taxation.

However, a large number of companies don't even mention FCF, while others have their 'Own brand' definitions.

CADBURY SCHWEPPES deducts *Net capital expenditure* as well as *Interest*, *Tax* and *Dividends* to arrive at FCF, while W. H. SMITH deducts *Dividends* after FCF.

But the company showing the most individuality on *free cash flow* must surely be BOOTS:

BOOTS *Extract from Financial review 2003*

The following summary of cash flow demonstrates the company's ability consistently to generate **free cash flow**.

Free cash flow is defined as the cash flow available to all providers of capital.

Summary of cash flows	£m 2003	£m 2002
Operating cash flows before exceptionals	590	792
Exceptional operating cash flows	(8)	(29)
Acquisitions/disposals of businesses	358	4
Purchase of fixed assets	(146)	(172)
Disposal of fixed assets	119	62
Disposal of own shares	3	8
Taxation paid	(197)	(139)
Free cash flow	**719**	**486**
. . .		

The following chart shows the amounts of free cash flow generated by the group for each of the last five years.

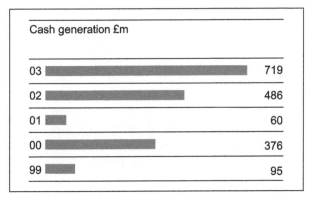

Cash generation £m	
03	719
02	486
01	60
00	376
99	95

Authors' comments on free cash flow

On page 226 is an edited version of Boots' *Group financial record 2003* using '*common sense*' to produce bottom line values of **[f]** the free cash flow in the years 1999 to 2003.

Boots' common sense free cash flow has been steady, as you would expect of this prosperous 'household name' retailer.

Boots 'own brand' definition, on the other hand, produces a 53% fall in its '*Own brand*' of free cash flow in 1999, followed by a 296% rise in 2000.

BOOTS *Edited extract from Group financial record 2003*

Cash flow statement	Authors' Notes	2003 £m	2002 £m	2001 £m	2000 £m	1999 £m
a Cash inflow from operating activities		582.3	722.4	664.4	753.7	601.9
b Net interest received/(Paid)		75.0	40.7	(22.6)	(9.8)	(24.9)
c Taxation		(196.7)	(139.2)	(167.4)	(154.4)	(112.4)
d = a +/− b − c	1	460.4	623.9	474.4	589.5	464.6
e Equity dividends paid		(238.3)	(234.5)	(224.0)	(216.3)	(207.1)
f = d − e	2	222.3	389.4	250.4	373.2	257.5

Authors' notes

1. Often called **'Gross cash flow'**
2. Often called **'Net cash flow'**

Cash flow ratios

Cash flow can be given **per share**:

Cash flow per share

$$= \frac{\text{(Attributable profits plus depreciation)}}{\text{Number of ordinary shares in issue}}$$

The definition used by *REFS* (*Really Essential Financial Statistics*, published by H S Financial Publishing Ltd, www.hsfinancial.com – see also page 290) is:

Cash flow per share

$$= \frac{\begin{array}{c}\text{(Cash flow from operating activities + return on}\\ \text{investments and servicing of finance − Taxation paid)}\end{array}}{\begin{array}{c}\text{Weighted average number of ordinary shares}\\ \text{in issue during the period}\end{array}}$$

Capex per share can then be compared with Cash flow per share. If this is done in terms of 'common sense' free cash flow, it will show how much of their '*disposable income*' the Board is spending on capital investment.

To show ABBEYCREST'S *Free Cash Flow* in 2002 and 2003, we take Abbeycrest's Consolidated cash flow statement on page 218 and rearrange it as shown on the next page. This also shows how the free cash flow was spent:

- **In 2002** Cash flow from operations plummeted to £1.8m, less than interest paid; FCF went negative (£2.8m), while Capex and an acquisition left the company with a (£5m) deficit.
- **In 2003** Cash flow from operations recovered to £6.1m, and FCF to £2.1m. Capex was 30% more than this, but

ABBEYCREST *Consolidated Cash Flow Statement 2003. Sequence of items rearranged*

	2003 £000	FCF	2002 £000
Net cash flow from operating activities	6,126		1,813
Net interest paid	(2,468)		(2,080)
Taxation	[F] (456)		(918)
Equity dividends paid	(1,045)		(1,627)
Common sense free cash flow	2,157	100%	(2,812)
Less:			
Capital expenditure and financial investment	(2,809)	(130%)	(1,158)
Acquisitions and disposals	−	−	(723)
Cash (outflow)/inflow before financing	(652)	(30%)	(4,693)
Financing – (new loan note, etc.)	2,437	113%	(321)
(Decrease)/Increase in cash in the year	1,785	83%	(5,014)

ABBEYCREST *Consolidated cash flow statement for the 6 months ended 31 August 2003*

	6 months to 31 August 2003 £000	6 months to 31 August 2002 £000	Year to 28 February 2003 £000
Net cash (outflow)/inflow from operating activities	**[A] (5,935)**	**[B] (12,014)**	6,126
Returns on investments and servicing of finance	**(773)**	(1,016)	(2,468)
Taxation	**(47)**	(46)	**[C] (456)**
Capital expenditure and financial investment	**(156)**	(1,367)	(2,809)
Acquisitions and disposals	–	–	–
Equity dividends paid	**(247)**	(1,144)	(1,045)
Cash outflow before financing	**(7,158)**	(15,587)	(652)
Financing . . .			

a new secured loan (less repayments) improved the cash position by nearly £1.8m.

'Sherlock Holmes' approach to cash flow

We call it the Sherlock Holmes approach because the cash flow statement often contains clues: clues on questions to ask, and where to look for the answers.

We will round off this chapter with examples of clues we found in ABBEYCREST's interim report for the six months ending 31 August 2003, shown above.

Clue No. 1

[A] *Almost £6m net cash outflow from operating activities! Golly gumdrops, the company must be haemorrhaging cash. No, hang on a minute,* **[B]** *there was a £12 million outflow in H1/02. Could it be a seasonal business?*

Look back at the directors' annual report:

ABBEYCREST *Directors' report 2003*

Principal activity
The principal activity of the group is the design, manufacture and distribution of gold and silver jewellery.

As the company manufactures, it may be building stock for Christmas. Details of changes in working capital will be in a note:

ABBEYCREST *Interim cash flow statement*

Note 1 Reconciliation of operating profit to net cash (outflow)/inflow from operating activities
. . .

Increase in stocks (£000)	(2,981)

This compares with (9,417) two years ago.

Does the chairman make any comment on stocks?

ABBEYCREST *Chairman's interim statement*

Review of activities
. . . Disposal of the excess stocks identified twelve months ago has continued well, with the emphasis being on addressing the more difficult stock to dispose of.

Clue No. 2

Why was £456,000 tax [C] paid in 2003, although Note 8 to the profit and loss account, below, showed a tax credit of £132,000?

Remember that a cash flow statement shows the amount of *tax actually paid in the period*, rather than the *tax charge for the period*, so it looks as though the previous year (2002) was profitable, but 2003 was not.

ABBEYCREST *Extract from the 2003 accounts*

	2003 £000
Note 8 Tax on profit on ord. activities	
UK Corporation tax	(69)
Foreign tax	257
Deferred tax	(331)
Tax charge in respect of the current year	(143)
Adjustment in respect of prior years	11
Total tax charge (credit)	(132)

Snippets of information

Always be on the lookout for snippets of information: they can be very important. In ABBEYCREST's case the last paragraph of the Chairman's statement in the Interim report to 31 August 2003 states:

ABBEYCREST *Extract from Chairman's statement in the Interim report to 31 August 2003*

... I am pleased to announce that I intend to split the roles of Chairman and Chief Executive ... with effect from 1 March 2004.

Research we did some years ago showed that 60% of Listed and USM companies that went bust had a combined Chairman and Chief Executive, compared with 45% of USM companies that survived, and less than 35% of listed companies.

Our view is that it is the duty of the chairman to replace the chief executive if the latter is not up to the job. This is rather difficult if they are one and the same person.

International Financial Reporting Standards

Introduction

IAS 7 is the equivalent of UK GAAP, FRS 1 with the same title. The main differences between the two standards relate to:

- IAS 7 requires cash flows to be grouped under only three headings (operating, investing and financing) as compared with nine under FRS 1.
- Whereas under FRS 1 the statements ends with 'cash', under IAS 7 the statement ends up with 'cash and cash equivalents'.

Classification of cash flows

IAS 7 requires cash flows ('inflows and outflows of cash and cash equivalents') to be grouped under *three* sub-headings:

1. operating activities – the principal revenue-producing activities of the entity and other activities that are not investing or financing activities;
2. investing activities – the acquisition and disposal of long-term assets and other investments not included in cash equivalents;
3. financing activities – activities that result in changes in the size and composition of the equity capital and borrowings of the entity.

Cash and cash equivalents

Cash comprises cash on hand and demand deposit (less bank overdrafts).

 Cash equivalents are defined as:

Short-term highly liquid investments that are readily convertible to known amounts of cash and which are subject to an insignificant risk of changes in value.

Example 26.1 shows a cash flow statement prepared under IFRs.

Example 26.1 Cash flow statement prepared under IFRS

	20X3			20X2
	£	£	£	£
Cash flow from operating activities				
Profit before taxation		576,103		x
Adjustments for:				
Depreciation		84,100		x
Investment income		(11,920)		(x)
Gain in value of investments		(8,450)		(x)
Profit on sale of investments		(2,960)		(x)
Gain in value of investment properties		(76,500)		(x)
Rental income		(25,000)		(x)
Interest expense		15,000		x
Preference dividend paid		10,000		x
Increase in inventories		(28,216)		(x)
Increase in trade and other receivables		(51,351)		(x)
Increase in derivatives		(4,978)		(x)
Increase in trade payables		6,549		(x)
Cash generated from operations		482,377		x
Preference dividend paid		(10,000)		(x)
Interest paid		(15,000)		(x)
Tax paid		(24,200)		(x)
Net cash from operating activities		433,177		x
Cash flows from investing activities				
Purchase of property, plant and equipment	(121,000)		(x)	
Proceeds on disposal of property, plant and equipment	82,000		x	
Proceeds on disposal of held for trading investments	80,260		x	
Purchases of available for sale investments	(25,000)		(x)	
Interest received	8,500		x	
Dividends received	3,420		x	
Rental income	25,000		x	
Net cash from investing activities		53,180		x
Cash flows from financing activities				
Repayments of borrowings	(50,000)		(x)	
Ordinary dividends paid	(80,000)		(x)	
Net cash used in financing activities		(130,000)		(x)
Net increase in cash and cash equivalents		356,357		x
Cash and cash equivalents at beginning of period		75,000		x
Cash and cash equivalents at end of period		431,357		75,000

Notes to the cash flow statement

Cash and cash equivalents

Cash and cash equivalents consist of cash in hand and balances with banks, and deposit accounts on 60-days' notice.

Cash and cash equivalents included in the cash flow statement comprise the following balance sheet amounts:

	20X3	20X2
	£	£
Cash on hand and balances with banks	31,357	5,000
Deposit accounts	400,000	70,000
Total cash and cash equivalents	431,357	75,000

This should be reconciled to items on the balance sheet

CHAPTER 27

Financial reporting for SMEs (small and medium-sized entities)

Introduction

The aim of this chapter is to provide an overview of accounting and disclosure concessions that are available to small and medium-sized companies. The widely-used abbreviation SMEs (which stands for small and medium-sized entities or enterprises) covers two quite distinct categories – small companies and medium-sized companies – as far as law and accounting are concerned. Below we refer separately to these two categories as different regulations apply to each one. Perhaps the most important characteristic of all SMEs is that they are privately-owned limited companies and tend to be owner-managed.

Small companies and concessions available

The Companies Act 1985 (CA 85) sets out a definition of a small company. This definition requires two sets of requirements to be satisfied. The first requirement relates to size and requires any two out of the following three criteria to be satisfied:

1. turnover must not be in excess of £5.6m;
2. gross assets (total of fixed assets and current assets) must not be in excess of £2.8m;
3. there should be no more than 50 employees.

Secondly, a company is not classed as 'small' if it is (or was at any time during the year) a plc **or** its business consisted of one or more of a number of excluded business categories relating to financial services and insurance **or** it was a member of a group that contains a plc or insurance or financial services company. So a small limited company

that is a member of a large plc group is not eligible for any small company reporting concessions.

A company that satisfies the above requirements is entitled to the following concessions:

- a reduced level of disclosure in accounts presented to shareholders;
- eligible to use the Financial Reporting Standard for Smaller Entities (often referred to simply as 'the FRSSE');
- eligible to file abbreviated accounts with the Registrar of Companies;
- exemption from the requirement to prepare and present a cash flow statement.

These are further referred to below.

A further concession available to many (but not all) small companies is the exemption from the requirement for a statutory audit. To qualify for this concession, a company must not only be 'small' (as described above) but it must also show that in the current year its turnover does not exceed £5.6m *and* its gross assets (fixed assets plus current assets) do not exceed £2.8m.

Disclosure concessions available to small companies under CA 85

A small company is not required to present the following information within its annual report:

- business review;
- financial risk management objectives and policies;
- number of employees;
- details of employee remuneration.

There are a number of other minor disclosure concessions under CA 85. However, the most significant disclosure concessions available are those offered in the Financial Reporting Standard for Smaller Entities (see below).

Abbreviated accounts

Companies that qualify as small *may* file abbreviated accounts with the Registrar of Companies. The minimum information that may be filed with the Registrar of Companies includes:

- an abbreviated balance sheet;
- selected notes to the accounts;
- a special auditor's report (except where the company is entitled to exemption from audit).

A profit and loss account need not be filed, nor is a small company required to disclose turnover or profit.

Many (but by no means all) small companies take advantage of this concession, as it allows the company an element of privacy over its financial affairs. To the user attempting to assess a company's finances this lack of information can be inconclusive and frustrating. However, it is always open to those who have commercial dealings with a company to request the full set of accounts which CA 85 requires to be made available to its shareholders.

The Financial Reporting Standard for Smaller Entities (FRSSE)

What is the FRSSE?

For companies that qualify as small under CA 85, the FRSSE is an alternative to full UK GAAP. The main concessions offered by the FRSSE relate to reduced disclosure of information in the annual report (additional to those offered by CA 85 and referred to above).

The latest version of the FRSSE is entitled 'The FRSSE (effective January 2007)'. It is effectively a 'one-stop shop' that combines requirements derived from accounting standards and with requirements derived from CA 85. The combined requirements are presented in an accessible way, arranged under clearly-labelled topic headings.

Use of the FRSSE is *optional*. Companies that elect to use it are *exempt* from the requirements of Financial Reporting Standards (FRSs), Statements of Standard Accounting Practice (SSAPs) and Abstracts (issued by the Urgent Issues Task Force). Small companies that do not opt for the FRSSE *must comply with full UK GAAP* (i.e. all relevant FRSs, SSAPs and Abstracts).

Topics covered in the FRSSE

The FRSSE includes accounting requirements for all areas likely to be important for small companies, including:

- revenue recognition;
- stocks and work-in-progress;
- fixed assets (tangible and intangible);
- financial instruments (shares, dividends and loans);
- hire purchase and lease transactions;
- related party transactions;
- contingent liabilities;
- events after the balance sheet date;
- share-based payments.

Does using the FRSSE affect the measurement of profit or assets?

Until recently, with very minor exceptions, adopting the FRSSE did *not* affect the measurement of profit or assets, although it has always offered the opportunity of simplified calculations in some areas. The concessions offered by the FRSSE related essentially to *disclosure issues*.

This approach has changed in the 2007 version where equity-settled share-based payment transactions (such as the granting to employees of share options) are dealt with by means of memorandum disclosure, and not as an expense to be charged in arriving at operating profit (which is what FRS 20 requires – see Chapter 9).

Equity-settled share-based payment transactions

Equity-settled share-based payment transactions, for example, share options granted to employees, simply require memorandum disclosure (by contrast with the complex and stringent accounting rules in FRS 20). Such transactions will not feature in the company's accounting entries unless and until optionholders take up their entitlement and subscribe for shares in the company by the payment of cash.

The notes to the financial statements should describe the principal terms and conditions of any equity-settled share-based payment arrangements that existed during the period, including:

- the number of shares;
- the number of employees and others potentially involved;
- the grant date;
- any performance conditions;
- over what period any performance conditions apply;
- any option exercise prices (where applicable).

The FRSSE refers also to 'cash-settled share-based payment transactions' but these are not referred to here as such transactions are more likely to apply to larger companies.

The International Financial Reporting Standard for SMEs

In February 2007, the International Accounting Standards Board (IASB) published an exposure draft of a proposed International Financial Reporting Standard aimed at small and medium-sized entities. This is a far longer and more detailed document than the FRSSE, and is an attempt to present a simplified version of full IFRS.

The UK Accounting Standards Board has issued this for public comment in the UK, and will then make a decision about its possible future use in the UK.

Medium-sized companies and concessions available

CA 85 makes limited concessions available for medium-sized companies. To qualify as medium, two sets of qualifying conditions must be satisfied, relating to size and legal status.

First of all, as regards size, two out of the following three conditions must be satisfied:

1. turnover must not be in excess of £22.8m;
2. gross assets must not be in excess of £11.4m;
3. there should be no more than 250 employees.

Secondly, a company is not classed as 'medium-sized' if it is (or was at any time during the year) a PLC **or** its business consisted of one or more of a number of excluded

business categories relating to financial services and insurance **or** it was a member of a group that contains a plc or insurance or financial services company.

Abbreviated accounts concession

A medium-sized company may file abbreviated accounts, which are essentially a full set of accounts, with the following omissions:

- turnover, cost of sales and other operating income may be omitted from the profit and loss account (assuming the company is using Format 1): effectively the profit and loss account commences with gross profit;
- the note providing analysis of turnover and profit by class of business and geographical markets.

It is likely that from a future date medium-sized companies will be required to include a note of the annual turnover figure. The relevant regulation under the Companies Act 2006 is yet to be finalised and published.

Business review concession

CA 85 requires medium-sized companies to publish a Business Review (see Chapter 4) as part of its Directors' report, but does not require the review to include details of non-financial key performance indicators (KPIs).

Small and medium-sized groups

Certain small and medium-sized groups are permitted an exemption from the requirement to prepare group (consolidated) accounts. In common with the above exemptions there are size and legal status criteria that apply. The size criteria are:

	Small	*Medium-sized*
1. Turnover not more than – net	£5.60m	£22.80m
Turnover not more than – gross	£6.72m	£27.36m
2. Gross assets not more than – net	£2.80m	£11.40m
Gross assets not more than – gross	£3.36m	£13.68m
3. Employees not more than	50	250

Two of the above three criteria must be met. The conditions may be met either on a gross basis, which simply requires the relevant numbers for each group company to be added together. Alternatively the calculation may be done on a net basis, which requires the effect of transactions between group companies to be adjusted for.

A group is not eligible for the exemption if any of its members is a plc or a company carrying out insurance activities or providing financial services (with limited exceptions).

> **The exemption from the preparation of group accounts option for *medium-sized groups* will be removed with effect from accounting periods beginning on or after 6 April 2008, as s. 398 of the Companies Act 2006 only provides an exemption option for small groups.**

A parent company that does not prepare group accounts must provide the following information by way of note. The notes below are intended as an overview of the applicable disclosures for most small and medium group situations. Detailed requirements are contained in Sch. 5, CA 85:

1. the name of each subsidiary undertaking;
2. the reason why the company is not required to prepare group accounts (i.e. exemption as small or medium-sized group);
3. for each subsidiary undertaking:
   - identify class of shares and nominal value held;
   - aggregate amount of capital and reserves at the end of the year;
   - disclose profit or loss for the year.

CHAPTER 28

Group accounts, acquisitions and mergers

Acquisitions of businesses

Introduction

Businesses may expand in a number of ways. Some grow organically, some expand by acquiring the businesses of others. Business acquisitions may result from:

- purchase of an unincorporated business such as a sole trader or partnership;
- purchase of a division of a company;
- purchase of a controlling shareholding in a company – by the payment of cash or issue of shares as consideration or a combination of these.

This chapter is concerned with the acquisition of a controlling shareholding in a company – this may relate to all of the shares or to a majority shareholding. In the latter case, the acquiring company does not acquire all of the shares; the shares held by others are usually referred to as a 'minority interest'.

This chapter includes two worked examples: a purchase of shares for cash and purchase by means of a share-for-share exchange.

Group accounts

Group structures and terminology

As mentioned above, one company (say, A Limited) may acquire a controlling interest in another company (say, B

Limited) by paying cash or issuing new shares. A Limited is referred to as a parent company (an alternative term sometimes used is 'holding company') and B Limited is referred to as a subsidiary.

A parent company–subsidiary relationship may come about in a number of ways, the most common of which is where A Limited acquires a majority of the voting rights of B Limited. The Companies Act 1985 includes a number of other situations but these rarely arise in practice, are complex and are not referred to in this chapter.

A *wholly owned subsidiary* is one in which all the share capital is held either by the parent company or by other wholly owned subsidiaries.

A *partially owned subsidiary* is one in which some of the share capital is owned outside the group. For an illustration of these terms, see Example 28.1. A parent company is also often termed the *holding company*, and, a parent company and its subsidiaries are referred to as a *group*.

Example 28.1 Partially and wholly owned subsidiaries

H is the parent company of a group of companies, all of which are incorporated in Great Britain:

- H holds 100,000 of the 100,000 ordinary shares of S
- H holds 7,500 of the 10,000 ordinary shares of T
- S holds 5,100 of the 10,000 ordinary shares of U
- T holds 1,000 of the 1,000 ordinary shares of V
- The H group may be depicted thus:

▶

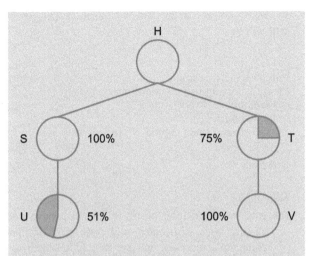

In law, the parent of a subsidiary is the parent of its subsidiary.

The H group consists of:

- H's wholly owned subsidiary S
- H's partially owned subsidiary T (in which there is a 25% minority)
- T's wholly owned subsidiary V (which in law is also a subsidiary of H, but colloquially a partially owned subsubsidiary of H)
- S's partially owned subsidiary U (in which there is a 49% minority).

In the past, all these relationships depended on voting control, but over the years the ingenuity of companies and their financial advisors to facilitate operation overseas, or in an attempt to keep companies off balance sheet (to hide either their liabilities or true profitability or their tendency to be loss-making), or simply to avoid tax, led to numerous devices which kept companies outside the group for purposes of the consolidated accounts. The Companies Act 1985 and FRS 2, Accounting for subsidiary undertakings, have done much to prevent this.

Group accounts

If, at the end of a financial year, a company is a parent company, group accounts have to be prepared, although small private groups and (prior to the Companies Act 2006) medium-sized groups are exempt (see Chapter 27).

Group accounts comprise:

- a consolidated balance sheet; and
- a consolidated profit and loss account,

dealing with the parent company and its subsidiary undertakings.

Group accounts should include also a consolidated cash flow statement (required by FRS 1) and a consolidated statement of total recognised gains and losses (required by FRS 3).

What has to be published?

The published group accounts should include the consolidated accounts referred to above, as well as the balance sheet of the parent company. Subsidiaries are normally shown in the parent company's own balance sheet at cost less any amounts written off for impairment.

Parent company's own profit and loss account

Under s. 230(3) of the Companies Act 1985, the parent company's profit and loss account may be omitted from the consolidated accounts providing the parent company's balance sheet shows the parent company's profit or loss for the year, as is shown by TT ELECTRONICS below. In practice one seldom if ever sees the parent company's own profit and loss account.

TT ELECTRONICS *Extract from note 25 to the 2003 accounts*

In accordance with the exemption allowed by Section 230 of the Companies Act 1985, the Company has not presented its own profit and loss account. A profit of £14.9 million (2002: £5.2 million) has been dealt with in the financial statements of the Company.

The group accounts under UK GAAP do not need to include the cash flow statement and statement of total recognised gains and losses of the parent company (contrast this with the situation under IFRS referred to at the end of the chapter).

The consolidated balance sheet

In simple terms a consolidated balance sheet shows all the assets and all the liabilities of all group companies whether wholly owned or partially owned. Where a partially owned subsidiary exists, its shareholders' funds are provided partly by the holding company and partly by the minority.

To illustrate the basic principles of consolidated accounts let us take the case of a parent company, H, with a partially owned subsidiary, S, and imagine that we wish to prepare the consolidated balance sheet for the H GROUP at 31 December 2003. H paid £340,000 cash for 200,000 of the 250,000 £1 ordinary shares of S on 1 January 1996.

The balance sheet of S at acquisition was:

S Balance sheet at 1 January 2001

	£000
Fixed assets:	
Freehold land and buildings	120
Plant and machinery	146
	266
Net current assets	169
	435
Ordinary share capital	250
Reserves	85
Ordinary shareholders' funds	335
7% Debenture	100
	435

H and S Balance sheets at 31 December 2003

	H £000	S £000
Fixed assets:		
Freehold land and buildings	150	120
Plant and machinery	250	180
	400	300
Shares in S	340	–
Net current assets	360	200
	1,100	500
Ordinary share capital	500	250
Reserves	480	150
Ordinary shareholders' funds	980	400
10% Unsecured loan stock	120	–
7% Debenture	–	100
	1,100	500

There are six steps to consolidating the two companies' balance sheets at 31 December 2003:

1. *Ascertain the goodwill* by comparing the cost to H of its investment in S with H's share of the equity share-

holders' funds of S at the date of acquisition. The goodwill will be:

	£000	£000
Purchase consideration		340
Parent company's share of ordinary shareholders' funds at date of acquisition:		
$^4/_5$ of Ordinary share capital	200	
$^4/_5$ of Reserves	68	268
Goodwill		72

Note that:
(a) Any pre-acquisition profits of S which have not already been distributed will form part of that company's reserves, and are thus represented by equity shareholders' funds taken into account in computing goodwill.
(b) Any distribution by S after it is acquired by H which is made out of pre-acquisition profits (i.e. reserves existing at acquisition) must be credited not to the profit and loss account of H as income, but to the asset account 'Investment in S' as a reduction of the purchase price of that investment.
(c) The accounting treatment of goodwill is dealt with in Chapter 14.

2. *Compute the holding company's share* of the undistributed post-acquisition profits of the subsidiary.

   This equals the parent company's proportion of the change in reserves since the date of acquisition:

   $$\frac{200,000}{250,000} \times (£150,000 - £85,000) = £52,000$$

   This, added to the parent company's own reserves, represents the reserves of the group which will appear in the consolidated balance sheet:

   $$£52,000 + £480,000 = £532,000$$

3. *Compute minority interests* in the net assets of S:

   $$\begin{array}{ccc} \text{Minority} \\ \text{interests} \end{array} = \begin{array}{c} \text{Minority} \\ \text{proportion} \end{array} \times \begin{array}{c} \text{Equity shareholders'} \\ \text{funds of S at} \\ \text{31 December 2003} \end{array}$$

   The minority interest in the equity shareholders' funds of S is:

   $$\frac{50,000}{250,000} \times £400,000 = £80,000$$

4. *Draw up the consolidated balance sheet*:
   (a) insert as share capital the share capital of the holding company;
   (b) insert the figures already computed for
      ■ goodwill (see 1 above) and
      ■ minority interests (see 3 above);
   (c) show as 'reserves' the total of the reserves of the holding company and the post-acquisition reserves of the subsidiary applicable to the holding company (see 2 above).
5. *Consolidate*: add together like items (e.g. add freehold land and buildings of the holding company and freehold land and buildings of the subsidiary) and show the group totals in the consolidated balance sheet. Omit, in so doing, the share capital of the subsidiary, reserves, and the investment in the subsidiary, which have already been taken into account in steps 1 to 3.

It will be seen (Example 28.2) that only the share capital of the parent company appears in the consolidated balance sheet. The share capital of the subsidiary has disappeared, one-fifth of it becoming part of 'minority interests' while the other four-fifths (£200,000), together with H's share of S's reserves on acquisition (£68,000) and the goodwill (£72,000) balance out the removal of H's balance sheet item 'shares in S' (£340,000).

Example 28.2 H GROUP Consolidated balance sheet at 31 December 1998

	£000
Fixed assets:	
Goodwill	72
Freehold land and buildings	270
Plant and machinery	430
	772
Net current assets	560
	1,332
Ordinary share capital	500
Reserves	532
Ordinary shareholders' funds	1,032
Minority interests	80
H's 10% ULS	120
S's 7% Debenture	100
	1,332

The consolidated profit and loss account

The format of the consolidated profit and loss account is similar to that for single companies (see Chapter 7). The total for each line is arrived by aggregation (or consolidation) and adjusted for inter-company items such as sales between one group company and another.

If the group contains partially owned subsidiaries, the minority interests in the profits of those subsidiaries have to be deducted at the consolidated profit after tax level.

Acquisitions and mergers

In the UK there are two methods of accounting for acquisitions (or business combinations):

1. acquisition accounting, and
2. merger accounting.

The rules for both methods are set out in FRS 6, Acquisitions and mergers, which restricts the use of merger accounting to rare situations. Acquisition accounting should be used for the majority of business combinations where a party can be identified as having the role of an acquirer.

Acquisition accounting

Earlier in the chapter we looked at an example that considered the principles of acquisition accounting. We look now at some of the detailed requirements of financial reporting standards.

Year of acquisition or disposal

In acquisition accounting, when a subsidiary is acquired (or disposed of) during the accounting period, the results of the subsidiary are included from the effective date of acquisition (or to the effective date of disposal), for example, RMC GROUP:

Purchased goodwill

FRS 10 defines purchased goodwill as the *difference* between

- the cost of the business that has been acquired, and
- the fair value of its identifiable assets less liabilities.

Purchased goodwill is sometimes described as '*goodwill on consolidation*'.

(Please refer also to Chapter 14.)

Determining fair values

FRS 7, Fair values in acquisition accounting, contains detailed rules for arriving at the cost of the business, as well as the fair value of the assets and liabilities.

Fair value rules

- Tangible fixed asset:
  (a) market value, if assets similar in type and condition are bought and sold on a open market; or
  (b) depreciated replacement cost, reflecting the acquired business's normal buying process and the sources of supply and prices available to it.
  The fair value should not exceed the asset's recoverable amount.
- *Intangible fixed asset* recognised in the accounts: replacement cost, normally its estimated market value.
- *Stocks*, including commodity stocks:
  (a) where trading is on a market in which the acquired business participates as both a buyer and a seller – current market prices;

  (b) other stocks, and work in progress – should be valued at the lower of replacement cost and net realisable value.
- *Quoted investments*: market price, adjusted if necessary for unusual price fluctuations or for the size of the holdings.

The fair values of monetary assets and liabilities (including provisions) should take into account the amounts expected to be received or paid, and their timing and, if significant, be discounted to present value.

A further worked example

Company A acquired company B by means of a share for share exchange. A issued 200,000 new £1 ordinary shares (valued at the time of the acquisition at £3 each i.e. at a premium of £2 above nominal value) in exchange for the entire share capital of B.
    The balance sheets of the two companies at the time of the acquisition were:

Before the combination

	A £000	B £000
Ordinary share capital	800	80
Reserves	280	340
	1,080	420
Net assets	1,080	420

Company A combined with Company B

Company A issues 200,000 new A £1 ordinary shares (standing at 300p each, a premium of 200p above par value) in exchange for the entire share capital of B.
    In acquisition accounting, the fair value of the net assets of B is assessed as £480,000, compared with the book value of £420,000, an increase (*uplift*) of £60,000.

For the purposes of the fair value calculations required under acquisition accounting, the fair value of the net assets of B is assessed as £480,000 (this assessment is required for the net assets of the *acquired* company only). Compared with book value of £420,000 this represents an uplift of £60,000.

After the businesses had combined

The consolidated balance sheet of A Group (A + B) would appear as:

	Note	£000
Ordinary £1 shares	1	1,000
Share premium account	2	400
Distributable reserves	3	280
		1,680
Net assets (excl. goodwill)	4	1,560
Goodwill	5	120
		1,680

Notes:

1. Company A's original £800,000 share capital plus the £200,000 shares A issued.
2. The premium of 200p per share on the 200,000 shares Company A issued.
3. Distributable reserves = Reserves of Company A (£280,000), plus the increase in Company B's reserves since acquisition (£nil, as the acquisition has only just taken place).
4. Under acquisition accounting, the net assets of B were taken at fair value of £480,000, rather than at book value of £420,000.
5. Goodwill is the amount by which the cost of the investment (£600,000) exceeds the fair value of the net assets acquired (£480,000).

Assets at the date of acquisition

The identifiable assets less liabilities of the acquired business (affecting the consequent goodwill calculation) should be those that existed at the date of acquisition, and should *not* reflect

- changes in asset values/liabilities resulting from the acquirer's intentions or future actions;
- impairments or other changes resulting from events subsequent to the acquisition;
- provisions for future operating losses or reorganisation costs to be incurred as a result of the acquisition (even if these were reflected in the purchase price).

The message from FRS 7 is clear – the effects of the above should be reflected in the group's operating profit/loss for the period after acquisition.

Provisional fair values

If possible, the identification and valuation of assets and liabilities should be completed by the date on which the accounts relating to the year of acquisition are approved by the directors.

CELLTECH *Extract from Note 21 to 2001 accounts: Acquisition of subsidiary undertakings*

(i) Medeva

Fair value adjustments
On 26 January 2000, the Group acquired Medeva PLC. Given the size and complexity of the acquisition, the fair values established in 2000 were provisional and gave rise to goodwill of £615.5m. The fair values have since been finalised and are presented below.

The assets and liabilities of Medeva acquired as follows:	Provisional value £m	Adjustments £m	Fair value £m
Fixed assets – tangible	67.7	2.8	70.5
Stocks	24.1	–	24.1
Debtors	71.3	2.1	73.4
Equity investments	15.1	(1.6)	13.5
Cash	17.0	–	17.0
Creditors	(145.2)	(1.4)	(146.6)
Loans and finance leases	(108.9)	–	(108.9)
Provisions for liabilities	(28.9)	(5.6)	(34.5)
Net assets acquired	(17.6)	(2.9)	(20.5)
Original goodwill			615.5
Adjustments (as above)			2.9
Goodwill – final			**618.4**

Example of a substantial acquisition

In 1999, WASTE RECYCLING made two major acquisitions from the Kelda Group (formerly Yorkshire Water) which tripled Waste's turnover. A note to Waste's accounts on the larger of the two acquisitions illustrates the main disclosures required for an acquisition classified by FRS 6 as 'substantial'.

WASTE RECYCLING *Extract from note to the financial statements, year ended 31 December 1999*

Note 28 Acquisitions

(a) Yorkshire Environmental Global Waste Management (YEGWM)
On 29 January 1999 the Company acquired the business of YEGWM for a total consideration of £181,278,000. Additionally, acquisition expenses of £1,601,000 were incurred. The results of YEGWM were as follows:

	[B] Date of acquisition to 31 December 1999 £000	[A] 1 January 1999 to date of acquisition £000
Turnover	59,962	6,535
Cost of sales	(44,743)	(5,540)
Administrative expenses	(3,751)	(706)
Operating profit	11,468	289
Taxation		(98)
Profit after taxation		191
Minority interests		(59)
Retained profit		132

[C] The profit after taxation for the preceding financial year ended 31 December 1998 was £4,709,000.
The following table analyses the book value of the major categories of assets and liabilities acquired:

[D]	Book value at date of acquisition £000	Accounting policy alignment £000	Revaluation adjustments £000	[E] Provisional fair value of net assets £000
Tangible fixed assets	48,372	(2,336)	(5,403)[1]	40,633
Debtors	11,147	–	(131)[2]	11,016
Cash balances	8,217	–	–	8,217
Creditors and accruals	(11,810)	–	(1,465)[3]	(13,275)
Borrowings	(10,850)	–	–	(10,850)
Deferred taxation	2,594	(2,709)	–	(115)
Provisions	(13,452)	2,616	–	(10,836)
Minority interests	(553)	–	–	(553)
Net assets acquired	33,665	(2,429)	(6,999)	24,237
[F] Goodwill				158,642
Consideration				182,879

Satisfied by

[G] Shares				181,278
Acquisition costs				1,601
				182,879

1. This adjustment represents a revision of the book values of landfill sites to reflect market royalty rates and the permanent impairment of the values of certain other fixed assets.
2. Additional bad debt provision.
3. Additional corporation tax provision and accruals for additional liabilities identified.

[H] . . . The provisional fair values represent the Directors' current estimates of the net assets acquired. However, in accordance with FRS7, the values may be revised as further information becomes available.

Where this is not possible, *provisional* valuations should be made. If necessary, these should be amended in the accounts of the following year with a corresponding adjustment to goodwill: see the CELLTECH extract earlier.

[A] A summarised profit and loss account of the acquired company from the beginning of its financial year to the date of acquisition.

[B] The post-acquisition results of the acquired company should be disclosed separately, where they have a major impact.

[C] The profit after tax and minorities for the acquired company's previous financial year.

[D] A table of book values and fair value adjustments, analysed as shown opposite.

[E] Where fair values can only be determined on a provisional basis at the end of the accounting period, this should be stated, and the reasons should be given.

[F] The amount of '*Purchased goodwill*' arising (in Waste's case £158.6m).

[G] Details of the consideration given, including any deferred or contingent consideration (none in Waste's case).

[H] Waste will have to disclose and explain any subsequent material adjustments.

Post balance sheet events

Where a material acquisition or disposal takes place shortly after the balance sheet date, it will be a post balance sheet event requiring disclosures under FRS 21, Events after the balance sheet date. For example NATIONAL GRID:

NATIONAL GRID *Note to the 2002 accounts*

Note 31 Post balance sheet event
On 22 April 2002 the Boards of National Grid Group and Lattice Group unanimously agreed and announced the terms of a recommended merger. Under the terms of the merger National Grid shareholders will retain their shares in National Grid (to be renamed National Grid Transco) and Lattice shareholders will receive 0.375 National Grid Transco shares for each Lattice share.
On completion of the merger, National Grid shareholders will hold approximately 57.3 per cent and Lattice shareholders will hold approximately 42.7 per cent of the issued share capital . . .
It is intended to account for the merger in accordance with merger accounting principles.

Merger accounting

With the introduction of FRS 6, Acquisitions and mergers, the use of merger accounting has become quite rare. The FRS restricts its use to business combinations where, by meeting strict criteria, the two companies concerned can demonstrate that the combination is a genuine merger, not a takeover of one by the other, for example, BP's merger with AMOCO.

Merger accounting is not referred to further, in view of its rareness under UK GAAP and the fact that it is prohibited under IFRS.

International Financial Reporting Standards

What do groups have to publish?

Groups may present consolidated accounts on the basis of IFRS either because they are required to (owing to being fully listed). Under UK law, the accounts of parent and subsidiaries may be prepared either on the basis of IFRS or on the basis of UK GAAP.

IFRS used throughout the group

Where IFRS is adopted *throughout the group*, the position as regards publication of accounts is as follows:

	Balance sheet	Income statement	Equity statement	Cash flow statement
Consolidated accounts (IFRS)	Required	Required	Required	Required
Parent company (IFRS)	Required	Exempt (provided s. 230 statement disclosed)	Required	Required

Where IFRS is used throughout the group, group and parent company information can be published alongside each other. For example, group and parent company balance sheet can both be published next to each other on the same page.

UK GAAP used for parent and subsidiaries

	Balance sheet	Income statement	Equity statement	Cash flow statement
Consolidated accounts (IFRS)	Required	Required	Required [IAS 1]	Required
Parent company (UK GAAP)	Required	*Exempt (provided s. 230 statement disclosed)*	Required [FRS 3]	*Exempt*

If the second approach is adopted, full UK GAAP accounting policies must be provided. The accounts must be kept completely separate from those of the group.

IFRS 3, Business combinations

A business combination is defined as 'the bringing together of separate entities into one reporting entity'. A business combination falling within the scope of the IFRS may be structured in a number of different ways and does not *necessarily* result in a parent–subsidiary relationship. For example, a business combination may involve the purchase of the net assets, including goodwill, of another entity rather than the purchase of its equity.

The main areas covered by IFRS 3 are:

- the method of accounting for business combinations (including measurement issues);
- accounting for goodwill – the standard prohibits the amortisation of goodwill acquired in a business combination, but requires such goodwill to be tested for impairment annually (or more frequently in certain circumstances).

We referred to the treatment of goodwill under IFRS in Chapter 14 (see page 114, Accounting policies of FIRST CHOICE HOLIDAYS).

Goodwill (the excess of the cost of the business combination over the acquirer's interest in the net fair value of the identifiable assets, liabilities and contingent liabilities) should initially be measured at cost. Subsequently, goodwill should be measured at cost less any accumulated impairment losses.

IFRS 3 prohibits systematic amortisation of goodwill and requires the acquirer to test goodwill for impairment annually or more frequently if events or changes in circumstances indicate that it might be impaired in accordance with IAS 36, Impairment of assets.

There are special rules when companies move across from UK GAAP to IFRS. Effectively, the net book value of the goodwill (determined under UK GAAP by applying FRS 10) is 'frozen' *at the company's date of transition to IFRS*. The date of transition is the first day of the relevant comparative year. The carrying amount must be tested for any impairment, and no amortisation is permitted after that date. Impairment tests will subsequently be required at least annually.

Example 28.3

Consider a company with a 30 September year end which decided to adopt IFRS for the year ending 30 September 2007. The company has a large balance on goodwill, all of which dates back several years.

The transition date is 1 October 2005. The net book value of goodwill under UK GAAP at that date is the amount to be carried forward into the IFRS balance sheet, subject to any subsequent adjustment for impairment (see illustration on page 285 regarding IFRS 3).

CHAPTER 29

Joint ventures, associates and foreign operations

Introduction

In the previous chapter we looked at group structures involving a parent company and one or more subsidiaries. In this chapter we look at groups that have investments in joint ventures, associates and foreign operations.

From an accounting viewpoint, consolidated accounts present the accounts of the group as though it were a single entity. Each item in the consolidated balance sheet and the consolidated profit and loss account represents the aggregate of the various line items, such as fixed assets, stock, turnover, etc. (subject to some adjustments for inter-company items) in the accounts of the parent and the individual subsidiaries.

As we saw in the previous chapter, a parent company has a controlling interest in a subsidiary, whether the shares in the subsidiary are wholly owned or partly owned. Not all investments in other companies, however, give rise to a controlling interest. Some investments simply carry an entitlement to vote at company meetings and receive whatever dividends the company declares. Others carry 'significant influence' (referred to below) on account of the size of the shareholding and other factors. Finally some investments give shared control, i.e. control of a company is shared between two or more investors.

As a general introduction to the more detailed discussion that follows below, the following table summarises in a very simplistic manner a number of investment levels, ranging from little or no influence through to control.

Accounting standards

FRS 9, Associates and joint ventures, contains the rules on accounting for associates and joint ventures.

Degree of influence or control	Example of shareholding size	Classification
Simple investment (little influence on investee)	Considerably less than 20% of the investee's total share capital	Trade investment (UK GAAP) or available-for-sale investment (IFRS)
Significant influence	20% or more	Associate
Control jointly with other investors	50% if two investors or 33.33% if three investors, etc.	Joint venture
Sole control	50.1% or more	Subsidiary

It recognises five types of interest:

1. a subsidiary (which we considered in Chapter 28);
2. a joint arrangement that is not an entity;
3. a joint venture;
4. an associate;
5. a simple investment (which we considered in Chapters 15 and 18).

This chapter deals with types 2, 3 and 4.

Joint arrangement that is not an entity

Where two or more entities (e.g. companies) participate in an arrangement to carry on part of their trade, that arrangement falls under this heading unless it carries on a trade or business of its own.

A joint arrangement will not be an entity if it is no more than a cost- or risk-sharing means of carrying out a process in the participants' trades or businesses: for example, a joint marketing or distribution network or a shared production facility.

A joint arrangement carrying out a single project (as, for example, occurs in the construction industry) tends to fall under this head, but the nature of such a joint arrangement may change over time: for example, a pipeline operated as a joint arrangement that initially provided a service only directly to the participants may develop into a pipeline business providing services to others.

Each party to a joint arrangement that is not an entity should account for its own share of the assets, liabilities and cash flows in the joint arrangement, measured according to the terms of that arrangement.

Joint venture

Where the investor holds a long-term interest and shares control under a contractual arrangement that arrangement is referred to as a joint venture.

The joint venture agreement can override the rights normally conferred by ownership interests with the effect that:

- acting together, the venturers can control the venture and there are procedures for such joint action;
- each venturer has (implicitly or explicitly) a veto over strategic policy decisions.

Definition

Where the investor holds a long-term interest and shares control under a contractual arrangement that arrangement is referred to as a *joint venture*.

The joint venture agreement can override the rights normally conferred by ownership interests with the effect that:

- acting together, the venturers can control the venture and there are procedures for such joint action;
- each venturer has (implicitly or explicitly) a veto over strategic policy decisions.

There is usually a procedure for settling disputes between venturers and, possibly, for terminating the joint venture.

The venturer should use the *gross equity method* to account for the joint venture.

Gross equity method

Under what is termed the gross equity method, all the amounts included under the equity method (see page 246) have to be shown and, in addition:

- *in the consolidated profit and loss account*, the venturer's share of their operating profit, [A] in the GUS illustration below, distinguished from that of the group, and
- *on the face of the group balance sheet*, the venturer's share of the gross assets, [B] in the GUS illustration below, and the gross liabilities [C] of its joint ventures.

GUS *Extracts from the 2003 accounts*

Consolidated profit and loss account

	Notes	2003 £m	2002 £m
Operating profit – continuing operations		452	381
Share of operating profit of BL Universal PLC (Joint venture)	**[A]**	**26**	**25**
Share of operating profit of associated undertakings		44	33
Loss on sale of fixed asset investments in continuing operations		–	(2)
Trading profit		522	437
. . .			

▶

Group balance sheet	Notes	2003 £m	2003 £m	2002 £m	2002 £m
Fixed assets					
Goodwill			2,436		1,422
Other intangible assets			178		192
Tangible assets			1,043		847
Investment in joint venture					
Share of gross assets	[B]	405		416	
Share of gross liabilities	[C]	(277)		(308)	
	[D]	128		108	
Loans to joint venture		82		87	
			210		195

Had it not been for the requirement to use the gross equity method, GUS would have shown the investment in BL Universal in 2003 as £128m (2002, £108m) **[D]** rather than spelling out the very substantial gross assets and liabilities involved.

This was often the case where there was a joint venture between the owners of land and builders/developers.

Where the venturer conducts a major part of its business through joint ventures, it may show fuller information provided all amounts are distinguished from those of the group (see Note 15 below).

	2003 £m	2002 £m
Fixed assets	795	813
Current assets	26	19
Creditors – amounts falling due within one year	(56)	(72)
Creditors – amounts falling due after more than one year	(506)	(541)
Shareholders' funds	259	219
Attributable to the Group	128	108

GUS *Extract from a note to the 2003 accounts*

Note 15 Investment in joint venture

	Shares £m	Loans £m	Total £m
Cost or valuation			
At 1 April 2002	108	87	195
Share of profit after taxation	5	–	5
Share of revaluation of investment properties	15	–	15
Repayment of loans	–	(5)	(5)
At 31 March 2003	128	82	210

The Group holds 50% of the ordinary share capital of BL Universal PLC. The Group's share of cumulative retained profits at 31 March 2003 is £22m (2002, £17m) and its share of turnover for the year, excluded from Group turnover, is £30.9m in 2002.

The consolidated balance sheet of BL Universal PLC is as follows:

Proportional consolidation and IFRS

It has been a long-standing practice in certain industries (e.g. oil exploration, engineering and construction) to account for certain types of joint venture using proportional consolidation; and this is recognised by the Companies Act. Proportional consolidation involves adding the investor's share of the joint venture to each line of the consolidated profit and loss account and balance sheet. This is not the same as consolidation of, say, a minority interest in a subsidiary, where what is added line by line is the whole of the subsidiary's figure (the minority interest being taken out separately).

IAS 31 (International Accounting Standard 31), Financial reporting of interests in joint ventures, permits but does not recommend the use of the equity method, on the grounds that proportional consolidation better reflects the substance and economic reality of a venturer's interest in a jointly-controlled entity. The ASB believes that it can be misleading to represent each venturer's joint control of a joint venture – which allows it to direct the operating and financial policies of the joint venture only with the consent of the other venturers – as being in substance equivalent to its having sole control of its share of each of that entity's assets, liabilities and cash flows. FRS 9 abolishes proportional consolidation, but the accounting treatment for joint arrangements which are not an entity is, arithmetically, virtually identical to proportional consolidation.

Joint ventures are often a means of sharing risks where the risks are particularly high. The amount involved can be considerable and the effect of failure spectacular.

W S ATKINS held a 20% stake in Metronet as part of a consortium of five companies responsible for upgrading, maintaining and running two-thirds of the London Underground network under the framework of a 30-year Public Private Partnership (PPP).

W S Atkins issued a press release on 18 July 2007. For further details on this press release, see Atkins Investor Relations on www.atkinsglobal.com.

Associates

Definition

Where the investor holds a *participating interest* and exercises *significant influence* the entity is an *associate*. This covers cases where the investor:

- has a *long-term interest* and
- is actively involved, and influential, in the direction of its investee through its participation in policy decisions covering the aspects of policy relevant to the investor, including decisions on strategic issues such as:
  - the expansion or contraction of the business, participation in other entities or changes in products, markets and activities of its investee;
  - determining the balance between dividend and reinvestment.

The investor should include its associates in its consolidated financial statements using what is called *the equity method* of accounting.

The equity method

Under the equity method:

1. Turnover does *not* include the turnover of associates.

See **[A]** in the DIAGEO consolidated profit and loss account below.

Where a group wishes to give an indication of the relative size of associates, it may give the associates' turnover in a note, or include it in an overall figure, provided the group's share of its associates' turnover is clearly distinguished.

For example, RIO TINTO includes its share of associates' (and joint ventures') turnover in *Gross turnover*, and then deducts them both to arrive at *Consolidated turnover*:

RIO TINTO *Extract from 2003 accounts*

Profit and loss account	2003 US$m	2002 US$m
Gross turnover (including share of joint ventures and associates)	11,755	10,828
Share of joint ventures' turnover	(1,820)	(1,662)
Share of associates' turnover	(707)	(723)
Consolidated turnover	9,228	8,443

---

2. The group's share of its associates' operating results should be included immediately after group operating profit, **[B]**.
3. Any amortisation or write-down of goodwill arising in associates should then be charged [DIAGEO had none].
4. The group's share of any exceptional items **[D]** should be shown separately. DIAGEO does so in a note:

DIAGEO *Extract from note to 2003 accounts*

Note 7 Exceptional items

. . .

Share of profits of associates The group's share of exceptional items in respect of associates comprised restructuring costs of £18 million incurred by General Mills and £3 million in respect of Moet Hennessy.

---

5. Below the level of trading profit [C], the group's share of the relevant amount for associates should be included within the amounts for the group, but may be shown separately in the notes: [D] and Note 7 (above); Interest payable [E] and Note 8 (not shown); Taxation [F] and Note 9 (not shown).

DIAGEO also shows details in *Note 6 Associates* (on the opposite page), together with *Dividends received by the Group* [G] and *Share of profits retained by associates* [H].

A group's share of associates' profits is only available to the group when it is paid out by the associates as dividends.

6. The group's share of the gains and losses of its associates should be included in the *Consolidated statement of total recognised gains and losses*, and should be shown separately under each heading, if material. See [I] on page 248.

Note that [I] = [G] + [H].

7. In the *Consolidated balance sheet* the group's share of the net assets of its associates should be included, and separately disclosed. Diageo has included it in *Investments* [J] giving details in Note 14, shown below.

DIAGEO *Extract from 2003 accounts*

Note 14 Fixed assets – Investments

	Investment in associates £million	Total £million
Cost		
At 30 June 2002	2,909	3,246
Exchange adjustments	(68)	(73)
Additions	63	304
Share of retained profits	186	192
Disposals	(55)	(129)
At 30 June 2003	3,035	3,540

Provisions/amortisation

At 30 June 2002	10	63
Amortisation of own shares	–	27
Created	–	7
Disposals	(9)	(38)
At 30 June 2003	1	59
Net book value		
At 30 June 2003	3,034	3,481
At 30 June 2002	2,899	3,183

8. The *cash flow statement* should include cash flows between the group and its associates, [K] and [L]:

DIAGEO *Extract from 2003 accounts*

Consolidated cash flow statement

		2003 £m	2002 £m
Net cash inflow from operating activities		1,970	2,008
Dividends received from associates	[K]	60	87
. . .			
Purchase of subsidiaries		(137)	(3,592)
Sale of subsidiaries and businesses		912	5,100
Sale of options on associates	[L]	58	–

9. Goodwill arising on the group's acquisition of its associates, less any amortisation or write-down, should be included in the carrying amount for associates but should be disclosed separately.

DIAGEO *Extract from 2000 accounts*

Consolidated profit and loss account

		Notes	Year ended 30 June 2003			Year ended 30 June 2002		
			Before exceptional items £million	*Exceptional items £million*	*Total £million*	*Before exceptional items £million*	*Exceptional items £million*	*Total £million*
Turnover	[A]	2	9,440	–	9,440	11,282	–	11,282
Operating costs		4	(7,411)	(168)	(7,579)	(9,176)	453	(9,629)
Operating profit		2	2,029	(168)	1,861	2,106	(453)	1,653
Share of associates' profits	[B][D]	6	478	(21)	457	324	(41)	283
	[C]		2,507	(189)	2,318	2,430	(494)	1,936
Disposal of fixed assets		7	–	(43)	(43)	–	(22)	(22)
Sale of businesses		7	–	(1,270)	(1,270)	–	821	821
Interest payable (net)	[E]	8	(351)	–	(351)	(399)	–	(399)
Pre-tax profit			2,156	(1,502)	654	2,031	305	2,336
Taxation	[F]	9	(539)	52	(487)	(511)	(121)	(632)
Profit after tax			1,617	(1,450)	167	1,520	184	1,704

Note 6 Associates

		2003 £million	2002 £million
Share of operating profit before exceptional items	[B]	478	324
Share of exceptional items	[D]	(21)	(41)
Share of interest payable (net)	[E]	(72)	(64)
Share of taxation	[F]	(138)	(87)
Equity minority interests		(1)	(1)
Dividends received by the group	[G]	(60)	(87)
Share of profits retained by associates	[H]	186	44

. . .

Consolidated statement of total recognised gains and losses

		Year ended 30 June 2003 £million	Year ended 30 June 2002 £million
(Loss)/profit for the year – group		(170)	1,486
Profit for the year – associates	[I]	246	131
		76	1,617

Exchange adjustments . . .

Consolidated balance sheet

		Notes	30 June 2003 £million	30 June 2002 £million
Fixed assets				
Intangible assets			4,288	5,434
Tangible assets			1,974	2,545
Investment in associates	[J]	14	3,034	2,899
Other investments			447	284
Current assets . . .			9,743	11,162

Interest held on a long-term basis

For an interest to be an associate the investor must have a long-term interest, i.e. the interest must be held other than exclusively with a view to subsequent resale. An interest held exclusively with a view to subsequent resale is:

- an interest for which a purchaser has been identified or is being sought, and which is reasonably expected to be disposed of within approximately one year of its date of acquisition; or
- an interest that was acquired as a result of the enforcement of a security, unless the interest has become part of the continuing activities of the group or the holder acts as if it intends the interest to become so.

Significant influence

For an investment to be an associate, its investor must exercise (not simply *be in a position to exercise*) significant influence over the investee's operating and financial policies. The investor needs an agreement or understanding, formal or informal, with its associate to provide the basis for its significant influence. An investor exercising significant influence will be directly involved in the operating and financial policies of its associate rather than passively awaiting the outcome of its investee's policies.

Active involvement in the operating and financial policies of an associate requires inter alia that *the investor should have a voice in decisions on strategic issues* such as determining the balance between dividend and reinvestment.

The investor's involvement in its associate is usually achieved through nomination to the board of directors (or its equivalent) but may result from any arrangement that allows the investor to participate effectively in policy-making decisions.

It is unlikely that an investor can exercise significant influence unless it has a substantial basis of voting power. A holding of 20% or more of the voting rights in another entity *suggests*, *but does not ensure*, that the investor exercises significant influence over that entity (FRS 9, paragraph 16).

International Financial Reporting Standards

There are no significance differences between UK GAAP and IFRS – both use the equity method for associates.

Foreign exchange

Introduction

Floating exchange rates bring both accounting problems and operating problems. This section will deal first with the accounting problems, and then look at what companies do to mitigate the adverse effects that currency fluctuations may have on their operations.

The main accounting problem

The main accounting problem is the rate (or rates) of exchange to be used in translating the accounts of foreign subsidiaries, associates and branches, which are kept in foreign currencies, into sterling when producing the consolidated accounts of a group.

The choice lies between:

- the *closing rate*: the spot rate of exchange at the balance sheet date;
- the *average rate* of exchange during the period; and
- the *historical rate*: the spot rate of exchange at the date of the transaction.

Various methods of translation use different combinations of these rates.

The UK Accounting Standard

SSAP 20 Foreign currency translation is concerned with:

- *individual companies* which enter directly into business transactions denominated in foreign currencies, and
- *groups* which conduct foreign operations through subsidiaries, associated undertakings or branches whose operations are based in a country other than that of the investing company, and whose accounting records are maintained in a currency other than that of the investing company.

Individual companies

When a company enters into transactions denominated in a foreign currency (i.e. a currency other than that in which the company's accounts are kept), SSAP 20 requires that they should normally be translated at the rate ruling at the date of each transaction, i.e. at the spot rate.

In the accounts of the individual company:

(a) *Non-monetary assets* (e.g. plant and machinery) will already be carried in the accounts in the company's reporting currency, having been translated at the time of acquisition.

(b) *Foreign equity investments*, being non-monetary assets, are normally shown at the rate of exchange ruling at the time the investment was made but, where financed by foreign currency borrowings, they may be translated at the closing rate. Any exchange differences on the investments are then taken to reserves, where the exchange differences on the foreign borrowings may be offset against them (SSAP 20, paragraph 51).

(c) *Monetary assets and liabilities denominated in foreign currencies* should be translated at the closing rate.

(d) All *exchange differences*, except those in (b) above, should be reported as part of the profit or loss for the year, for example, differences arising from variations in exchange rates between the dates of invoicing in a foreign currency and the dates of payment. It is comparatively rare for such differences to be 'material' and nothing is normally disclosed.

Example 29.1 illustrates the treatment of four simple transactions involving foreign currency.

Example 29.1 Treatment of foreign transactions by an individual company

ABLE is a hypothetical UK company whose accounting year ends on 31 December. During the year, Able:

		Rate of exchange
(i)	Purchases hock from a West German company, Weinburger GmbH, on 31 October for €20,000	£1 = €1.6
	Pays Weinburger GmbH on 30 November	£1 = €1.52
	Goods remain in stock at 31 December	
(ii)	Sells cider to Prague and Pilsen, a Czech company, for 420,000 Koruna Debt remains unpaid at 31 December	£1 = 42 Koruna (Crowns)
(iii)	Borrows on long-term loan from a Swiss bank SFr750,000 on 1 April	£1 = SFr3.0

(iv)	Purchases plant and machinery from a US company for $480,000 on 15 August	£1 = US$1.50
	Pays on 30 September	£1 = US$1.60

On 31 December exchange rates are:
£1 = €1.475
£1 = 42 Koruna
£1 = SFr2.50
£1 = US$1.55

The company maintains its bank account in sterling and buys or sells foreign exchange as needed on the spot market.

Under SSAP 20 the transactions of Able will be treated as follows:

(i) The purchase will be recorded in purchases and creditors at the rate ruling on 31 October, £1 = €1.6. The hock will appear in stock at a book cost of £12,500 and the eventual cost of sales will also be £12,500. When the account is paid, the rate has fallen to £1 = €1.52, so it is necessary to pay £13,158 to buy the necessary currency.

An exchange loss of £658 (£13,158 − £12,500) will be charged to the profit and loss account for the year.

(ii) The sale is translated at the rate ruling at the date of the transaction, £1 = FFr10.50, giving a sales and debtor figure at transaction date of £10,000. At the end of the year, the debtor is a monetary item and retranslated at the closing rate, £1 = 40 Koruna = £10,500.

The resulting exchange gain of £500 (£10,500 − £10,000) will be credited to the profit and loss account for the year.

(iii) The loan will initially be translated at the transaction rate of £1 = SFr3.00, i.e. as £250,000. At the year end the loan will be translated at the closing rate £1 = SFr2.50, i.e. as £300,000.

The exchange loss of £50,000 (£300,000 − £250,000) may be treated as 'financing' and *may be* disclosed separately as part of 'other interest receivable/payable and similar income/expense'.

(iv) The fixed asset will be translated at the transaction rate of £1 = $1.50, i.e. as £320,000. The asset will continue to appear at this cost unless it is revalued. Depreciation will be charged on £320,000. Payment for the machine will take (at £1 = $1.60) £300,000.

The gain of £20,000 (£320,000 − £300,000) will be credited to the profit and loss account for the year and will appear separately if considered material.

In Able's statement of accounting policies, the treatment of these purchases and sales would be explained in a note similar to that in ML LABORATORIES' accounts, illustrated below:

ML LABORATORIES *Extract from accounting policies 2003*

Foreign currency translation
Foreign currency transactions are translated into sterling at the rate prevailing at the date of the transaction. Assets and liabilities at the year end are translated into sterling at the rate prevailing at the balance sheet date. The resulting exchange differences are dealt with in the profit and loss account.

Group accounts

Where a company has foreign subsidiaries, associates, joint ventures or branches, the '*closing rate net investment method*' is normally used in translating local currency financial statements. Under this method:

(a) *Balance sheet* items should be translated into the currency of the holding company at the 'closing rate' (the spot rate on the balance sheet date). Where this year's closing rate differs from the previous year's closing rate, the differences arising from the retranslation of the opening *net investment* at this year's closing rate should be taken to reserves and will appear in both the statement of recognised gains and losses and the movements in shareholders' funds (see pages 88–9).

The *net investment* is the holding company's proportion of the subsidiary or associates' share capital and reserves. Long-term indebtedness between members of the group should be treated as part of the net investment. The translation process is illustrated in Example 29.2.

Example 29.2 Translation of an overseas subsidiary's accounts

On 31 December 2000, INJECTION MOULDERS PLC acquired a small foreign manufacturing company, RURITANIAN PLASTICS, to expand its operations into Ruritania, and paid asset value, 60m Ruritanian dollars (R$), for it. At the time the exchange rate was R$10 = £1, so the sterling cost was £6m.

During the first year of operation as a subsidiary Ruritanian Plastics made a profit after tax of R$10m, and the R$ fell to R$12.5 = £1. Ruritanian Plastics' actual and translated balance sheets for 2000 (R$10 = £1) and 2001 (R$12.5 = £1) were:

Year ended 31 December	2000		2001	
	R$m	£000	R$m	£000
Fixed assets	100	10,000	100	8,000
Current assets	20	2,000	32	2,560
	120	12,000	132	10,560
5 year State loan	50	5,000	50	4,000
Current liabilities	10	1,000	12	960
	60	6,000	62	4,960
Shareholders' funds	60	6,000	70	5,600

The difference between the opening net equity of R$60m translated at R$10 = £1 (the closing rate in the 2000 accounts) and at R$12.5 = £1 (the 2001 closing rate) is £6m – £4.8m = £1.2m, which would be taken from group reserves at 31 December 2001 as an exchange translation difference.

The profit of R$10m (represented in the absence of any capital input or dividends by the difference between opening and closing shareholders' funds) has been translated in the group accounts at the closing rate of R$12.5 = £1 to produce £0.8m.

The fall in sterling terms in the net equity of Ruritanian Plastics from £6m to £5.6m is made up of the exchange translation loss of £1.2m less the £0.8m profit for 2001, i.e. £0.4m.

(b) *Profit and loss account* items should be translated using either the average rate for the accounting period or the closing rate and the method chosen should be applied consistently.

Any difference between translation at the average rate and the closing rate should be taken to reserves.

The rate used can make a considerable difference to the reported profit: for example, if a German subsidiary made a profit of €13.5m during a year in which the rate of exchange fell from €1.55 = £1 at the beginning of the year to €1.35 = £1 at the end of the year, averaging €1.5 = £1 because most of the fall occurred in the last three months, on an average basis the group accounts would include German profits of £9m; on a closing rate basis they would include £10m.

If the closing rate method is used, no difference will arise between the profit or loss in sterling terms used for profit and loss account purposes, and the result of translation for balance sheet purposes. If the average rate is used there will be a difference, which should be recorded as a movement on reserves. The method used should be stated in the accounts. The advantage of using the average rate is that the translated results correspond more nearly to those given by management accounts prepared (say) on a monthly basis. Indeed to reflect those results even better, DIAGEO uses the *weighted* average rate of exchange (on the basis that it takes account of seasonal fluctuations in profitability):

DIAGEO *Accounting policies 2003*

Foreign currencies
The profit and loss accounts and cash flows of overseas subsidiaries and associates are translated into sterling at weighted average rates of exchange, other than substantial exceptional items which are translated at the rate on the date of the transaction. The adjustment to closing rates is taken to reserves.

(c) *Foreign exchange borrowings*: where borrowings have been used to finance equity investment in foreign subsidiaries or associates, differences arising on their translation (at the closing rate) due to currency movements during the period may be offset against differences arising from the retranslation of the opening net investment, as is explained by SYGEN INTERNATIONAL (see below).

SYGEN INTERNATIONAL *Extract from accounting policies 2003*

(h) Foreign currencies
The results of overseas subsidiaries are translated into sterling at average exchange rates and assets and liabilities are translated using rates at the balance sheet date. Exchange differences which arise on translation are dealt with through reserves.

Differences arising on the translation of foreign currency borrowings which hedge group equity investments in foreign enterprises are taken directly to reserves to the extent of corresponding exchange differences on translation of the related net investment. The tax on those exchange differences which are taken directly to reserves is also recorded as a direct movement on reserves.

Hyperinflation

Urgent Issues Task Force (UITF) Abstract 9 is concerned with accounting for operations in hyperinflationary economies. The Abstract requires adjustments to be made when incorporating operations in hyperinflationary economies into consolidated accounts where the distortions caused by hyperinflation are such as to affect the true and fair view given by the accounts. In any event, adjustments are required where the cumulative inflation rate over three years is approaching or exceeds 100% (a level widely accepted internationally as an appropriate criterion). The Abstract discusses acceptable methods of handling the problem, one of which is to translate the results of operations in hyper-inflationary economies using a relatively stable currency as the functional currency.

One group which operates in countries suffering very high rates of inflation, even hyperinflation, is LONMIN (formerly LONRHO) (see later).

Where restrictions prevent the transfer of cash from one part of the business or group to another, a note to the cash flow statement should specify the amounts involved and explain the circumstances (see page 221).

The temporal method

Where, and only where, the trade of a subsidiary is a direct extension of the trade of a holding company, for example, a subsidiary acting purely as a selling agency in a foreign country, the temporal method of translation should be used in consolidation:

- all transactions should be translated at the rate ruling on the transaction date or at an average rate for a period if this is not materially different;
- non-monetary assets should not normally be retranslated at the balance sheet date;
- monetary assets and liabilities should be retranslated at the closing rate; and
- all exchange gains and losses should be taken to the profit and loss account as part of the profit and loss from ordinary activities.

Current UK practice under UK GAAP

UK companies have mostly used the average rate rather than the closing rate in translating overseas profits, and state which method is used in their accounting policies.

Mitigating the effect of currency fluctuation

Exchange rate movements are difficult to predict.

Examples 29.3–29.5 show the range of the UK's main trading currencies against sterling over a ten-year period.

Currency	High	Low	Range
Euro	1.27	1.72	78p–58p
US$	1.42	1.85	70p–54p
Yen	135	237	0.74p–0.42p

The way in which companies have sought to protect themselves against the effect of these and other currency fluctuations, both on their earnings and on their balance sheets, is explained in Chapter 23.

Although selling currency forward does protect the sterling value of future foreign income, doing so can have adverse effects if the foreign currency then strengthens rather than weakens. For example, if a UK motor manufacturer covers the US dollar forward, when its European competitors do not, and the US dollar strengthens, they will have scope for cutting their prices in the USA, while UK manufacturers will not.

Protecting the balance sheet can be done in a variety of ways, the most obvious one being to borrow in the foreign currency. If the foreign subsidiary does the borrowing, the net equity investment in the subsidiary will be reduced. If the parent company borrows in the foreign currency and switches it into sterling, it will have a gain (or loss) to offset against any loss (or gain) on

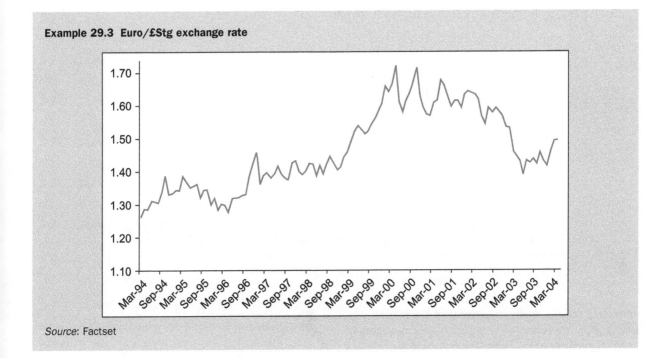

Example 29.3 Euro/£Stg exchange rate

Source: Factset

Example 29.4 US$/£Stg exchange rate

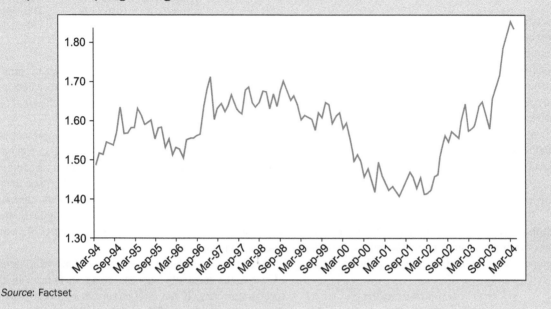

Source: Factset

Example 29.5 The Yen/£Stg exchange rate

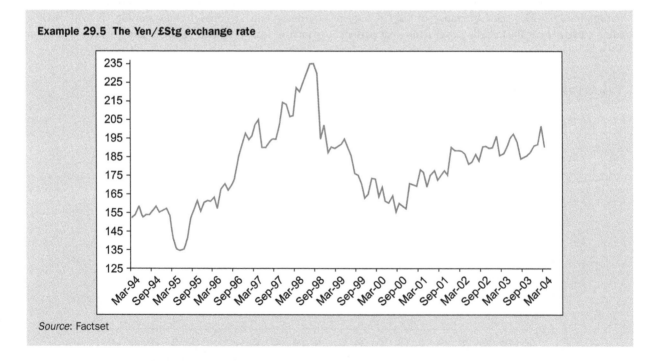

Source: Factset

translating the net equity investment of the foreign subsidiary. If interest rates in sterling are higher than those in the foreign currency the parent company will also make a profit on the differential.

Beware of companies that trade in currency futures, unless they have in-house expertise, tight controls, and a deep pocket.

Remember BARINGS, a merchant bank with an impeccable reputation, brought down by failure of management to control a rogue trader in Singapore.

What the analyst should study

As has been seen, information about foreign currency tends to be scattered around in reports and accounts. A suggested sequence for the analyst to follow is:

1. *Accounting policies on foreign currencies*
   Check that, as required by SSAP 20, differences on unmatched foreign borrowings are dealt with in the P & L account and not taken direct to reserves. Before SSAP 20, some companies borrowed in a hard currency (e.g. Deutschmarks or Swiss francs) to reduce their cost of borrowing for investment in the UK. The lower interest rates (broadly reflecting the lower expectations of inflation) increased the companies' profits and, when the foreign currency inevitably strengthened, they debited the increase in the sterling value of their borrowings direct to reserves. This method of enhancing the profits was short-sighted and often very costly. For example the WEIR Group managed to lose £3.6m on a DM denominated loan originally worth £6.3m, and the loss would have been even greater if the company hadn't arranged early repayment.

   Note also if there has been any change in accounting policy, as this can be a way of enhancing the year's results.

   There seems nothing strange or changed about LONMIN's accounting policies, but the rate changes during 2002–03 could have given more cause for worry.

	2003	2002
Average exchange rates:		
Sterling	0.62	0.68
South African rand	7.88	10.65
Zimbabwe dollar	1,000.00	415.97

	2003	2002
Closing exchange rates:		
Sterling	0.60	0.64
South African rand	6.97	10.54
Zimbabwe dollar	1,000.00	640.00

But information is never all in one place:

> **LONMIN *Note to the 2003 accounts***
>
> **Note 2 Group operating profit**
> . . .
> Group operating profit is stated after charging/ (crediting):
>
> | | 2003 | 2002 |
> |---|---|---|
> | | $m | $m |
> | Operating lease charges | 1 | 1 |
> | Depreciation charges | 46 | 39 |
> | Foreign Exchange profits | (6) | – |

2. *Note analysing operating profit*
   It is here that differences arising from variations in exchange rates between the dates of invoicing in a foreign currency and the dates of payment, and on monetary items, should be (but are not always) shown where material. Most companies, including LONMIN, show nothing.
3. *Statement of recognised gains and losses and movements in shareholders' funds*
   Check whether the adjustments for currency fluctuations are material in relation to (i) the profit for the financial year and (ii) the transfer (from profit and loss account) to reserves

> **LONMIN Accounting policies 2003**
>
> **Foreign currencies**
> Subsidiaries that keep their accounts in currencies other than their functional currency remeasure them into the functional currency by the temporal method prior to consolidation. This results in non-monetary assets and liabilities being recorded at their historical cost expressed in the functional currency whilst monetary assets and liabilities are stated at the closing exchange rate. Differences on translation are included in the profit and loss account.
>
> The principal US dollar exchange rates used in the financial statements, expressed as the foreign currency value of one US dollar, are as follows:

> **LONMIN *Statement of total consolidated recognised gains and losses 2003***
>
> **Statement of total consolidated recognised gains and losses for the year ended 30 September**
>
> | | 2003 | 2002 |
> |---|---|---|
> | | $m | $m |
> | Profit for the year – Group | 75 | 187 |
> | – Associates | (1) | (2) |
> | Total recognised (losses)/ gains relating to the year | 74 | 185 |

LONMIN *Reconciliation of movement in equity interests*

Reconciliation of movement in equity interests for the year ended 30 September

	2003 $m	2002 $m
Total recognised (losses)/ gains relating to the year	74	185
Dividends	(101)	(101)
	(27)	84
Capital return	(361)	
Share buyback	–	(128)
Shares issued on exercise of share options	–	3
Net (reduction)/increase in equity interests in the year	(27)	(402)
Equity interests at 1 October	675	1,077
Equity interests at 30 September	648	675

4. *If exchange adjustments found are large*

   Look for further information elsewhere. Wherever a balance sheet or cash flow statement note explains the change in an accounting item over the year (e.g. fixed assets, provisions or cash), if foreign currency is involved there may be a 'Currency translation difference'. It is here that depositing money in a soft depreciating currency (as POLLY PECK did) or borrowing (at a low rate of interest) in appreciating currency (as WEIR, mentioned above, did) would come to light.

5. *The reconciliation of group operating profit to net cash flow from operations*

   The reconciliation of group operating profit to net cash flow from operations does not usually show any exchange translation differences, but it may. This is likely to happen where a group translates 'profits, losses and cash flows' from overseas subsidiaries at average rate rather than closing rate (as TT ELECTRONICS did in its 2003 accounts).

TT ELECTRONICS *Extract from reconciliation of group operating profit to net cash flow from operating activities*

	2003 £million	2002 £million
. . .		
Exchange translation differences	(1.1)	(3.6)

6. *Again, if the figures seem significant . . .*

   Look for comments in the financial review, if there is one, or in the chairman's statement or possibly in the directors' report, or even elsewhere in the notes. Where exchange rates have a significant effect, further information may include tables of exchange rates.

7. *Study the note on contingent liabilities*

   Most companies did not in the past consider the potential liability in relation to swaps. But the note on contingent liabilities may today provide interesting information.

8. *Study any note on derivative financial instruments*

   FRS 13, Derivatives and other financial instruments, (see page 186) calls for a good deal of information on the use being made of derivatives and similar financial instruments. BP included more than a page on the matter in its accounts.

9. *Look for any indication of significant exchange rate changes having an effect on profitability*

   Look also for any indication of the risks/costs/benefits of using financial instruments.

   Activities on a global scale inevitably involve many types of risk. Few companies spell this out quite so clearly or at such length as BP. Their annual report for 2003 illustrates the complexity of the subject (the italics are ours).

BP *Extracts from the financial review 2003*

Financial risk management
The group co-ordinates certain key activities on a *global basis* in order to optimise its financial position and performance. These include the *management of the currency*, maturity and interest rate profile of finance debt, cash . . .

Market risk
Market risk is the possibility that *changes in currency exchange rates*, interest rates or oil, natural gas and power prices will adversely affect the value of the group's financial assets, liabilities or expected future cash flows . . .

Currency exchange rates
Fluctuations in exchange rates can have significant effects on the group's reported profit. The effects of most exchange rate fluctuations are absorbed in business operating results through changing cost competitiveness, lags in market adjustment to movement in rates, and conversion differences accounted for on specific transactions. For this

▶

reason *the total effect of exchange rate fluctuations is not identifiable separately in the group's reported profit.* The main underlying economic currency of the group's cash flows is the US dollar. This is because BP's major products are priced internationally in US dollars. BP's *foreign exchange management policy is to minimise economic and significant transactional exposures arising from currency movements against the US dollar.* The group co-ordinates the handling of foreign exchange risks centrally, by netting off naturally occurring opposite exposures whenever possible, to reduce the risks, and then dealing with any material residual foreign exchange risks.

Interest rates

. . .

The group is exposed predominantly to US dollar LIBOR (London Inter-Bank Offer Rate) interest rates as *borrowings are mainly denominated in, or are swapped into, US dollars.*

10. *Consider the state of any overseas economies*
    Probably equally if not more important for the profitability of foreign operations than a weak exchange rate is the state of the economy in the foreign countries concerned. If the weak exchange rate reflects a weak economy, then adverse trading conditions may be more damaging for profits than translation.

LONMIN *Extract from 2003 Financial Review*

Analysis of results

. . .

gold mining operations in Zimbabwe were sold

. . .

Costs in US dollars were higher than in 2002 due to a combination of the strengthening in the South African rand average exchange rate of 26% and higher smelting costs following the explosion of the new smelter in December 2002.

International Financial Reporting Standards

IAS 21, The Effects of Foreign Exchanges Rates, is a complex standard. The terminology and explanation of concepts is quite different from those in SSAP 20 although for most groups the general view is that the practical impact is broadly similar apart from differences in certain areas, for example, the treatment of goodwill and calculation of gains and losses on disposal of foreign operations. IAS 21 provides disclosure of more information compared with SSAP 21.

In the UK, companies who have adopted FRS 26, Financial instruments: recognition and measurement are required to adopt a converged standard FRS 23 that is identical to IAS 21. However, companies that have not adopted FRS 26 are not allowed to adopt FRS 23 and most still use SSAP 20. Nothing is straightforward!

BP *Extracts from Note to 2003 accounts on Derivatives*

25. Derivative financial instruments
In the normal course of business the group is a party to derivatives with *off balance sheet risk*, primarily to manage its exposure to foreign currency exchange rates and to interest rates, including the management of the balance between floating rate and fixed rate debt.

The group also manages certain of its exposures to movements in oil, natural gas and power prices. In addition *the group trades derivatives* in conjunction with these risk management activities.

Risk management
Gains and losses on derivatives used for risk management purposes are deferred and recognised in earnings or adjustments to carrying amounts when the underlying debt matures or the hedged transaction occurs. . . .

The unrecognised and carried forward gains and losses on derivatives used for hedging are shown in the following table:

	Unrecognised			Carried forward in the balance sheet ($million)		
	Gains	Losses	Total	Gains	Losses	Total
Gains and losses at 1 January 2003	526	(450)	76	352	(28)	324
of which accounted for in income in 2003	96	(51)	45	200	(14)	186
Gains and losses at 31 December 2003	331	(130)	201	1,003	(425)	578
of which accounted for in income in 2002	98	(28)	70	438	(75)	363
Gains and losses at 1 January 2002 . . .						

CHAPTER 30

Historical summaries, ratios and trends

Historical summaries

Variations in form and content

In 1964 the Chairman of the Stock Exchange wrote to the chairmen of all listed companies asking for various items of information to be included in their reports and accounts. One of the items which 'might be included' was 'Tables of relevant comparative figures for the past ten years'.

Apart from this request, listed companies are under no obligation to provide any form of historical summary: there is no FRS or SSAP, and no uniformity of content, layout, or period covered, and some smaller companies don't bother.

The majority of companies give a five-year summary; most of the remainder show ten years, although a few choose a different period, usually for a specific reason; for example, LONRHO's 'Financial Record' for many years went right back to 1961, the year their then chief executive, Tiny Rowland, joined the company. Renamed LONMIN, the group now shows only five years.

Because there is, as yet, no standard on historical summaries, the content varies enormously. For example, PROTHERICS, the result of a merger between two tiny biotechnology companies, Therapeutic Antibodies Inc. and Proteus International plc, in September 1999, show only two basic items in the table below.

But, if read in conjunction with the Chairman's statement: '*in the last six months of the year to 31 March 2003, the company traded profitably*', the figures suggest that Protherics may well be a company worth following.

Of course, Protherics had no earnings per share or dividends to report: most companies give rather more information, and some give a great deal more.

GLAXOSMITHKLINE, for instance, devotes three pages to its five-year record, as well as six pages of quarterly trends for the most recent year. Some companies include information of particular relevance to their type of business: for example, TESCO, in their five-year record (see opposite), show the number of stores, total sales area, and a number of other statistics which provide the reader with growth ratios some of which are not available from the accounts.

Have a look at TESCO's five-year record. Do you think that *Turnover per employee* and *Profit per employee* have grown satisfactorily between 1999 and 2003?

BP is among a number of oil companies which give useful statistics, including statistics on refinery throughput, crude oil and natural gas reserves, capital expenditure and acquisition, and is among companies which now provide historical cash flow data.

PROTHERICS *Annual Report 2003*

Financial Summary

	2003 £000	2002 £000	2001 £000	2000 £000	1999 £000
Turnover	11,270	7,924	4,186	1,598	2,847
(Loss)/profit on ordinary activities after taxation	(238)	2,867	(6,206)	(15,454)	(13,017)

TESCO *Extracts from five-year record*

		1999	2000	2001	2002	2003
. . .						
Operating margin[1]	**[A]**					
UK		5.8%	5.9%	6.0%	6.0%	6.0%
Rest of Europe		4.1%	3.7%	4.0%	4.1%	5.2%
Asia		(1.3)%	(0.2)%	0.5%	2.1%	3.5%
Total Group		5.6%	5.5%	5.6%	5.6%	5.7%
. . .						
Return on shareholders' funds[5]	**[B]**	21.3%	20.9%	22.7%	23.2%	23.3%
Return on capital employed[6]	**[B]**	17.2%	16.1%	16.6%	16.1%	15.3%
UK retail productivity	**[C]**					
Turnover per employee		151,138	156,427	161,161	165,348	162,457
Profit per employee		8,771	9,160	9,649	10,002	9,748
Wages per employee		15,271	15,600	16,087	16,821	17,020
UK retail statistics						
Number of stores		639	659	692	729	1,982
Total sales area – 000 sq ft		15,975	16,895	17,965	18,822	21,829
Average store size (sales area – sq ft)[8]		25,627	26,641	27,636	28,576	29,455
Full-time equivalent employees[9]		104,772	108,409	113,998	121,272	133,051
. . .						

Tesco's Notes to above summary

1. Operating margin is based on turnover exclusive of VAT
   . . .
5. Underlying profit divided by average shareholders' funds
6. Profit divided by average capital employed excluding net debt
   . . .
8. Average store size excludes Express and TS stores
9. Based on average number of full-time equivalent employees in the UK

Our comments on Tesco's five-year record 1999–2003

[A] UK on a plateau. Rest of Europe improving. Asia turned profitable in 2001
[B] All unreliable, due to *Immediate write-off* of goodwill prior to FRS 10, and *not* reinstated
[C] UK retail productivity, adjusted for inflation. In £ of 1999:

	1999	2000	2001	2002	2003
RPI in February (see Appendix 3)	163.7	167.5	172.0	173.8	179.3
Factor to divide by each year	1.000	1.023	1.051	1.062	1.095
Turnover per employee	151,138	152,910	153,340	155,695	148,362
Profit per employee	8,771	8,954	9,180	9,418	8,902
Wages per employee	15,271	15,249	15,306	15,839	15,543

*In real terms, wages per employee actually fell in 2000
and 2003*

There is a growing tendency for companies to omit the normal table of historical information altogether in favour of often colourful diagrams of a few salient items. TAY HOMES, in its annual report for 2000, devoted half a page to presenting six items of basic information in six clever little blue-washed diagrams in a way that didn't immediately draw attention to the large losses made in the previous year, nor to nil dividends in 1999 and 2000.

The majority of listed companies manage to show between 25 and 35 items in a single-page five-year record.

A few companies, like WATERMARK, provide no historical information at all.

No FRS planned

A Financial Reporting Standard would be welcome on historical summaries, but because they fall outside the statutory accounts, there appear to be no plans for one.

The main difficulty facing the shareholder or analyst who tries to interpret a five- or ten-year summary is lack of consistency. We will consider this under five heads:

1. Inflation;
2. Changes in accounting standards;
3. Accounting changes made by the company;
4. Changes in the business environment;
5. Changes in the composition of the group.

Inflation

It used to be reasonable to regard a pound sterling today as the same as a pound last year and a pound next year. Inflation has made this concept of a stable currency (referred to in the US as the *uniform dollar concept*) seriously misleading.

To read a ten-year record as though currency were stable is to obtain a false picture, and would be just as misleading as the company chairman who makes much of 'yet another year of record profits' when they have advanced a mere 2% compared with a 3% or 4% rate of inflation.

We show, in the TESCO example on page 259, how, by adjusting by the RPI, the effects of inflation can be stripped out.

Changes in accounting standards

The first of the Accounting Standards Board's standards, FRS 1, Cash flow statements, was published in September 1991. We are now up to FRS 29 in force, and there is hardly an area of company accounts that hasn't been affected by one or more of these standards.

Take, for instance, goodwill. FRS 10, Goodwill and intangible assets, required goodwill arising in accounts periods ending after 23 December 1998 to be capitalised and amortised (see page 109). This change affected most groups, since most had previously chosen to account for goodwill by *immediate write-off against reserves*, which was (absurdly) the *officially preferred method* before FRS 10.

Companies may, under FRS 10, choose to reinstate goodwill previously written off as though it had been capitalised and amortised throughout. In this case a five- or ten-year summary could, and probably would, show comparable figures throughout. But the ASB 'does not require reinstatement', and the large majority of listed companies have not done so.

For example TESCO:

TESCO *Extracts from 2003 accounts*

Note on accounting policies

Goodwill
Goodwill arising from transactions entered into after 1 March 1998 is capitalised and amortised on a straight line basis over its useful economic life, up to a maximum of 20 years.
  All goodwill entered into prior to 1 March 1998 has been written off to reserves.

Note 11 Intangible fixed assets

	2003 £m	2002 £m
Net carrying value At 22 February 2003	890	154

Note 24 Reserves

. . .
The cumulative goodwill written off against the reserves of the Group as at 22 February 2003 amounted to £718m (2002 – £718m).

Prior to FRS 10, Return on capital employed (ROCE) and similar ratios were often considerably inflated in acquisitive companies by *immediate write-off* of goodwill. And these ratios will continue to be inflated in the historical summaries of companies like Tesco (with £718m written off against reserves) for many years to come.

Accounting changes made by the company

Accounting changes made by the company can make a significant difference to reported profits.

Take, for example, THORNTONS, the Derbyshire-based chocolate manufacturer and retailer, which changed the expected useful life of its shop-fits to reflect an operational change of policy:

THORNTONS *Finance director's review 2000*

Accounting standards and policy changes

. . .

Our change in strategic emphasis will result in a slower shop-opening programme and fewer shop refits, which means that capital investments already made will last longer.

We have, therefore, revised the depreciation policy on fixtures and fittings from four to five years. The net impact on profit is a gain of almost £2 million this year, and we expect a net gain of £1 million next.

Almost £2m was a significant amount in a year when pre-tax profit halved from £11m to £5.5m and the company, under new management, was wisely cutting back on capital expenditure.

Changes in the business environment

Changes may be imposed on the company: for example, changes in the rate and/or method of taxation, as was the case with the reduction of ACT in the 1990s and its subsequent abolition.

Changes in the composition of the group

Where a group either grows other than internally or deliberately gets rid of activities, year-on-year comparability is bound to be affected. The changes can be carried out in several ways:

■ acquisitions,
■ disposals,
■ termination of a specific activity.

Acquisitions

FRS 3, Reporting financial performance, requires profit and loss account figures down to the operating profit level to be split *inter alia* into (a) continuing activities and (b) acquisitions.

Few companies do this in any five- or ten-year summary, simply lumping the figures together as continuing activities. You can safely assume that data represent total sales from all activities including new activities developed internally and acquisitions and that the operating profits include such activities. We discuss the rules on new acquisitions on page 237.

Continuing and discontinued operations

FRS 3 requires the subdivision in the profit and loss account of results down to operating profit level into continuing operations, acquisitions and discontinued operations.

It also requires separate disclosure, after operating profit and before interest, of:

■ profits or losses on the sale or termination of an operation;
■ costs of a fundamental reorganisation or restructuring having a material effect on the nature and focus of the reporting entity's operations; and
■ profits or losses on the disposal of fixed assets.

The FRS does not mention five- or ten-year summaries, which therefore do not *have* to do this.

Most but not all do divide turnover and operating profit into those from continuing operations and those from discontinued operations. Most do not show profits or losses on the disposal of fixed assets.

In a simple case (like that of BENSONS CRISPS on the next page) one has little difficulty seeing what happened and when. In 1994, the entire business was unprofitable at the operating profit level; and operations with a turnover of £5.501m discontinued in that year are said to have lost £880,000.

In more complex cases (such as ALLDAYS, shown on page 262) it may be difficult to tell whether there has been one disposal or several over a period of years.

ALLDAYS' turnover figures would be consistent with there having been just one discontinuance of activities (in

BENSONS CRISPS *Extract from five-year record 1998*

Summarised profit and loss accounts

	1998 £000	1997 £000	1996 £000	1995 £000	1994 £000
Turnover					
Continuing operations	38,011	34,514	32,797	31,184	30,182
Discontinued operation	–	–	–	–	5,501
	38,011	34,514	32,797	31,184	35,683
Operating profit/(loss)					
Continuing operations	3,332	2,875	2,544	928	(2,690)
Discontinued operation	–	–	–	–	(880)
	3,332	2,875	2,544	928	(3,570)

. . .

ALLDAYS *Extract from five-year record 1998*

Five year record

	1998 £000	1997 £000	1996 £000	1995 £000	1994 £000
Turnover:					
Continuing operations	493,826	455,801	410,427	378,925	348,894
Discontinued operations	203,832	181,705	166,175	118,911	91,676
Total turnover	697,658	637,506	576,602	497,836	440,570
Operating profit before exceptional items:					
Continuing operations					
Alldays:	14,720	19,492	15,064	12,086	7,949
Trademarket	590	1,518	1,650	1,602	1,940
Total – continuing operations	15,310	21,010	16,714	13,688	9,889
Discontinued operations					
W&P Foodservice	3,434	4,582	4,031	3,389	2,281
Wholesaling activity	–	–	2,754	3,261	3,840
Other	–	–	427	427	427
Total – discontinued operations	3,434	4,582	7,212	7,077	6,548
Total operating profit before exceptional items	18,744	25,592	23,926	20,765	16,437

1998). The analysis of operating profit makes it clear that there was an earlier discontinuance; and that the figures for 1996 and earlier represent both sets of activities since discontinued.

Just as there is little consistency in *what* is disclosed in a historical summary, there is no one order of *columns* which may, as in the ALLDAYS example, run in reverse chronological order from left to right (showing the most recent figures first), or may run in the other direction (as with BRUNEL HOLDINGS).

Brunel has seen a gradual whittling away of operations but, after years of painful restructuring, the group may now possibly be out of the wood. In the words of the present chairman, appointed a little over two years ago:

BRUNEL HOLDINGS *Extract from 2000 report and accounts*

Five Year Record	1996	1997	1998	1999	2000
Turnover (£m)					
Continuing operations	73.3	77.2	77.3	65.5	72.0
Discontinued operations	115.0	65.0	22.4	6.6	–
Total	188.3	142.2	99.7	72.1	72.0
Operating profit (£m)					
Continuing operations	4.6	5.3	2.9	(6.9)	0.4
Discontinued operations	2.4	2.1	–	(0.5)	–
Total	7.0	7.4	2.9	(7.4)	0.4

BRUNEL HOLDINGS *Extract from Chairman's 2000 statement*

Prospects
Today, Brunel is a more tightly controlled, more disciplined and more focused Group. We view the next twelve months with a sense of quiet optimism.

ALLDAYS, on the other hand, has run into deep trouble:

ALLDAYS *Extract from Directors' 2000 report*

Results and dividends
The consolidated profit and loss account, set out on page 16, shows a retained loss after interest, tax and exceptional charges of £65,276,000 (1999: loss of £90,659,000). [and, surprise surprise] The directors do not recommend the payment of a dividend (1999: nil).

ALLDAYS no longer includes a five-year record in its annual report and accounts.

When a company omits or reduces the information that it provided last year, always ask yourself

'Why?'

If you can find no good reason, treat it as a warning signal.

The first time we came across this was many years ago, but it's a good example nevertheless (if you live long enough, you will have seen it all before):

BURMAH OIL *Details of ship chartering*

	£million
1971	
Tanker in-charters	204
Tanker out-charters	127

1972
Tanker in-charters had been lumped in with other contractual commitments in a total of £470 million, and the note went on to say that 'a substantial part of these commitments is already matched by tanker out-charters and other long term arrangements'.

1973/74
When the tanker charter market subsequently collapsed, Burmah's unmatched in-charter commitments ran up huge losses for the company and it had to be rescued by the Bank of England.
    This was a classic example of a rogue trader bringing a company down. The person running Burmah's tanker chartering at the time was, we vaguely recall, a gentleman called Culukundis who, after the disaster, didn't feel he'd done anything wrong.

But to get back to ALLDAYS, there was a good reason for omitting the five-year review. A new chairman and a new chief executive had been appointed towards the end of 1999, and five of the 'old guard' directors had since left. We presume the new team wanted to disassociate themselves from the (very murky) past.

Ratios

The key to using ratios is selectivity, not saturation.

Choice of ratios

With the profit and loss account, balance sheet and cash flow statement each containing a minimum of 10 to 20 items, the scope for comparing one item with another is enormous, so it is important to be selective, both to limit the calculations required and, more importantly, to make the presentation of the selected ratios simple and readily understandable. No decision maker wants a jungle of figures, so the ratios chosen should be the key ones, logically grouped.

Ratios can conveniently be divided into

- *operating ratios*, which are concerned with how the company is trading, and take no account of how the company is financed;

- *financial ratios*, which measure the financial structure of the company and show how it relates to the trading activities;
- *investment ratios*, which relate the number of ordinary shares and their market price to the profits, dividends and assets of the company.

Some companies include a table of key ratios in their report and accounts, and a few, like UNILEVER (page 265), opposite explain their definitions. This sort of table can be useful for looking at trends within the company concerned but, if you have the time and want to make inter-company comparisons, it may be preferable to work out your own ratios by a standard method.

In describing these ratios we give what we regard as the most useful and practical definition of each component.

Although there is an increasing trend towards standardisation, individual analysts do not always agree on definitions, while companies do not all define ratio components in the same way.

Why capital-based ratios are unreliable

Ratios like ROCE, Debt/Equity and Return on shareholders' funds have been distorted by inflation, which has made historical cost (HC) values increasingly irrelevant. As David Tweedie (formerly the chairman of the ASB) pointed out, to show a building at its HC of £20m when the bank had taken it as security for a £60m loan is clearly neither true nor fair.

And, more importantly in companies with an acquisitive history, the *immediate write-off* method of accounting for purchased goodwill has made millions and millions of pounds of shareholders' money simply disappear from the balance sheet, reducing shareholders' funds and thus increasing the return on them.

As UNILEVER pointed out in a note to its five-year record, shown below, 'Return on shareholders' equity is substantially influenced' by the Group's policy, prior to 1998, of *immediate write-off*, and 'Return on capital employed and net gearing are also influenced but to a lesser extent.'

Earnings per share

Here we are spoilt for choice. You can have basic e.p.s., IIMR/UKSIP e.p.s. (page 80) and any 'Own Brand' e.p.s. a company or broking house likes to define. Of course David

---

MAIN RATIOS

Indexed by type

Operating ratios	Page
Operational gearing	181
Profit margin	75
Return on capital employed (ROCE)	75*
Working capital ratios	147–150

Financial ratios	
Cash flow per share	226
Financial gearing; leverage effect	180–181*
Liquidity: current and quick ratios	148

Investment ratios	
Dividend yield	87
Earnings per share (e.p.s.)	79–85
Price/Earnings ratio (P/E or PER)	86

* Unreliable

UNILEVER *Extract from Five-year record*

Key ratios	€million **2003**	€million 2002	€million 2001	€million 2000	€million 1999
Return on invested capital (%) (Note 1)	**12.5**	9.8	8.7	6.2	16.5
Net profit margin	**6.5**	4.4	3.3	2.2	6.7
Net interest cover (times) (Note 2)	**6.7**	4.5	3.1	5.0	308.0
Adjustment for depreciation and amortisation	**2.8**	2.5	1.8	3.2	85.9
Net interest cover based on EBITDA (times)	**9.5**	7.0	4.9	8.2	393.9
Ratio of earnings to fixed charges (times)	**4.6**	3.6	2.6	3.1	8.0
Funds from operations . . .					

Note 1 . . . Invested capital is the sum of tangible fixed assets and fixed investments, working capital, goodwill and intangible assets at gross book value and *cumulative goodwill written off directly to reserves under an earlier accounting policy.*

Note 2 [Authors' note]: The very large figure for interest cover (times) in 1999 is due to a very small figure for interest paid.

Tweedie was right to make it all-inclusive – so it couldn't easily be fudged.

But it's a shame that the ASB decided to call it *'Basic'*, which it isn't, rather than *'All-inclusive'*, which it is. A serious and misleading misuse of the English language. If you aren't sure, ask yourself 'Is my "basic" salary all-inclusive?' We doubt it except, possibly, in a roaring bear market.

How e.p.s. can be 'smoothed' a little

In the years BT (Before Tweedie) there was a great deal of scope for fudging the figures. Now there is much less, but still some. To help e.p.s. up/(down) a company can:

- Decrease (increase) various provisions, for bad debt etc.
- Be slack (strict) on writing down old or surplus stock.
- Put intangible assets on the balance sheet, but don't depreciate, do annual impairment reviews instead.
- When reviewing annually, be optimistic (pessimistic) about the value of each intangible.
- Extend (shorten) *'useful lives'* to reduce (increase) the depreciation charge.
- Defer (accelerate) bringing home profits from overseas to reduce (increase) tax on remission.

Now some of these measures may be taken in good faith (e.g. THORNTONS) as a matter of policy, increasing the

number of years between retail outlet refurbishments from four to five (see page 261). And it's always a good idea to be rather more 'prudent' in good years, but the analyst and investor should watch out for signs of profit enhancement, which may include:

- Plausible rather than reasonable reasons for a change in accounting policies or practices.
- Threats of being taken over, a galvanising reason for reporting, or forecasting the best profits you can.
- Reporting profits only a whisker above last year's results. The company may have strained every muscle to avoid a fall in profits, particularly if it has an unbroken record. Using up all the company's 'spare fat' in one year makes it more likely that the company will fall out of bed the following year if trading conditions don't improve.

Two modern ratios

Before we move on from ratios we would like to consider two relatively new ones:

1. fixed charges cover;
2. total return to shareholders.

Older hands will remember the way property development companies went down like ninepins in 1989–90, when the UK property market virtually dried up.

Those that survived, as at least one shrewd property analyst had predicted, were the ones that had sufficient rental income to cover their fixed costs until times got better.

Whether this experience gave W.H. SMITH the idea we do not know, but we like the ratio they have come up with:

Fixed charges cover

Other companies may use the ratio internally, but this is the only company we have spotted publishing it in the annual report and accounts:

W.H. SMITH *Extract from 2000 accounts*

Note 11 Fixed charges cover

	2000 £m	1999 £m
Interest income	(6)	(14)
Operating lease rentals	154	141
Property taxes	32	30
Other property costs	11	9
Total fixed charges	191	166
Profit before tax	140	134
Profit before tax and fixed charges	331	300
Fixed charges cover	**1.7x**	**1.8x**

Fixed charges cover is calculated by dividing profit before tax and fixed charges by total fixed charges

---

W.H. SMITH also includes the fixed charge cover in its five-year summary.

Total return to shareholders

This has become popular in more recent years for use as a criterion for extra remuneration to directors and senior managers, for example BOOTS:

BOOTS *Extract from 2003 report*

Financial review

. . .

Total shareholder return (TSR) of the company over the last five years compared with those of our peer companies were as follows:

Five years to 31st March 2003	%
1. Smith & Nephew	123.9
2. Alliance UniChem	24.0
3. Reckitt Benckiser	21.4
4. Tesco	13.1
5. GUS	(17.1)
6. Debenhams	(17.4)
7. Boots	**(24.0)**
8. WH Smith	(24.2)
9. Kingfisher	(35.6)
10. Marks & Spencer	(37.8)
11. J Sainsbury	(39.3)

Debenhams replaced SmithKlineBeecham but appears as a peer company for the first time as it has completed five years as a listed company. Position seven this year is an improvement of two places compared with last year. Our five-year TSR of (24.0)% represents (5.3)% on an annualised basis. Over a ten-year period our equivalent annualised return was 5.7%.

Although this is a good way of comparing companies it is hardly original; the concept of total return has been central to UK portfolio performance measurement since 1971 or earlier. And it is too historic to be of any great value to the analyst.

What we naively don't understand is why bonuses should be handed out during a bear market, when the share price and shareholders are taking a thrashing.

We are highly distrustful of incentive schemes which do not align the interests of directors and senior management with the interests of shareholders.

Trends

It is frequently a worthwhile, even profitable, exercise to set alongside one another, growth in:

- turnover;
- profit before tax;
- earnings per share;
- dividend per share.

If they are wildly different, the cause should be investigated. In the sixth edition we looked at MITIE GROUP, a relatively small cleaning and maintenance contractor, saying that it was 'taking advantage of the trend towards out-sourcing such services' while at the same time expanding by making a series of small acquisitions.

As is shown in the first extract below, from Mitie's 1995 group statistical record, growth between 1990 and 1995 was spectacular:

- turnover was up almost 703% in five years;
- pre-tax profit (up 604%) had nearly kept pace; but
- because of acquisitions for paper (issuing new Mitie shares to the vendor, rather than paying cash), e.p.s. had only grown 165%;
- from a very low base, and nine times covered, dividends had increased 500%, which must have pleased the long-term shareholders.

Taking a subsequent period, 1996 to 2000, shown in the second extract overleaf:

- the growth in turnover had slowed down a little, but still an impressive increase of 115% in four years;
- profit before tax, up 205%, grew almost twice as fast as sales;
- the increase in e.p.s. of 153% was quite a lot less than the rise in pre-tax profit, due to acquisitions for paper;
- dividends grew by 150%, roughly in line with e.p.s.;
- dividend cover had remained at around 4 × throughout the five years. The low payout ratio of around 25% left 75% invested in the group to help finance Mitie's continued growth.

In other words the group was exhibiting ratios typical of a highly profitable, but more mature group.

Common size statement

Another way of looking at these figures is to draw up a *Common size statement*. All the earliest year's values are rebased at 100 and each subsequent year's value for each item is divided by the increase in the Retail Price Index (RPI); see overleaf.

MITIE GROUP *Extract from Group statistical record 1995*

	1995 £000	1994 £000	1993 £000	1992 £000	1991 £000	1990 £000	Increase 1990–1995
Turnover	125,183	101,732	72,994	52,276	32,699	15,594	702.8%
Profit on ordinary activities before taxation	4,571	3,361	2,402	1,808	1,231	649	604.3%
. . .							
Earnings per share	12.2p	8.5p	6.6p	5.8p	5.5p	4.6p	165.2%
Dividend per share	3.0p	2.25p	1.75p	1.375p	1.0p	0.5p	500.0%

Earnings and Dividend per share figures have been re-stated to reflect the sub-division of shares referred to in Note
. . .
  The results of merger accounted acquisitions are reflected in full in the year of acquisition and subsequent years but only the year prior to acquisition has been re-stated on a comparable basis.

MITIE GROUP *Extract from Group statistical record*

	2000 £000	1999 £000	1998 £000	1997 £000	1996 £000	Increase 1996–2000
Turnover	346,514	264,455	236,293	209,425	161,149	115.0%
Profit on ordinary activities before taxation	19,240	14,508	11,110	8,210	6,302	205.3%
. . .						
Earnings per share	8.1p	6.5p	5.1p	4.0p	3.2p	153.1%
Dividend per share	2.0p	1.6p	1.2p	1.0p	0.8p	150.0%

Earnings and Dividend per share figures have been re-stated to reflect the sub-division of shares in 1997 and 1998
. . .

MITIE GROUP *Common size statement 1996–2000 and Average annual growth*

	2000	1999	1998	1997	1996	Average growth p.a.
Turnover	215.0	164.4	146.6	130.0	100.0	21.1%
Profit on ordinary activities before tax	305.3	230.2	176.2	130.3	100.0	32.2%
. . .						
Earnings per share	253.1	203.1	159.4	115.0	100.0	26.1%
Dividend per share	250.0	200.0	150.0	125.0	100.0	25.8%

International Financial Reporting Standards

UK companies presenting their first financial statements under IFRS have presented five-year summaries where the numbers for the current and previous year are presented on an IFRS basis, and for the first three years on a UK GAAP basis.

The Invensys Annual Report for 2006 contains useful disclosures on pages 121 and 122 (www.invensys.com).

CHAPTER 31

Inflation

Introduction

In the 1970s, when inflation was galloping along in double figures (see Example 31.1), two fruitless attempts were made to introduce inflation accounting.

The first method, *Current purchasing power (CPP) accounting*, which simply adjusted figures for the rise in the Retail Price Index, was eminently sensible. It was also the accounting profession's proposed system.

But the government, apparently fearful of runaway inflation if everything was indexed, rejected CPP and appointed a committee headed by Francis Sandilands to find something better.

The Sandilands committee came up with a different system, *Current Cost Accounting (CCA)*, which was very complicated (even the step-by-step guide *CCA the Easy Way* ran to 145 pages of A4) and proved unworkable in practice, and CCA ended up in the bin. Francis Sandilands was knighted.

Because both these methods have been tried and abandoned, there is a temptation to treat the subject of inflation as irrelevant. Dormant might be a better word: if the Chancellor fails to keep the lid on inflation, or some future government resorts to government's old tricks of promising the earth, and paying for it by printing money, then the whole subject will be back on the agenda.

But even with inflation bumbling along at 2% or 3%, as it has for the last ten years (see Example 31.2, which is on the same scale as Example 31.1), sterling has lost 23% of its value between 1994 and 2003.

The shortcomings of historical cost (HC) accounting apply at even quite modest rates of inflation.

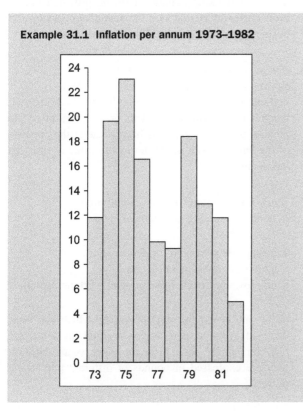

Example 31.1 Inflation per annum 1973–1982

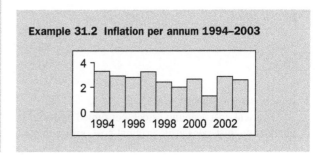

Example 31.2 Inflation per annum 1994–2003

Historical cost (HC) accounting

HC accounting with stable prices

In a time of stable prices, the historical cost system works well. What an asset cost is seldom in dispute, and although the directors have to assess the expected useful lives of fixed assets, and their likely residual value, there is limited scope for subjective judgement.

Furthermore, the quality of historical cost accounts has steadily improved over the years, largely thanks to the efforts of the ASB, which has considerably reduced the number of options available.

Though problems do still remain, few other than accounting theorists would seriously suggest that historical cost be abandoned as the basis of accounting in periods of little or no inflation.

But inflation may creep up again. If it does, it will be important to understand the weaknesses of HC accounting.

HC accounting with inflation

In a period of 'inflation', historical cost accounting has five main weaknesses:

1. *Depreciation is inadequate for the replacement of fixed assets.*
   Historical cost accounting seeks to write off the cost of fixed assets over their effective lives. In a period of stable prices, sufficient cash could be set aside over the life of an asset to replace it at its original cost. In times of inflation, insufficient is provided in this way to enable the business to replace its assets. For example, where an asset is written off on a straight line basis over ten years, the total provisions for depreciation as a percentage of cost (in constant pounds) are:

Inflation rate	Depreciation as % of cost
5%	79.1%
10%	64.4%
15%	53.8%

2. *Cost of sales is understated.*
   In historical cost accounts, stock consumed and sold is charged against sales at its original cost, rather than at the cost of replacing it. But, in order to retain the same stock level, the company has to finance the difference entirely out of profits after tax. This is perhaps most easily understood if we add a few figures. Assume that the company has in stock items which cost £4,000. It sells them for £6,000, incurring overheads of £1,600, and replaces them at a cost of £4,400. Corporation tax is payable at, say, 30%.

   HC accounts will say that the company has made a profit of £400 (£6,000 – £4,000 – £1,600) on which it will pay corporation tax of £120, leaving a net profit after tax of £280. But out of this the company has to meet the additional cost of replacement (£400), so it will be left with minus £120.

3. *Need for increase in other working capital is not recognised.*
   In most companies, amounts for debtors are greater than those for creditors, so, on an unchanged volume of business, 'debtors minus creditors' increases with inflation, requiring extra money to be provided for working capital. Historical cost accounts fail to recognise that this extra working capital has to be provided out of profits after tax to maintain the operating capacity of a business.

4. *Borrowing benefits are not shown.*
   Borrowings are shown in monetary terms, and if nothing is repaid, and nothing further is borrowed, borrowings appear stable. This is a distortion of the picture, because a gain has been made at the expense of the lender (since in real terms the value of the loan has declined).

5. *Year-on-year figures are not comparable.*
   In addition to being overstated due to

   - inadequate provision for depreciation,
   - understated cost of sales, and
   - no provision for increase in other working capital,

   profits are stated in terms of money which has itself declined in value. Similarly, sales and dividends are not comparable with those of other years, because they are expressed in pounds of different purchasing power.

Key point

The reporting of profits in inflated pounds gives a far too rosy impression of growth in profitability

- **This lulls both managers and shareholders into thinking that their company is doing much better than it really is;**
- **It encourages unions and employees to expect wage increases that are unmatched by real (as opposed to reported) profit growth; and**
- **It encourages government measures that are harmful to the long-term prosperity of companies, for example, price controls or excess profits tax made on a completely false impression of profitability.**

It is somewhat difficult, without making proper adjustment, even in times of modest inflation, to estimate profits, earnings and dividends, and their trend in real terms, as is shown by THE BODY SHOP below.

To allow for inflation it is necessary to restate these figures at the price levels ruling at a particular point in time. Two obvious points are 1999 (the beginning of the five years) or 2003 (the end). We have chosen to convert everything to 1999 prices, using the February index for each year.

Not only do the adjusted figures look less promising, the year-on-year change looks much less happy. We see, for instance, that in real terms:

- turnover fell between 2001 and 2003
- dividends fell 9% in real terms between 1999 and 2003.

The impact of modest inflation

It is worth looking in more detail at the impact that even quite modest rates of inflation have on the value of money if they persist for several years. See Example 31.3 overleaf.

Between 1960 and 2000 inflation averaged a touch over 6.9% compound; but it was extremely variable in rate (from a low of 1.3% p.a. to a peak of over 25%); and it was throughout that period very difficult to predict what the rate of inflation would be a year later.

It wasn't always like this. Prior to the Second World War prices had changed surprisingly little in a hundred years. By 1940, prices were a shade over twice their 1840 level.

THE BODY SHOP *Extract from Group Five Year Summary 2003*

	2003 £m	2002 £m	2001 £m	2000 £m	1999 £m
As reported					
Turnover (excluding exceptional turnover)	**378.2**	379.6	374.1	330.1	303.7
Operating profit (before exceptional items)	**26.9**	26.7	29.4	33.0	24.6
Earnings per ordinary share (excluding exceptionals)	**7.5p**	7.8p	9.5p	10.7p	7.0p
Dividends per share	**5.7p**	5.7p	5.7p	5.7p	5.7p
Adjustment factors					
RPI February (company's year end)	**179.3**	173.8	172.0	167.5	163.7
Factor to adjust to £1999	**0.913**	0.942	0.952	0.977	1.000
Adjusted figures					
Turnover (excluding exceptional turnover)	**345.3**	357.6	356.1	322.5	303.7
Operating profit (before exceptional items)	**24.6**	25.2	28.0	32.2	24.6
Earnings per ordinary share excluding exceptionals	**6.8p**	7.3p	9.0p	10.5p	7.0p
Dividends per share	**5.2p**	5.4p	5.4p	5.6p	5.7p

Example 31.3 Effect of inflation on the value of £1

Annual rate of inflation	After 5 years	After 10 years	After 20 years
2½%	88.3p	78.1p	61.0p
5%	78.3p	61.3p	37.6p
7½%	69.6p	48.5p	29.5p

But, as Example 31.4 shows, the effect of inflation on the value of money since 1940 and, in particular, since 1970, has been staggering.

Example 31.4 The RPI at 5-year intervals (1915 = 100)

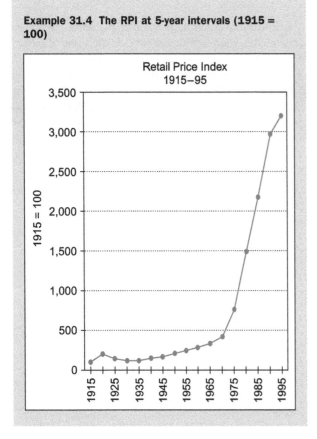

The effect of inflation on the investor in fixed-interest stocks

Anyone who bought £100 of Government, irredeemable, 3½% War Loan when it stood at par in the 1940s by 2004 saw it standing at about 72, which reflected interest rates and inflationary expectations at the time. If one adjusted the original £100 by the subsequent movement in the RPI (which was about 28 times its 1940 level), and expressed £100 in 2004 pounds, one got about £2,800. In real terms the investor had lost over 97% of his capital: horrifying! Since then, interest rates have fallen and inflationary expectations are much less.

In 1940 the RPI was 6.6 (taking 1987 = 100) and in March 2004 was 184.6 which represents an increase of 2,697%.

Appendix 5 provides tables showing the effect of inflation in the UK on the Retail Price Index.

The future if high (over 10%) inflation returns

Until the purpose of inflation accounting is agreed no system of inflation accounting is likely to be introduced successfully.

Consequently, HC accounts will continue

- to lull many managers and shareholders into thinking that their companies are doing better (sometimes considerably better) than they really are, and
- to encourage unions and employees to seek wage increases that are not justified by real (as opposed to reported) profits.

Furthermore, unless the system so developed produces accounts acceptable to the Inland Revenue for tax purposes and which become the *only* accounts a company produces, there will continue to be a problem. The production of *two* sets of accounts will always pose the question 'Which one is to be believed?'

CHAPTER 32

Half-yearly reports (interim reports)

Background

Introduction

For many years, listed companies have been required to prepare and publish interim reports. The Listing Rules of the UK Listing Authority set out minimum disclosure requirements but in practice there have been huge variations in the amount of information contained in interim reports of different companies.

In 1999, the Accounting Standards Board (ASB) published a Best Practice Statement entitled 'Interim Reports'. The status of the document was that it was 'designed as a formulation and development of best practice; it is intended to have persuasive rather than mandatory force and it is not an accounting standard'.

As the ASB put it: 'In the interests of good financial reporting its use is commended by the Financial Reporting Council, the Hundred Group of Finance Directors, the London Stock Exchange and the Irish Stock Exchange.'

In July 2007, the Statement was retitled 'Half-yearly Reports' and updated and revised as a result of the new UK Disclosure and Transparency Rules.

We start in this chapter with the situation as it has been until recently, and then we refer to the implications of the UK Disclosure and Transparency Rules for fully-listed companies.

UK Listing Rules

The rules reflect the European Union Directive on Interim Reports, which requires each listed company to prepare a report on its activities and profit and loss for the first six months of each financial year.

Later in the chapter we consider how the new UK Disclosure and Transparency Rules will have an impact on interim reports (which may be described as 'Half-yearly Reports') of fully listed companies whose full financial year starts on or after 20 January 2007.

ASB Statement of Best Practice

The 1999 version of the statement was intended for voluntary use. We refer later in the chapter to the changed status of the July 2007 version.

This statement is intended for voluntary use.

It suggests that Interim Reports should be drawn up employing the same principles and practices as those used for annual reporting.

They should *include*:

(a) a narrative commentary;
(b) summarised profit and loss account;
(c) balance sheet;
(d) cash flow statement;
(e) a statement of total recognised gains and losses, where relevant.

And should *provide* details of:

(a) acquisitions and discontinued operations;
(b) segmental information;
(c) exceptional items;
(d) comparative figures for the corresponding interim period and for the previous full financial year.

Companies are encouraged to make their interim reports available with 60 days of the interim period end.

Auditors' review

One of the recommendations of the Cadbury Report on Corporate Governance was that interim reports should be reviewed by the Company's auditors.

The review process, which is **'best practice' rather than mandatory**, is described in a Bulletin *Review of Interim Financial Information*, issued by the Auditing Practices Board.

Many smaller companies and some larger ones, don't have their interim reports reviewed, and it is open to debate as to whether the benefits of a review justify the costs.

In those companies where the auditor *has* reviewed the interim information, his report will appear in the company's interim report. The prescribed format of the report is, in some people's views, both long winded and pedantic. For example, the Review report by the auditors to the Ready Mix Concrete Group RMC takes up more than half a page of A4, and gets its own page. Here is an abridged version:

RMC *Extract from Review report by the auditors*

Introduction
We have been instructed by the Company to review the financial information which comprises . . . We have read the other information contained in the Interim Statement and considered whether it contains any apparent misstatements or material inconsistencies with the financial information.

Directors' responsibilities
The Interim Statement . . . is the responsibility of, and has been approved by the Directors. The Listing Rules of the FSA, require that the accounting policies and presentation applied to the interim figures should be consistent with those applied in preparing the preceding annual accounts except where any changes, and the reasons for them, are disclosed.

Review work performed
We conducted our review in accordance with the guidance contained in Bulletin 1999/4 issued by the Auditing Practices Board . . .
 A review consists principally of making enquiries of Group management and applying analytical procedures. . . . A review excludes audit procedures such as . . . It is substantially less in scope than an audit . . . and therefore provides a lower level of assurance than an audit. Accordingly we do not express an audit opinion . . .

Review conclusion
On the basis of our review we are not aware of any material modifications that should be made to the financial information as presented for the six months ended 30 June 2003.

Chartered Accountants
London
5 September 2003

With so many disclaimers in the report, the boards of some companies may decide that an auditors' review is hardly worth the candle.

Following the new UK Disclosure and Transparency Rules, the Auditing Practices Board will bring in revised reporting requirements regarding auditors' review statements on half-yearly reports.

Practical issues

Accounting policies

The ASB Statement expects interim reports to be prepared on the basis of accounting policies used in the previous annual accounts. Where there has been any change, this should be spelt out (e.g. DIAGEO):

DIAGEO *Note to the Interim Statement 2004*

1. New accounting policies
The group has adopted the reporting requirements of FRS 17 – Retirement benefits . . . from 1 July 2003. The financial information included in this interim statement also complies with . . . the amendment to FRS 5 – Reporting the substance of transactions.

Major transactions

Although not specifically mentioned, it is clearly desirable that interim statements should report other major transactions such as the redemption or conversion of shares or the purchase of a company's own shares and their subsequent cancellation, for example:

DIAGEO *Note to the interim statement 1999*

8. Repurchase of shares
In July 1998, 3m B shares were redeemed at a cost of £15m. On 1 August 1998, the company converted the remaining B shares into 12m ordinary shares at a price of 725 pence per share. In October 1998, the company purchased, and subsequently cancelled, 10.5m ordinary shares at an average price of 555 pence per share for an aggregate consideration of £59m.

Exceptional items

As explained earlier, interim statements are not audited, and in the past, when they were not reviewed either, it is possible that the stringent look which is given to the balance sheet at the end of the year, and the consequent making of adequate provisions, did not occur at the half-year. It perhaps still does not, and this tends to mean that adverse exceptional items are somewhat more likely to be included in the second half of a year than in the first half. But where they are found in the first half year figures they may be material as is demonstrated by DIAGEO:

DIAGEO *Note to the interim statement 2003*

3. Exceptional items

	Six months ended 31 Dec 2003 £m	Six months ended 31 Dec 2002 £m
Operating costs		
Seagram integration	(19)	(89)
Guinness UDV integration	–	(15)
	(19)	(104)

Half year on half year comparisons

It is obvious that a careful item by item comparison of this year's interim figures (H1/Year 2) with last year's interim figures (H1/Year 1) will help with assessing how the company is doing. It should also prompt questions about the cause of any sudden jump.

But it is rather less obvious that the same comparison should be made of H2/Year 2 with H2/Year 1, because companies hardly ever publish their second half figures.

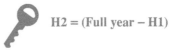

$$H2 = (\text{Full year} - H1)$$

Second half figures have to be calculated, but the effort can be very worthwhile, revealing information that might otherwise be overlooked.

For example, LOCKER GROUP, where the Chairman's statement in the annual report to 31 March 2000 did not mention that the Group had plunged into loss in the second half, but this is easily deduced:

LOCKER GROUP *Second half results*

Operating profit reported

	£000
Six months to 30 September 1999	1,758
Year ended 31 March 2000	482
Operating loss in second half, deduced	**(1,276)**

Seasonal businesses

According to the ASB 'Fluctuating revenues of seasonal businesses are generally understood by the marketplace and it is appropriate to report them as they arise'. What, in the past, may have been less well known, is the effect on the balance sheet and cash flow statement (which traditionally were not disclosed), for example, THORNTONS:

THORNTONS *Half yearly fluctuations due to seasonality*

	Reported		Deduced
	H1 2003 28 weeks to 11 January 2003 £000	Full year 2003 52 weeks to 26 June 2003 £000	H2 2003 24 weeks to 26 June 2003 £000
Consolidated profit and loss account			
Turnover	104,684	167,095	62,411
H1 and H2 adjusted to 26 weeks	97,206		67,612
Operating profit	12,698	9,444	(3,254)
Margin	12.1%	5.7%	[Zilch]
Consolidated balance sheet			
Cash at bank and in hand	15,471	4,522	
Bank loans (etc.) due within one year	(11,155)	(7,915)	
Consolidated cash flow statement			
Cash inflow from operating activities	21,414	24,860	3,446

H2 and H1 compared

Operating profit in H2 was about £15.9m lower than H1. The knock-on effect in the balance sheet was a fall of about £10.9m in cash, with short-term loans and overdraft falling by only £3.2m.

H1's Christmas sales dominate, in spite of H2's Easter eggs.

Company strategy

The Chairman, in his Statement in the 2003 annual report, said '. . . high temperatures during the final week before Easter and the hottest June since 1976 seriously depressed sales over Easter and Father's Day'. The company usually breaks even in H2.

The new Disclosure and Transparency Rules (DTR)

Introduction

DTR are the rules which the Financial Services Authority have developed in the UK in order to implement the EU Transparency Obligations Directive. The reporting aspects of these rules are mandatory for fully-listed companies only (*not* AIM-listed ones) and must be applied for financial years starting on or after 20 January 2007.

DTR apply to full-year reports and half-yearly financial reports. The comments below refer to half-yearly reports only.

Interim (half-year) reports

Interim reports will have to be published *two months* after the end of the interim period.

As regards the content of interim reports:

- listed companies reporting under IFRS will be required to apply IAS 34, Interim Financial Reporting;
- listed companies reporting under UK GAAP (e.g. listed companies without subsidiaries who currently are permitted to choose between UK GAAP and IFRS) will be required to apply the ASB's Statement on Half-yearly Reports (issued July 2007), which updates and replaces the previous statement (Interim Reports, issued September 1999).

Minimum contents of half-yearly financial reports – fully listed companies

For fully-listed companies the half-yearly report must contain:

- a condensed set of financial statements;
- an interim management report;
- a responsibility statement.

Fully-listed companies preparing consolidated accounts will be required to prepare interim financial reports which comply with IAS 34, Interim financial reporting. Some companies are already complying with IAS 34 but many are not. For the latter, complying with IAS 34 will result in more extensive disclosures than they are providing at present.

Minimum contents of half-yearly financial reports – AIM listed companies

AIM companies continue to be regulated by separate rules and will not be affected by the extended reporting rules of DTR. The rules for AIM companies require half-yearly interim reports to be published within *three months* of a period end.

Minimum content is:

- a balance sheet;
- an income statement (assuming IFRS is adopted);
- a cash flow statement;
- comparative figures for the corresponding period in the previous financial year.

AIM companies are not required to comply with IAS 34 but may adopt it on a voluntary basis.

CHAPTER 33

UK GAAP and IFRS compared

Introduction

The Accounting Standards Board and the International Accounting Standards Board (and its predecessor) have been working closely together for many years. As a consequence, UK GAAP has been moving closer to International Financial Reporting Standards (IFRS) for longer than is popularly imagined. For example, FRS 12 on Provisions was issued in 1998 – this standard is absolutely identical to IAS 37 issued at the same time. Other standards such as FRS 11 on Impairment and FRS 15 on Tangible fixed assets are broadly similar to their international equivalents (IAS 36 and IAS 16).

In this chapter we make a high-level comparison between UK GAAP and IFRS and divide this into three parts:

1. areas where UK GAAP and IFRS are identical;
2. areas where UK GAAP and IFRS are broadly similar but where differences remain;
3. areas where UK GAAP and IFRS are markedly different.

Where UK GAAP and IFRS are identical

The earliest example of this was accounting for provisions, FRS 12 and IAS 37 respectively, referred to above (see Chapter 19).

More recent examples are:

- Presentation of financial instruments – FRS 25/IAS 32 (Chapters 22 and 24);
- Disclosure of financial instruments – FRS 25 and FRS 29/IAS 32 and IFRS 7 (Chapter 22)*;
- Recognition and measurement of financial instruments – FRS 26/IAS 39 (Chapters 15, 18, 22, 23)*;
- Events after the balance sheet date – FRS 21/IAS 10 (Chapter 25);
- Share-based payment – FRS 20/IFRS 2 (Chapters 9 and 24);
- Earnings per share – FRS 22/IAS 33 (Chapter 10);
- Foreign currency – FRS 23/IAS 21 (Chapter 29)*.

The new converged UK GAAP standards are not mandatory for all categories of company, so many unlisted UK companies are still using all or parts of 'unconverged' UK GAAP standards.

In addition, the publication in July 2007 of FRED 41, Related party disclosures, will result in convergence with IAS 24.

Where UK GAAP is similar but where differences remain

In many areas, although there are some differences of detail (mainly relating to presentation and disclosure), the broad practical effects are similar.

These areas include:

- Accounting for defined benefit pension costs – FRS 17/IAS 19 (Chapter 9);
- Accounting for tangible fixed assets – FRS 15/IAS 16 (Chapter 13);
- Stock/Inventories – SSAP 9/IAS 2 (Chapter 16);
- Construction contracts – SSAP 9/IAS 11 (Chapter 16);
- Revenue recognition – FRS 5/IAS 18 (Chapter 8).

Where UK GAAP and IFRS are markedly different

The more significant differences between UK GAAP and IFRS are set out in the following table:

Topic	UK GAAP treatment	IFRS treatment
Balance sheet format and terminology *(Chapters 7 and 12)*	These are presently dealt with in CA 85; Sch. 4 (in future in Regulations supporting the Companies Act 2006).	Dealt with in IAS 1 which is far less prescriptive than Schedule 4.
Performance reporting *(Chapters 7 and 11)*	Profit and loss formats and terminology are dealt with in CA 85, Sch. 4 and FRS 3.	Income statement formats and terminology are dealt with in IAS 1.
	FRS 3 requires a Statement of total recognised gains and losses.	IAS 1 requires a Statement of changes in equity and allows a choice of two formats: columnar format statement *or* statement of recognised income and expense.
	FRS 3 includes a stringent definition of 'discontinued operations'.	IFRS 5 refers to presentation of 'discontinued operations' but the definition and presentation differs from FRS 3.
	FRS 3 requires *fundamental* errors to be accounted for by way of restatement (as though the error had never occurred) and prior year adjustment. The effects of material errors should be reflected in the profit and loss account without restatement.	IAS 8 prohibits the inclusion of *material* errors in the income statement.
Exceptional items *(Chapter 8)*	FRS 3 includes definitions for exceptional items.	IAS 1 does not refer to the term 'exceptional item' although it requires separate disclosure (either on the face of the income statement or in the notes) 'when items of income and expense are material' and gives examples of circumstances that would give rise to separate disclosure.
	FRS 3 requires all exceptional items to be charged or credited in arriving at operating profit with three specific exceptions.	
Cash flow statements *(Chapter 26)*	FRS 1 requires cash flows to be grouped under nine sub-headings.	IAS 7 requires cash flows to be grouped under three sub-headings.
	The statement should reconcile to cash.	The statement should reconcile to cash and cash equivalents.
	FRS 1 specifies a number of exemptions from its scope.	IAS 7 contains no scope exemptions.
	FRS 1 requires 'net debt' disclosures.	IAS 7 specifies disclosure of breakdown of cash and cash equivalents, and reconciliation to the balance sheet.
Deferred tax *(Chapter 20)*	Deferred tax may not be provided on revaluation surpluses, or gains on disposal where rollover relief is likely to be claimed.	Deferred tax must be provided on these 'temporary differences'.
	Deferred tax balance may be discounted.	Discounting is not permitted.
	Tax reconciliation required is to 'current' tax.	Tax reconciliation is to total tax expense (current tax plus deferred tax).
Goodwill (including purchased goodwill arising in the accounts of an individual company) *(Chapter 14)*	FRS 10 gives choice for positive goodwill between systematic amortisation and carrying an unchanged amount subject to annual impairment review.	IFRS 3 prohibits systematic amortisation. The amortisation charge is replaced by a charge for impairment (whenever the impairment review reveals impairment).
Research and development costs *(Chapter 14)*	Where 'development cost criteria' are satisfied, accounting policy choice is between capitalisation and immediate write-off.	Where IAS 38 criteria satisfied, capitalisation is mandatory.

▶

Topic	UK GAAP treatment	IFRS treatment
Investment properties *(Chapter 13)*	SSAP 19 requires investment properties to be revalued in the accounts each year at open market value (SSAP 19.11) with changes in market value taken to investment revaluation reserve, subject to limited exceptions.	IAS 40 allows a choice between the 'fair value model' and the 'cost model'. The fair value model requires property to be measured at its fair value reflecting market conditions at the balance sheet date with changes in value recognised in the income statement for the period. The cost model would require investment properties to be stated at cost less any accumulated depreciation and any impairment losses.

The future

The convergence programme has temporarily been put on hold. The following are four examples of exposure drafts issued some time ago with the aim of further converging UK GAAP with IFRS. To date, these have not been converted into definitive Financial Reporting Standards:

1. FRED 28, Inventories; Construction and service contracts – issued May 2002 to converge with IAS 2, IAS 11;

2. FRED 37, Intangible assets – issued July 2005 to converge with IAS 38;
3. FRED 38, Impairment of assets – issued July 2005 to converge with IAS 36;
4. FRED 36, Business combinations – issued July 2005 to converge with IFRS 3.

Further announcements are awaited from both the Accounting Standards Board and the government. It is possible (but by no means definite) that full convergence will be achieved by, say, 2010/11.

CHAPTER 34

Adopting IFRS for the first time

The impact of the change from UK GAAP to IFRS

We summarise the main differences between UK GAAP and IFRS in Chapter 33. These differences become critical in a company's first set of accounts prepared under IFRS, because shareholders and analysts will have seen previous accounts for that company prepared under UK GAAP. No doubt initially many users of accounts were confused by profits and earnings per share of a different magnitude as between UK GAAP and IFRS (many may continue to be confused particularly when they look at complex and lengthy IFRS accounts in sectors such as banking).

The profits and assets may *appear* to be different under IFRS, but these differences are due to differing measurement bases and the requirements of particular International Financial Reporting Standards where these differ from their UK GAAP counterparts (see Chapter 33).

 What is vital to appreciate is that the underlying value of the business remains the same, as do its cash flows.

Consider a simple example. Under UK GAAP, suppose a company reported an operating profit of £520,000 whilst under IFRS the operating profit amounted to £450,000. There could be several possible reasons for the different figures. Suppose here that there are only two reasons:

1. Under UK GAAP there was no charge for share-based payment as FRS 20 was not mandatory for the period in question, but under IFRS 2 there was a charge of £135,000.

2. Under UK GAAP there was a £65,000 charge for amortisation of goodwill under FRS 10, whilst under IFRS there was no charge (and no impairment was identified).

This information could be summarised in a simple UK GAAP/IFRS profit reconciliation, as follows:

	£000
UK GAAP operating profit	520
Amortisation of goodwill	65
Share-based payment expense	(135)
IFRS operating profit	450

As mentioned above, there is no impact whatsoever on cash flows. The respective profits can be reconciled to cash flows as follows (refer to Chapter 26 for explanation of reconciling items for stock and debtors, etc.):

	UK GAAP	IFRS
	£000	£000
Operating profit	**520**	**450**
Increase in stock/debtors etc.	115	115
Depreciation	85	85
Amortisation of goodwill	65	–
Share-based payment expenses	–	135
Operating cash flow	**785**	**785**

Timing of IFRS implementation and different categories of companies

In the UK, a major problem for analysts and other users of accounts is that different companies have varied considerably as regards implementation of IFRS. In fact many still use UK GAAP as they are not yet required to adopt IFRS (see Chapter 2).

Fully-listed companies

For fully-listed companies, the first set of consolidated accounts which had to be prepared under IFRS was for the first period that commenced on or after 1 January 2005. For companies with December year ends, the first IFRS accounts were for the year ended 31 December 2005, whilst for companies with March year ends the first set of IFRS accounts covered the year ended 31 March 2006.

AIM-listed companies

AIM-listed companies were permitted (but not required) to adopt IFRS for accounts periods beginning on or after 1 January 2005. For AIM-listed companies, IFRS did not become mandatory until accounts periods beginning on or after 1 January 2007. Whilst many AIM-listed companies adopted IFRS at the earliest opportunity, most did not. An AIM-listed company with a June year end which adopts IFRS at the latest date permitted by the London Stock Exchange would prepare its first set of accounts under IFRS in respect of the year to 30 June 2008.

Unlisted companies (including Plus Market companies)

A number of these companies have already adopted IFRS, but it is probably safe to say that the overwhelming majority continue to adopt UK GAAP (and will do so until the regulators force them to adopt IFRS).

So the dilemma for analysts is quite simple – what price comparability? All we can say with confidence is that all year ended 31 December 2007 consolidated accounts of fully-listed and AIM-listed companies will be prepared on the same basis – IFRS.

The impact of IFRS 1, First-time adoption of IFRS

In the first year a company adopts IFRS, it must apply a crucial accounting standard IFRS 1, First-time adoption of International Financial Reporting Standards.

IFRS 1 and restatement of UK GAAP comparatives

To understand the importance and implications of IFRS 1, consider a simple example. Suppose an AIM-listed company with a 31 December year end will adopt IFRS for its 2007 accounts. It will therefore have prepared its accounts for the year ended 31 December 2006 under UK GAAP, and this is the last period for which it is allowed to use UK GAAP according to the requirements of the London Stock Exchange.

AIMCO PLC *Transition example*

1/1/06		31/12/06	31/12/07
Final year UK GAAP Statements			
Comparative period IFRS		First IFRS Statements	
Transition Date			*Reporting Date*

Its accounts for the year ended 31 December 2007 will be prepared on the basis of IFRS. The 2006 comparatives for the income statement, balance sheet, equity statement and cash flow statement will have to be restated in accordance with IFRS (even though the 2006 accounts were prepared and signed off under UK GAAP). This restatement can be a complex business as it will involve going back to the beginning of the comparative period, i.e. 1 January 2006, and restating the various items in the balance sheet at that date in accordance with IFRS. That date is referred to in the standard as 'transition date'. So the first thing that IFRS 1 does is set out a stringent set of rules which companies must follow in order to restate all their comparatives. In principle this should mean that the 2007 and 2006 IFRS numbers are comparable.

This is generally the case, but in restricted situations IFRS 1 may allow the original comparatives under UK GAAP to be left in unchanged. This usually relates to situations where it may be almost impossible to determine reliable restated comparatives because, for example, earlier period valuations are not available or because new systems were not in place at that time.

IFRS 1 – disclosing the impact of IFRS

In the example above, IFRS 1 requires the company to explain how IFRS has impacted on its reported numbers. It does this by requiring the company to present a number of reconciling disclosures:

- a reconciliation between the reported profit for the year ended 31 December 2006 under UK GAAP and the equivalent profit under IFRS (which forms the basis of the restated comparatives in the 2007 accounts);

- a reconciliation between the equity (= net assets) at the transition date of 1 January 2006 between the previously reported UK GAAP numbers and the numbers restated under IFRS;

- a reconciliation between the equity (= net assets) at comparative balance sheet date of 31 December 2006 between the previously reported UK GAAP numbers and the numbers restated under IFRS.

Two published accounts examples appear below – illustrating the two main ways that the above reconciliations can be presented.

ROYALBLUE GROUP PLC *Extract from annual report and accounts year ended 31 December 2005*

Note 23 – Explanation of transition to IFRS

These are the Company's and the Group's first consolidated financial statements prepared in accordance with IFRSs. The accounting policies referred to in note 2 have been applied in preparing the consolidated financial statements for the year ended 31 December 2005, the comparative information for the year ended 31st December 2004 and the preparation of an opening IFRS balance sheet at 1st January 2004, the Company's and the Group's date of transition to IFRS.

In preparing its opening IFRS balance sheet and comparative information for the year ended 31st December 2004, the Company and the Group have adjusted amounts reported previously in financial statements prepared in accordance with UK GAAP.

An explanation of how the transition from UK GAAP to IFRS has affected the Company's and the Group's financial position and financial performance is set out in the following tables and notes accompanying them. There have been no changes to the Company's or the Group's cash flows as a result of the transition.

		Group		Company	
		31st December 2004	1st January 2004	31st December 2004	1st January 2004
Equity as at:	*Note*	£000	£000	£000	£000
Total equity reported under UK GAAP		26,753	21,525	20,599	16,999
Intangible assets; product development capitalised	a	6,511	6,224	–	–
Deferred tax liability; product development capitalised	a	(1,953)	(1,867)	–	–
Staff benefits; share-based payments	b	(22)	(93)	17	–
Deferred tax asset; share-based payments	b	370	570	–	–
Dividends payable	c	1,851	9,941	1,851	9,941
Total equity reported under IFRS		33,510	36,300	22,467	26,940

▶

For the period:	Note	Group 31st December 2004 £000	Company 1st January 2004 £000
Profit for the period reported under UK GAAP		7,607	5,773
Product development; capitalisation and amortisation	a	287	–
Product development; change in tax charge	a	(86)	–
Share-based payments; expensed in the income statement	b	(343)	–
Share-based payments; change in tax charge in the income statement	b	(240)	–
Profit for the period reported under IFRS		7,225	5,773

An explanation of how the transition from UK GAAP to IFRS has affected the Group's earnings per share for the share for the 12 months to 31st December 2004 is in the table below.

	Under UK GAAP	Effect of transition to IFRS	IFRS
Basic earnings per share	23.9p	(1.2p)	22.7p
Diluted earnings per share	23.4p	(1.1p)	22.3p

a Research and development – IAS 38 Intangible Assets[1]

Under UK GAAP all expenditure on research and development was expensed as incurred. Under IFRS, research expenditure is recognised as an expense as incurred but costs incurred on product development are capitalised as intangible assets when it is probable that the development will provide economic benefit, considering its commercial and technological feasibility, resources are available for the development and costs can be measured reliably. Other development expenditures are recognised as an expense as incurred. Capitalised product development expenditure is amortised over the expected useful life. A deferred tax liability arises on the product development expenditure that has been capitalised.

b Employee benefits – IFRS 2 Share-based payment; IAS 19 Employee benefits[2]

The primary change is that IFRS 2 requires that the fair value for share incentives to employees be estimated and charged to the income statement over the vesting period of the incentive. This only applies to share incentives granted and awarded since November 2002 and not vested at 1st January 2005. The standard also required that the potential tax benefit to employing companies from share incentives being exercised in the future be recorded as a deferred tax asset based on the intrinsic value of all the incentives at the balance sheet date. Tax charges and credits are only reflected in the income statement for incentives granted after November 2002 for which the fair value is charged to the income statement.

c Dividends payable[3]

Under IFRS dividends are charged to the income statement when paid or approved and not in the period to which they relate as required previously by UK GAAP. This typically results in dividends being deducted from equity in a later period.

Authors' notes

1. Under UK GAAP, capitalisation of development costs is optional (they may be charged to the profit and loss account as incurred, usually referred to as 'expensed') but under IFRS capitalisation is mandatory (see Chapter 14).
2. Under UK GAAP, the share-based payment standard FRS 20 did not become mandatory until accounts periods starting on or after 1 January 2006, so this was an important reconciling difference for these accounts.
3. The proposed dividend adjustment is no longer relevant. However UK balance sheets prior to 31 December 2005 were required to include a dividend creditor for proposed dividends, and at that time this was a significant difference between UK GAAP and IFRS. Today the UK GAAP rules are identical to IFRS.

MANAGEMENT CONSULTING GROUP PLC *Extract from annual report and accounts year ended 31 December 2005*

Note 28. Restatement of financial information under International Financial Reporting Standards (extracts)
This is the first year that the Company has presented its financial statements under IFRS. The following disclosures are required in the year of transition. The last financial statements under UK GAAP were for the year ended 31 December 2004 and the date of transition to IFRS was therefore 1 January 2004.

The standards giving rise to changes to the Group's consolidated results on transition from UK GAAP to IFRS and their financial impact are as follows:

IFRS 2 Share-based Payment[1]
Under IFRS 2, the Group recognises a charge for the fair value of outstanding share options granted to employees after 7 November 2002. The charge has been calculated using the stochastic option pricing model and the resulting cost has been charged to the income statement over the relevant option vesting periods, adjusted to reflect actual and expected levels of vesting. There was no charge to the profit and loss account in 2004 under UK GAAP in relation to share options granted to employees. The impact of IFRS 2 is a reduction in retained earnings as at 1 January 2004 of £0.2 million and a pre-tax charge of £0.4 million for the year ended 31 December 2004. A deferred tax asset of £0.2 million was recorded in the year ended 31 December 2004 in relation to the share option scheme.

IFRS 3 Business Combinations[2]
Under IFRS, goodwill is no longer amortised but held at carrying value in the balance sheet and tested annually for impairment (with a specific requirement to be tested at the date of transition) and when there are indications of impairment. The goodwill amortisation under UK GAAP of £3.8 million charged during the year has been reversed under IFRS. All goodwill has been tested for impairment for the year ended 31 December 2004 and at the transition date in accordance with IFRS, and no adjustment was deemed necessary . . .

Under the transitional rules of IFRS 1, the Group has taken advantage of the option not to apply IFRS 3 retrospectively to business combinations that took place before the date of transition. As a result, goodwill arising from past business combinations is recorded initially in the opening balance sheet at the amortised carrying value under UK GAAP on that date.

IAS 10 Events after the Balance Sheet Date[3]
IAS 10 requires that dividends are recognised in the period in which they are declared. This is different to UK GAAP where the proposed dividend is recognised in the profit and loss account. The final proposed dividend for 2003 of £0.9 million has been reversed out of the opening balance sheet and recorded at the amount paid in the year ended 31 December 2004. Similarly, the final proposed dividend for 2004 of £1.2 million has been reversed from the income statement.

IAS 19 Other Long-term Benefits
Deferred employee bonuses awarded in respect of the year ended 31 December 2004 but not payable in cash and shares until 31 December 2007, are accounted for under IAS 19 as deferred long-term benefits, and will be expensed to the income statement over the subsequent three year deferral period under IFRS. Under UK GAAP they are charged in full to the profit and loss account in 2004 . . .

IAS 38 Intangible Assets
IAS 38 requires computer software costs, including development costs, to be classified as intangible assets. Capitalised software of £0.4 million is reclassified at 31 December 2004 as intangible assets, which continue to be amortised over three years or the life of the software contract if shorter. The opening balance sheet under IFRS includes a similar reclassification of £0.4 million.

▶

IAS 21 The Effects of Changes in Foreign Exchange

Under IFRS, translation differences arising from the date of transition to IFRS that are permitted to be taken to reserves must be tracked in a separate foreign exchange reserve. Foreign exchange taken to reserves relating to translation of foreign equity investments must be recycled to the income statement on disposal of the investment.

The Group has elected to take the exemption, permitted under the transitional rules, of not applying IAS 21 retrospectively; this has allowed the Group to reset to zero its historic foreign exchange reserve at 1 January 2004 of £12.3 million by means of a reclassification to retained earnings. The gain or loss on any subsequent disposal of a foreign subsidiary will be adjusted only by these accumulated translation adjustments arising after 1 January 2004.

Authors' notes

1. Under UK GAAP, the share-based payment standard FRS 20 did not become mandatory until accounts periods starting on or after 1 January 2006, so this was an important reconciling difference for these accounts.
2. The goodwill exemption available when a company adopts IFRS for the first time, and changes from GAAP accounting to IFRS accounting, is used almost universally. In the final year of UK GAAP amortisation of goodwill is charged to the profit and loss account. This accounting treatment is prohibited by IFRS so when the comparatives are restated for the first year of IFRS, this amortisation charge is removed.
3. The proposed dividend adjustment is no longer relevant (see the previous example above).

29. Restatement of Group financial information under International Financial Reporting Standards[4]

(a) Reconciliation of income for the year ended 31 December 2004

	Previously reported under UK GAAP £000	IFRS 2 Share based payment £000	IFRS 3 Business combinations £000	IAS 10 Dividend £000	Other £000	Restated under IFRS £000
Revenue	119,248	–	–	–	–	119,248
Cost of sales	(60,270)	(144)	–	–	–	(60,414)
Gross profit	58,978	(144)	–	–	–	58,834
Selling costs	(30,362)	(86)	–	–	–	(30,448)
Goodwill amortisation	(3,792)	–	3,792	–	–	–
Administrative expenses excluding goodwill amortisation	(16,275)	(209)	–	–	534	(15,950)
Operating profit	8,549	(439)	3,792	–	534	12,436
Finance costs	(34)	–	–	–	–	(34)
Profit before tax	8,515	(439)	3,792	–	534	12,402
Tax	(2,995)	160	(920)	–	(190)	(3,945)
Retained profit after tax	5,520	(279)	2,872	–	344	8,457
Dividends	(1,221)	–	–	296	–	(925)
Profit for the period	4,299	(279)	2,872	296	344	7,532
Earnings per share – basic	3.0p					4.6p
Earnings per share – diluted	3.0p					4.5p

(b) Reconciliation of equity as at 1 January 2004 (date of transition to IFRS)

	Previously reported under UK GAAP £000	IFRS 2 Share based payment £000	IAS 10 Dividends £000	IAS 38 Intangible assets £000	IAS 21 Foreign exchange reserve £000	Restated under IFRS £000
Non-current assets						
Goodwill	69,206	–	–	–	–	69,206
Other intangible assets	–	–	–	390	–	390
Property, plant and equipment	1,649	–	–	(390)	–	1,259
Total non-current assets	70,855	–	–	–	–	70,855
Current assets						
Trade and other receivables	7,910	–	–	–	–	7,910
Goodwill amortisation	9,738	–	–	–	–	9,738
Total current assets	17,648	–	–	–	–	17,648
Total assets	88,503	–	–	–	–	88,503
Current liabilities						
Trade and other payables	(19,084)	–	–	–	–	(19,084)
Dividend to shareholders	(944)	–	944	–	–	–
Current tax liabilities	(3,987)	–	–	–	–	(3,987)
Total current liabilities	(24,015)	–	944	–	–	(23,071)
Net current assets/(liabilities)	**(6,367)**	**–**	**944**	**–**	**–**	**(5,423)**
Non-current liabilities						
Retirements benefits obligation	(13,213)	–	–	–	–	(13,213)
Non-current tax liabilities	(3,655)	–	–	–	–	(3,655)
Long-term provisions	(1,884)	–	–	–	–	(1,884)
Non-current accruals	(1,028)	–	–	–	–	(1,028)
Total non-current liabilities	(19,780)	–	–	–	–	(19,780)
Total liabilities	**(43,795)**	**–**	**944**	**–**	**–**	**(42,851)**
Net assets	**44,708**	**–**	**944**	**–**	**–**	**45,652**
Equity						
Share capital	47,198	–	–	–	–	47,198
Share premium account	38,009	–	–	–	–	38,009
Share to be issued	2,166	–	–	–	–	2,166
Share compensation reserve	–	177	–	–	–	177
Own shares held by employee share trust	(970)	–	–	–	–	–
Translation reserve	(12,338)	–	–	–	12,338	–
Other reserves	12,747	–	–	–	–	12,747
Retained earnings	(42,104)	(177)	944	–	(12,338)	(53,675)
Total equity	**44,708**	**–**	**944**	**–**	**–**	**45,652**

(c) Balance sheet as at 31 December 2004

[Not reproduced – similar format to 1 January 2004]

Authors' notes (continued)

4. The ROYALBLUE example above showed the UK GAAP to IFRS adjustments in single columns in a vertical format. Most companies use the alternative format shown above for MANAGEMENT CONSULTING GROUP. This shows the effect of each adjustment on each line in the income statement and the balance sheet. Analysts prefer this presentation because it provides more information than the lesser-used alternative 'vertical' format.

Explaining the impact on key ratios

As explained above, IFRS 1 requires explanation in words and numbers of the impact of adopting IFRS. This information is, of course, provided only in the first full set of accounts under IFRS, but as indicated below, useful insights can be obtained by going back through company websites – many companies retain IFRS conversion information.

Another useful way of explaining the impact of IFRS is to compare ratios in the final year of UK GAAP and what those ratios would have revealed had they been calculated on the basis of IFRS.

For example, in the finance sector CATTLES PLC included in its 21 June 2005 IFRS briefing (see also below) a slide entitled 'Key ratios – 2004'. This listed the following six ratios and in each case stated the number calculated under UK GAAP and the number calculated under IFRS:

1. bad debt charge as a percentage of closing net receivables (consumer division);
2. return on average net receivables (consumer division);
3. cost to income ratio;
4. gearing ratio;
5. interest cover;
6. average cost of funds.

Making use of company websites

Many leading UK companies used their websites to explain the likely impact of IFRS well before publishing the first full statutory accounts. Much of this information has been archived and can still be accessed from websites.

Examples of earlier slide presentations include:

- WHITBREAD PLC – Changes to financial reporting under IFRS, Presentation and conference call 3 August 2005;
- DAIRY CREST PLC – Presentation of the Impact of Restating Accounts from UK GAAP to International Financial Reporting Standards, 25 May 2005;
- CATTLES PLC – IFRS briefing, 21 June 2005;
- AWG PLC – International Financial Reporting Standards, Presentation to analysts, 12 September 2005.

The following are extracts from a company presentation explaining the impact of the transition from UK GAAP to IFRS:

Headline impact – 2004/5

£m	Profit earned for ordinary shareholders	Net assets
Share-based payments	(1.9)	2.6
Pension accounting	(13.4)	(311.8)
Income tax (inc. deferred tax)	(1.7)	(137.4)
Depreciation/goodwill amortisation	8.3	7.4
Dividends		54.6
Net impact	(8.7)	(384.6)

Key metrics adjusted for IFRS – 2004/5

	UK GAAP	IFRS	Movement
PBIT (£m)	313.7	296.9	(16.8)
PBT (£m)	249.4	222.8	(26.6)
PAT (£m)	176.9	168.2	**(8.7)**
EPS (pence) Adjusted basic	64.08	58.68	(5.40)
Net assets (£m)	2,208.4	1,823.8	**(384.6)**

New disclosure opportunities under IFRS – some examples

Many users of IFRS accounts are beginning to appreciate the additional information that is coming through as compared with what was previously provided under UK GAAP. Some of this is tucked away in various notes and not always easy to find. Some individual notes are extremely lengthy and patience is required in looking for valuable information.

The following are examples of areas where the note under IFRS may help to shed light on important commercial issues and sometimes help users to get a quick grasp of areas where companies may be vulnerable to changes in markets and general economic factors.

1. **Impairment of goodwill and intangibles**
   Key assumptions for value in use calculations
   - revenue volumes
   - revenue prices
   - operating costs
   - growth rate assumptions
   - growth in perpetuity
   - discount rate.

2. **Critical accounting estimates and judgements**
   - estimated impairment of goodwill
   - impairment of assets
   - income taxes
   - post employment benefits

   - restructuring provisions
   - inventory provisions.

3. **Impact of transition from UK GAAP to IFRS**
   - profit
   - equity (net assets)
   - presentation of cash flows.

   Note – this information is provided for the first year of IFRS only and will not appear in subsequent years.

4. **Other areas**
   Notes to the financial statements which may contain additional useful information compared with UK GAAP relate to:
   - share-based payment
   - segment reporting
   - related parties (key management personnel disclosures)
   - inventories.

CHAPTER 35

Putting it all together

Introduction

To illustrate how we go about analysing a company we have chosen an AIM (Alternative Investment Market) company, CHARTERHOUSE COMMUNICATIONS, which has already had an exciting but at times perilous record since it joined AIM in 1996.

Since AIM was launched in June 1995, well over 2,900 companies have been admitted. At 31 December 2007, there were 1,694 companies on AIM; 114 had gone on to the main market and the remainder had left the market for various reasons.

AIM is a high risk/high reward area. The downside is 100%, but the upside can be much more.

Charterhouse Communications

[*Note*: The authors' comments are in square brackets.]

Question 1: What does the company do?

The annual report gives a list and detailed descriptions of Charterhouse's publications under the headings:

- mortgage publications
- wealth enhancement.

[We note that the highly successful *REFS* (*Really Essential Financial Statistics*) is among the publications, and that the company owns a small bookseller.]

Question 2: How large is Charterhouse?

Monday's *FT* gives market capitalisation, or you can work it out.

Market cap = Called up share capital
× Current share price
= 294,762,143 Ord 1p shares × 1.63p
= £4.8m

(Details of share capital: see Note 18 to the accounts.)

Question 3: Recent history?

The annual report contains *Financial Highlights* for the last five years.

Financial Highlights
Group revenues and results for the last five years are as shown:

	2003 £000	2004 £000	2005 £000	2006 £000	2007 £000
Turnover	10,235	9,361	9,643	9,570	9,891
Loss before tax	(266)	(294)	(248)	(797)	(3,119)
Profit before tax, amortisation and exceptional items	619	586	632	83	212

The basis for showing results before the amortisation of goodwill and intangible assets, and before exceptional items, is set out under 'Presentation of group results' in the Directors' Report.

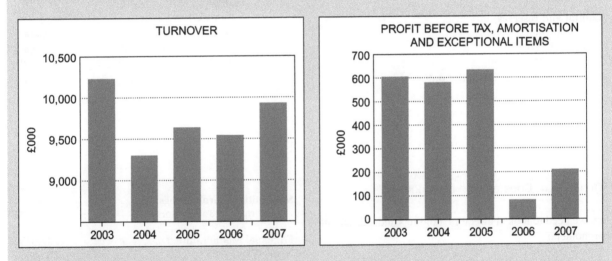

Highlights – Reduction of debt and refinancing
The Group sold three non-core parts of the business during the year – *Independent Research Services, What Investment* magazine and website, and a freehold property previously used by its subsidiary Brand & Co – for a net total of £0.9m.

There were cost savings in key areas, including staff reductions and switching to the London Stock Exchange for the data to power the Group's directories. Along with exceptional cash management, this meant that debt was further reduced.

At 31 May 2007 net debt stood at £4.1m, compared with £5.8m at the end of the previous financial year. Furthermore, the Group's debt was substantially decreased again after the year-end, with the placing of shares in July 2007 raising a further £2.5m.

As a result, the Group has now refinanced with its bank, securing a new loan of £2.75m payable over six years and an overdraft facility of £0.5m.

The effect of the placing of shares in July 2007 and the refinancing in August 2007, had they been applied to the audited May 2007 balance sheet, would have turned the Group's net liabilities into a net assets balance sheet.

	Group 2007 £000	Placing and refinancing £000	Pro-forma Group 2007 £000
Fixed assets			
Intangible assets	3,243	–	3,243
Tangible assets	122	–	122
	3,365	–	3,365
Current assets			
Stocks	59	–	59
Debtors: amounts due within one year	2,252	–	2,252
Debtors: amounts due after one year: deferred taxation	156	–	156
Cash at bank and in hand	98	1,395	1,493
	2,565	1,395	3,960
Creditors: amounts due within one year	(7,308)	2,469	(4,839)
Net current liabilities	(4,743)	3,864	(879)
Total assets less current liabilities	(1,378)	3,864	2,486
Creditors: amounts due after more than one year	(928)	(1,364)	(2,292)
Net (liabilities)/assets	(2,306)	2,500	194
Capital and reserves			
Called up share capital	1,233	1,715	2,948
Share premium	–	785	785
Profit and loss account	(3,539)	–	(3,539)
Equity shareholders' (deficit)/funds	(2,306)	2,500	194

Question 4: Does anyone have control?

Here we need to look at directors' holdings and substantial shareholders:

CHARTERHOUSE *Extract from 2007 Directors' Report*

Directors and their share interests

P M Strong	733,652	0.25%
I H Elliott	28,541,709	9.68%
G C Gamble	18,698,468	6.34%
R S Leighton	1,180,000	0.40%
A J Peters	10,204,208	3.46%
		20.13%

[Percentage holdings not given, calculated by authors.]

Substantial shareholdings
. . . interests of 3% or more

Financial Media Limited	29.90%
Nigel Wray	20.58%
David Newton	9.62%

Let's see what we can also find out by trawling through the press cuttings from back copies of the *Investors Chronicle*.

INVESTORS CHRONICLE *Cuttings since 1998*

3 April 1998
Charterhouse was formed in 1988 as a management buyout from Publishing Holdings, under the direction of its two leading lights MD Ivan Elliott and publishing director Geoffrey Gamble . . . Charterhouse is seasonally loaded towards the second half, largely as a result of heavy personal finance advertising ahead of the end of the tax year.
  [Company year end is May.]

9 October 1998
With increased competition in financial services, *What Mortgage?, What Investment?* and other organs may benefit from higher advertising.

18 December 1998
In August Charterhouse paid £550,000 cash for Brand & Co. Brand sells business books and distributes publications – the Stationery Office accounts for a quarter of its revenue.
  It was hardly a major deal but not a major cost either, as Brand brought with it £200,000 of cash and a £100,000 freehold property.
  It also turned in profit of £120,000 in the year to end-October 1997 and, not surprisingly, 'will be immediately earnings enhancing' for Charterhouse.

25 June 1999
Bid talks have ended at financial magazine publisher Charterhouse Communications.

24 September 1999
Final results £1.39m pre-tax (£0.91m). Advertising revenues were buoyant. There are funds available for acquisitions.
  [Going to burn a hole in their pocket?]

18 February 2000
Interims £0.34m (£0.28m). Consistent growth record is being maintained. New website should be profitable by the end of the year. Results only included £88,000 from Home Study Company *Independent Research Services.* The £8.4m acquisition is expected to enhance earnings per share this year by 16%.
  [It did burn a hole in their pocket.]
  Post-results profit taking knocked 12p off the shares, leaving them at 68p.

PRICE (p)	1p Ords vs FTSE All-Share vs norm eps						(Scale 16)
	97	98	99	00	01	02	03

	97	98	99	00	01
HIGH	9.75	14	36.8	82	37
LOW	6.25	8.25	10.5	27.5	29
AVE PER	12.2x	18.1x	26.3x	37.0x	22.0x

RELATIVE %	
1M	+11.6
3M	−19.0
6M	−18.0
1Y	−27.5
Beta rel	−0.52

Record results for the year to 31 May 2000 were assisted by organic growth and earnings-enhancing acquisitions . . . With a strong product offering, at 45p it looks good value.

20 October 2000

Smaller company tips

Charterhouse Communications
BUY at 43¹⁄₂p
. . . Charterhouse has grown steadily, rocketing to a high of 82p a share earlier this year . . . While its price has fallen back to 43¹⁄₂p, the company's acquisition strategy looks set to ensure that it continues to move in the right direction by maximising its resources across a range of products . . . this looks like a good time to buy.
   [The directors didn't think so.]

16 February 2001
Half year results: Pre-tax profits £0.66m (£0.68m). Price 26p. Long awaited acquisition of HS Publishing failed to halt a collapse in sentiment as the Group will fail to meet expectations for the full year.
   [The following week the MD did put a toe in the water, buying 85,000 shares at prices between 22p and 24p, with more directors' purchases further down. The MD caught the bottom two years later, buying 250,000 shares at 1p each.]

12 December 2003
CHARTERHOUSE'S 2002–03 RESULTS would have been a lot worse but for its six mortgage publications (the previous year included an exceptional goodwill amortisation charge of £7.84m).
   Reduced marketing of the *Successful Personal Investment* part-work also hit sales.
   [FD sold more than 42% of his holding. Let's have a look at the share price graph from *REFS*.]

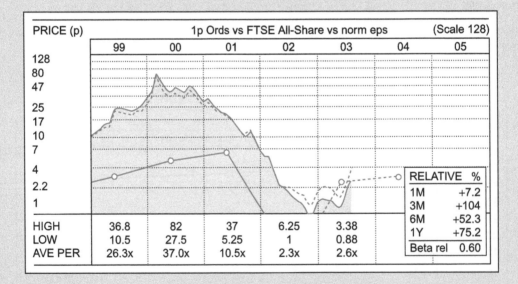

13 January 2006
Charterhouse continues to work hard for Lloyds Bank. At end-May, it still had to pay back a £2.51m secured loan over the next four years, plus interest. As cash flow is less than this, working capital is being squeezed. But, from June 2006, the company will save £250,000 a year by obtaining its data information feeds for Company REFS from the London Stock Exchange, rather than Hemscott. Last year's turnover was made up of £6m of advertising income, with the balance coming from magazine and book sales.

Ord price: 2.38p			Market value: £2.93m	
Touch: 2–2.75p			12-month High: 3.88p Low: 2p	
Dividend yield: nil			PE ratio: na	
Net asset value: 1.18p			Net debt: 378%	

Year to 31 May	Turnover (£m)	Pre-tax profit (£m)	Earnings per share (p)	Dividend per share (p)
2004	9.36	−0.29	−0.37	nil
2005	9.64	−0.25	−0.36	nil

Any other information?

Geoff Gamble, Managing Director of Charterhouse since 1999, and a founding partner of the business, indicated at the time of the placing that he wishes to step down from the Board. Accordingly, the Board is seeking a suitable replacement for the position of Managing Director. In the meantime he retains his role as MD.

Summary

- The refinancing has transformed the balance sheet which now shows net assets of £194,000 compared with a £2.3 million deficit.

- There are some very good publications in the company's portfolio, but they are mostly in the turbulent mortgage market.
- REFS in now being marketed online.
- The auditors report is no longer qualified. A replacement is being sought for Geoff Gamble, who is standing down as MD; a founder partner of the company and MD since 1999.

Conclusion

CHARTERHOUSE COMMUNICATIONS remains a speculative investment. Much will depend on the new MD and the successful marketing of REFS.

Appendices

The following Standards, UITF Abstracts and Exposure
Drafts were current on 30 November 2007:

Date of Issue

Standards

ASB	Foreword to accounting standards	Jun 1993
FRS 1	Cash flow statements	Sep 1991
FRS 2	Accounting for subsidiary undertakings	Jul 1992
FRS 3	Reporting financial performance	Oct 1992
FRS 4	Capital instruments	Dec 1993
FRS 5	Reporting the substance of transactions	Apr 1994
FRS 6	Acquisitions and mergers	Sep 1994
FRS 7	Fair values in acquisition accounting	Sep 1994
FRS 8	Related party disclosures	Oct 1995
FRS 9	Associates and joint ventures	Nov 1997
FRS 10	Goodwill and intangible assets	Dec 1997
FRS 11	Impairment of fixed assets and goodwill	Jul 1998
FRS 12	Provisions, contingent liabilities and contingent assets	Sep 1998
FRS 13	Derivatives and other financial instruments	Sep 1998
FRS 14	Earnings per share	Oct 1998
FRS 15	Tangible fixed assets	Feb 1999
FRS 16	Current tax	Dec 1999
FRS 17	Retirement benefits	Dec 2000
FRS 18	Accounting policies	Dec 2000
FRS 19	Deferred tax	Dec 2000
FRS 20	Share based payment	Apr 2004
FRS 21	Events after the balance sheet date	May 2004
FRS 22	Earnings per share	Dec 2004
FRS 23	The effects of changes in foreign exchange rates	Dec 2004
FRS 24	Financial reporting in hyperinflationary economies	Dec 2004
FRS 25	Financial instruments: Disclosure and presentation	Dec 2004
FRS 26	Financial instruments: Recognition and Measurement	Dec 2004
FRS 27	Life Assurance	Dec 2004
FRS 28	Corresponding amounts	Oct 2005
FRS 29	Financial instruments: Disclosures	Dec 2005
FRSSE	Financial Reporting Standard for Smaller Entities (effective January 2007)	Jan 2007
FRSSE	Financial reporting standard for smaller entities (effective January 2007)	Jan 2007

Urgent Issues Task Force (UITF)

ASB	Foreword to UITF Abstracts	Feb 1994
Abstract No.:		
4	Presentation of long-term debtors in current assets	Jul 1992
5	Transfers from current assets to fixed assets	Jul 1992

9	Accounting for operations in hyper-inflationary economies	Jun 1993
11	Capital instruments: issuer call options	Sep 1994
15	Disclosure of substantial acquisitions	Jan 1996
19	Tax on gains and losses that hedge an investment in a foreign enterprise	Feb 1998
21	Accounting issues arising from the proposed introduction of the euro	Mar 1998
22	Accounting for acquisition of a Lloyd's business	Jun 1998
23	Application of the transitional rules in FRS 15	May 2000
24	Accounting for start-up costs	Jun 2000
25	National Insurance contributions on share option gains	Jul 2000
26	Barter transactions for advertising	Nov 2000
27	Revisions to estimates of the useful economic life of goodwill and intangible assets	Dec 2000
28	Operating lease incentives	Feb 2001
29	Website development costs	Feb 2001
31	Exchanges of businesses or other non-monetary assets for an interest in a subsidiary, joint venture or associate	Oct 2001
32	Employee benefit trusts and other intermediate payment arrangements	Dec 2001
33	Obligations in capital instruments	Feb 2002
34	Pre-contract costs	May 2002
35	Death in service and incapacity benefits	May 2002
36	Contracts for sales of capacity	Mar 2003
38	Accounting for ESOP trusts	Dec 2003
39	Members' shares in Co-operative Entities and similar instruments	Feb 2005
40	Revenue recognition and service contracts	Mar 2005
41	Scope of FRS 20	Apr 2006
42	Re-assessment of embedded derivatives	Apr 2006
43	The interpretation of equivalence for the puroses of Section 228A of the Companies Act 1985	Oct 2006
44	FRS 20 – Group and treasury share transactions	Feb 2007
45	Liabilities arising from participating in a specific market – waste electrical equipment	Feb 2007

Non-mandatory statements

Half-yearly financial reports	Jul 2007
Preliminary announcements	Jul 1998
Operating and financial review	Jan 2006

ASB Statement of Principles

| Statement of principles for financial reporting | Dec 1999 |

Accounting Standards Committee

The following standards issued by the ASC continue in force:

SSAP 4	Accounting for government grants	Apr 1974
SSAP 5	Accounting for value added tax	Apr 1974
SSAP 9	Stocks and long-term contracts	May 1975
SSAP 13	Accounting for research and development	Dec 1977
SSAP 19	Accounting for investment properties	Nov 1981
SSAP 20	Foreign currency translation	Apr 1983
SSAP 21	Accounting for leases and hire purchase contracts	Aug 1984
SSAP 25	Segmental reporting	Jun 1990

Appendix 2 – International Accounting Standards (IAS) and International Financial Reporting Standards (IFRS)

As at 30 November 2007

Number	Title
IAS 1	Presentation of financial statements
IAS 2	Inventories
IAS 7	Cash flow statements
IAS 8	Accounting policies, changes in accounting estimates and errors
IAS 10	Events after the balance sheet date
IAS 11	Construction contracts
IAS 12	Income taxes
IAS 14	Segment reporting
IAS 16	Property, plant and equipment
IAS 17	Leases
IAS 18	Revenue
IAS 19	Employee benefits
IAS 20	Accounting for government grants and disclosure of government assistance

IAS 21	The effect of changes in foreign exchange rates
IAS 23	Borrowing costs
IAS 24	Related party disclosures
IAS 26	Accounting and reporting by retirement benefit plans
IAS 27	Consolidated financial statements and accounting for investments in subsidiaries
IAS 28	Accounting for investments in associates
IAS 29	Financial reporting in hyperinflationary economies
IAS 30	Disclosures in the financial statements of banks and similar financial institutions
IAS 31	Financial reporting of interests in joint ventures
IAS 32	Financial instruments: Disclosure and presentation
IAS 33	Earnings per share
IAS 34	Interim financial reporting
IAS 36	Impairment of assets
IAS 37	Provisions, contingent liabilities and contingent assets
IAS 38	Intangible assets
IAS 39	Financial instruments: Recognition and measurement
IAS 40	Investment property
IAS 41	Agriculture

Number	Title
IFRS 1	First-time adoption of IFRSs
IFRS 2	Share-based payment
IFRS 3	Business combinations
IFRS 4	Insurance contracts
IFRS 5	Non-current assets held for sale and discontinued operations
IFRS 6	Exploration for and evaluation of mineral resources
IFRS 7	Financial instruments – disclosures
IFRS 8	Operating segments

Appendix 3 – Useful website addresses

www.icaew.co.uk   Institute of Chartered Accountants in England & Wales

www.icas.org.uk   Institute of Chartered Accountants of Scotland

www.accaglobal.com   Association of Chartered Certified Accountants

www.cimaglobal.com   Chartered Institute of Management Accountants

www.icsa.org.uk   Institute of Chartered Secretaries and Administrators

Companies Act 2006 guidance – Guidance on electronic communications with shareholders published February 2007: www.londonstockexchange.com/aim

Useful link for AIM companies: http://www.londonstockexchange.com/en-gb/pricesnews/statistics/factsheets/aimmarketstats.htm

www.aia.org.uk   The Association of International Accountants

www.frc.org.uk   Financial Reporting Council

Accounting Standards Board (including SORPs), Urgent Issues Task Force, Auditing Practices Board, Financial Reporting Review Panel – useful summaries and press notices as well as full texts of authoritative documents.

www.iasb.org   International Accounting Standards Board

www.berr.gov.uk   Department for Business, Enterprise and Regulatory Reform

www.opsi.gov.uk   Office of Public Sector Information (Acts of Parliament, Statutory Instruments, Draft Statutory Instruments)

www.ft.com/home/uk   Financial Times (Excellent website – click on Site Map to see detailed contents. Search facility from 5 year archive. Information about companies by sector.)

www.business.timesonline.co.uk   The Times online (Comprehensive website covering wide range of business issues. Information on different industry sectors. Facility to search for information on specific companies, including ratio analysis (linked to Hemscott).)

www.fsa.gov.uk   The Financial Services Authority

www.iod.com   Institute of Directors (Policy information and advice – corporate governance, fact sheets on roles of directors (including non-executives), etc.)

www.companieshouse.gov.uk   Companies House

Appendix 4 – Present value

£1 received in a year's time is worth less than £1 received today, because £1 available today could be invested to earn interest for the next 12 months. If £1 now could be invested at a rate of interest i (expressed as a decimal), it would be worth £$(1 + i)$ in a year's time. If the £$(1 + i)$ at the end of the year was left invested, it would be worth £$(1 + i) \times (1 + i) = $ £$(1 + i)^2$ at the end of the second year, and £$(1 + i)^3$ at the end of the third year, and so on; i.e. it would earn compound interest at the rate of i per annum.

Present value is like compound interest in reverse: the value of £1 received in a year's time is worth £$1 \div (1 + i)$ now, and £1 in two years' time is worth £$1 \div (1 + i)^2$ now, and so on. For example, if i (known as the discount rate) is 10% p.a., then the present value of £1 received in a year's time is £$1 \div (1 + 0.10) = $ £0.9091. Similarly the present value of receiving £1 in two years' time is:

$$£1 \div (1 + 0.10)^2 = £0.8264$$

and £1 in three years' time is:

$$£1 \div (1.10)^3 = £0.7513,$$

and £1 in n years' time is £$1 \div (1.10)^n$.

Tables *of present values* are available for various rates of interest and periods of years. The table below is a very simplified and abbreviated version.

Present value tables refer to the value of 1, rather than the value of £1, because they can be used for any currency: the 1 may be $1, €1 or 1 of any other currency you care to name.

The present value concept (which is also the basis of discounted cash flow, DCF) can be applied to any streams of future income and to repayments of capital. For example, £20 nominal of 5% loan stock redeemable in three years would be worth the interest payments of £1 at the end of each year plus the £20 in three years' time, all discounted at 10% per annum, to give a present value of:

$$\frac{£1}{(1.1)^1} + \frac{£1}{(1.1)^2} + \frac{£1}{(1.1)^3} + \frac{£20}{(1.1)^3}$$

$$= £(0.909 + 0.826 + 0.751 + 15.026)$$

$$= £17.512$$

The calculation of the present value of a steady stream of income can be assisted by the use of annuity tables, an annuity of 1 for n years simply being an annual payment of 1 for n years; such a table is set out below.

In our previous example, the present value of £1 per annum for three years, discounted at 10%, could have been obtained from the annuity table: three years at 10% = 2.487.

In practice, interest on fixed-interest securities is usually paid half-yearly in arrears (i.e. at the end of each half-year), and so the half-yearly discount rate, which is the square root $(1 + i)$, is used to discount each half-yearly interest payment. For example, £100 of 5% Loan Stock with three years to redemption, discounted at 10% per annum, would have a present value of:

$$\frac{250}{(\sqrt{1.10})} + \frac{250}{(\sqrt{1.10})^2} + \cdots + \frac{250}{(\sqrt{1.10})^6} + \frac{10}{(1.10)^3}$$

$$= 2.3837 + 2.2728 + \cdots + 1.8784 + 75.1315$$

$$= £87.8734.$$

Annuity table: present value of 1 in n years' time

n	1%	2%	3%	4%	5%	10%	15%
1	0.990	0.980	0.971	0.962	0.952	0.909	0.870
2	0.980	0.961	0.943	0.925	0.907	0.826	0.756
3	0.971	0.942	0.915	0.889	0.864	0.751	0.658
4	0.961	0.924	0.889	0.855	0.822	0.683	0.572
5	0.951	0.906	0.863	0.822	0.784	0.621	0.497
10	0.905	0.820	0.744	0.676	0.614	0.386	0.247
20	0.820	0.673	0.554	0.456	0.377	0.149	0.061

Annuity table: present value of an annuity of 1 for *n* years

Rate of interest (the discount rate)

n	1%	2%	3%	4%	5%	10%	15%
1	0.990	0.980	0.971	0.962	0.952	0.909	0.870
2	1.970	1.942	1.913	1.886	1.860	1.736	1.626
3	2.941	2.884	2.829	2.775	2.723	2.487	2.283
4	3.902	3.808	3.717	3.630	3.546	3.170	2.855
5	4.853	4.713	4.580	4.452	4.329	3.791	3.352
10	9.471	8.983	8.530	8.111	7.722	6.145	5.019
15	13.865	12.849	11.938	11.118	10.380	7.606	5.847

Appendix 5 – Retail Price Indices since 1950

A full listing of the Retail Price Index (RPI) is published on www.statistics.gov.uk/rpi. Please refer here for fully up-to-date figures.

Accountancy, the monthly journal of the Institute of Chartered Accountants in England and Wales, publishes a ten-year table each month and the *Investors Chronicle* includes figures for the last three months under Economic Indicators.

Appendix 6 – Problems and solutions

Problem 1.1

Elcho (Mossdale) Ltd is a small company manufacturing a simple safety device. Chairman and managing director, Mr Charles Farnesbarn, is offered a two-year contract by JQB, a do-it-yourself chain, which would double the current production and turnover of the company. It would be necessary to acquire additional plant and machinery costing £60,000. To do this, Farnesbarn seeks overdraft facilities from the company's bankers. Currently, the company has an overdraft limit of £50,000 and Farnesbarn is seeking to increase this to £110,000.

Profit after tax to turnover is running at 2.6%, so Farnesbarn is looking for profits to increase by, perhaps, £25,000 per annum. He presents his bank manager with accounts for the last trading year – see alongside. Although such facilities would earn the bank 3% or 4% over base rate on the amount outstanding, the bank manager is of a

mind to reject Farnesbarn's request. Suggest three reasons why that might be so.

For solutions to problems, see below, pages 303–11.

Problem 2.1

How would you tell whether a company was (a) a public or (b) a private limited company; or (c) was one limited by guarantee; or (d) was an unlimited company?

Problem 3.1

Q is the wholly owned subsidiary of X Group, a listed company. Q's share capital includes 100m £1 3.5% cumulative preference shares. You hold 10,000 £1 cumulative preference shares. Is X bound to pay the dividend on your shares?

Problem 4.1

Grouch Group is seeking to dispose of one of its less profitable subsidiaries to management (as a management buy-out). The asking price is £10m. The management team plans to form a company, Hopeful plc, and is prepared to invest £2m in the form of ordinary share capital; and a venture capital company has offered to put up either (i) £8m as a medium-term loan at 10% fixed; or (ii) £6m as a medium-term loan at 9% fixed and £2m in the form of ordinary share capital.

A business plan suggests that Hopeful will produce profits before interest of from £750,000 to £1,400,000. Ignoring tax, (a) calculate the profits available to management on their investment under scenarios (i) and (ii) for the range of profits projected; (b) depict this in a chart; (c) calculate the return earned (i) by management and (ii) by the venture capital company on the same bases.

Problem 5.1

Fleetwood has a fleet of 20 identical Ajax 1.6 litre motor cars purchased as follows:

1 January 1998	5 at	£10,000
1 January 1999	5 at	£11,000
1 January 2000	5 at	£12,000
1 January 2001	5 at	£12,500

Useful economic life is four years at the end of which sales proceeds are expected to be 40% of cost. These are the only motor vehicles.

Show the balance sheet item 'Motor vehicles' and its make-up as at 31 December 2001.

Problem 6.1

Companies hold fixed asset investments for a variety of reasons.

(i)   Suggest five possible reasons; and
(ii) Explain why it is important for the reader of accounts to have as clear an idea as possible of the reasons for any significant holding.

Problem 7.1

You are given the following extract from a group's accounts:

15. Stocks		
	2002	2001
	£m	£m
Raw materials and consumables	0.1	0.2
Finished goods and		
goods for resale	28.2	26.0
Residential developments		
Land	1,004.5	835.6
Development and		
construction costs	507.8	419.6
Commercial, industrial and		
mixed development properties	166.4	160.0
	1,707.0	1,441.4

(i)   Provide a brief description of the group.
(ii) What do the figures suggest? Where would you look for confirmation (or otherwise) of your hypothesis?
(iii) Imagine that Land included an estate which cost £56m, which, six months later, the group no longer plans to develop, but which it proposes to hold as a fixed asset investment. Suitably sized parcels of the estate will be offered to other developers subject to long leases. The estate is included above at cost; but its realisable value is now estimated to be only £40m. How should the proposed change be handled in next year's accounts; and why?

Problem 8.1

Companies hold current asset investments for a variety of reasons. You are asked: (a) to suggest five possible reasons; and (b) to explain why it is important for the reader of accounts to have a clear idea of the reasons for any significant holding.

Problem 9.1

Just before Christmas, a fund manager decides that he would like to purchase £10m of UK stocks, but the funds will not be available until February.

The FT-SE 100 Index stands at 4,000 at the end of December and he is looking for it to rise 5% over the next month. The fund manager wants to limit the price he has to pay in the future to a value of 4,100.

The fund manager decides to purchase 250 (£10m ÷ (4,000 × (£10)) March 4,000 calls for 100. Each contract represents £10 per index point movement.

1. What is his initial outlay?
2. What is the maximum amount risked by the manager?
3. If on 15 February it becomes clear that the £10m will not after all be available but the market has risen to 4,155, what can the investment manager do?

Problem 10.1

(a) Distinguish clearly between:
    (i)   an accrual and a provision;
    (ii) income in advance and a deposit;
    (iii) a commitment and a contingent liability.

(b) Provide examples of each.
(c) Explain the significance of each to an analyst seeking:
    (i)   to estimate a group's future cash flows/liquidity;
    (ii) to consider its viability in the medium term.

Problem 11.1

Examining the report and accounts of a group, you find that the effective rate of tax (i.e. taxation as a percentage of pre-tax profits) is:

(a) much less, or
(b) much greater,

than the normal rate of UK corporation tax.
    Suggest in each case why this might be so. Where would you look for further information? Why is this important?

Problem 12.1

The basic earnings per share of a listed company, PG, in 2001 are stated to be 71.4p.

1. How would you expect this figure to have been calculated?
2. How might you use the figure of earnings per share, i.e. with what might you compare it?
3. What other types of e.p.s. are likely to be found in published accounts, and why?

Problem 13.1

Given these extracts from the 1995 accounts of CORDIANT, explain in simple terms why the cash generated by operations was so much less in 1995 than in 1994:

Consolidated statement of cash flows:			
Year ended		31 Dec	31 Dec
		1995	1994
	Note	£m	£m
Net cash inflow from operating activities	16	16.6	58.9

Note 16
16. Reconciliation of operating profit to net cash inflow from operating activities

	Year ended 31 Dec 1995 £m	Year ended 31 Dec 1994 £m
Operating profit	28.3	44.5
Depreciation	25.7	25.7
(Profit) loss on sale of tangible fixed assets	(1.5)	0.2
Increase in work in progress	(9.4)	(8.0)
Increase in debtors	(54.8)	(77.8)
Increase in creditors	38.6	86.1
Utilisation of property provisions	(10.3)	(11.8)
Net cash inflow from operating activities	16.6	58.9

Problem 14.1

Given the extracts below from the five-year summary of a group, provide a short commentary.

Problem 15.1

1. What do you understand by 'a going concern'?
2. What responsibilities do
    (a) directors
    (b) auditors
    have in relation to this?
3. Why does it matter to investors?

Problem 16.1

Given the extract opposite from Note 10 to the 2003/04 interim statement of DIXONS GROUP, compute (a) the operating profit and (b) net cash (outflow)/inflow from operating activities for the 24 weeks to 3 May 2003. Comment on what you find.

Extracts from 5-year summary

	1996	1995	1994	1993	1992
	£m	£m	£m	£m	£m
Turnover	1,083.6	1,079.1	1,045.5	1,139.3	1,179.8
Profit from retail operations	102.0	87.2	65.2	43.0	10.0
Exceptional items	1.2	–	(6.4)	(31.4)	–
Profit for the financial year	74.6	61.6	38.9	0.4	10.8
Earnings per share	17.8p	14.8p	9.4p	0.1p	2.6p
Dividend per share	7.2p	6.3p	5.5p	5.0p	5.0p
Total net assets	532.0	484.2	447.3	423.9	438.3
Number of stores	435	433	431	425	736
Net selling space (000 sq ft)	5,268	5,005	4,815	4,704	6,452

DIXONS *Note to the Interim Statement 2003/04*

10. Reconcilition of operating profit to net cash inflow (outflow) from operating activities

	28 weeks to 15 Nov 2003 £million	28 weeks to 9 Nov 2002 £million	52 weeks to 3 May 2003 £million
Operating profit	102.4	89.4	278.4
Depreciation	64.9	60.5	118.2
Amortisation of goodwill and own shares	2.4	2.4	4.2
Share of profit of associated undertaking	–	(2.0)	(2.0)
Profit on disposal of fixed assets	(7.7)	(6.3)	(9.8)
Net (utilization of)/additions to provisions and impairment	(6.4)	(1.1)	9.2
(Increase)/decrease in stocks	(335.6)	(230.8)	(25.1)
(Increase)/decrease in debtors	(12.3)	(20.5)	17.9
Increase/(decrease) in creditors	320.2	104.7	(50.6)
	127.9	(3.7)	340.4

Problem 17.1

Share prices are used by investors and analysts for a variety of purposes.

1. Name four widely used ratios based on the market price(s) of equity shares.
2. Suggest four other ways in which an investor or analyst might use the price history of a share.
3. Explain four ways of obtaining share prices and suggest the advantages of each.

Solution 1.1 Elcho (Mossdale)

Three reasons why the bank might reject Farnesbarn's request:

1. An extra £60,000 is not enough.

The bank manager is likely to say to himself: 'They are asking for £60,000. Let us see how much they really need.'

	£	£
A. New machine		60,000
B. Current overdraft limit	50,000	
Overdraft at balance sheet date	48,150	
This must bring difficulties; to be safe, they really need another, say,		10,000
C. Working capital:		
Additional raw material stock, say,	5,000	
Finished goods, say	12,000	
Debtors, say 2 months	100,000	
	117,000	
Less: Additional creditors, say,	40,000	
That looks like		77,000
A total of		£147,000

These figures certainly won't be accurate, but one thing one can say for certain is that £60,000 is not enough.

Trawling for information (and watching carefully his customer's reaction), the bank manager might well ask:

- How is the present limit working?
- What are delivery arrangements . . . are you going to be holding much stock for them?
- What about payment terms? How long credit have they asked for?

On the other hand, he might simply say to himself: 'Either they haven't done their homework; or they know full well that they need more and they plan to break the news as a nasty shock later.'

Neither scenario is likely to commend the proposition to him.

2. Farnesbarn's profit estimate seems to be based on simplistic logic:

'On turnover of £600,000 per annum we make £15,785 after tax', he seems to suggest. 'If we double sales we should make twice that.'

But that ignores:

(i)   the price to be paid by JQB (which is likely to be less (possibly much less) than that paid by smaller

customers for the same items). If the price paid is substantially less than other people pay, sales *volume* (hence the total material and labour costs) is going to be more than double with a doubling of turnover;

(ii)   the cost structure of the business, i.e. the variability of cost (see Chapter 10); hence:

(iii) the profit margin (or profit) likely to be achieved (almost certainly different from that on existing business);

(iv)   the additional interest which would be payable at 15%.

Either (i) Farnesbarn has not got the necessary information; or (ii) he does not see its significance; or (iii) both.

And that certainly will not have impressed the bank.

3. JQB:

- Undue dependence on one customer is risky. There is no sign that Farnesbarn recognises this.
- Has Farnesbarn investigated JQB?

He does not say so; but he would earn a black mark if he had not.

- The bank will almost certainly know more (or be in a position to find out more) about JQB's credit standing than Farnesbarn. They may also know things about JQB's trading methods which Farnesbarn may not, e.g. that after the first couple of years the contract price is likely to be driven down so hard that the business becomes unprofitable.
- Can JQB break the contract for any reason, e.g. late delivery, poor workmanship? i.e. what are the risks involved? Is Farnesbarn aware of them?

Other possible reasons:

- **The bank manager may himself be under pressure.** He may be limited in what he can lend in certain business areas; and he will have a limit to his discretion beyond which he must seek head office approval.
- **The history of Elcho's past dealings** with the bank may not make the proposal one which he should be seen to endorse, e.g. the overdraft was nearly at limit at balance sheet date. Is there a history of bounced cheques; or requests to bend the limit to pay wages etc.?
- **Elcho's assets** do not provide very convincing security. In any case, lending to the company will be based less on its assets than on its forecast future trading. And Farnesbarn does not appear to have done his homework.

His forecast is therefore unlikely to be accurate, and that would worry any banker.

■ **What happens at the end of two years?**

How likely is it that the contract will continue at a similar level of profitability?

If not, can the output from the new plant and machinery be sold elsewhere at a profit?

Or is it special purpose plant? Might it be necessary to sell it (at well below book value?), to write it down sharply or even write it off altogether?

Solution 2.1

One can tell whether a company is (a) a public or (b) a private limited company from its name. A company whose name ends 'plc' or 'PLC' or Public Limited Company is a public company; one whose name ends with 'Ltd' or 'Limited' is a private company.

One cannot tell from its name alone whether a company is limited by shares or limited by guarantee; it is necessary to study the company's memorandum of association.

And it is quite difficult to tell whether a business with a name like 'Home Wreckers' is a business name of an individual or a partnership or an unlimited company. If it is an unlimited company it will be possible to inspect its file at Companies House and study its memorandum. Such companies are quite rare.

To an investor the advantage of a quote driven market is that there should always be a market in which he can deal, although the size may be limited. In an order driven market the investor avoids the cost of the spread, but he can only buy if there are sellers, and vice versa.

Solution 3.1

Preference shares carry a fixed rate of dividend, but unlike the holders of loan capital, who can take action against a company in default of interest payments, preference shareholders have no legal redress if the board of directors decides to recommend that no preference dividends should be paid.

However, if no preference dividend is declared for an accounting period, no dividend can be declared on any other type of share for the period concerned, so the subsidiary cannot pay an ordinary dividend to its holding company.

Cases have arisen where, though the subsidiary is very profitable, the holding company says it wishes to retain those profits, and no dividends, preference or ordinary, have been paid for a number of years. In these circumstances the preference shareholders may become entitled to vote at shareholders' general meetings. But this is little comfort, unless it gives them a majority of the votes, which is unlikely.

Solution 4.1

	£	£	£	£	£	£	£	£
(a) and (c) Profits before interest	750,000	800,000	900,000	1,000,000	1,100,000	1,200,000	1,300,000	1,400,000
Scenario (i)								
Interest at 10% on £8m	800,000	800,000	800,000	800,000	800,000	800,000	800,000	800,000
Return earned by venture capital company (%)	10.00%	10.00%	10.00%	10.00%	10.00%	10.00%	10.00%	10.00%
Profits available to management	(50,000)	0	100,000	200,000	300,000	400,000	500,000	600,000
Return earned by management (%)	−2.50%	0.00%	5.00%	10.00%	15.00%	20.00%	25.00%	30.00%
Scenario (ii)								
Interest at 9% on £6m	540,000	540,000	540,000	540,000	540,000	540,000	540,000	540,000
Profits due to equity owned by venture capital company	105,000	130,000	180,000	230,000	280,000	330,000	380,000	430,000
Total to venture capital company	645,000	670,000	720,000	770,000	820,000	870,000	920,000	970,000
Return earned by venture capital company (%)	8.06%	8.38%	9.00%	9.63%	10.25%	10.88%	11.50%	12.13%
Profits available to management	105,000	130,000	180,000	230,000	280,000	330,000	380,000	430,000
Return earned by management (%)	5.25%	6.50%	9.00%	11.50%	14.00%	16.50%	19.00%	21.50%

(b)

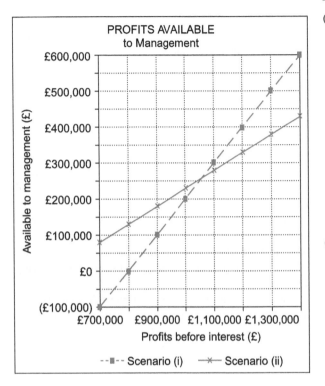

PROFITS AVAILABLE
to Management

Available to management (£)

Profits before interest (£)

--■-- Scenario (i)   —*— Scenario (ii)

Solution 5.1

Fleetwood: Balance Sheet as at 31 December 2001			
	Note	2001 £	2000 £
Fixed assets:			
...			
Motor vehicles	1	145,375	117,000

Notes:

1. Fixed assets	Cost	Depreciation to date	Net
	£	£	£
Motor vehicles			
2001	227,500	82,125	145,375
2000	165,000	48,000	117,000

Solution 6.1

(i) Companies hold fixed asset investments for a variety of reasons, among them:

(a) as a consequence of acquiring control of other companies (i.e. subsidiaries) and 'running them';

(b) as a way of entering into some sort of joint operation (i.e. a joint venture or consortium);

(c) as an investment to generate income (as an investment trust does);

(d) for protection, e.g. life policies on senior employees;

(e) as a means of gaining a foothold (a prelude to a possible bid);

(f) for self-aggrandisement on the part of the directors, e.g. works of art.

(ii) It is important for the reader of accounts to have a clear idea of the reasons for any significant holding:

(a) to understand how the holding and income from it will be treated in the accounts. As will be seen, the treatment of subsidiaries is quite different from that of associated companies;

(b) to predict future actions on the part of the board (e.g. a bid);

(c) to judge board behaviour (pictures, racehorses, yachts and aircraft may not be the most profitable use of funds).

Solution 7.1

(i) The items (a) land and (b) development and construction costs suggest these are the accounts of a group engaged in construction and residential property development; but there appears also to be activity in commercial, industrial and mixed development property.

(ii) The figures suggest that there was an expansion of the land bank; and that development costs in progress grew 21% either:

(a) because of stock building to meet a perceived **improvement** in the market; or

(b) because of stock was unsold because of a **deterioration** in the market for residential property.

It should be possible to identify which of these is the probable cause by studying:

- the directors' report;
- the chairman's statement;
- any financial review;

- notes to the accounts, in particular any analysis of turnover and profit;
- the cash flow statement.

The accounts are, in fact, those of TAYLOR WOODROW for 2002. Their financial review explained:

Housing

The housing businesses located in the United Kingdom, North America, Spain and Gibraltar all had a successful 2002 . . .

Construction

Taylor Woodrow Construction has continued its good performance . . .

(iii) The issue of transfers from current assets to fixed assets was considered by the UITF which, in July 1992, issued Abstract 5, *Transfers from current assets to fixed assets.*

The UITF was concerned, in the then current economic climate, that 'companies could avoid charging the profit and loss account with write-downs to net realisable value arising on unsold trading assets. This could be done by transferring the relevant assets from current assets to fixed assets at above net realisable value, as a result of which any later write-down might be debited to revaluation reserve.'

The UITF agreed that in respect of such transfers, the current asset accounting rules should be applied up to the effective date of transfer (the date of management's change of intent). The transfer should then be made at the lower of cost and net realisable value. Thus the land that cost £56m should be transferred to fixed assets at £40m, and the shortfall charged to the profit and loss account.

Solution 8.1

(a) Possible reasons why companies hold current asset investments include:

(i)   to set aside (and earn interest on) money later required to pay taxation;
(ii)   to save towards a planned expansion, refurbishment, or reorganisation;
(iii) to cover contingencies (e.g. a shortfall in receipts);

(iv)   to assure potential joint venture partners that the company, while not in the same league in size terms as they are, can fund its share of future operations (found for example in oil exploration and development);
(v)   as a more general store of value;
(vi)   to earn income (there being no better use of funds in the short term);
(vii) where required under the terms of a contract, or by statute, as with insurance funds;
(viii) where the group acts as its own insurer (because cover is impossible to obtain or prohibitively expensive, e.g. certain types of disaster cover), as large sums could be needed urgently.

(b) It is important for the reader of accounts to have a clear idea of the reasons for any significant holding of current asset investments because:

- Money which is tied up (under, say, (vii) or (viii) above) is not available to support general operations.
- Money set aside for a purpose (e.g. taxation) is earmarked.
- If money currently earning income is used for non-income-generating activities, income will fall.
- If large sums of money are invested:
  (a) has management clear plans as to their use? or
  (b) has the business become a 'cash cow', a generator of cash which it cannot itself usefully employ?
  (c) is management simply sitting on money that it does not know what to do with (black mark!)?

Solution 9.1

1. The initial outlay is

   $(250 \times 100 \times £10)$.

2. That is also the maximum amount risked.
3. If the index rises to 4,155, the fund manager can sell the option back to the market realising a profit of £137,500 ($55 \times 250 \times £10$). With over a month left to expiry there would also be some time value left, say 25 index points. In this case the manager would sell the options back to the market for 180 index points, an overall profit of £200,000 ($80 \times 250 \times £10$).

Solution 10.1

(a) (i) An accrual is a known liability where there is no uncertainty as to either the timing or the amount of the future expenditure required in settlement.

By contrast, a provision is a liability of uncertain timing or amount. Whilst the Companies Act 1985 contains a definition of provision, companies must also satisfy the required conditions in FRS 12 before a provision may be recognised in the balance sheet. The two key conditions are:

- the company has an obligation which it will probably be required to settle, and
- a reliable estimate can be made of the amount of the obligation.

(ii) Income in advance represents income received which at the date of the balance sheet had not been earned; whereas a deposit either represents money paid by a customer/client as an earnest (or a sign) of good faith or, in the case of a financial institution, customers' money which earns interest for them.

(iii) A commitment is a financial obligation which a company has already contracted for but which does not satisfy the criteria to be recognised as a provision.

A contingent liability is a possible obligation that arises from past events and whose existence will be confirmed only by the occurrence of one or more uncertain future events that are not wholly within the company's control. A contingent liability may also relate to a present obligation that arises from a past event but which is not recognised in the balance sheet because it does not satisfy all the conditions set out in FRS 12.

(b) Examples:

(i) Of an accrual: rent of £24,000 per annum payable quarterly in arrear on 31 March, 30 June etc. Company makes up its accounts to 30 April 1999, having paid rent up to 31 March. Rent of £2,000 (i.e. one month) will be accrued.

Of a provision: a restructuring provision representing expenditure which is to be incurred on a major reorganisation which was publicly announced prior to the balance sheet date.

(ii) Of income in advance: a magazine publisher receives prepayment in respect of annual subscriptions to journals. At the end of the year £213,000 represents journals to be supplied in future years.

(iii) Of a commitment: capital expenditure contracted for at the balance sheet date to the extent that this has not been provided for in the accounts; exposed foreign currency commitments; commitments under operating lease agreements.

Of a contingent liability: guarantee of bank borrowings; pending legal action against the company.

(c) In seeking to estimate the effect on a company's future cash flows and its viability in the medium term:

(i) Accruals are rarely of much significance. As to provisions, their background and adequacy should be considered, as well as their size, what calls they will bring on the company and when.

(ii) There is a tendency for companies hard-pressed for cash to spend what is in effect other people's money. In an ideal world deposits would be banked separately in a 'client/customer account', and never used for purposes of the company until such times as they were earned. This is not an ideal world. Solicitors and travel agents may work like that; other businesses tend not to. For example, a magazine publisher selling discounted three-year subscriptions would be in trouble if he spent receipts in the year they were received; he would then be relying on future receipts to provide copies to people who had already paid for them, in much the same way governments were able, in the early years of schemes, to treat pensions on a pay as you go basis; but once a large pensioner population built up, the costs escalated and there were no funds to fall back on.

(iii) Capital commitments require financing. The wise finance director ensures that this is planned and negotiated in advance. Some even explain what has been done in the financial review.

Solution 11.1

The effective rate of tax (i.e. taxation as a percentage of pre-tax profits) might be: (a) much less, or (b) much greater, than the normal rate of UK corporation tax because of:

Cause	Effect
Adjustments to previous years	(a) or (b)
Disallowed expenses	(b)
Capital gains	(a)
Loans	(b)
Losses and loss relief	(a) or (b)
Overseas income	(a) or (b)
Exceptional items	(a) or (b)

An abnormal tax charge should be explained in the note on taxation.

An abnormal tax charge is important because it directly affects after-tax profits, and hence earnings per share, the P/E ratio and cover. And, less obviously, the effect is not proportionate. For example, take a company with pre-tax profits of £100m which has 1000m 10p ordinary shares. If the effective tax rate is 30%, tax is £30m and the after-tax profit £70m. Were that rate to increase (because, say, a greater proportion was earned overseas and subject to higher rates of tax) to 35%, the after-tax profits would fall (on the same income) to £65m, i.e. by 5/70 = 7.14%.

Solution 12.1

1. Earnings per share (e.p.s.) are the amount of profit on ordinary activities, after tax and all other charges, that has been earned for each ordinary share:

$$\text{e.p.s.} = \frac{\text{Profit attributable to ordinary shareholders}}{\text{Number of ordinary shares in issue}}$$

Adjustments are necessary where there is
- a scrip (bonus) issue or share split, or
- an issue of shares in an acquisition, or
- a rights issue

during the period. These adjustments are explained on page 84.

2. One might use the e.p.s. figure:
   - in computing a price earnings ratio;
   - to compute cover or dividend payout ratio;
   - in assessing earnings growth;
   - as a basis in estimating future earnings.

   Where dilution may arise (because of, say, convertibles, warrants or options) it may be necessary to show the fully diluted earnings.

3. Some companies compute their own preferred versions (as well) because they feel their method of calculating

earnings provides better comparability (or because they do not like hefty charges for exceptional items reducing their apparent earnings) or show earnings on an IIMR basis (for much the same reasons).

Solution 13.1

The 1995 net cash inflow from operating activities of CORDIANT was less than that in 1994 because:

- The two principal components of cash inflow from operations tend to be:
  1. Operating profit: which was only £28.3m, against £44.5m in 1994; and
  2. Depreciation: unchanged at £25.7m.
- But cash flow is also affected by increased working capital demands:
  1. Increase in work in progress (£9.4m in 1995; £8.0m in 1994);
  2. Increase in debtors (£54.8m in 1995, £77.8m in 1994); and while the increase in creditors £38.6m operated in the reverse direction, it was far less than the increase of £86.1m the previous year. Had the increase in creditors been only £38.6m in 1994, the working capital requirement would have been £47.5m greater, and the cash generated from operations not £58.9m but £11.4m.
- In each year property provisions were utilised (£10.3m in 1995 and £11.8m in 1994). These had already been charged against the profits of earlier years, but the cash was not spent until 1995 and 1994 respectively.

Solution 14.1

- The first clue is the reference to 'stores'. This is a fairly substantial store company with just over 400 stores (averaging 12,350 sq ft). It was in fact STOREHOUSE which previously owned BHS and Mothercare.
- A major change occurred in 1993:
  (a) The number of stores fell from 736 to 425.
  (b) There were exceptional items in both 1993 and 1994 (£31.4m and £6.4m respectively). This looks like the closure or sale of stores.
  (c) The dividend of 5p against earnings of 2.6p in 1992 suggests there was a marked drop in profitability around that time.
- Turnover was drifting sideways (it increased in the last two years from £1,045.5m to £1,083.6m, i.e. by 3.6%,

and in the last year by 0.4%, which did not keep up with inflation.
- That was despite adding two new stores in each year and 263,000 sq ft of selling space in the last year.
- Profit margins, however, improved markedly, year by year:

	%
1992	0.85
1993	3.77
1994	6.24
1995	8.08
1996	9.41

Solution 15.1

1. A going concern is a company or other enterprise which does not intend or need either:
   - to go into liquidation or
   - to curtail the current level of operations significantly.

2. (a) The directors are responsible for making appropriate enquiries to satisfy themselves that company and group have adequate resource to continue in operational existence for the foreseeable future before continuing to adopt the going concern basis of accounting;
   (b) It is the auditors' responsibility to form an independent opinion on the financial statements. Were they to consider the company was not a going concern the accounts would present a true and fair view only if they were prepared on a 'gone concern' basis and provided adequate explanations – otherwise the auditors would qualify their report.

3. The matter is important to investors because the value of shares in a break-up is only a fraction of that as a going concern. Typically the yield on an equity investment is far less than that on fixed-interest securities for the simple reason that equities are expected to grow in value (to provide a hedge against inflation). A business which ceases to be a going concern is certainly not a hedge against inflation. It is a dead duck.

Solution 16.1

DIXONS *Note to the Interim Statement 2003/04*

Workings: deducing figures for 24 weeks to 3 May 2003

	28 weeks to 15 Nov 2003 £million	28 weeks to 9 Nov 2002 £million	52 weeks to 3 May 2003 £million	24 weeks to 3 May 2003 £million
Operating profit	102.4	89.4	278.4	189.0
Depreciation	64.9	60.5	118.2	57.7
Amortisation of goodwill and own shares	2.4	2.4	4.2	1.8
Share of profit of associated undertaking	–	(2.0)	(2.0)	–
Profit on disposal of fixed assets	(7.7)	(6.3)	(9.8)	(3.5)
Net (utilization of)/additions to provisions and impairment	(6.4)	(1.1)	9.2	10.3
(Increase)/decrease in stocks	(335.6)	(230.8)	(25.1)	205.7
(Increase)/decrease in debtors	(12.3)	(20.5)	17.9	38.4
Increase/(decrease) in creditors	320.2	104.7	(50.6)	(155.3)
	127.9	(3.7)	340.4	344.1

Solutions:

	28 weeks to 15 Nov 2003 £million	28 weeks to 9 Nov 2002 £million	52 weeks to 3 May 2003 £million	24 weeks to 3 May 2003 £million
(a) Operating profit	102.4	89.4	278.4	189.0
(b) Net cash inflow/(outflow)	127.9	(3.7)	340.4	344.1

Comment:
It seems that in cash flow terms Dixons is highly seasonal. From May to early November 2002 the net cash flow from operating activities was negative (taking the average of the two years, around £100m outflow); whereas from November to April (which of course includes Christmas) it was highly positive (in 2002/03 the cash inflow was £344.1m net).

In part this is because operating profits are seasonal (£89.4m in the first half of 2002/03 against £189.0m in the second half). But it is the stocks, debtors and creditors which create much of the cash flow seasonality: increasing sharply in the first half and falling back again in the second.

Solution 17.1

1. Four widely used ratios based on the market price(s) of equity shares are:
   (a) Dividend yield (%) = (Net dividend in pence per share ÷ Ordinary share price in pence) × 100.
   (b) Price/Earnings Ratio (P/E ratio or PER), which is the market price of the ordinary share divided by the earnings per share

   i.e. PER = Share price ÷ e.p.s.

   (c) Price earnings growth factor (PEG) is a yardstick introduced by Jim Slater in *The Zulu Principle*. The PEG is a measure of whether a share looks overrated or underrated:

   PEG = Price/Earnings ratio ÷ Prospective growth rate of e.p.s.

   (d) Increase (decrease) in price (normally the closing price) on the day, week, month or year:

   (Share price at end of period ÷ Share price at end of previous period × 100) − 100%

2. Four other ways in which an investor or analyst might use the price history of a share are:

- to draw a chart depicting the share's price behaviour;
- to compare the behaviour of an individual share against (a) the FT-SE 100 or (b) the All-Share Index;
- to compare the behaviour of an individual share with that of its sector index or of another share in the same sector;
- to value the portfolio for any purpose, e.g. inheritance tax purposes or to project the capital gains tax that would be payable on the sale of a holding.

3. Four ways of obtaining share prices are:
- Look up the price in the City pages of the *FT* or of any good daily paper. Where a daily paper is already purchased or is available in a library, this involves no additional cost; but it is tiresome to keep track of a large number of prices.
- Look the price up on teletext (this again involves no additional cost assuming one has a TV with teletext) or use a teletext board in a PC (once purchased, with appropriate software this will update prices automatically at a stated time daily, free; and it is possible to watch prices during the day updated every couple of hours).
- Download prices from a modem-based service like Prestel or watch them live using that service.
- Purchase data from a data source, say, weekly on disk or CD-ROM.

Index